Second Edition

Measuring and Managing Patient Satisfaction

William J. Krowinski, PhD, and Steven R. Steiber, PhD

AHA books are published by American Hospital Publishing, Inc., an American Hospital Association company

This publication is designed to provide accurate and authoritative information in regard to the subject matter covered. It is sold with the understanding that neither the authors nor the publisher is engaged in rendering legal, accounting, or other professional service. If legal advice or other expert assistance is required, the services of a competent professional person should be sought.

The views expressed in this publication are strictly those of the authors and do not necessarily represent official positions of the American Hospital Association.

Library of Congress Cataloging-in-Publication Data

Krowinski, William J.
   Measuring and managing patient satisfaction / William J. Krowinski and Steven R. Steiber. — 2nd ed.
       p.   cm.
   Steiber's name appears first on earlier edition.
   Includes bibliographical references and index.
   ISBN 1-55648-157-8
   1. Patient satisfaction. 2. Patients—Attitudes. 3. Medical care surveys. I. Steiber, Steven R. II. Title.
   [DNLM: 1. Patient Satisfaction. 2. Attitude to Health. 3. Research Design. 4. Questionnaires.   W 85 K93m 1996]
RA399.A1S74   1996
362.1'068—dc20
DNLM/DLC
for Library of Congress   96-22064
                                                                                             CIP

Catalog no. 136108

©1996 by American Hospital Publishing, Inc.,
an American Hospital Association company

All rights reserved. The reproduction or use of this book in any form or in any information storage or retrieval system is forbidden without the express written permission of the publisher.

Printed in the USA

AHA is a service mark of the American Hospital Association used under license by American Hospital Publishing, Inc.

Text set in Century Textbook

3.5M—9/96—0444

Audrey Kaufman, Senior Editor
Patricia Fiene, Developmental Editor
Lisa Weder, Editor
Peggy DuMais, Assistant Manager, Production
Marcia Bottoms, Director, Books Division

Contents

List of Figures and Tables iv
About the Authors vii
Preface ix
Acknowledgments xi
Chapter 1. Customer Satisfaction and Its Implications 1
Chapter 2. Defining the Terms of Patient Satisfaction 29
Chapter 3. Service Encounters and Satisfaction Outcomes 51
Chapter 4. Potential Pitfalls in the Research Process 67
Chapter 5. Research Design 77
Chapter 6. Sampling 87
Chapter 7. Qualitative Research 97
Chapter 8. Quantitative Research 121
Chapter 9. Self-Report Questionnaires 145
Chapter 10. Telephone Questionnaires 159
Chapter 11. Reliability and Validity 181
Chapter 12. Evaluation Designs 191
Chapter 13. The Evaluation Plan 207
Chapter 14. Analysis of Research Data 217
Chapter 15. Plotting a Course of Action 231
Appendix A. Table of Random Numbers 245
Appendix B. Distribution of t 251
Appendix C. Chi-Square Test 253
References 255
Index 263

List of Figures and Tables

Figures

Figure 1-1. The Cost of Dissatisfaction for a Typical Hospital 10
Figure 1-2. The Cost of Dissatisfaction for a
Typical Primary Care Provider 11
Figure 1-3. Health Care Advisory Board Assumptions for Hypothetical
Cost–Benefit Analysis of Money-Back Guarantee Program 13
Figure 1-4. Patient Loyalty without Service Guarantee 14
Figure 1-5. Patient Loyalty with Service Guarantee 15
Figure 1-6. A Model of Service Quality Improvement and Profitability 16
Figure 1-7. Impact of Quality Expenditures on Percent Disappointed 18
Figure 1-8. Increase in Activity over Prior Year 26
Figure 1-9. More Patient Satisfaction Activity 27
Figure 2-1. Recent Hospitalization 30
Figure 2-2. Family Doctor 31
Figure 2-3. Sources of Good and Bad Surprises 32
Figure 2-4. Overall Patient Satisfaction with a Provider 36
Figure 2-5. Full Listing of Inpatient Questions 39
Figure 2-6. Statistically Important *Categories* of Inpatient Questions 40
Figure 2-7. Full Listing of Outpatient Questions 41
Figure 2-8. Statistically Important *Categories* of Outpatient Questions 41
Figure 2-9. Full Listing of Physician's Office Patient Questions 42
Figure 2-10. Statistically Important *Categories* of Office Patient Questions ... 42
Figure 3-1. Service Delivery System 52
Figure 3-2. Statistically Important Categories of Inpatient Questions 57
Figure 3-3. Overall Inpatient Experience: Mean Ratings in Rank Order 59

List of Figures and Tables

Figure 3-4. Structure of the Quality Perception Model 60
Figure 3-5. Quality Perception Model (Inpatient) 61
Figure 3-6. Scatter Plotting of Association between Nursing and Overall Quality 62
Figure 5-1. Preliminary Research Plan: XYZ Ambulatory Surgery Center Patient Satisfaction Study 83
Figure 5-2. Revised Research Plan: XYZ Ambulatory Surgery Center Patient Satisfaction Study 84
Figure 7-1. Interview Guide 103
Figure 7-2. Empathic Interviewing 106
Figure 7-3. Summarizing and Prefacing Technique 106
Figure 7-4. Prompting Technique 107
Figure 7-5. Focus Group Leader's Opening Remarks 111
Figure 8-1. Types of Quantitative Research Questions 123
Figure 8-2. Double-Barreled Questions 125
Figure 8-3. Use of Jargon and Abbreviations 126
Figure 8-4. Branching Question 127
Figure 8-5. "Does Not Apply" Response Alternative 127
Figure 8-6. Global Question with Open-Ended Follow-Up 128
Figure 8-7. Vague Questions 129
Figure 8-8. Explaining the Purpose of Personal Questions 130
Figure 8-9. Biased Questions 131
Figure 8-10. Biased Response Categories 131
Figure 8-11. Changing Question Wording 132
Figure 8-12. Exhaustive Response Options 134
Figure 8-13. "Other" as a Response Option 135
Figure 8-14. Mutually Exclusive Response Categories 135
Figure 8-15. Mutually Exclusive Response Grouping 136
Figure 8-16. Two- and Five-Level Satisfaction Scales 137
Figure 8-17. Service Attribute Scaling 138
Figure 9-1. Horizontal versus Vertical Format 147
Figure 9-2. Letter of Transmittal 149
Figure 9-3. Notification Handout 152
Figure 9-4. Prenotification Postcard 153
Figure 9-5. Postcard Follow-Up 153
Figure 9-6. Follow-Up Letter 154
Figure 10-1. Question-and-Answer Sheet 162
Figure 10-2. Reducing Scale Levels for Telephone Surveys 165
Figure 10-3. Alternative to Truncating Scales 166

Figure 10-4. Ranking Question 167

Figure 10-5. Telephone Ranking Question 167

Figure 10-6. Incorporating Response Categories into Questions 168

Figure 10-7. Telephone Income Question 169

Figure 10-8. Questionnaire Format 170

Figure 12-1. Third Variables 193

Figure 12-2. Education as a Spurious Variable 193

Figure 12-3. Education as a Confounding Variable 193

Figure 12-4. Potential Effects of Extraneous Variables 194

Figure 12-5. Six Evaluation Designs 198

Figure 12-6. Five Trend Lines with Different Patterns 202

Figure 12-7. One Group Interrupted Time Series Design
(ADZ Urgent Care Centers) 202

Figure 12-8. Control Group Interrupted Time Series Design (Comparison of the West and East Side Urgent Care Centers) 205

Figure 14-1. Scatter Plot of x and y 224

Figure 14-2. Relationship between x and y 226

Figure 15-1. Setting Satisfaction Priorities 233

Figure 15-2. Creating an Index of Quality 235

Figure 15-3. How a Quality Index Moves 236

Figure 15-4. Significant Increases in Key Drivers 237

Figure 15-5. Flowchart the Processes 238

Figure 15-6. Model for Improvement 239

Figure 15-7. Internal Metric Translation 240

Figure 15-8. Identifying Outliers for Action 241

Figure 15-9. Closing the Management Loop 243

Tables

Table 6-1. Confidence Intervals for Market Samples of Various Sizes 90

Table 8-1. Distribution of Responses for Satisfaction Question 137

Table 8-2. Quality Scaling 138

Table 8-3. Frequency Scaling 139

Table 8-4. Graphic Scaling 140

Table 8-5. Likert-Type Scaling 141

Table 9-1. Likert-Type Scaling 147

Table 11-1. Paired Measured and True Satisfaction Scores 182

Table 13-1. Comparison of Measurement Methods with Data Accuracy, Expense, and Feasibility Criteria 210

Table 14-1. Likelihood of Returning 220

About the Authors

William J. Krowinski, PhD, BCD, is a research consultant and clinical practitioner in Erie, Pennsylvania. He has held faculty positions at Gannon University and the University of Pittsburgh, where he taught research methods and statistics. Dr. Krowinski was previously employed by Hamot Health Systems of Erie and the Health Education Center of Pittsburgh, where he managed research functions. He holds his doctorate from the University of Pittsburgh.

Steven R. Steiber, PhD, is a senior vice-president and health care practice director of Opinion Research Corporation (formerly known as Quality Expectations, Inc.), an international market research organization based in Princeton, New Jersey. Prior to 1996, Dr. Steiber was president of Quality Expectations, Inc., a health care consulting group. Dr. Steiber was senior vice-president for research and development with the Gallup Organization following its merger with Allied Research Associates between 1986 and 1988. Prior to the merger, Dr. Steiber was chief executive officer of Allied Research Associates, and between 1979 and 1981, he was senior research associate with the American Medical Association's Center for Health Policy Research. He holds a doctorate from the University of Arizona and has served on two other academic faculties. His research has appeared in most major health care publications.

Preface

Health services providers today are confronted by two principal challenges. The first is to gain insight into what is important to the patients they serve. The second is to "move the needle," or make measurable changes in the patients' experience of the health care encounter.

With this as a backdrop, *Measuring and Managing Patient Satisfaction* was first published by American Hospital Publishing, Inc., in 1991. Much has changed in the field since then, and new tools and methodologies are available to the health services researcher. The authors, therefore, have extensively revised, expanded, and refined the text in order to provide a more current perspective to the reader. Like the first edition, however, this second edition is truly a collaborative effort, with both authors contributing equally to the final product. The order of authors' names connotes no difference in contribution.

Measuring and Managing Patient Satisfaction was written with both the health care professional and the researcher in mind. It accommodates the questions and needs of both by offering an overview from start to finish of all elements important to patient satisfaction. The lessons and case studies presented will help the reader not only measure patient satisfaction more accurately but also manage patient satisfaction more effectively. The present edition of this book expands its scope to include a broader range of health experiences and applications, with examples drawn from inpatient, outpatient, emergency room, and physician office settings. By following the steps outlined in the chapters, the reader should be able to customize the methods to virtually any service setting. The net result of such effort, we hope, will be twofold: greater competitiveness of the provider and better service for the customer.

Acknowledgments

A book like this does not come into being without the input and assistance of many individuals and organizations. We acknowledge the efforts of the many researchers whose works we have cited, in particular the efforts of Ware, Rust, Linder-Pelz, Campbell, Stanley, Jones, and Sasser. We are also indebted to the many health services providers who have given of their time and whose experience has informed this book. Outstanding among those who have helped in and supported the research important to this project are Vanderbilt University Medical Center, Baton Rouge Medical Center, Lafayette General Medical Center, Condell Medical Center, and Florida Hospital. Special thanks also for their input to Richard Anton, Ina Albert, Robert Barriger, Larry Wolcott, and Deborah Ross.

We are indebted to Audrey Kaufman, Pat Fiene, and Lisa Weder of American Hospital Publishing, Inc., without whose support, input, and critical comment this book would not have been possible. Thanks also go to Gary Koeske of the University of Pittsburgh for his thoughtful review and comments on chapter 11. The editorial and graphic assistance of Victoria Stember is gratefully acknowledged, as is the assistance of Teri Sardina, Desiree Skey, and Denise Gould.

CHAPTER ONE

Customer Satisfaction and Its Implications

In the years since publication of the first edition of *Measuring and Managing Patient Satisfaction*, there has been increasing incentive for providers to be more in touch with, and more attentive to, the full spectrum of health care customers. Thus, whereas the first edition of this book focused on the end user/patient in a hospital setting, the present edition broadens its purview to include other customer groups and other provider settings. As in the first edition, the focus is on the patient, but patient satisfaction is examined within the context of a more complex, customer-oriented model of the health care service experience.

As this edition goes to press, it is still appropriate to raise some of the same questions that the first edition addressed: Why has customer satisfaction become so important to business in general and to health care in particular? What happens when customers (or patients) become dissatisfied? How does a service provider prevent or remedy customer dissatisfaction? Where does patient satisfaction fit into the overall evaluation of, or report card on, health care, which also includes measures of clinical efficacy, clinical efficiency, and financial cost? What are the best ways to measure, and consequently manage, patient satisfaction?

To begin to answer these questions, this chapter reaffirms, through empirical evidence and theory, the importance of patient satisfaction and patient-centered care. After examining customer satisfaction and quality improvement models from a general business standpoint, the chapter analyzes specific implications for health care, where the customers may include not only patients but also their families, employers, and insurers. Subsequent discussion focuses on additional implications of a satisfied patient for health outcomes as well as business outcomes. The evolving roles and increasing demands of employers, insurers, and others are explored, as is the perspective of government and other third-party regulators and watchdog groups. Finally, the chapter examines the role of patient satisfaction as a competitive positioning strategy.

No business premise should be accepted wholly without question. To this end, the chapter begins by reviewing the importance of placing the customer/patient at the center of business decisions and service delivery. In this respect, the competitive provision of health services is no different from the competitive provision of business services in virtually any other sector of the economy.

The Evolution of Customer-Centered Service

Even a casual review of the business literature shows that customer satisfaction is considered by most to be at the core of good business practices that lead to corporate success. Customer satisfaction fits into a larger, customer-centered model of quality improvement systems and practices. As with many of the ideas that American business has come to prize, the development of customer-centered service with its focus on customer satisfaction has followed the lead of the Japanese, who were the first to embrace the work of American economist W. Edwards Deming, a pioneer in creating modern models for quality improvement processes. Deming assisted Japan in the postwar reconstruction of its economy, which afforded a laboratory for testing new ideas. The customer-centered service model that Deming advocated, and Japanese companies adopted, yielded such excellent results in the marketplace that American companies followed suit.

Deming and Customer-Centered Service

Following World War II, while other business analysts were hewing to a model of productivity improvement that rewarded more efficient processes, W. Edwards Deming was building models of statistical quality control. Deming argued that simply finding cheaper parts or fewer steps for completing a given task was not enough. The answer to improved productivity, he believed, lay in a total rethinking of the organization, from mission statement through production.

Deming blended scientific and humanistic approaches to business management and leadership, holding quality as a core value. His ideas were consolidated into 14 key points, which ranged from redefining the mission and philosophy of the organization to moving away from the narrow practices of price shopping and short-term profit taking (Walton, 1986).

Although Deming's major points did not address the role of customer satisfaction per se, many of his points about the constant improvement of products presaged Thomas Peters and Robert Waterman's later encouragement to "stick close to the customer" for new product and product enhancement ideas. In his early lectures to Japanese executives, Deming cautioned against following the existing U.S. model of production. Instead, he argued, the Japanese should consider the customer to be at the core of production line processes, from the point at which raw materials enter the factory to the point at which the product leaves the gates (Yates, 1992).

Juran and Quality Management

Joseph Juran, a contemporary of Deming, wrote the book that has become the standard reference on statistical quality control. The fourth edition of *Juran's Quality Control Handbook* (Juran and Gryna, 1988) defines the language and describes how to apply a wide range of quality improvement tools, many of them statistical. Where does customer satisfaction research fit into this model? In Juran's "spiral of progress in quality" model, market research into customer needs and wants is the starting point for service (or product) design. A series of nine development, design, sourcing, marketing, and other production steps follows, with final tests or inspections performed as the service (or product) is introduced to the customer. At the point where the service (or product) is introduced into the market, the business collects feedback from customers through formal research and complaint management. With service modifications growing out of this feedback, the service moves around and up the spiral, the entire multistage process beginning again with external customer market research.

Peters and Waterman's Search for Excellence

In their 1982 best-seller, *In Search of Excellence*, Thomas J. Peters and Robert J. Waterman, Jr., introduced what to many was a refreshing concept regarding American business. The concept stated very simply that certain outstanding ("excellent") companies outperformed, outsold, and outproduced the rest because they had created and nurtured uniquely positive corporate cultures. Employees within these cultures were more innovative, more productive, and more responsive to their customers than employees in other cultures. The outcome of combined superior efforts was excellence: growth where others shrank, profits where others lost money, and significant successes where others failed.

Of the many important lessons presented by Peters and Waterman in their analysis of American business, one in particular stands out: "Stay close to the customer." Excellent companies not only perform better because they listen to the customer, many also "get their best business ideas from customers. That comes from listening, intently and regularly" (Peters and Waterman, 1982, p. 14). For excellent companies, the obsession with listening to the customer is no accident; it is a conscious commitment. In the years since Peters and Waterman's groundbreaking book, Peters and others within the quality movement have furthered the cause of excellence with more concrete recipes for improving, enhancing, and perpetuating "best practices."

In his more recent titles, Peters has built on the basic theme of orienting business practices to the customer, advocating regular solicitation of customer feedback as a means of gauging present performance as well as of assessing the marketability of new products or services. In all sectors of the economy, Peters contends, "it is possible, not just desirable, to deal imaginatively and speedily with the customer in a market chockablock with good products, good services, and good competitors from here, there, and heaven knows where else" (Peters, 1994, pp. 227–28). His notion for incorporating the customer's point of view into product or service design embraces the core philosophy of the quality movement.

The quality movement in U.S. business, which had its origins in Deming and others, emphasizes "catching employees in the act of doing things right." A fundamental tenet of the quality movement is that quality does not result simply from finding a way to engineer errors to an increasingly lower level; rather, quality resides in engineering positives to an increasingly higher level for any given product or service. With the former method, quality is measured by the number of "things gone wrong," or TGW. Peters recommends that this perspective be turned upside down to measure the number of "things gone right," or TGR. Minimizing TGW, he argues, is necessary but not sufficient for quality improvement. The beauty of the TGR perspective, besides moving businesses away from "bad appling" or "finger-pointing" as methods of quality improvement, is that it forces providers to find ways to impress their customers. Customer satisfaction goes up proportionately and measurably, while market leadership also rises by raising the ante for all other providers.

The Malcolm Baldrige National Quality Award

Although American business leadership initially turned a deaf ear to Deming's guidelines for corporate productivity and success, the Japanese listened, even going so far as to develop a prize for corporate excellence in Deming's name. In the United States, the name of another business leader—Malcolm Baldrige—became synonymous with quality business practices. (The more cynical reader might infer that Baldrige was chosen over Deming to avoid calling attention to America's late arrival on the quality scene.)

Baldrige was a former Secretary of Commerce after whom President Ronald Reagan named an award on August 20, 1987, through the Malcolm Baldrige National Quality

Improvement Act (P.L. 100-107). The act designated a national quality prize and some basic guidelines for its award, but the details of how the score was to be tallied were left to the National Bureau of Standards (known at present as the National Institute of Standards and Technology, or NIST). Using a 1,000-point scoring system, the award offers points for achievement in many areas, including customer orientation. In fact, 300 of the 1,000 points are designated for customer satisfaction issues, as the representative list below indicates:

- Identifying customer requirements
- Managing the customer relationship
- Establishing customer service standards
- Demonstrating commitment to customers
- Resolving customer complaints
- Measuring customer satisfaction
- Demonstrating customer satisfaction
- Benchmarking customer satisfaction (Garvin, 1991, pp. 80–83)

Although the Baldrige Award has focused on larger, for-profit corporations, its influence has been widespread, as interest in excellence has spawned alternative applications of the Baldrige criteria. A Health Care Pilot of the Baldrige Award was conceived in 1993, and activities were subsequently launched in 1994 and 1995 (Malcolm Baldrige National Quality Award, 1995). The criteria of the Health Care Pilot award in many ways parallel those of the original award, but the point allocation and substantive focus of the satisfaction components are different. In the overall 1,000-point value listing, for instance, 25 points are allocated to "employee/health care staff well-being and satisfaction." Section 7.0 of the criteria addresses the health care provider's systems for examining, and measuring the extent to which it is meeting, patients' and other stakeholders' requirements and expectations. It brings satisfaction more explicitly into play, with 250 points allocated across the following dimensions:

- Patient and health care market knowledge
- Patient/stakeholder relationship management
- Patient/stakeholder satisfaction determination
- Patient/stakeholder satisfaction results
- Patient/stakeholder satisfaction comparison (Malcolm Baldrige National Quality Award, 1995)

In this format, the Baldrige Award extends the concept of *customer* beyond those who receive services (the patients) to include those who work in the health care setting and other stakeholders. *Stakeholders* are defined by the award group as "customers other than the patient," such as patient family members and friends, insurers, employers, other providers, and community residents at large. Given the broader interpretation of *customer*, it would appear that the Baldrige committee wants to encourage providers to go beyond merely measuring patient satisfaction and expectations and to assess the needs of the larger community. Quality, then, becomes a way for a provider to become more fully integrated into the market and community it serves. As complicated as these components may appear, they are only a partial picture of the overall quality improvement system that the Baldrige Award encourages among providers. The criteria also include the development of internal systems for process management, the charting of organizational performance, and more.

Health care providers need not work in a vacuum as they seek to implement Baldrige-based quality improvement mechanisms. In addition to the customary consulting firms, health-related companies such as Abbott Laboratories are offering value-added consulting services to those among their customer base who wish to implement the more "nuts-and-bolts" components of quality improvement. Having implemented programs of its own designed around the Baldrige criteria, Abbott is in a unique position to work closely with providers who embrace this same vision. Indeed, providers focused on quality improvement should expect no less from their suppliers.

Focus on Quality versus Focus on Award Winning

Both theoretically and empirically, true quality improvement activities enhance competitiveness in the marketplace. This competitive position can pay off in very tangible ways, but enhanced quality does not necessarily come from mere adherence to published guidelines such as those of the Baldrige Award. Furthermore, the guidelines do not guarantee market success, despite their grounding in quality improvement principles. Most would agree that quality improvement activities offer only long-term payoffs, and that to look for short-term market share, profitability, or even productivity gains is unreasonable. This lesson was learned the hard way by the Wallace Company, which went bankrupt in 1992, owing in part to the high levels of spending necessitated by striving for and ultimately winning the Baldrige Award in 1990 (Hill, 1993). Cadillac, a 1990 recipient of the Baldrige Award, found that it had slipped from fourth place in customer satisfaction ratings in 1989 to eighth place in 1990, according to an industry standard report from J. D. Powers (Garvin, 1991, p. 84).

These Baldrige Award winners are not the only ones with corporate egg on the face. Florida Power & Light spent millions of dollars to compete for the Japanese Deming Prize, only to find that the commensurately rising costs resulted in an embarrassing hue and cry from ratepayers. The program was subsequently shelved (Wiesendanger, 1993). The simple fact is that many programs of quality improvement do not yield parallel improvements in productivity and therefore profitability. In fact, typically productivity is able to keep pace with quality improvement only in manufacturing or in standardized service businesses (Rust, Zahorik, and Keiningham, 1995, p. 58).

Drucker and Customer Acquisition and Retention

The measurement of customer (patient) satisfaction is but one of the information sources on which business management decisions will be made. Peter Drucker (1995) argues that for a time, business combined data about customer satisfaction with other data in what came to be economic business decision-making models. But many of these models have been engineered beyond what the data can deliver. Such has been the case with traditional job cost accounting, which attempts to quantify the basic time and materials costs of delivering a specific product or service to the customer. The net result is a model that allows management to identify an appropriate charge to the customer and to identify where costs can be trimmed so that the company can become more cost competitive in delivering products or services. An example of cost trimming to increase cost competitiveness can be seen in the current health care delivery environment. Many health services suppliers (insurers, hospital corporations, and others) are looking at costs, clinical outcomes, and economies while paying little attention to patient satisfaction.

Using American banks as an example, Drucker brings customer satisfaction back to center stage of the business model in the following analysis:

> Banks, for instance, have been trying for several decades to apply conventional cost-accounting techniques to their business—that is, to figure the techniques of individual operations and services—with almost negligible results. Now they are beginning to ask, Which one activity is the center of costs and of results? The

answer: serving the customer. The cost per customer in any major area of banking is a fixed cost. Thus it is the yield per customer—both the volume of services a customer uses and the mix of those services—that determines costs and profits. Retail discounters, especially those in Western Europe, have known that for some time. They assume that once a unit of shelf space is installed, the cost is fixed and management consists of maximizing the yield thereon over a given time span. Their focus on yield control has enabled them to increase profitability despite their low prices and low margins. (Drucker, 1995, pp. 56–57)

Drucker's central argument is that acquiring the customer comes first, retaining the customer comes second, and maximizing profitability from the consequent relationship comes third. These principles have clear implications for health care: as providers move into managed care under a service-oriented model, customer satisfaction will be critical to success. It will not be the cost of services that will have to be managed so much as the cost of acquiring and retaining the customer.

Patient and Provider Benefits of Customer Satisfaction

Of course, health care is not quite so straightforward as other service or industrial sectors. The health care customer may be the end user/patient, but looking over this customer's shoulder are employers, insurers, regulators, friends and family of the patient, and others. Given the wide spectrum of customers, how does the health services provider usefully approach customer (patient) satisfaction?

It is axiomatic that good clinical practices lead to good clinical outcomes. Care paths, patient-centered care, and other operating models have attempted to improve outcomes. But in the process, another benefit is added—better outcomes lead to higher levels of patient satisfaction. And then the synergy begins in earnest, because enhanced levels of patient satisfaction in turn lead to still better clinical outcomes, if only because satisfied customers are more apt to follow medical advice than less satisfied customers. In effect, "high-touch" health care becomes not just a market position but a solid clinical and business practice.

The successful health services provider places the customer at the center of its organizational strategy (Peterson, 1988, p. 3). The best way to keep the customer in that number one position is to measure and manage each employee's interface with the customer while that customer is under the provider's care. The challenge faced by health services management, then, is to ensure that all service providers and managers deliver the specific outcome for which the customer contracts. Superior or "excellent" companies supplement this basic effort with additional service dimensions that attempt to exceed customers' expectations. All providers are challenged to provide superior service, and the best way to do that is through well-directed management and measurement of customer satisfaction.

All this talk about satisfaction makes it sound like a good idea; it is only reasonable to say that it is desirable to offer superior service that satisfies the customer. But cost-conscious health care managers may also respond that they have a budget to balance, the nursing staff must be reduced, and some of the very customers to be satisfied have insurers that reimburse 67 cents or less on the dollar for services offered. Moreover, under the emerging rules of managed care, every service encounter is debited against a fixed fee that is paid just once a year. In today's financially strained environment, providers might well argue against allotting dollars to customer satisfaction programs if satisfaction means only that the customer will be happier. But the fact is that customer satisfaction is tied to some very grounded dimensions like brand loyalty, perceived quality, market share, and other financially rooted outcomes, common to virtually all businesses. In health care, these dimensions translate into better health and business outcomes, such as improved patient compliance with treatment regimens, increased loyalty to a provider, and fewer malpractice suits.

Improved Compliance with Treatment Regimens

Research reported in the professional literature over the past three decades confirms that satisfied patients follow medical recommendations better than dissatisfied patients. As a consequence, satisfied patients benefit more directly from medical diagnoses and treatment regimens (DiMatteo and DiNicola, 1982; Ley, 1982; Pascoe, 1983).

Compliance with medical advice is strongly associated with satisfaction with the patient–provider interaction. Ley (1982, p. 242) cites a wide body of research supporting a statistical association between compliance and satisfaction with consultation, communications, and medical care received overall. Simply understanding what the doctor says is a good predictor of satisfaction with communications. Med Ad News, an industry reporting group, suggests that as much as $100 billion a year is spent to remediate complications arising out of poor compliance, and that poor compliance arises principally from poor understanding of the doctor's, the pharmacist's, or the pharmaceutical company's communications with the patient. Med Ad News cites consumer research showing that only 58 percent of patients surveyed reported receiving any information from their doctors and only 35 percent reported receiving any information from their pharmacists, yet only about 10 percent reported ever asking questions. Med Ad News further posits that as many as half of patients who fill their prescriptions fail to take the medications properly (Med Ad News, 1995).

Properly prescribed medication, given for appropriate indications and taken as recommended, can spell the difference between normal recovery and prolonged or complicated bouts of disease. As a specific application of the more general rule of compliance, satisfied patients have been reported to be more compliant. Were Mary Poppins a quality improvement professional, she might have changed her maxim to "A spoonful of satisfaction helps the medicine go down." In many cases, delivering a satisfactory experience can be equated with meeting a patient's psychosocial/service needs, and this kind of satisfaction can have a demonstrable impact on health. Under the emerging rules of capitated care, patient satisfaction of this sort will have significant financial implications for the provider. Less compliant patients will have lower rates of recovery and will consume disproportionately more resources per health care episode than their more compliant counterparts.

Increased Loyalty to Providers

A review of two hospital case studies, reported by Woodside, Frey, and Daly (1989), suggests that there is a clear statistical link between overall satisfaction with recent inpatient care and the reported likelihood of returning for any subsequent care needs. Although the Woodside analysis uses only correlation, which is not a true predictive statistical measure, the clear suggestion is that satisfaction and return likelihood tend to move together. That is, customers who report high overall satisfaction also tend to report high return visit intentions. The authors report that many of the same factors were strongly correlated with each of these two outcomes, with nursing care being the most strongly associated.

In a national study we conducted in the mid-1980s and reported in the first edition of this book (Steiber and Krowinski, 1990, p. 21), we found the same general relationship, but again, only through correlation. When predictive models using multiple regression are applied, it becomes clear that the factors predictive of repeat visit intentions are not precisely the same factors as those predictive of overall satisfaction. Even so, the two outcomes have some common predictors. (Chapter 3 gives more detailed information about predictive models that use multiple regression.)

As Ware and Davies (1983) report, the contribution of a previous satisfactory experience to future decisions on seeking care is likely to vary from one decision to another, for it is subject to other kinds of variables, such as type of care sought, travel time, the age and sex of the patient, emergency or nonemergency nature of the problem, and so on. In particular, the decision to seek care in the first place is more likely to be motivated by the actual level of clinical need than by degree of satisfaction with a prior service experience. That is, as a condition reaches a patient-perceived threshold of activity, then a provider is sought. For instance, only if a cold becomes an intractable infection will a doctor's counsel be sought, or only if a wound appears sufficiently deep or bleeding sufficiently profuse will an emergency room or acute care center visit seem warranted.

In their analysis of patient loyalty to primary care physicians, Ware and Davies (1983, p. 294) found that consumers tend to be "hot" or "cold" about a physician; 71 percent in their survey reported seeing the same doctor as reported in an initial interview for either all (hot) their subsequent needs or none (cold) of their needs. Ware and Davies divided the entire patient response base of this study into two groups: patients who saw the same physician in the future for 50 percent or more of primary care needs (loyal), and patients who saw the same physician for less than 50 percent of primary care needs (switchers). Satisfaction with the initial provider was then coded using a summary scale on which patients were classified as experiencing high, middle, and low satisfaction. Among those who were highly satisfied, the percentage of consumers who reported switching providers was 42 percent, whereas 66 percent of those in the low-satisfaction category reported switching providers. Those who were in the middle range of satisfaction also were in the middle range for switching behavior—52 percent.

Ware and Davies found a similar pattern in disenrollments for prepaid health plan members. Among those with the highest levels of satisfaction, the reported annual disenrollment was only 3.5 percent, but among those with the lowest levels of satisfaction, the reported disenrollment rate was 30.0 percent. An ongoing, regular source of care is the greatest support for wellness and well-being. Patients are more committed to a sustained relationship with a primary care physician when they are satisfied that their interpersonal needs and medical needs are met.

Fewer Malpractice Suits

Although much attention is given to "informed consent" in the contemporary litigious health care environment, informed consent is only part of the larger picture of provider–patient communication. It is difficult to find a definitive empirical study linking patient dissatisfaction to litigious intent, but anecdotes from surgeons and their lawyers suggest that the best indicator of patients' willingness to sue is not medical malfeasance, but garden-variety dissatisfaction. Brown and Swartz (1989) found that satisfied patients were more likely to follow medical orders and less inclined to file malpractice claims. Kravitz, Rolph, and McGuisan (1991, p. 2087) cite a large body of data that suggests two general patterns in malpractice claims: "First, most cases of physician negligence never result in malpractice claims. Second, many malpractice claims are filed in the absence of physician negligence." Although some clinical processes are associated with more than their proportionate share of malpractice episodes, Rolph, Kravitz, and McGuisan (1991) suggest that a physician's past history of malpractice claims is a relatively poor predictor of future malpractice suits. Communication breakdowns, however, are among the more important underlying causes of malpractice claims.

These studies suggest that customer satisfaction is one of the better forms of malpractice "insurance." Some providers have applied this premise to grievance management, citing evidence that addressing patient complaints before they become major issues should reduce litigation incidence and that the source of a complaint is often the service encounter that led to the outcome, rather than the outcome itself (*Hospitals*,

1987; Rudnick and Dougherty-Draper, 1987; Sommers and Thompson, 1983). In fact, some recommend that litigation prevention simply boils down to better communication. Nowhere is the price of poor communication more clearly shown than in the following example.

In June 1990, the American College of Healthcare Marketing Institute reported in its newsletter, *HealthMarketing,* a classic case in which professional neglect itself would have been insufficient to spur litigation and an award for damages had not customer "disservice" intervened. The case, which began as a fairly routine surgical procedure, became more complicated when the patient experienced postoperative pain. A subsequent X ray showed that a 6-inch hemostat had been left in the patient's body after an invasive procedure. With the early alert and presumably minimal complications, the patient's problem was rectified by a recision and removal of the offending clamp.

According to patient reports, the patient did not intend to sue the hospital following the second surgical procedure and a return home for recovery. The story might have ended there had the surgical unit communicated with the billing department. Instead, the patient received an invoice in the mail for the *second* surgical procedure. In a subsequent legal confrontation, the judge awarded the patient $95,000 for the mishap. This case underscores not only the importance of positive patient relations as an intervening variable when problems do occur, but also the financial cost of dissatisfaction when customer relations break down.

Brook, Brutoco, and Williams (1975) further suggest that the generally litigious environment of health care further erodes the physician–patient relationship, resulting in a lower level of satisfaction on the part of the patient. That is, a spiraling effect occurs, in which lower satisfaction in the patient population increases the likelihood of malpractice suits and an increase in malpractice suits further diminishes overall patient expectations for a satisfactory experience. However, the good news, according to Brook, is that the trend away from a traditional authority-versus-dependence (doctor–patient) relationship and toward empowerment of the patient should lead to patients being more willing to take more control over their own well-being and therefore to seek a potentially healthier outcome.

The Financial Consequences of Dissatisfaction

The patient who is sufficiently dissatisfied to sue a provider following treatment is a public relations nightmare, costing the hospital goodwill and damaging its reputation from the moment the press reports the story to the community. The case begins to cost the hospital real dollars from the first billable legal hour, with costs mounting until the final disposition of the case, when the hospital may see a larger price tag on dissatisfaction in the form of an adverse judgment. Even when professional liability insurance covers much of the cost of the judgment, the provider incurs other direct costs, either in ancillary staff time and related charges or in increased premiums for insurance in the future. All of these costs detract from the bottom line.

Malpractice suits are dramatic and obvious examples of financial loss due to customer dissatisfaction. Less obvious are the unspoken grievances, the cases in which dissatisfied patients do not seek legal recourse but, because of a lack of a forum in which to air their grievances, remain dissatisfied. What are the real costs of this type of dissatisfaction?

Impact on the Hospital

In a study across 51 medical-surgical hospitals and with a response base of more than 15,000 patients, Nelson, Rust, Zahorik, Rose, Batalden, and Siemanski (1992, p. 6) were able to show statistical links between hospital service performance and hospital financial performance. In a multivariate examination, the authors demonstrated that patient satisfaction with the discharge process, physician care, and ancillary care had a positive and statistically significant impact on three financial outcomes—earnings, net revenue, and return on assets. The authors concluded that "work on quality improvement today can be viewed as an investment in the long-term survival and growth of the hospital.... [T]he path to higher profitability begins with improving quality as perceived by the key customers of the hospital" (p. 12).

Hospital marketing executives surveyed in the late 1980s indicated that only 75.6 percent of their annual volume of patients were "brand loyal"—meaning that the executives expected only three in every four patients would return for their next health care need (Steiber and Krowinski, 1990, p. 4). The remaining one in four was lost for various reasons. Some patients were lost for unavoidable reasons, such as moves out of the market, restriction changes in health insurance, or unavailability of specific medical services. Others were lost because the first service encounter simply did not meet their minimum expectations. The figure cited by hospital marketing executives appeared markedly higher than in many industries, where the usual attrition rate is 10 to 15 percent per year. Assuming that hospital marketing executives need not be quite so pessimistic, what are the expected costs of dissatisfaction for the typical hospital?

Figure 1-1 offers an example of a "typical" community-based hospital of 174 beds with a "typical" discharge volume of 5,864 patients per year. (*Typical* is a national statistical average in this case.) The rule of thumb on the future needs cycle for hospitals is that about one in every five households in America has a hospital inpatient stay each year. So, of those discharged in the present year, the typical hospital has the potential to see one in five within the following year:

$$5{,}864 \text{ patients} \times 0.20 = 1{,}173$$

The figure is, of course, higher for households with seniors present and relatively lower in younger households, particularly those with no children present. Now, consider the impact of patient dissatisfaction on the potential 1,173 returns. The basic unit is the household rather than the patient, because patient dissatisfaction is presumed to affect household, not just individual, health care purchase activity. However, customer dissatisfaction grows beyond the specific incident, person, or household. In the mainstream service economy, the Technical Assistance Research Programs (TARP) show that customer dissatisfaction spreads beyond the current event through the conversations that

Figure 1-1. The Cost of Dissatisfaction for a Typical Hospital

- Typical hospital size: 174 beds*
- Typical annual discharges: 5,864*
- Typical annual repeat volume likely: 1,173**

- Assume rate of disloyalty: 12.5%
- Assume length of stay: 7.1 days*
- Assume base revenue per patient day: $1,364
- Assume dissatisfied customer tells 9.5 others: (1 + 9.5)

12.5% × (1 + 9.5) × 1,173 × 7.1 days × $1,364

Potential lost annual revenue: $14,907,197

*Source: American Hospital Association, 1993.
**Source: Data archives, Quality Expectations, Inc., 1995.

disgruntled customers have with friends and acquaintances. An unsatisfactory experience comes to be a sign of low quality of the provider and the provider's services. Findings by TARP show that the average dissatisfied customer tells between nine and ten other people about the unsatisfactory experience, and one in every eight customers with a service problem will recount the event to more than 20 individuals. By comparison, the satisfied customer talks about a positive experience with only three to four other individuals (Peterson, 1988, pp. 3–4).

Figure 1-1 shows how potential problems associated with negative customer experiences for the typical hospital grow:

$$(5,864 \text{ patients} \times 0.20) \times (1 + 9.5) = \$12,314$$

The rest is simple accounting. Figure 1-1 shows the financial conclusion that the typical hospital will reach when the average base revenue per inpatient day is $1,364 and the average length of stay is 7.1 days:

$$(5,864 \text{ patients} \times 0.20) \times (1 + 9.5) \times (\$1,364 \times 7.1) = \$119,257,575$$

$$(5,864 \text{ patients} \times 0.20) \times (1 + 9.5) \times (\$1,364 \times 7.1) \times 12.5\% = \$14,907,197$$

These figures account for just the first year. The problem moves forward with a hospital into future years and future revenues as well.

Impact on the Physician's Office

Figure 1-2 shows how a model similar to that applied to hospitals can be applied to a primary care physician's office practice. The numbers change, because although the revenue per utilization experience is dramatically lower than the revenue from a hospital day, the average household has many more opportunities to visit a physician's office than a hospital in a given year. In this particular case, the same dissatisfied patient represents 3.1 household visits for the physician per year at an average office visit charge of $43.70 (American Medical Association, 1994).

It is likely that loyalty is markedly higher, given the fact that only 1 percent of consumers in a nationwide survey are "very dissatisfied" and an additional 4 percent are "somewhat dissatisfied" (Steiber, 1988b, p. 79). Even so, fully 22 percent are only "somewhat satisfied," which suggests that the low end of the service industry continuum may be a reasonable assumption for disloyalty, or switching physicians. Figure 1-2 shows a 5 percent rate of disloyalty and the consequent cost, in the following year, of dissatisfaction to a primary care physician's practice. To be conservative and to

Figure 1-2. The Cost of Dissatisfaction for a Typical Primary Care Provider

- Typical practice size: 6,400*
- Typical office visit charge: $43.70*
- Typical annual visits per household: 3.1**

- Assume rate of disloyalty: 5.0%
- Assume dissatisfied customer tells only family/household members

$5.0\% \times 6,4000 \times \$43.70 \times 3.1$

Potential lost annual revenue = $43,350.40

*Source: Center for Health Policy Research at the AMA, 1994.
**Source: Data archives, Quality Expectations, Inc., 1995.

recognize the finite sphere within which consumer conversations about any given physician may occur, the TARP multiplier of 9.5 added lost households is not included in these calculations. Even so, the annual revenue at risk from dissatisfaction for the typical primary care physician totals in excess of $43,000.

With the increasing scrutiny of insurers, business coalitions, and regulators, satisfaction affects not only patient loyalty but also contract awards or renewals. Given the relatively unforgiving nature of the marketplace, there are good reasons to attempt to move the patient satisfaction indicator higher.

Dissatisfaction has farther-reaching implications than the loss of a customer: it also damages the provider's good name, because satisfaction is tied to customers' perceptions of quality. Recall that satisfaction and perceived quality are statistically related to one another. Low perceived satisfaction in any context leads to both diminished brand loyalty and low perceived quality.

By extension, as low perceived quality and/or low satisfaction drives away business, market share will suffer (Ouchi, 1982; Phillips and others, 1983). Most service businesses cannot replace lost customers fast enough to stem the inevitable tide. Experience in other industries further shows that quality perceptions and customer satisfaction are closely tied to the profitability of businesses (Clifford and Cavanaugh, 1985, p. 259; Jacobson and Aaker, 1987). In the end, then, customer satisfaction has a very clear impact on the bottom line. Those providers in any business who keep the customer satisfied will see an enhanced image of quality as a direct and immediate consequence. Customer satisfaction is no longer simply the nice or right thing to do; it is the only good business choice in today's highly competitive environment. And the good news is that just as dissatisfaction can magnify itself in working against growth and financial success, so satisfaction can be amplified by selective investment and marketing.

The Financial Benefits of Addressing Dissatisfaction

Effective customer satisfaction programs not only attempt to deliver health care experiences that exceed customer expectations, they also try to address the complaints of dissatisfied customers. Why is it in the provider's best interests to encourage complaints from recently treated patients? Once a patient complains about a service shortfall, the patient has re-created the opportunity for the provider to address and rectify the grievance. The real question, then, is how a provider might create an incentive for dissatisfied patients to air their complaints. One such incentive is the "money-back guarantee."

Money-Back Guarantees

Many providers may look at the money-back guarantee or other incentive as appropriate only for other service or product businesses, reasoning that health care is "above all that." Some also fear that a program could prove disastrously costly, despite the fact that the Health Care Advisory Board (1988, p. 96), reporting on seven hospitals with money-back guarantee programs in place, showed that the average annual direct cost in rebates had been only about $1,000 per facility. Still, the question arises as to why a health service provider would voluntarily raise the specter of dissatisfaction, let alone incur added cost.

The logic behind money-back programs and corporate cultures that wish to address dissatisfaction is to find problems so that they can be remedied. The Health Care Advisory Board offers a cost–benefit analysis of how a program offering a potential $100 refund would help ensure enhanced patient business in the future. Figure 1-3 shows the plan's basic assumptions, which highlight the overall volume of patients in play,

Figure 1-3. Health Care Advisory Board Assumptions for Hypothetical Cost–Benefit Analysis of Money-Back Guarantee Program

1. A 550-bed hospital admits 15,000 inpatients per year.
2. Thirteen percent of all patients are dissatisfied with the service they received.
3. Average revenue per patient admission is $5,000.
4. Variable costs associated with hospital procedures are 50 percent of revenues.
5. Sixty-three percent of dissatisfied customers will complain without prompting.
6. With the service guarantee, the hospital can raise the percentage of dissatisfied customers complaining to 73 percent.
7. Ninety-one percent of dissatisfied noncomplainers will not buy from the same institution again.
8. In general, 26 percent of complaining customers are satisfied with the business's response to their complaint.
9. With the service guarantee, the hospital can raise the percentage of complaining customers who are satisfied with the response they get to 36 percent.
10. Nineteen percent of complainants whose complaints are not satisfactorily resolved will buy from hospital again; 54 percent of complainants whose complaints are satisfactorily resolved will buy from the hospital again.

anticipated levels of dissatisfaction, levels of actual complaints with and without a guarantee program, and the increased revenue available if complaints were brought to the surface so that they might be resolved. Note that the surfacing of grievances is at the heart of the matter.

Figures 1-4 and 1-5 offer a side-by-side analysis of how the two scenarios, one without a guarantee and one with, result in a bottom line. The scenario in figure 1-4, without a service guarantee, shows that patients with unresolved complaints are the most likely never to return to the hospital for services. The sources of these unresolved complaints are as follows:

- 91 percent of patients who are dissatisfied but do not complain
- 81 percent of patients who complain but see no satisfactory resolution
- 46 percent of patients who complain and see a satisfactory resolution but still will not return

These 1,540 patients (total) and the associated average revenue generated for each repeat purchase ($5,000) result in an anticipated loss of $7,700,000 in revenue owing to dissatisfaction.

Unlike the previous examples, this revenue projection does not detail how the dollar amount per dissatisfied customer—$5,000—is derived. However, the projection does offer a clear picture of the dollars forgone by not giving more dissatisfied customers an opportunity to express and remediate their grievances.

Figure 1-5 offers a somewhat brighter future, with incremental revenue and profit gained with the at-risk amount of the guarantee program, which results very simply in more complaints voiced. Figure 1-5 shows that the guarantee encourages 1,424 complaints to be raised, compared to 1,228 complaints expressed in the setting without a service guarantee. The difference between these two contributes directly to the volume of repeat business to be expected from these 196 returning patients (1,424 − 1,228 = 196). It is anticipated that these additional returning patients will generate approximately $435,000 in added revenues, of which approximately 50 percent will go directly to the bottom line. The cost incurred through the guarantees themselves is only $4,000. With a return on investment (ROI) of $217,500 in profit, the program not only would have satisfied more patients but also would have generated an incremental ROI of

Chapter 1

Figure 1-4. Patient Loyalty without Service Guarantee

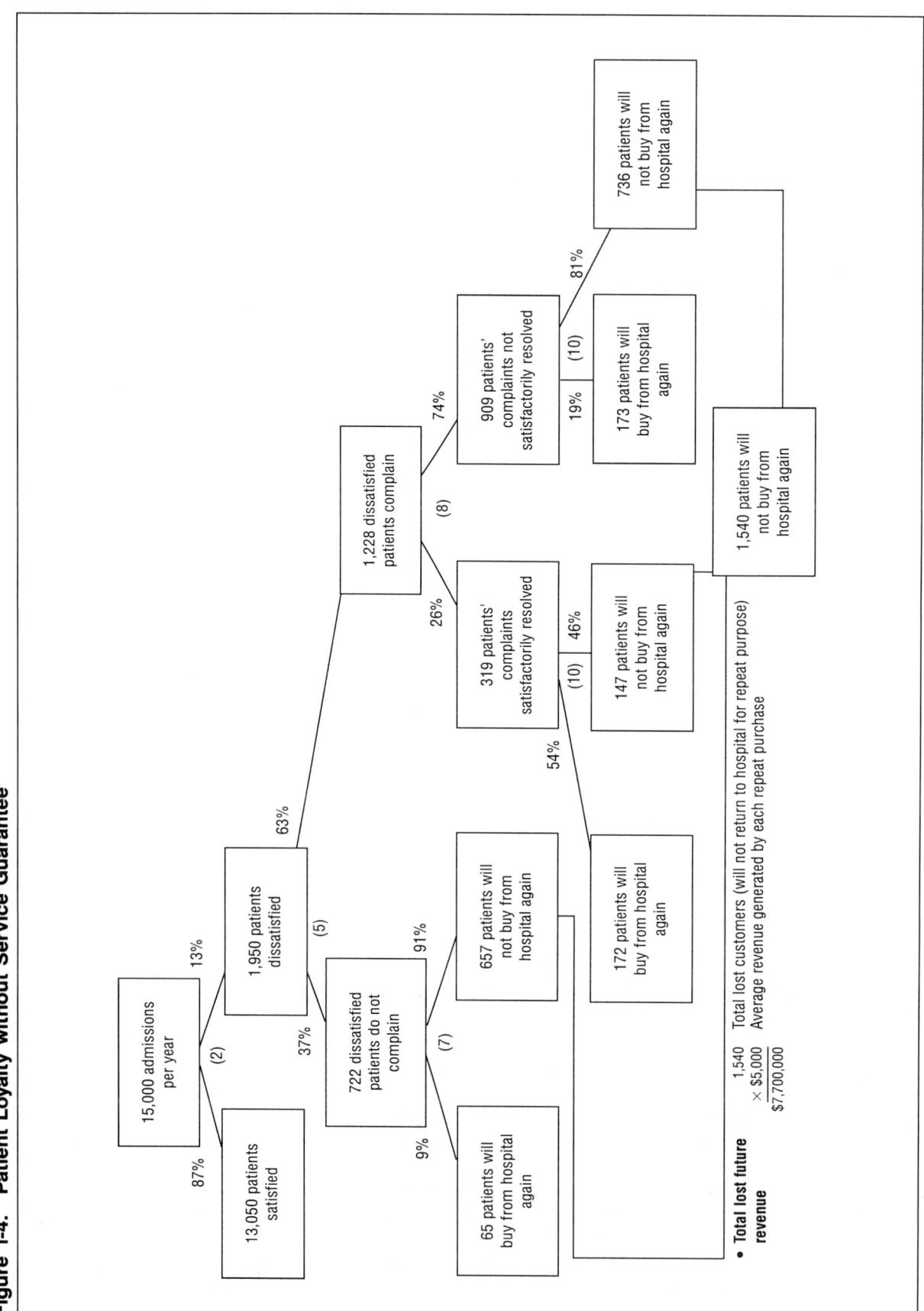

Note: Numbers in parentheses refer to the assumptions in figure 1-3.

Figure 1-5. Patient Loyalty with Service Guarantee

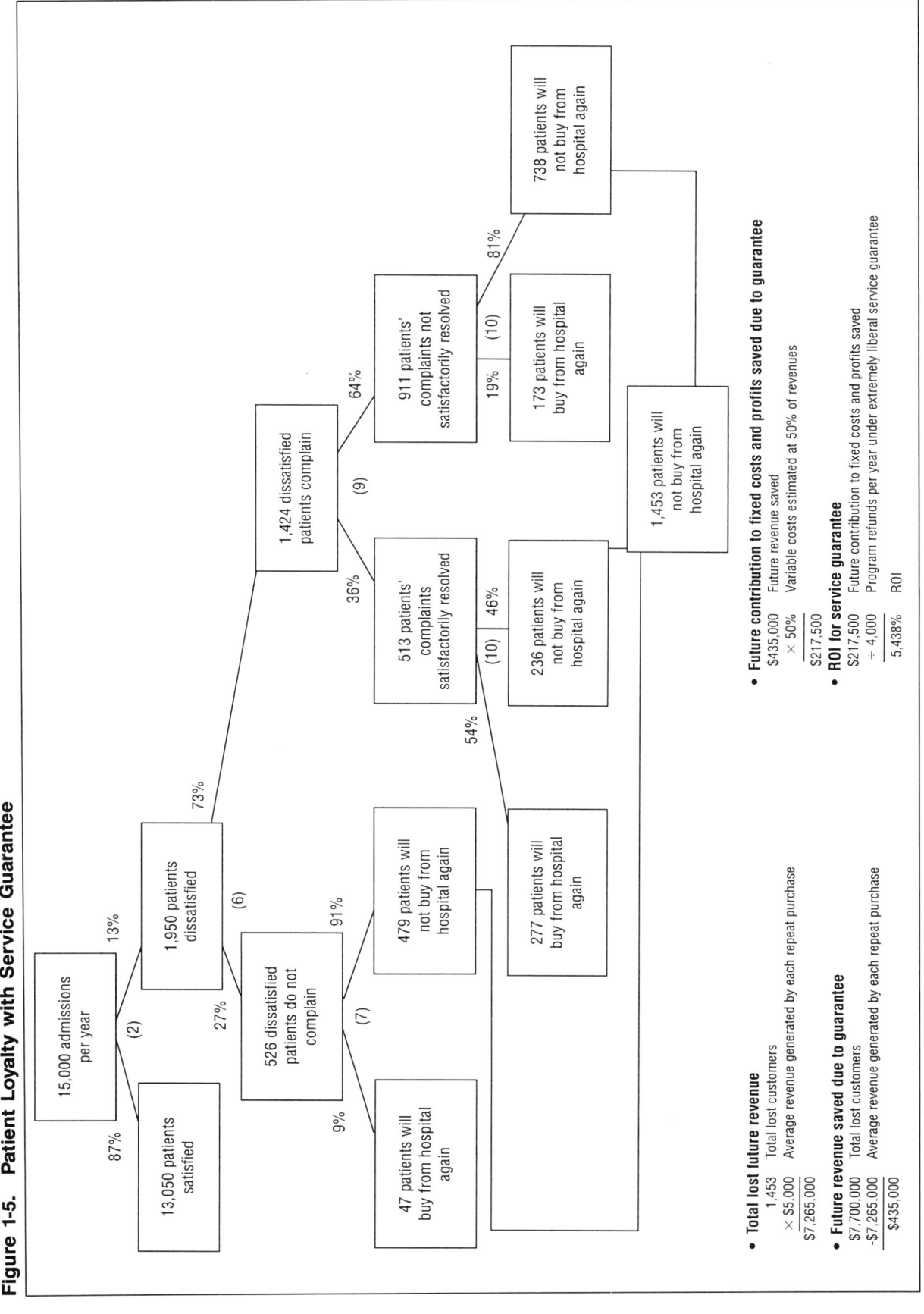

Note: Numbers in parentheses refer to the assumptions in figure 1-3.

5,438 percent ($217,500 ÷ $4,000). It is unlikely that a hospital could find any other programs that rival this level of expected return and have such a modest risk.

The Financial Return on Quality

Quality improvement efforts have a history of being viewed by many managers as expenses instead of investments. To put quality improvement efforts into a productive perspective, it is useful to document the financial "return on quality." Rust, Zahorik, and Keiningham (1995) use quantitative models to show a financial benefit associated with quality improvement, and by extension customer satisfaction measurement exercises.

A Quantitative Model

The general model with which we are concerned is shown in figure 1-6. Notice that the top box, "Improvement Effort," is the program that initiates actual changes in

Figure 1-6. A Model of Service Quality Improvement and Profitability

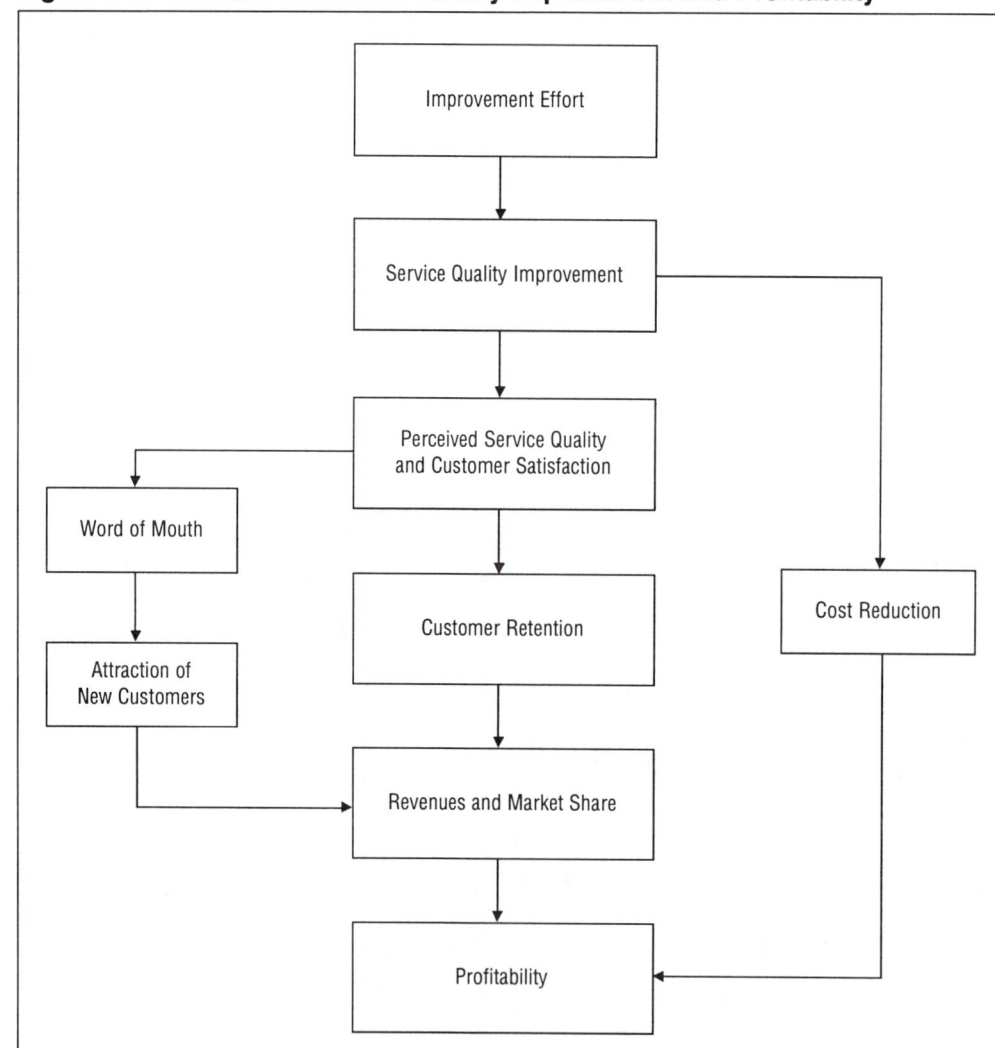

Source: Rust, R. T., Zahorik, A. J., and Keiningham, T. L. Return on quality (ROQ): making service quality financially accountable. *Journal of Marketing* 59:58–70, Apr. 1995. Reprinted with permission from American Marketing Association, Chicago, IL.

the way a service provider does business ("Service Quality Improvement"). This "Service Quality Improvement," in turn, spins off two changes. The first is an immediate "Cost Reduction" through presumed efficiencies on the right-hand side of the figure, which drops revenue to the bottom line ("Profitability"). But "Service Quality Improvement" also is recognized by customers through the next box in the main trunk of the figure, "Perceived Service Quality and Customer Satisfaction."

This perceptual shift favorably affects both the customer's own likelihood of returning for future needs ("Customer Retention") and the customer's subsequent messages to others about the experience ("Word of Mouth"). Both "Customer Retention," acting directly, and "Word of Mouth," acting indirectly through "Attraction of New Customers," work to create new "Revenues and Market Share." All these actions therefore work collectively to enhance profitability for the service provider.

The figure does not show the specific statistical analysis initially required in order to focus on the element(s) that will offer enhancements to customer satisfaction, but it is possible to make some inferences based on the patient satisfaction research literature. For most hospital inpatient applications, this focus typically resides somewhere within the nursing function; for physician's offices, it rests in the patient–physician interaction; and for emergency room encounters, it may rest in the amount of time spent waiting or in customer perceptions of the attending physician(s). These elements probably come as no surprise to most health care professionals. (The precise methodology required to come to the correct focus for any given facility is described in greater detail in chapter 3.)

In this model, the financial return on quality can come from one of three elements as reflected in the three vertical paths of the figure: (1) cost reduction, (2) customer retention, and (3) attraction of new customers. Although Rust and others concede that quality improvement does not always usher in productivity improvements (and the consequent cost reductions), this is one point where listening to the customer and designing more user-friendly services can enhance organizational effectiveness, not merely customer happiness. These "cost reductions" and consequent cash savings flow to the bottom line of the model. The main trunk of this model shows that quality improvement will enhance customer satisfaction, which in turn will bring the customer back for any future needs, thereby reinforcing revenues, market share, and profitability. Finally, moving to the left branch, Rust and others agree with TARP that "word of mouth" translates in financial terms into revenue and market share.

It is understood that this model may leave many health care professionals somewhat skeptical, particularly those who have not seen any improvement on their own patient satisfaction surveys to date. Without a focus on what is important to the customer and without a sensitive measure of incremental improvements, however, it is difficult to say whether it is the model that is not working or the quality improvement effort that is not working. In Rust and others' own research, in the hotel industry, the focus first is on bathrooms as a driver of customer satisfaction. Within this category, the cleanliness of a bathroom is the number one priority. For a physician's office, a parallel case might include a focus on the amount of time spent waiting; for inpatient care, a focus might be on nurses' personal attention to patients; for a rehabilitation setting, a focus might be on a physical therapist's explanation to a patient of the goals of a therapeutic regimen. Each of these areas of service, if it measurably improves over time, should ultimately have a positive impact on business outcomes such as overall perceived quality, the likelihood of repeat business, or the likelihood of referral. This is what is meant by a "driver" of overall quality outcomes.

The hotel chain in Rust and others' case study then reflected on how to improve bathroom cleanliness most directly, finally deciding to have cleaning personnel spend more time cleaning bathrooms. This labor cost investment could easily be calculated, as could the relationship between cleaner bathrooms and enhanced satisfaction and the likelihood that a customer would choose to stay in one of the chain's hotels again.

Figure 1-7 shows the relationship between the investment in cleaning labor costs and declining customer dissatisfaction. The nonlinear nature of this relationship is to be expected; the returns on quality are at their greatest with the first dollars spent. Additional expenditures offer incrementally lower returns to the point of negligible contribution to customer satisfaction or lack of dissatisfaction (on the right-hand side of the figure).

Could a similar model be applied to health care? The answer is yes, but with some qualifications. For a physician's office visit, the implications of customer satisfaction for practice growth are relatively clear, but for a health system or hospital, the implications of customer satisfaction are not quite as straightforward. In the former case, a physician can get away with keeping patients waiting inordinately long in the reception area only if there is no competition for the patients' business or if the rest of the service is extraordinarily good. However, the markets in which there is no competition are rapidly vanishing, and the practices that actually offer extraordinary service are not as common as practitioners may believe. In the case of the health system or hospital-based provider, service delivery becomes more complex. The service provided by a given health care professional may become intertwined with the services provided by other professionals, with the result that any one staff member's contribution to a poor (or good) service experience becomes less clear.

Some of this complexity will diminish, however, as capitation and managed care enrollment panels come to dominate most markets. Ask any present insurer what an improvement of 1 percent in reenrollment rates would do for the bottom line, and it becomes clear how well a model such as that of Rust and others can work for the customer-oriented provider.

Physicians and Patient Satisfaction

Physicians have always had an incentive to maintain satisfaction among their patients. Early on, it may have been felt as an ethical obligation to meet more than just the

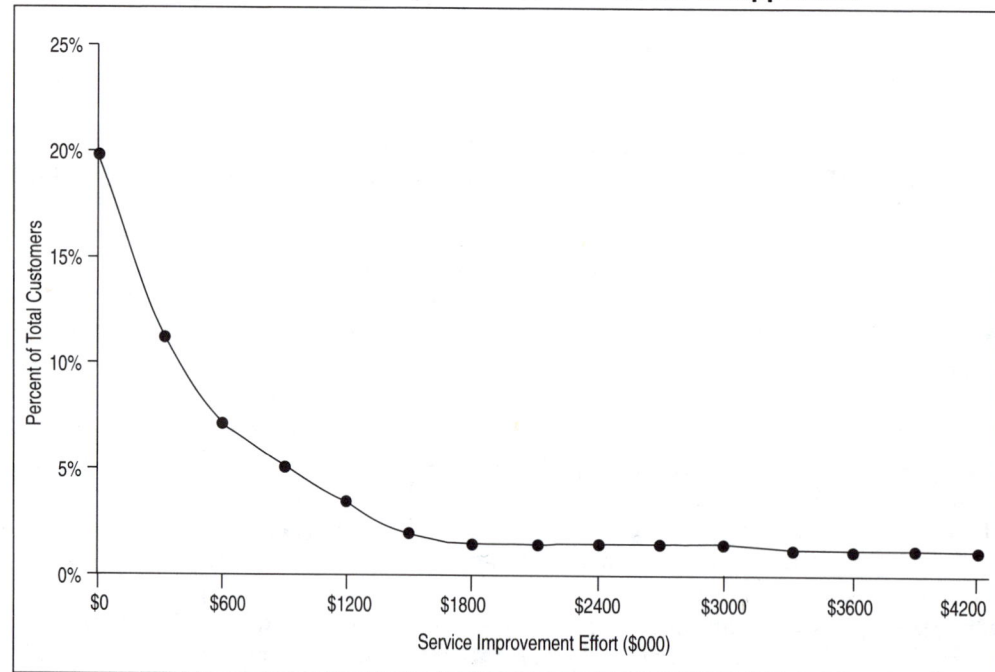

Figure 1-7. Impact of Quality Expenditures on Percent Disappointed

Source: Rust, R. T., Zahorik, A. J., and Keiningham, T. L. Return on quality (ROQ): making service quality financially accountable. *Journal of Marketing* 59:58–70, Apr. 1995. Reprinted with permission from American Marketing Association, Chicago, IL.

health care needs of the patient. Some physicians incorporated this "high-touch" approach into their day-to-day practice activities. But in medicine's "pre-oversupply" days (with a watershed from about 1975 through 1980), there was little financial risk for the physician who did not embrace the virtues of patient-centered care. Long reception room waits and a "doctor knows best" mentality were pervasive prior to the mid-1970s. With an increase in the numbers of physicians, hospital beds, and health care facilities during the 1970s, however, patient satisfaction became a competitive issue. Providers who could fulfill the patient's service agenda were more likely to retain the patient and grow the business. Providers who did not meet customer expectations may also have had viable practices, but viability would have depended on the local competition for the patient's attention.

Enter the present competitive environment, with its increasingly strong dose of managed care and associated capitated payment systems, negotiated fees for service or per diems, and physicians as employees on salaries. Market forces are becoming codified into financial incentive packages for providers, including primary care physicians and specialists. These packages quantify the extent to which the patient's clinical as well as service experiences are managed in such a way as to create an optimal matching of patients' expectations with clinical necessities (Franks, 1992). Neil Schlackman (1994, p. 18) explains it this way:

> Many components of quality, e.g., access, appropriateness of care, the technical competence with which a procedure is performed, patient satisfaction with care and service, and outcomes can and should be measured. Increasingly, healthcare consumers — both employers and patients — are becoming involved in determining the course of healthcare services. This is an important development. Yet, with consumer involvement, it has become even more evident that there is a wide gap between technically possible quality and the quality actually achieved in the daily practice of medicine. Thus, there is an increased need to justify what and how medicine is practiced and reward those who do it "right."

Physicians with significant percentages of their practices paid by managed care will be among the first to see the virtues of customer satisfaction, but all employed (salaried) physicians will follow this precedent (de Lafuente, 1994, p. 36). Daniel Zismer (1994, p. 39) offers a very simple formula for integrating patient satisfaction into physicians' incentives within the managed care framework. Zismer recommends that for a hypothetical family practice physician with 30 percent of total income derived from an incentive structure, 10 percent of that incentive structure should come directly from performance goals built around measured patient satisfaction.

TakeCare, one of Colorado's largest health maintenance organizations, has invested heavily in a patient satisfaction system that rewards physicians who meet or exceed patients' expectations. For some physicians, the mere implementation of a patient satisfaction dimension was a radical step. As Gaughan and Muneta (1993, p. 6) suggest, "Before TakeCare began their survey, many physicians had no idea how long the average patient had to wait for an appointment or sit in their waiting rooms." Now, physicians track performance on patient satisfaction dimensions.

Purchaser Demands for Patient Satisfaction

The patient is the customer who receives the services purchased in a health care delivery setting. But the patient is not the only individual who puts dollars on the table to cover the costs of those services. In fact, in some cases, the patient is not at all at risk for the cost of care (although such patients are vanishing about as quickly as most endangered species of the Serengeti Plain). Other players and purchasers with a fiscal interest in the patient's care are looking over the patient's shoulder to analyze the service interaction. What do the purchasers want to see?

Insurers' Stake in Patient Satisfaction

Employers and insurers have begun to build their health care purchasing decisions more rationally and quantifiably around perceived "value." Although buyers using these "value-based purchasing" decisions do not necessarily place patient satisfaction at the center of their decision-making processes, satisfaction is at least part of their decision-making equations. Value is defined as a blend of such variables as cost, outcomes, volume, and patient satisfaction.

Perhaps the most obvious item on an insurer's agenda is *lower cost* of the health services provided to the insurees. A second item on insurers' agenda, *higher quality* (in the form of better outcomes), dovetails with health care's long history of quality assurance programs and standards (although it is important to distinguish contemporary quality improvement from the "bad apple" legacy of quality assurance). In effect, insurers receive a certain minimum standard for quality without asking for it, but many also are seeking better success rates, greater efficacy, and enhanced wellness. These standards are set by other third parties, to whom health services providers must report, and the insurer is the beneficiary of this process. Healthier patients and better outcomes for those who must seek a provider's care simply are less costly for an insurer to maintain.

A third item of interest to insurers is *higher volume* of procedures, because it reduces the contracting/transaction costs traditionally associated with working with a large number of smaller providers versus a smaller number of larger providers. However, a higher volume of procedures is important to insurers not so much for economies of scale as for the increased proficiency of the practitioners performing those procedures. It is presumed that better outcomes accrue with practice, and with the consequent higher volume of procedures. To the extent that high proficiency will at least somewhat correlate with the patient's perception of the service experience, there may be some tie-in with patient satisfaction.

A fourth item of interest is *patient satisfaction*. Enlightened self-interest suggests that if patients are more satisfied with providers, then the enrollees will be more satisfied with the health plan. Thus, patient satisfaction serves all parties' interests in customer retention. This is, perhaps, why insurers were so quick to jump on the health care reform bandwagon for a consumer report card when the first rallying cry was sounded from Washington, DC (Priest, 1993). However, patient satisfaction is also an important value-based selling tool that offers synergies with employers' enlightened self-interests.

Employers' Stake in Patient Satisfaction

Employers and other health services purchasers are looking for quality of care on behalf of their employees or enrollees. But differences emerge in the definition and measurement of quality. Those participating in an early Woods Hole, MA, think-tank session came to a consensus about what purchasers are looking for—something the participants called a "patient's quality of life." Unfortunately, purchasers tend to be most comfortable with dimensions they can quantify, and quality of life is a bit elusive, to say the least. To providers, purchasers sometimes seem to be trying to procure health care as if they were buying heavy equipment for the factory. Providers point out that health care purchases are quite different.

Because purchasers value quantitative measurement, they tend to evaluate health care in terms of mortality, morbidity, the cost of care episodes, and the extent to which other costs, such as insurance and disability, can be reduced (Geigle and Jones, 1990). Patient satisfaction likewise can be quantified, and so it can enter the equation. But purchasers find it a challenge to square patient satisfaction with the dollars expended. The difficulty of measuring patient satisfaction in dollars and cents may explain the anecdotal evidence suggesting that patient satisfaction is not at the top of purchasers' list of quality elements. Purchasers may also be swayed by the fact that low satisfaction does not appear to involve any measurable costs. In addition, there is, as yet, no true standard that purchasers can use to compare one provider with another. In local markets in which report cards have been mandated by business coalitions or larger employers, true standards may be emerging.

There are hazards in simply jumping to a standardized, value-based, patient-satisfaction selling tool. Offering comparable data across provider institutions is useful only to the leader. It does nothing to help providers who have low scores. (Chapter 3 defines the parameters of a working model for measuring and managing patient satisfaction, something we call "value-based engineering.")

In lieu of concrete data, what can employers/health services purchasers rely on? Nationwide research suggests that employers are sensitive to the price they will pay for reduced premiums if the choices become too restrictive. The "price" is the increased number of complaints they must field through the human resources director's office from employees who discover their personal physician or favored hospital is no longer in the care plan. Many employees have preexisting ties to providers (both physician and hospital), and these employees tend to be less satisfied when they do not have access to the providers of their choice under the most favorable pricing structures available to them. Moreover, if employees must spend more time traveling for care or are dissatisfied with the providers on the preferred panel, their dissatisfaction with their insurance plan can negatively affect their perceptions of their employer. As a consequence, employee (patient) satisfaction enters their value-based purchasing equation just as it enters the equation of the insurer. Once purchasers/employers are in a position to compare apples with apples, then price (measured as complaints or, conversely, patient satisfaction) may emerge as a more tangible — and therefore more important — criterion.

Purchasers' Drive for Quality Measurement

It has nearly always been the case that larger employers get more of what they want from their vendors than smaller employers, but health care is a bit challenging even for large purchasers. Historically, large purchasers have offered the most generous health benefits packages to their employees, which means that larger employers also have seen the most severe increases in costs to maintain these "lavish" offerings. It is not simply costs that employers are attempting to contain; it is the whole health care agenda they now are trying to manage more effectively, and this, as we have demonstrated, includes patient satisfaction.

Xerox Corporation was one of the early pioneers in demanding more from its health care insurers. It was joined in 1993 by four other national employers: Allied Signal, Ameritech, GTE, and Pepsico ("Health Care Policy Standards," 1993). These "big five" have required that their health maintenance organizations become accredited by the National Committee for Quality Assurance; and other employers (General Electric, IBM, Mercantile Stores, and USAir), while not necessarily aligning themselves with the big five, have followed suit.

In an effort to make good health care purchasing decisions, some businesses have formed coalitions to compile and share health care information. Large employers with national operations can develop provider evaluations that enable them to compare and choose from among a nationwide array of insurers. Recognizing that most health care purchasing choices are made at the local market level, however, most business coalitions that are developing comparative information for decisions are in metropolitan markets. Some comparative studies are subsidized by the larger employers themselves, and some are required of the providers within their own budgets. These coalitions have accumulated a variety of outcomes information to help employers and their employees make better choices from among available options. The intent is to help all parties make more informed cost-benefit decisions that ultimately have the potential to affect the cost of health care.

One of the first such initiatives, the Greater Cleveland Health Quality Choice Program, in 1989 started to compile value-based purchasing data on medical costs, clinical outcomes, and patient satisfaction (Greater Cleveland Health Quality Choice Program, 1995, pp. 7–8). Data collected through this program were made available to all business purchasers. Although this program has its detractors, it has served as a model for other business coalitions nationwide.

In many markets, only the largest businesses have sufficient clout to enforce compliance with a reporting system on providers of managed care plans. In Chicago, for example, a dozen local businesses operating through the Midwest Business Group on Health created a "buyers' guide" on responsiveness of health plans, costs, physician credentials, eligibility requirements, cost of coverage, and employer/employer satisfaction (Oloroso, 1994, pp. 1, 58).

Employers are not necessarily using these initiatives to hold providers' feet to the fire. In some cases, employers are looking to partner with health care providers. In effect, health care providers are increasingly being treated as suppliers, and businesses want to be able to measure the quality of what they receive as well as to help set the standards (Bergman, 1993, p. 38). As a result, many providers have begun to share information derived from their own quality improvement initiatives. One such initiative, the Picker/Commonwealth Program for Patient-Centered Care, grew out of Beth Israel Hospital's quality improvement activities.

The Picker Institute and Patient-Centered Care

In 1987, the Picker/Commonwealth Program for Patient-Centered Care was initiated on the campus of Beth Israel Hospital in Boston. Its principal goal was to embrace the perspective of the patient both in assessing "through the patient's eyes" satisfaction with the clinical care and service received and in designing health care quality improvement efforts. Although many survey standards have incorporated rating scales per se, the Picker method is novel in that in most areas of inquiry, it simply identified whether specific services occurred, resulting in a simple dichotomy of yes, an event occurred, or no, the event did not occur.

Question areas of the Picker surveys (both inpatient and ambulatory) address seven basic dimensions of care or service:

- Respect for patients' values, preferences and expressed needs
- Coordination of care and integration of services within an institutional setting
- Communication between patient and providers; dissemination of accurate, timely, and appropriate information; and education about the long-term implications of disease and illness
- Physical care, comfort, and alleviation of fears and anxiety
- Emotional support and alleviation of fear and anxiety
- Involvement of family and friends
- Transition and continuity from one locus of care to another (Gerteis and others, 1993)

Patient Satisfaction and Regulators

In its 1994 standards, the Joint Commission on Accreditation of Healthcare Organizations (Joint Commission, or JCAHO) built patient satisfaction more explicitly into its review processes. This approach, initially begun as part of the Quality Initiative, has since been codified by the Joint Commission into a series of core processes that are summarized by the tag lines "doing the right thing" and "doing the right thing well."

Although with a shorter track record and with a focus on health insurers, the National Committee for Quality Assurance (NCQA) has attempted to test some of the basic tenets of the Health Plan Employer Data and Information Set (HEDIS). In early 1995, the NCQA completed a one-year pilot project among 21 health insurers. It has released preliminary findings that are suggestive of a model, or report card, that insurers and providers/insurers can productively apply. Patient satisfaction with issues such as access, convenience, and other service perceptions figures into this model.

State and federal regulators have not yet clearly outlined the role of patient satisfaction, but these payers will not be idle as they review care received by Medicare and Medicaid recipients. Some states, such as Maryland, Minnesota, Pennsylvania, and Vermont, also have picked up the health care reform ball dropped by the federal government and run with it.

The Joint Commission

In its express mission "to improve the quality of care provided to the public," the Joint Commission has embraced the major tenets of continuous quality improvement. Within this context, patient satisfaction has a clear role in the commission's 1995 standards. Although the Joint Commission is judicious in avoiding mandates for specific methodologies, question designs, or other tactical issues of patient satisfaction measurement, it does spell out the overall processes within which patient satisfaction is embedded.

Among the leadership standards of the Joint Commission (1994, p. 275), patient satisfaction is interpreted in the following ways:

- LD.1.3.3: Services are designed to be responsive to the needs and expectations of patients and/or their families/decision makers.
- LD.1.3.3.1: The organization gathers, assesses, and takes appropriate action on information that relates to the patient's satisfaction with the services provided.

Some of the more substantive elements of these standards are spelled out in a Joint Commission example:

> Concurrent and retrospective surveys of patient satisfaction are conducted. Patients are queried on appropriate aspects of the organization's performance through telephone interviews, questionnaires or interviews. The organization evaluates the data it collects in relation to its major clinical care activities and support functions. In particular, dimensions of performance—appropriateness, availability, continuity, effectiveness, efficacy, efficiency, safety, and timeliness of services—are analyzed. Based on the results of analysis of the patient satisfaction surveys, the organization refocuses its services and/or redesigns the existing process of providing services as appropriate. (Joint Commission, 1994, pp. 275-76)

Within the larger context of organizational performance, the Joint Commission (1994, p. 227) encourages providers to be attentive to the needs and expectations of staff as well as patients. This attentiveness translates into the following process standards:

- New processes are designed well (P1.2)
- The design is based on: (P1.1.1)
  - The organization's mission, vision, and plans (P1.2.1.1)
  - The needs and expectations of patients, staff, and others (P1.2.1.2).

As an example, the Joint Commission offers the case of a provider determining through an assessment conducted among staff and patients that a given service area must be expanded to include an additional, complementary specialty. Patients, their families, physicians, and other staff members are consulted in some fashion for input on appropriate design and practice guidelines. The "best practices" of other institutions are also consulted in order to learn from the experiences of others. It is clear from the Joint Commission examples that such external consultation is not simply a comparison of internal performance or needs with a national "average," or norm. Instead, continuous quality improvement theory and the Joint Commission encourage the charting of one's present and future performance against the best practices as available in the health care arena. (One might add a wry reminder that Olympic gold medals are not awarded to the individual who finishes ahead of the average competitor but to the first-place finisher.)

Although an argument could be made that these process standards are grounded in "managing patient satisfaction," the Joint Commission also specifically mandates "measuring patient satisfaction," although the patient is not the only one with input into satisfaction measurement. The Joint Commission (1994, p. 233) encourages the following measures:

- The organization collects data about: (P1.3.3)
  - The needs and expectations of patients and others and the degree to which these needs and expectations have been met (P1.3.3.1)
  - These data relate to the relevant dimensions of performance (P1.3.3.1.1)

Feedback from the patient, "patients' families and/or significant others, surrogates, and those responsible for the payment of care" is important in designing and refining services. Surveying should assess, from multiple perspectives, what a service is to be and how well the design has been executed. In short, the Joint Commission encourages providers to see if they are "doing the right thing" and "doing the right thing well."

The National Committee for Quality Assurance and HEDIS

Focusing specifically on managed care organizations, the NCQA began assessing managed care organizations' quality of care and services. Through an array of internal and external review mechanisms, NCQA has consolidated its criteria into the Health Plan Employer Data and Information Set. In 1991, HEDIS version 2.0 was first used in initial accreditation reviews of health maintenance organizations (HMOs), and in January 1994, NCQA used this tool as the core of a one-year national report card pilot project involving 21 managed care plans. In 1996, HEDIS 3.0 will have been released, and NCQA plans to review at least half of the estimated 550 HMOs in the United States.

The HEDIS system assesses performance on a range of measures that include member satisfaction, quality of or access to care, physician credentials, utilization of services and membership, and finance issues. "Member satisfaction" consists of the following major dimensions, covered in a standardized questionnaire format:

- Overall evaluation or recommendation of the plan
- Access to medical care
- Thoroughness of examinations
- Ease of accessing the physician of choice
- Physician's interest in the patient and patient's condition

The HEDIS system seems to afford a platform for value-based selling and purchasing. That is to say, national employers can use the data on a comparative shopping basis to identify the "best" plans with which they will contract on behalf of their employees (NCQA, 1996). Less clear is whether the system affords a platform for value-based engineering. In other words, do the plans themselves gain insights into what is important to the patient/enrollee, or do they simply gain a relative sense of performance in light of minimum, maximum, and mean scores for the standardized dimensions?

NCQA is one of the most ambitious national efforts among those designing and applying patient satisfaction as a report card, and it is credible because it has a relatively large sample base for each plan included. It does not yet include all health plans, of course, but the reporting base is growing. Other report cards from local business coalitions or other national purchasing groups also have embraced patient satisfaction as a core indicator on which to base contracting choices. The Cleveland Health Quality Choice Program (described earlier in this chapter) is among the noteworthy examples of those employer coalitions (in partnership with hospitals and physicians) that have developed a standardized patient satisfaction tool as an important part of their report card to metropolitan Cleveland area businesses. Beyond patient satisfaction, the Cleveland project also focuses on mortality and morbidity indicators for hospital-based providers in the market.

Patient Satisfaction and the Competition

With purchasers, patients, and others demanding patient satisfaction programs, providers and insurers have rushed to comply. This fact is backed up by the most recent *National Hospital Marketers' Survey,* a nationally representative survey of hospital-based marketing executives that is conducted annually by Quality Expectations, Inc., in Evanston, IL.* The 1995 survey represents 201 marketing executives drawn from a stratified random sample to represent hospitals by both bed size and geographic distribution across the 48 contiguous states. The survey shows that virtually all hospitals have some form of patient satisfaction measurement system in place. Nearly as many have a quality improvement system in place, but whether patient satisfaction measurement is fully informing patient satisfaction management systems is not clear. However, the bottom line for capturing negotiated contracts is clear: at the very least, it is critical to show that patient satisfaction/quality measurement is in place and that levels of performance are comparable to those of other providers within the choice set. Because there are no universal standards yet, these mandatory performance standards may prove sufficient over the near term. However, over time, the standards are likely to be elevated.

Patient Satisfaction and the Hospital

The 1995 *National Hospital Marketers' Survey* also shows that many hospitals are increasing their patient satisfaction efforts. When hospital marketers were asked a series of questions about relative rates of growth in key marketing activities, nearly seven in ten of the 201 respondents (69.8 percent) cited patient satisfaction research as an area with at least "somewhat more activity" than last year (see figure 1-8).

A second tier of activity forms around managed care contracting and public relations, with at least somewhat more activity reported by 61.3 percent and 59.0 percent of marketers, respectively. The greatest push for managed care is in the western United States and in the largest facilities (500+ beds). Public relations shows more activity in the South and among the smallest providers (fewer than 100 beds). Uniformly flat among all market segments is hospital-to-hospital relations (horizontal integration), with only 55.9 percent of respondents reporting more activity than in the previous year.

---

*Please note that in 1996, Quality Expectations, Inc., changed its corporate name to Opinion Research Corporation, and that all references to Quality Expectations, Inc., refer to years prior to this name change.

Figure 1-8. Increase in Activity over Prior Year

Percentage of marketing executives indicating somewhat more and much more activity than last year.

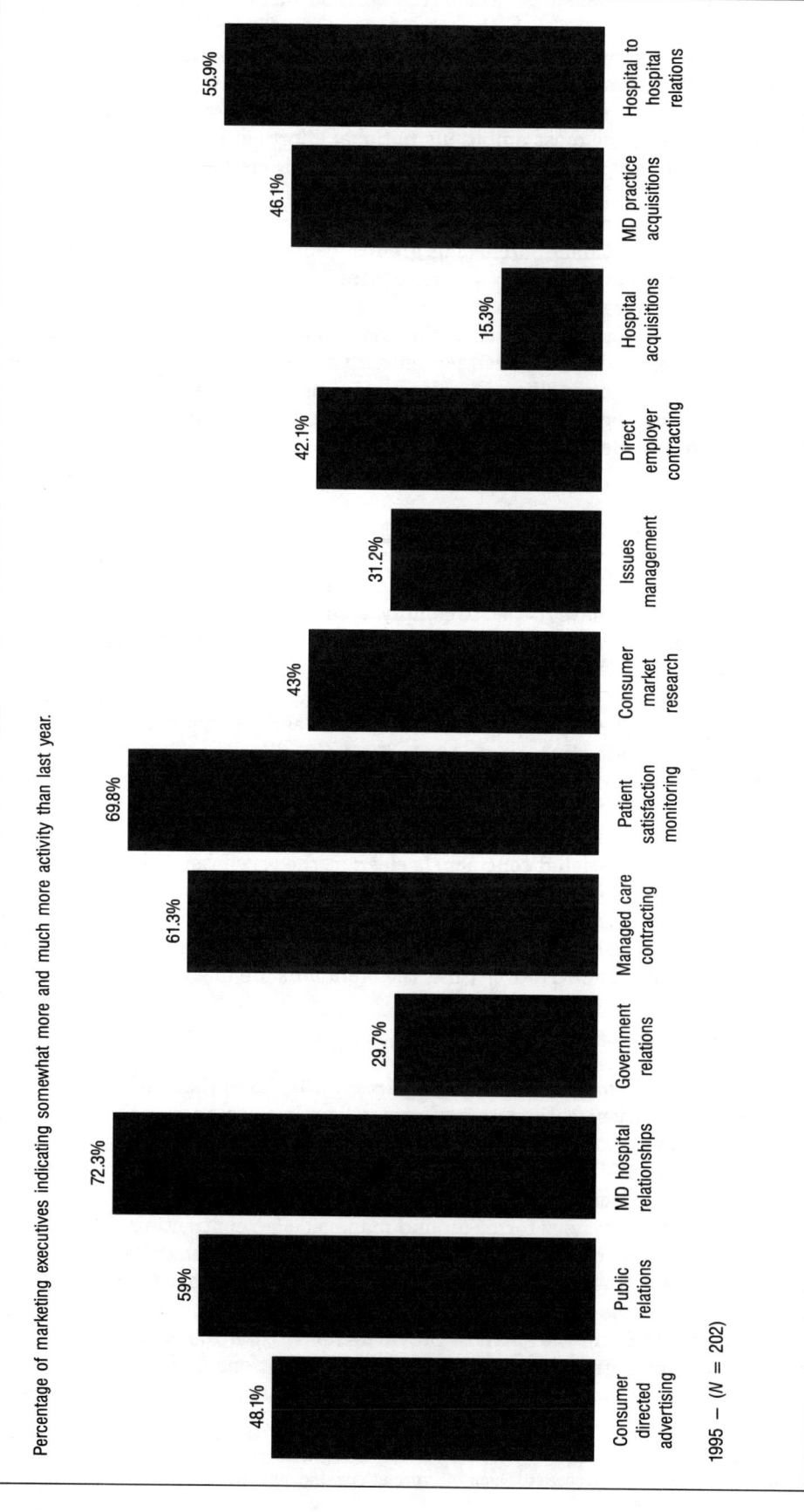

Source: *National Hospital Marketers' Survey*, Quality Expectations, Inc., 1995.

Note that integration, or physician–hospital relationships, heads the list as a key growth strategy for many health care providers. Fully 72.3 percent of marketers overall report seeing somewhat more integration activity or a great deal more integration activity than in the preceding year. Continued integration with physicians will fuel this growth, which in turn will have implications for the patient satisfaction monitoring systems that providers have in place. Most contracts with physicians have begun to include compensation-related components that explicitly set standards for patient satisfaction.

The providers most actively engaged in these vertically integrative activities have 300 to 499 beds (88.5 percent of 300–499-bed institutions have at least "somewhat more") and are in the north-central United States (where 78.2 percent had at least "somewhat more"). Although this integration does not seem to elevate actual physician practice acquisition to the same level (currently at 46.1 percent with at least "somewhat more activity"), it is noteworthy that acquisition is up from the 38.8 percent mark of only a year ago.

At the opposite end of the activity continuum is hospital acquisitions, with only 15.3 percent of marketers reporting at least somewhat more acquisitions activity and nearly as many (11.4 percent) reporting somewhat less acquisitions activity. Joining this lowest tier of activity are government relations, with only 29.7 percent of respondents reporting at least somewhat more activity, and issues management, with only 31.2 percent of respondents reporting somewhat more activity. This relatively low level of activity is probably due, in part, to the fading out of health care reform.

As early as 1990, when the first edition of this book was released, almost all hospitals had in place some form of patient satisfaction feedback system, if for no other reason than to qualify for selective insurance or reimbursement channels. From 1993 to the present (1995), the *National Hospital Marketers' Survey* has monitored increasing activity in patient satisfaction measurement as well. Figure 1-9 shows that activity levels measured by the most recent survey top levels in the prior years measured. Although the data are relatively thin, the 1995 survey also shows that patient satisfaction may be the focus of increased activity with more of it contracted externally to research and other vendors.

In 1995, fully 55 percent of hospital-based marketing executives reportedly contracted externally for some form of market research, compared with only 39.8 percent reporting such contracts in the year prior. Of those contracting in 1995, 26.1 percent reported that the most recent contract research project was focused on patient satisfaction—more than double the 12.5 percent reporting this activity in 1994.

Figure 1-9. More Patient Satisfaction Activity

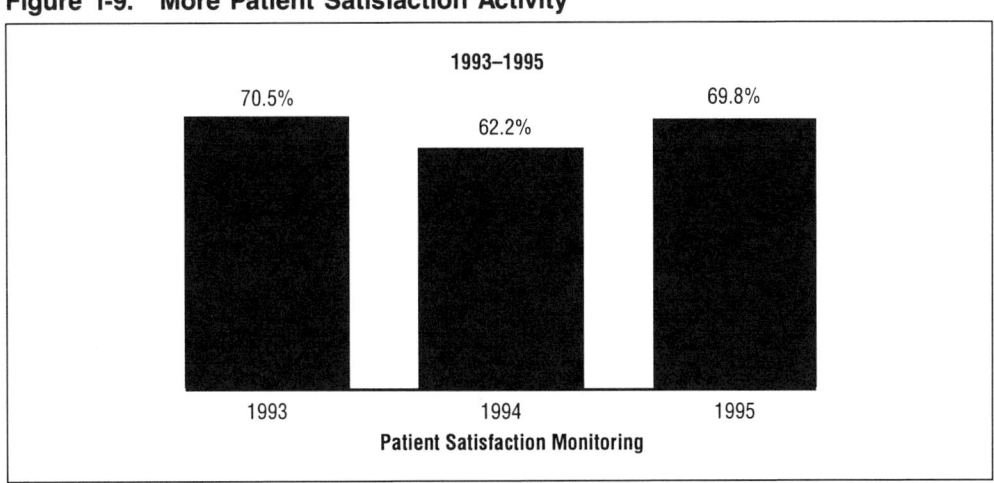

Source: *National Hospital Marketers' Survey,* Quality Expectations, Inc., 1995.

Telephone-based surveying was the most commonly contracted research activity overall in 1995, followed by mail survey, at 22.2 percent of research. When the contracted project had patients as its focus, however, mail was the preferred medium, with 37.9 percent of providers reporting mail, as opposed to 41.4 percent reporting telephone research. For patient satisfaction research specifically as well as for all hospital-based marketing generally, qualitative methodologies or alternatives to telephone and mail surveys account for very little of the activity reported.

Summary

Patient satisfaction, once an issue of modest importance to many professionals in the health care sector, is now of primary concern to virtually all health care professionals. Major reasons for the increase in efforts to measure and manage patient satisfaction include increased competition among health care providers; new demands for patient satisfaction from employers, insurers, regulators, and others; and the recognition that satisfying patients can lead to better health and business outcomes. Providers' increasing financial investment in patient satisfaction and measurement appears commensurate with the heightened interest in the patient's opinion.

CHAPTER TWO

Defining the Terms of Patient Satisfaction

It is safe to say that all patient satisfaction surveys measure *something* from the customer's point of view, but it is not an academic question to ask exactly what, in fact, the surveys measure. What is patient satisfaction? What is quality? What is brand loyalty? And how do these dimensions tie in to more conventional measures of clinical outcomes? Once these basic questions are answered, how does one design or adapt a patient survey system that (1) gives insight into how to enhance patient satisfaction measurably, (2) allows tracking of movement in patient satisfaction over time, and (3) has a role in a larger model of clinical management?

Measuring and managing patient satisfaction is especially challenging because the health care environment is highly regulated and highly competitive. Providers not only must maintain the highest clinical standards, they also must deliver service that satisfies the customer. The two dimensions are, indeed, distinct, but they are not mutually exclusive. One may provide top-flight clinical care while at the same time providing a satisfactory customer experience. However, to meet this dual challenge, a provider must have a full understanding of what constitutes both clinical excellence and customer satisfaction.

This chapter seeks to define customer satisfaction by examining several models of the concept. To provide an understanding of how customers form perceptions of satisfaction, the chapter examines a series of encounters in different health care service environments from the customer's point of view and analyzes the encounters using a basic psychological framework. Finally, the chapter looks at the role of patient satisfaction within the larger picture of pharmacoeconomic analysis.

Generally High Satisfaction Rates among Patients

Talk to any health care professional about customer satisfaction, and chances are that the first topic that surfaces is not customer satisfaction but customer complaints. To many health care workers, providing satisfaction means making a dissatisfied customer satisfied or taking care of the many gripes that customers are presumed to have. Yet research shows that most patients are at least somewhat satisfied with the care they receive (Fitzpatrick and Hopkins, 1983, p. 298). In fact, most of the "surprises" patients report are positive (Nelson and Larson, 1993). The larger challenge, then, is not to create converts from dissatisfied customers but to maximize the varying levels of satisfaction that may already exist among customers.

Note, for example, the high satisfaction rates reported in a 1996 national survey of recently hospitalized patients. On a 5-point, Likert-format scale ranging from "very dissatisfied" to "very satisfied," 90 percent of respondents reported that they were at least "somewhat satisfied" (Opinion Research Corp., 1996). The charting of these patient responses in figure 2-1 shows that the majority of patients (65 percent) are not just satisfied but "very satisfied." When this percentage is compared to the 3 percent who are "very dissatisfied" and the 3 percent who are "somewhat dissatisfied," a generally positive picture of patient experience emerges. Although this survey assessed patient satisfaction retrospectively and by using a telephone interview as the survey instrument, both of which conditions can result in more positive scores, the ratings are consistent with the authors' research among providers nationally. Most patients reportedly are mostly satisfied with their hospital care.

An assessment of satisfaction with family physicians shows even greater levels of patient satisfaction. Figure 2-2 shows that fully 63 percent of patients who have a regular source of primary care are "very satisfied" with the care they receive from those physicians. An additional 22 percent are "somewhat satisfied" and 6 percent are "neutral". Only 9 percent are "somewhat dissatisfied" or "very dissatisfied" (Opinion Research Corp., 1996). One should bear in mind that this survey measures the physician–patient relationship, which is more focused and personal than the relationship between a patient and a hospital. Responses also represent the net evaluation of a relationship that, in many cases, has taken years to solidify. Moreover, it is easier for patients who are dissatisfied with a physician to switch practitioners than for patients who are dissatisfied with a hospital to switch hospitals. These reservations notwithstanding, most patients are reportedly mostly satisfied with their family physicians.

Figure 2-1. Recent Hospitalization

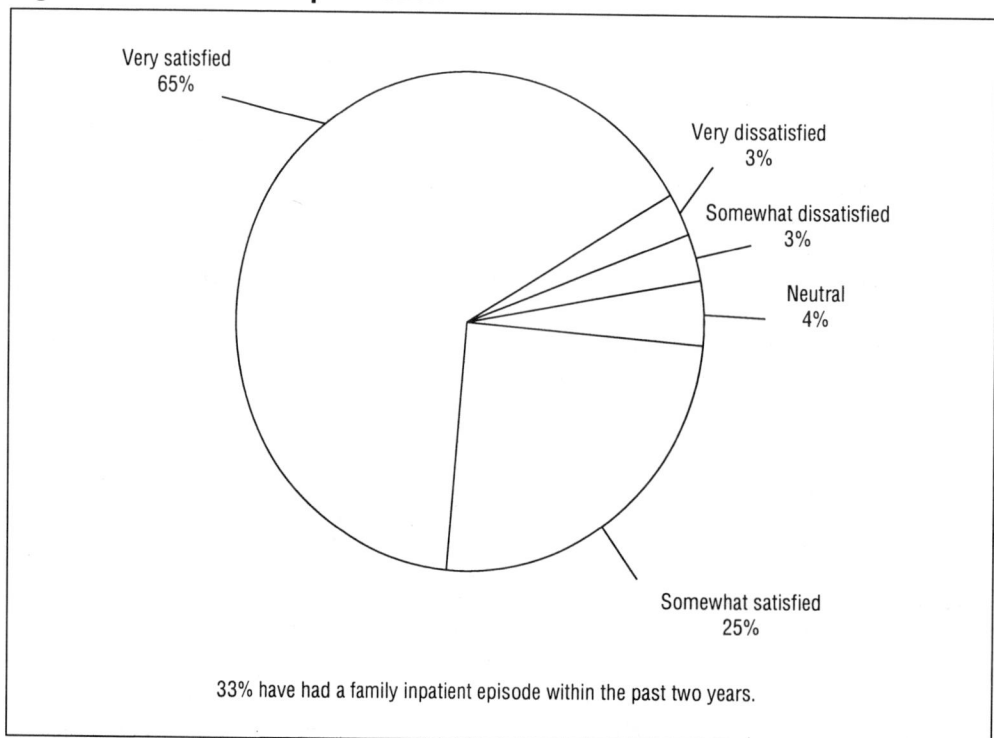

33% have had a family inpatient episode within the past two years.

Source: *National Healthcare Consumer Survey,* Opinion Research Corporation, 1996.

Figure 2-2. Family Doctor

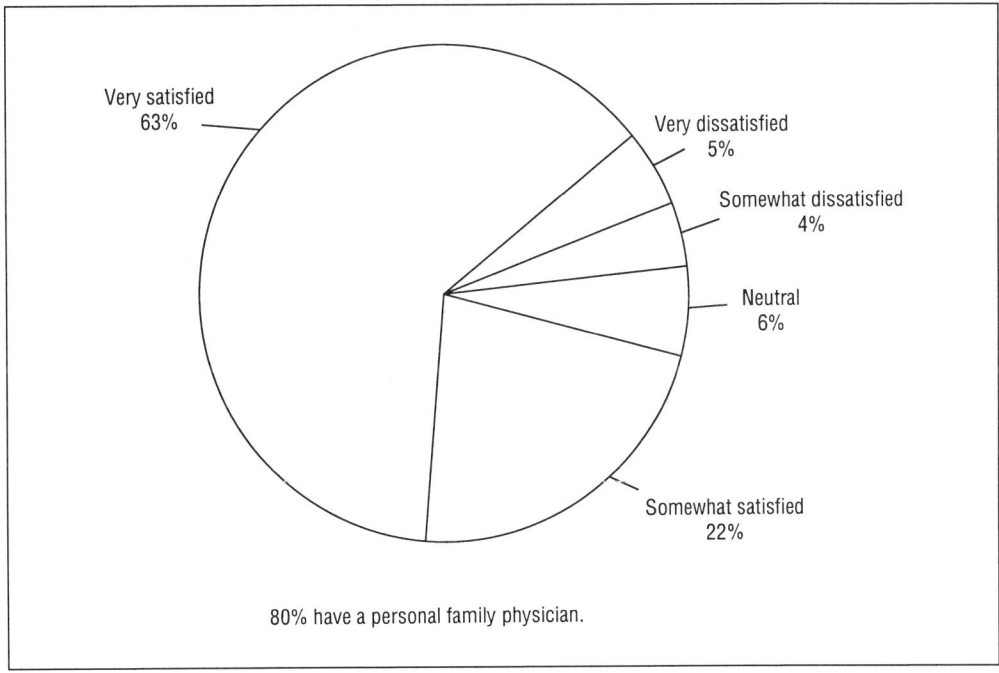

Source: *National Healthcare Consumer Survey*, Opinion Research Corporation, 1996.

Positive and Negative Surprises

What are the sources of patients' satisfaction or dissatisfaction with a provider—whether hospital or physician? Satisfaction in any service encounter is, in part, based on the individual's expectations before the encounter as well as on the nature of the encounter itself. In an indirect exploration of quality expectations, Nelson and Larson (1993) asked 15,019 patients discharged from 12 acute care, medical-surgical facilities, "Did anything happen during your stay in the hospital that surprised you?" (In this context, *surprises* are departures from what the patient expected.) Verbatim responses from 2,160 of the patients were coded by two independent, trained analysts. The results are displayed in figure 2-3.

Note that only five of the dimensions on the figure have both positive and negative net evaluations vis-à-vis expectations and surprises. In each case, the positive surprises outweigh the negative. When all positive and all negative surprises are totaled, the positive surprises again outweigh the negative surprises, with 66 percent of all respondents reporting positive surprises, compared with 54 percent reporting negative surprises. (These figures sum to more than 100 percent because patients could report both positive and negative surprises as well as multiple negative or positive surprises.) Using multiple regression techniques (explained in chapter 3), the authors found that positive surprises were associated with a significantly better overall evaluation of the hospital stay. Negative surprises, on the other hand, predicted poorer evaluations of the hospital stay. Among those patients reporting both negative and positive surprises, their overall evaluations of the hospital stay were poorer than those reporting only positive surprises and also poorer than those reporting no surprises at all. Evidently, negative surprises carry the greatest weight.

The 54 percent of patients reporting negative surprises (of the total 2,160 patients who reported any surprises at all) appear to make up approximately 7.8 percent of the total base of 15,019 patients in the 12-hospital survey. It may be no coincidence that this figure is essentially the same as the combined percentage of "somewhat dissatisfied" and "very dissatisfied" responses from the national telephone survey (see figure 2-1).

This research, which suggests a role to be played by surprises vis-à-vis expectations, also is consistent with the findings of Swan, Sawyer, VanMatre, and McGee who suggest that "[t]he set of future outcomes anticipated by an individual are his/her expectations and become a standard by which the individual will compare the actual outcomes that result from choice [made to achieve individual goals]..." (1985, p. 8).

Swan and others suggest further that patients possess a second set of expectations concerning fairness and equity in treatment situations. When a patient enters a health care service situation, they suggest, that patient carries the dual set of expectations of outcome and expectations of equitable treatment, and those expectations

Figure 2-3. Sources of Good and Bad Surprises

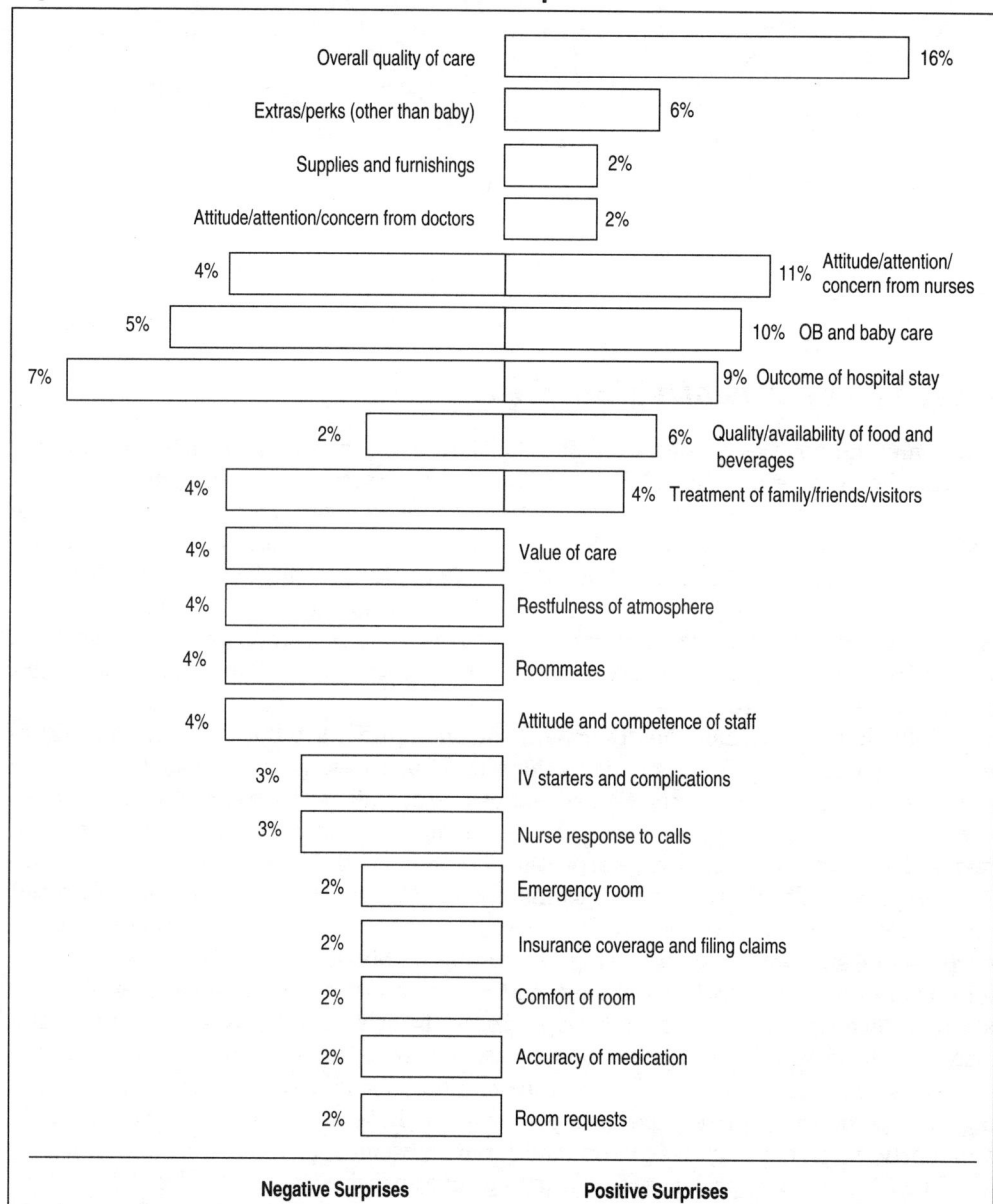

Source: Nelson, E. C., and Larson, C. Patients' good and bad surprises: how do they relate to overall patient satisfaction? *Quality Review Bulletin* 19(3):89–94, Mar. 1993. Reprinted with permission from the Joint Commission on Accreditation of Healthcare Organizations, Oakbrook Terrace, IL.

are fulfilled to a greater or lesser extent during the service encounter. Providers then can maximize patient satisfaction by working toward a positive fulfillment of the patient's expectations. In broad view, patient satisfaction might be characterized as the net result of patient expectations filtered through perceptions the patient acquires during and after the service encounter. A definition of patient satisfaction that would assist in quality management decisions, however, is much more difficult to attain.

Patient Satisfaction Defined

The previous section looked at patient satisfaction in relation to expectations in encounters with physicians and hospitals. From this dual perspective on two kinds of patient-provider relations—patient-hospital and patient-physician—we can begin probing more deeply into the nature of patient satisfaction.

Solicitations of patients' general likes and dislikes frequently take the form of questions such as "How did you like the physician?" or "How did you like your hospital stay?" When patients respond to these inquiries, what do they mean when they say, "I was satisfied"? Although it is difficult to define patient satisfaction and the associated cognitive processes, a clear definition of patient satisfaction is an essential starting point for good research. Without a clear definition and associated theory, patient satisfaction research is merely the proverbial "shooting in the dark."

Pascoe's Contrast and Assimilation Models

Gregory Pascoe (1983) offers a two-part definition that incorporates the expectations that patients bring to an encounter. In simple encounters, the patient enters the health care situation with expectations, and the perceived difference between expectations and experience offers net satisfaction (or dissatisfaction). This explanation of the perception process is referred to as the *contrast model*. When a patient's health care experience exceeds his or her expectations, the experience is satisfactory; when the experience falls short of expectations, the experience is unsatisfactory.

In general, patients do not like what they do not understand. This principle may account for the fact that in most evaluations of medical personnel, patients typically place importance on effective communication skills. However, it is also true that patients who are confronted with a situation that they do not fully understand (frequently the case in health care) may adjust their ultimate expectations and consequent evaluations downward if the experience falls short of their original expectations. This *assimilation model* may help explain why patient satisfaction with most clinical personnel is very high. When asked about their physician, traditional patients who have a "doctor knows best" perspective often accept responsibility for not understanding rather than fault the provider.

The assimilation model also explains the lower levels of satisfaction typically reported for readily understood dimensions of the health care experience, such as food services and availability of parking. Because these dimensions are commonplace and familiar, patients have clearer initial expectations of them and are less likely to lower their original expectations out of lack of experience with them.

Linder-Pelz's Ten Attributes of Health Care

Another definition of patient satisfaction is offered by Susan Linder-Pelz in her review of the patient satisfaction literature. To Linder-Pelz, patient satisfaction is "positive evaluations of distinct dimensions of the health care. (The care being evaluated might be a single clinic visit, treatment through an illness episode, a particular health care setting or plan, or the health care system in general)" (Linder-Pelz, 1982, p. 578).

Linder-Pelz suggests that satisfaction must be understood within a context in which a variety of elements may be more or less satisfying to the patient. She then moves beyond the simple model by identifying health care as a service experience with ten attributes that can be used to assess satisfaction from the patient's point of view:

1. Accessibility/convenience
2. Availability of resources
3. Continuity of care
4. Efficacy/outcomes of care
5. Finances
6. Humaneness
7. Information gathering
8. Information giving
9. Pleasantness of surroundings
10. Quality/competence

Linder-Pelz's model provides a more general perspective on customer satisfaction, one that both derives from and fits into a variety of other industries. Analysts in these other industries also have sorted out the salient attributes that define other, more general service experiences. This broader orientation gave rise to SERVQUAL, a more general model that has become the foundation of a survey standard applicable in many service sectors.

SERVQUAL

SERVQUAL (short for "services quality") is a battery of standardized questions that affords a broad-based and sensitive means of measuring customer experiences across a wide range of service experiences. For each question item, the scale dissects the customer's perspective into three general categories: expectations, importance, and performance. The ten dimensions of SERVQUAL consist of the following aspects of a service encounter:

- Tangibles
- Communication
- Competence
- Access
- Courtesy
- Understanding, knowing the customer
- Responsiveness
- Reliability
- Security
- Credibility

In a typical administration of SERVQUAL, each of the ten aspects is rated according to the expectations of the customer, the importance to the customer, and the performance perceived by the customer. The following examples illustrate how these three categories can be applied to items intended to rate communication as an aspect of a service encounter.

- *Expectations:* "A provider should communicate well with patients." (Patient rates relative agreement on a 7-point scale.)
- *Importance:* "A provider who communicates well [is important]." (Patient rates relative importance on a 7-point scale.)
- *Performance:* "[Name of provider] communicates well with me." (Patient rates relative agreement on a 7-point scale.)

The significant success of SERVQUAL, originally developed by Parasuraman and colleagues and others outside the health care arena (1985, 1986, 1988) to measure *customer experience*, has led some researchers to apply it to *patient satisfaction* measurement efforts. Among them are Bowers and others (1994), who added two health care-related dimensions—outcomes and caring—derived from qualitative research among recently discharged acute care hospital patients.

In a self-administered survey completed by 308 patients discharged from a southeastern medical hospital, Bowers and others discovered through multiple regression the following statistically significant predictors of overall patient satisfaction:

- Caring
- Communication
- Reliability
- Accessibility
- Knowing the customer
- Responsiveness

Note that five of the six significant predictors are also dimensions identified by SERVQUAL. Although the sample base (the 308 patients) was relatively modest for a regression model containing 12 independent variables, the results suggest that SERVQUAL covers most of the elements important in health care service encounters—or, at least, a hospital inpatient experience. It is important to note, however, that one aspect very important to patients—"caring"—is not a part of the SERVQUAL model. As Bowers and colleagues conclude, health care may be at least qualitatively different from other services as an experience because of the level of risk and the personal, intimate involvement on the part of the patient.

Some researchers have more serious reservations about using SERVQUAL as a tool for measuring patient satisfaction. In a review of current literature on patients' evaluations of quality and satisfaction, Kathryn Taylor concluded that patient satisfaction researchers should

> refrain from using the SERVQUAL scale as a basis for surveys designed to measure service quality perceptions. Evidence that calls into question both the appropriateness of measuring service quality by measures of disconfirmation and the efficacy of the SERVQUAL scale to capture disconfirmation perceptions is growing. Specifically, the use of the expectations portion of the SERVQUAL scale appears to offer little in the way of psychometric efficacy and may actually impede the collection of data.... (Taylor, 1994, p. 233)

In effect, Taylor has suggested that not only does SERVQUAL not account for the appropriate dimensions of the health service experience, but it also poorly measures those dimensions for which it does account.

James McAlexander and others (1994) concur with Taylor's conclusions. Based on their analysis of patient satisfaction with dental services, McAlexander and others also found that use of the SERVQUAL instrument for measuring expectations from the patient's point of view added no insights beyond what could be gained from the simple performance questions already available in SERVQUAL. This observation may be due to the uniformly high expectations that health care customers have of their providers—that is, the performance category, seen from the patients' point of view, already assimilates their high expectations. In the interests of a shorter survey instrument, the authors recommend simply dropping the expectations questions from any research effort.

Fiebelkorn's Model

Sandra Fiebelkorn (1985) also has developed a customer service model that has application to health care. Figure 2-4 represents how the average customer/patient arrives

Figure 2-4. Overall Patient Satisfaction with a Provider

Overall satisfaction with provider
↑
Service encounters
↑
Service attributes
↑
Positive and negative events

Source: Adapted from Fiebelkorn, S. L. Retail service encounter: model and measurement. In: J. A. Czepiel, M. R. Solomon, and C. F. Surprenant, editors. *The Service Encounter: Managing Employee/Customer Interaction in Service Businesses.* Lexington, MA: Lexington Books, 1985, p. 183.

at a generally satisfactory or unsatisfactory evaluation of encounters with a provider. *Overall customer satisfaction with a provider* arises from the customer's evaluations of specific experiences, or *service encounters,* with providers. These service encounters in turn are evaluated on the basis of *service attributes* of the encounters or events. Finally, service attributes are evaluated on the basis of a sifting of *positive and negative events* that serve as cues of the quality of each service attribute (Fiebelkorn, 1985, pp. 182–83).

Building now in reverse, from the ground up, the net evaluation of a service attribute is the sum total of the negatives and positives weighted by the significance associated with each of the events that makes up the attribute. The same summation across service attributes gives rise to an overall evaluation of the provider, one element of which is satisfaction. Finally, the net evaluation of all service encounters while the customer is in the provider setting gives rise to an overall evaluation of the provider, key elements of which are satisfaction, overall quality, repeat visit likelihood, and referral.

To illustrate, we can apply this model to patient encounters with a nurse, a typical service encounter that affects overall satisfaction across most inpatient settings. Specific *service attributes* of the encounter might include the response time of the nurse when needed, or some aspect of communication with the nurse about the medical condition. A number of *positive or negative events* may allow the patient to evaluate the overall responsiveness of the nurse; for example, the nurse's response time to a call button on the morning of the patient's first day and the delivery of morning medications on the afternoon of the second day. The timeliness and accuracy of the nurse's performance during all events will help the patient evaluate the nurse's responsiveness, which, along with a host of other *service attributes,* will help the patient draw a conclusion about a specific nurse or the nursing team in general. Finally, the nurse's performance in the context of other *service encounters* in the provider setting will contribute to the final, overall evaluation of the provider, one element of which is *patient satisfaction with the provider.*

Patient Satisfaction Categories, Attributes, and Processes

As we probe deeper into customer satisfaction models, we might ask, How does the typical patient experience a health service? The answer is, very much as that person experiences any other service or social encounter. A customer typically identifies first the salient categories of an experience or environment and then, within the categories, the defining processes or attributes. That is, having first come to terms with the structure of an encounter, an individual seeks to reckon with the processes. For example, people first attempt to comprehend the nature of a speaker before the nature of that person's communication, or the nature of an office before the demands of the officeholder.

The typical service experience is a complex web or series of discrete structural and process challenges to the uninitiated. As an example, imagine arriving at your first meeting of an organization you have just joined – the Committee for XYZ. It may be that those in charge of the meeting anticipate newcomers and have a formal mechanism for greeting you that would facilitate your introduction into the environment. But if no such formal system exists, what do you do?

If you are like most people, you will attempt to identify the proper entrée, perhaps a person of authority or a greeting station, so that you may determine what is to happen, when it is to happen, and what other information you need to assimilate yourself into the organization's meeting. You walk up to someone stationed at a table that has a sign indicating that it is the registration station. Then you introduce yourself and say, "I'm here for the meeting of the Committee for XYZ." The person behind the table extends a hand and says, "Good evening. We've been looking forward to meeting you." You respond, "Could you tell me who's in charge of newcomers' registration?" "I'm in charge," says the person behind the table. "Could you please take a moment to complete this form? After you've finished, I'll introduce you to some people who can help explain what we're planning to accomplish at tonight's meeting."

Although this is a brief introduction to a service encounter or a social setting, it illustrates some of the psychological elements that are generalizable to the patient experience and therefore to building an assessment tool from the patient's point of view. The first step as anyone is introduced into an unfamiliar environment is to gain comfort in the environment by identifying its salient categories. For example, your implicit agenda on entering the meeting room for the Committee for XYZ was to find where to access the meeting (the registration table), how to further determine within this context whose counsel should be sought out (the person in charge), and how to complete the appropriate next steps (filling out the form and meeting those who will facilitate further assimilation into the group). This taxonomic approach is generalizable to most other service encounters or social experiences. Individuals gain comfort first from identifying the structural or categoric patterns of a new experience and then become more familiar with the categories through an understanding of the attributes of the categories. Individuals further evaluate how they feel about the categories by evaluating the attributes of the categories as well as the processes inherent in the categories.

The patient experience can best be considered an interrelated one in which attributes define processes as well as categories, and categories describe the structure of experience while processes describe the threads that knit the structure together into a larger corporate culture. A non–health care example may demonstrate this point more clearly. The registration table of the meeting of the Committee for XYZ defines the access *category* for the encounter. An *attribute* of the person at the table is hierarchical; someone is in charge. Your introduction into this initial category is facilitated by communication, a *process*. You will therefore be able to evaluate the specific attribute of this category according to the effectiveness of the communication as well as other processes. Likewise, you will be able to evaluate another attribute of the category on a number of processes, such as the paperwork you were asked to complete.

In the health care environment, processes (beyond communication) can include timeliness, cycle time, efficacy, efficiency, and others. To some extent, these processes are borrowed from the Joint Commission on Accreditation of Healthcare Organizations' perspective on the core processes of providers. One could extend this list by referring to Linder-Pelz's list of ten elements of satisfaction. If an analyst allows the data to naturally cluster into categories, or groupings of elements that are held in common by patients, these groupings tend to be best represented by the structural categories of the patient experience, not the core processes. For the inpatient experience, these categories typically include a subset of the following, with the possible addition of categories:

- The structural access elements such as parking and signage
- The emergency department as an access point
- The admitting department as an access point
- The patient's room and immediate surroundings
- The nursing staff
- The physician staff
- The ancillary and other staff
- The dietary services
- The discharge stage
- The billing process

For outpatient experiences, emergency patient experiences, and physician's office experiences, the list of possible categories tends to be shorter or a subset of those listed for the inpatient experience.

Factor Analysis

How can we state that patients will look for categories in their experiential environment and then, within categories, begin to assess the processes or attributes that define them? One could simply ask patients, and in fact we have done so in qualitative research such as focus groups and in-depth interviews. The results typically indicate that patients commonly define service highlights (or "lowlights") based on encounters with designated personnel, designated departments, or designated locations. Where designations are relatively unclear, patients attempt to superimpose a structural label on them. For instance, patients may encounter a variety of staff, such as nurses, physicians, and technicians, and will attempt to define staff as best they can when unclear about who holds what position.

Patients talk about their experiences in terms like the following: "They have wonderful nurses at St. Elsewhere Hospital," "The doctors at XYZ Clinic are great," or "The physical therapists at the rehab clinic were very helpful." Patients may go on to say, "The nurses really cared about me as a person," or "My doctor listened to my questions and made sure I understood the answers," or "The therapists know just how hard to push me as I recover." These typical patterns suggest a reference first to *categoric* distinctions reflecting the quality of service, followed by an *attribute* or *process* definition of the experiences. Although this paradigm may seem compelling because it is consistent with many readers' own experiences, hard evidence is needed to back it up.

How can one be certain that patients do not first define processes or attributes that are important, and then define categories within certain process categories? In short, what is the underlying structure of the patient experience?

A multivariate statistical technique called *factor analysis* allows the researcher to capture the larger patterns of individuals' experiences to identify the bigger picture. By using individuals' responses to a series of questions, factor analysis allows the researcher to identify the larger, common elements that help define respondents' perspectives. Taking all questions into account at once, factor analysis seeks to group items together with other items that behave in the same way, to generate the smallest number of categories possible to explain all of the variations in all of the variables. In the case of patients, a small number of categories—typically three to six—is enough to explain most of the variability in the health care experience. The ultimate number of factors depends, in part, on the underlying structure of the patient experience (simple or complex), the number of questions (the variables) in the database, and the number of patients responding to the questionnaire (the sample size).

For example, if patients' responses to questions suggested an underlying, larger dimension of patient experience that could be called "communication," then factor analysis would lump together many individual evaluations, or responses to individual questions, into this single factor. Because communication is a process, the analyst might look for other groupings of processes—for example, efficiency, efficacy, and flow, or cycle time. If, on the other hand, the larger underlying structure were best defined by the categories the inpatient encounters, then the factors would include admitting personnel, nurses, physicians, food services, or other groupings defined by departments.

Hypothetical Case Study 2-A: Inpatient Experiences

The items listed in figure 2-5 offer a brief description of 38 questions included in an inpatient survey for XYZ Medical Center. These wide-ranging questions reflect inquiries into processes and departments, as well as attributes of service. To simply inquire into the underlying structure of the questions and allow the data to "speak for themselves," the researcher might begin with a method called principal components analysis (PCA). PCA allows the researcher to let the data show how every question item relates to every other question item in the entire survey at the same time. Ultimately, the questions sort themselves out into a smaller number of groupings according to the common associations among all the questions. (Readers who desire a more detailed explanation of PCA are referred to Bryant and Yarnold, 1995.)

Figure 2-5. Full Listing of Inpatient Questions

Room ready when you needed it?	Physician care and concern?
Security of parking lots?	Accessibility of your physician?
Valet parking services?	Physician's ability to keep family informed?
Signs on how to get to main entrance?	Coordination of testing and procedures?
Internal signs directing you?	Skill of person who drew your blood?
Respect for privacy in the room?	Courtesy of person who drew your blood?
Intercom system at your bedside?	Courtesy of volunteer staff?
Television in your room?	Promptness of transport staff?
Quiet of your room?	Staff identified themselves in your room?
Cleanliness of your room?	Your sense of security at the facility?
Courtesy of housekeeping?	Timeliness of meals served?
Skill of nursing staff assigned?	Quality of your food?
Nurses' communication with you?	Correctness of food you ordered?
Care and concern shown by nurses?	Variety of food you ordered?
Nursing staff's ability to solve your problems?	Temperature of food served?
Nurses' response to call buttons?	Physician's release from hospital in a timely fashion?
How well nurses did their jobs?	Discharge instructions from nurses?
Physician's willingness to listen to/answer your questions?	Time it took you to leave the hospital?
Physician's ability to keep you informed?	Information you received about billing?

Figure 2-6 shows how a factor analysis sorted the question items from figure 2-5 into six common groupings. Although factor analysis does not stop at just these six groupings, statistical examination shows that additional groupings, or factors, would explain nothing more of patients' overall perceptions of their experiences. And the 28 question items that define these factors lead to the conclusion that the ten excluded items offer no additional insight into the inpatient experience.

The grouping that accounts for the most important opinions of the patients in this survey database is in the first category. The remaining groupings are in descending order of importance. Categoric distinctions define these groupings, beginning with the most important of them, nursing. The questions that form the basis for nursing are those that best capture the nurse–patient relationship from the perspective of the patient. Other statistics not presented (for example, the amount of variance explained by each factor) show quite clearly that nursing is not only the first element that patients consider in defining their inpatient experience but also far more important than any of those that follow: physicians and other hospital staff, meal service, security and parking and signage, discharge and billing, and room environment. In a subsequent application of a related statistical method, confirmatory factor analysis (CFA), which assesses the utility of these groupings in describing the relationships among patient experiences, no other groupings or divergences from these initial six emerge. (This factor analysis of the inpatient experience will be reexamined in case study 3-A of chapter 3.) Although the actual wording of question items can influence how they are grouped in factor analysis, this exercise suggests that structure is the larger force at work in the patient's perceptual frame of reference.

Hypothetical Case Study 2-B: Outpatient Experiences

Figure 2-7 lists 30 questions that were part of a survey among recent outpatients at a medical center. This analysis is somewhat hindered by the tremendous diversity of the outpatient experience, where any ten patients may potentially have ten entirely

Figure 2-6. Statistically Important *Categories* of Inpatient Questions

1. Nursing
   - Skill of nursing staff assigned?
   - Nurses' communication with you?
   - Care and concern shown by nurses?
   - Nursing staff's ability to solve your problems?
   - Nurses' response to call buttons?
   - How well nurses did their jobs?

2. Doctors and Staff
   - Physician's willingness to listen to/answer your questions?
   - Physician's ability to keep you informed?
   - Physician care and concern?
   - Accessibility of your physician?
   - Courtesy of volunteer staff?
   - Coordination of testing and procedures?

3. Meal Service
   - Timeliness of meals served?
   - Quality of your food?
   - Correctness of food you ordered?
   - Variety of food you ordered?
   - Temperature of food served?

4. Parking and Signage
   - Security of parking lots?
   - Valet parking services?
   - Signs on how to get to main entrance?
   - Internal signs directing you?

5. Discharge and Billing
   - Discharge instructions from nurses?
   - Time it took you to leave the hospital?
   - Information you received about billing?

6. Room Environment
   - Intercom system at your bedside?
   - Television in your room?
   - Quiet of your room?
   - Cleanliness of your room?

different experiences within ten different diagnostic or therapeutic services. But in using the data to help understand the larger dimensions that the patient defines in the outpatient experience, it is not the actual services so much as the common entry points that seem to offer structure to the outpatient experience. That is, structure once again seems to be the larger dimension underlying the total outpatient experience.

The 30 question items are reduced to the five factors and 15 question items of figure 2-8, and the most important grouping again is not a process or attribute element, but rather the categoric element of registration. According to this analysis, it is outpatients' first impressions, formed during the registration process, that contribute most to defining their overall experience with a facility. But their last impression, formed during billing, is also quite important. The remaining three categories of any importance in defining the outpatient experience are radiology services—perhaps the common denominator of outpatient care; the internal physical environment; and the external physical environment.

Figure 2-7. Full Listing of Outpatient Questions

Informed of ER delays?	Convenience of facility's location?
Care and concern of ER physicians?	External signage directing you to facility?
Care and concern of ER nurses?	Ability to find parking?
Cleanliness of ER?	Ease of finding where to go at facility?
Thoroughness of ER physician's exam?	Cleanliness of facility inside?
ER nurses answered your questions?	Comfort of temperature inside?
ER physicians answered your questions?	Respect for your privacy?
ER instructions for follow-up care?	Skill of radiology staff?
Treated as a person in ER?	Follow-up instructions from radiology staff?
Courtesy of scheduling staff?	Skill of laboratory staff?
Clarity of instructions during scheduling?	Courtesy of laboratory staff?
Skill of person handling registration?	Follow-up instructions from laboratory staff?
Courtesy of person handling registration?	Information you received about billing process?
Explanation of financial matters?	Clarity of bill received?
Speed and efficiency of registration process?	Amount of bill you personally paid?

Figure 2-8. Statistically Important *Categories* of Outpatient Questions

1. Registration
   - Skill of person handling registration?
   - Explanation of financial matters?
   - Speed and efficiency of registration process?

2. Billing
   - Information you received about billing process?
   - Clarity of bill received?
   - Amount of bill you personally paid?

3. Radiology
   - Skill of radiology staff?
   - Courtesy of radiology staff?
   - Follow-up instructions from radiology staff?

4. Outside Environment
   - Convenience of facility's location?
   - External signage directing you to facility?
   - Ability to find parking?

5. Inside Environment
   - Ease of finding where to go at facility?
   - Cleanliness of facility inside?
   - Comfort of temperature inside?

Hypothetical Case Study 2-C: The Physician's Office

The health care experience of greatest longevity for the patient is usually the patient's association with his or her own personal physician. Figure 2-9 shows the list of 29 questions that were part of this hypothetical (sanitized) survey. Factor analysis was used to identify which of these elements come together to define the overall point of view of the patient. Fully 25 question items were required to define six important factors in figure 2-10. It probably comes as no surprise that the figure shows the defining element of a physician's office visit to be the physician himself or herself.

Figure 2-9. Full Listing of Physician's Office Patient Questions

Time wait to appointment date?	Skill and knowledge of physician?
Courtesy of scheduling?	Time spent with physician?
Efficiency of scheduling?	Physician's office follow-up with you?
Clarity of instructions during scheduling?	Physician's explanation of tests?
Convenience of appointment?	Concern shown by nurse?
Adequacy of external signage?	Skill and knowledge of nurse?
Availability of parking?	How well nurse answered questions?
Cost of parking?	Explanations for home care?
Cleanliness of facility?	Number of bills received?
Time spent checking in?	Clarity of bills?
Courtesy of check-in personnel?	Questions about charges answered completely?
Efficiency of check-in?	Accuracy of bills?
Explanation of financial matters at check-in?	Pain management while at facility?
Time wait to see the physician?	Pain experienced since visit?
Concern shown by physician?	

Figure 2-10. Statistically Important *Categories* of Office Patient Questions

1. Doctors
   - Time wait to see the physician?
   - Concern shown by physician?
   - Skill and knowledge of physician?
   - Time spent with physician?
   - Physician's office follow-up with you?
   - Physician's explanation of tests?

2. Financial Matters
   - Explanation of financial matters at check-in?
   - Number of bills received?
   - Clarity of bills?
   - Questions about charges answered completely?
   - Accuracy of bill?

3. Scheduling
   - Courtesy of scheduling?
   - Efficiency of scheduling?
   - Clarity of instructions during scheduling?
   - Convenience of appointment?

4. Check-in Process
   - Time spent checking in?
   - Courtesy of check-in personnel?
   - Efficiency of check-in?

5. Nursing
   - Concern shown by nurse?
   - Skill and knowledge of nurse?
   - How well nurse answered questions?

6. Facility
   - Adequacy of external signage?
   - Availability of parking?
   - Cost of parking?
   - Cleanliness of facility?

The other elements that define the physician's office visit in this case study include, in descending order, financial matters, scheduling, check-in process, nursing, and the facility itself. Although these additional five categoric elements are important, it is the long-standing relationship that the patient has with the physician that categorically defines that patient's perception of the visit. This holds true even though that same patient's major complaint may have to do with the price of an office visit or waiting time required before seeing the physician. The conclusion appears to be consistent with the first two case studies on inpatient and outpatient experiences. Structure seems to be the larger dimension underlying the doctor's office experience (although in these examples, structure is defined by specific roles, like "physician" or "nurse," in at least two cases).

Quality and Satisfaction: Statistical Interrelationships

In the examples used to this point, the patient's evaluation of the service experience has been treated at a very general level. Patient satisfaction, patient evaluation of quality, patient report of repeat visit likelihood—all are evaluations, but it may be appropriate in this chapter to recognize some of the semantic and empirical differences and commonalities across these responses. Quality, satisfaction, and loyalty (and, by inference, word-of-mouth referrals) are distinct, yet at the same time they are highly interrelated from the patient's point of view. In a national study, patients' ratings of quality and satisfaction with inpatient care were so strongly associated statistically that the rating of one dimension was able to "predict" the rating of the other in approximately half the cases (Steiber, 1988c). In statistical terms, approximately half the variance of the two dimensions is shared in common. In the same study, satisfaction shares approximately 18.5 percent of its variance in common with repeat business likelihood (loyalty), and more than 22 percent of the variance in quality is shared by loyalty.

Bolton and Drew (1991) suggest that satisfaction and quality are related in the following manner. *Quality* is a long-term and evolving perception on the part of a customer, whereas *satisfaction* entails a perceptual evaluation of a specific, discrete transaction. Cronin and Taylor (1994) agree. Their findings, based on specific health services data, also show that patients' perspective on provider service quality is relatively durable, in comparison to their feelings of satisfaction, which tend to be episode-specific. Service experiences that yield a satisfactory or unsatisfactory outcome will either affirm or disaffirm a patient's standing perspective on quality. The net result of this relationship is a strong, but not perfect, statistical association between the two measures. Our own experience further suggests that models predicting patients' perspectives on service quality will have some, but not all, elements in common with those predicting overall satisfaction.

Some customers will come back from force of habit or because of insurance constraints, while others will come back because their physicians tell them to come back. These repeat customers are "brand loyal." In today's competitive market, fewer and fewer customers can be counted on to follow any of these paths blindly. To achieve brand loyalty in a crowded market, services must meet—or exceed—the customer's expectations.

On any given day, as many as 800,000 patients are discharged from a hospital (American Hospital Association, 1993, p. xxxiii). In our experience, for every ten patients a hospital discharges home, three to four of those households (the patient or a household member) will have another inpatient experience within the next two years (Opinion Research Corp., 1996). As many as seven of those households will have an inpatient, outpatient, or emergency room experience. In the physician's practice, the clear majority of patients treated today will return for some reason within the next year. But not all hospitals will see the patients return for their next medical need.

In a patient research project reported in 1987, Lourdes Hospital, in Paducah, KY, found that nearly three of every four patients rated the hospital's services as "good to excellent." "Poor" ratings were in the single digits, yet the hospital was in jeopardy of losing more patients than the single-digit rating would indicate. In fact, only 87 percent of discharged patients overall claimed that they would use the hospital again (Schoenfeldt, Seale, and Hale, 1987). Clearly, that leaves 13 percent who would not return—much higher than the single-digit number one would expect. Obviously, more than just the dissatisfied customers were walking.

Admittedly, referral likelihood may be related to these other perceptual outcomes in a negative sense. Someone who is dissatisfied with a service experience or with the perceived quality of the experience is more likely to talk about it with others than someone who has had a satisfactory experience. Our own experience linking health status with service evaluations suggests a weaker, although still measurable, link. The difficulty lies in finding acceptable measures of health status itself. Although objective measures of health status are difficult to link statistically with perceptual measures, patient-perceived outcomes are nominally associated with selected measures of service that reflect the rapport between patient and provider.

Davies and Ware (1988) suggest that the patient's opinion of quality is often statistically associated with more objective or clinical measures of quality. Meeting the customer's standards for service, then, may be an effective way not only to garner greater repeat business but also to improve the perception of clinical delivery of service. Davies and Ware offer some basic points to support this linkage:

- Bias from personal characteristics is not so strong as to invalidate consumers' ratings of interpersonal or technical quality of their care.
- Consumers' ratings of technical quality do reflect, at least in part, how many services they received.
- For common problems, consumers can distinguish between the technical aspects of care judged good and less good by physicians.
- Interpersonal features of care do not obscure consumers' ability to distinguish levels of technical process for common outpatient problems.
- Whatever "quality" means to consumers, their perceptions of quality affect their choices among health care alternatives.
- Consumers' reports (as distinct from ratings) hold considerable promise for quality assessment and assurance activities.

Patient Satisfaction, Efficacy, and Value

Managed care is often credited with being the impetus behind a great many changes in health care. Among these changes is a shift toward the development of prospective tools to be used in clinical management. If the ultimate goal of health care is to provide wellness or health maintenance of the patient rather than intervention in an illness episode, then new treatment modalities may be indicated. The provider must rise above the present acute care episode to gain the longer view of health status and quality of life. Add to this the financial constraint of capitation, and there must also be a recognition of the maintenance of value over the long run.

Patient satisfaction has a role in such analyses inasmuch as patient-perceived outcomes can be at least one of the bases for evaluating efficacy; for example, patient satisfaction certainly is a component of quality of life. In addition, it is generally accepted that outpatient treatments are more desirable than inpatient treatments, that it often is more desirable to receive home care than clinically delivered care, and that it is desirable to minimize discomfort or pain to the patient whenever possible. One can also compare treatment modalities within any specific clinical setting as well, seeking the optimal means for providing care to the patient. This has given rise to "care paths," "care maps," and "clinical pathways."

There are various ways to measure the value and efficacy of outcomes in relation to the costs involved in producing them. Four common approaches are the cost-effective analysis, the cost–benefit analysis, the cost-minimization analysis, and the cost–utility analysis.

Cost-Effective Analysis

Cost-effective analysis uses statistical methods to compare the relative costs associated with one or another approach with some net outcome, such as quality of life, reduction in pain, or patient satisfaction. A cost-effective analysis is easiest to conduct when the outcomes can be tangibly counted or otherwise quantitatively compared to derive some sense of the relative cost per unit of effect of one treatment versus another. What the researcher hopes to generate in a cost-effectiveness study is information that reflects how many cures are produced per dollar spent or how much health is generated by the dollars expended or how much satisfaction is enhanced by dollars expended. (Recall the "return on quality" analysis in chapter 1.)

A cost-effective analysis also can give rise to a common expression of the association between the cost and the outcome, called a "cost-effectiveness ratio." This ratio can answer the question, How much investment yields how much cure or improvement under one treatment versus the competing treatment? If one treatment is more costly than another, it is also important to ask if the outcome actually is worth the added investment, because not all investments yield the same quantity of return. In fact, investments beyond a given threshold actually may begin to reverse an otherwise positive effect. For example, the first 2,000 calories of sustenance in diet A may yield a very desirable outcome, but the next 2,000 calories will begin to reverse the desirable effect by encouraging obesity. And, of course, patient satisfaction or quality of life measures also may be included as variables to be evaluated.

Cost–Benefit Analysis

The distinguishing feature of a cost–benefit analysis is that both the inputs and the outputs are measured in dollars. When one looks at the outcome, one also looks at the relative costs associated with the usual course of a disease state. In the case of asthma, for example, it is possible to develop a profile of the typical asthmatic patient and the average number of acute episodes that result during the course of a year when the condition goes untreated for that time. Tracking a group of such "control" individuals over time would yield this information. Then two other experimental groups could be compared with this control group.

Suppose, for example, that the first group receives from a physician a prescription inhaler that is considered highly efficacious in halting the onset of acute symptoms and that the inhaler is used as needed. Further suppose that the second group receives both the inhaler and a coordinated program of informational materials and educational counseling on health style and other elements that can help prevent acute episodes. For a cost–benefit analysis, the researcher must, for the first group, calculate the costs of the physician's office visit (for diagnosis and prescription of the inhaler) and the drug over a specified period of time. Added to these costs are the cost of the inhaler and the costs associated with the average number of acute episodes, hospitalizations or visits to the emergency room. In the case of the second group, the researcher assesses the charges associated with a physician's office visit, diagnosis and prescription of the inhaler, the cost of the drug over a specified period of time, and the costs of producing the informational materials. Time costs associated with administration of an educational program for the asthmatic patients are also assessed. By comparing the outcomes produced by the different regimens with the inputs (costs), one can measure the benefits.

A program that uses cost–benefit analysis is under way at Merck, which to date has signed an agreement with at least one of its managed care clients for a shared risk arrangement in the treatment of benign prostatic hyperplasia, the progressive enlargement of the prostate. In this agreement, Merck will supply its indicated drug for this condition, Proscar, at a mutually determined charge for diagnosed patients with the following guarantee: Merck will reimburse all costs for prescription administration should patients with conditions qualifying under the terms of the agreement who have been complying with the drug regimen require prostate surgery within a specified time period. Clearly, Merck has conducted a cost–benefit analysis that indicates that the number of cases per thousand patients in which surgery will be required and the associated costs are sufficiently small that it will still earn a profit on the use of its drug. Merck's approach is in sharp contrast to the more traditional approach drug companies have taken to managed care clients, such as discounting on volume purchase or bundling of drugs to offer price incentives. Not cited in the literature, although potentially important, is the patients' perception of surgical and recovery experiences compared with long-term, noninvasive recovery–patient satisfaction.

For each of these dimensions, the data may not always be complete, so the researcher must rely on published data or assumptions. In many cases of cost–benefit analysis, it is also appropriate to construct decision trees or models of the course of action of a typical patient and the associated responses from health care providers. These models can become even more sophisticated as one recognizes that dollars invested at the outset of a program are also nominally more expensive than dollars invested later. "Present dollar value" corrections must then be introduced in order to maintain a valid analysis. Another consideration that poses some difficulty to cost–benefit analysis is that patient satisfaction or quality of life issues may be part of the end result of any given study. How does one translate either satisfaction or quality of life into dollars and cents?

Muirhead (1994) points out that behavioral or neurologic drug interventions are among the most difficult to gauge in this context, because most of their outcomes are judged in terms of quality of life measures. If a new drug intervention, for instance, helps mainstream patients, there may be a very straightforward cost reduction. But what other costs are now associated with the mainstreamed patient once he or she is outside the institutional setting? Are there other custodial costs, or perhaps the cost of episodic health interventions when compliance is less than optimal? These kinds of costs should also be factored into the model, if possible, once data become available. In the meantime, they suggest the difficulty of incorporating future contingencies into health care cost models.

Cost-Minimization Analysis

Cost-minimization analysis is a specialized application of cost–benefit analysis that is useful when two therapeutic interventions offer equivalent outcomes, the only appreciable difference being their cost. For example, the price per dose of one drug may be far greater than the cost of another, but if fewer doses are required, then the costs for each therapy can be calculated and compared to find a preferred treatment. Or if two minor surgical procedures – for instance, a hernia repair – offer the same successful medical outcome, but one procedure is done on an outpatient basis and the other requires an overnight stay in the hospital, then again, the costs for each can be compared for a judgment.

One of the challenges of cost-minimization analysis is that two alternative procedures or drug interventions rarely offer precisely the same medical outcome. In the case of drugs, the outcomes would be virtually indistinguishable if the two prescriptions in question were for a generic compound identical to an old, standard brand-name drug. Drugs competing within the same therapeutic class but without the same formula, however, rarely have precisely the same medical profile. One will have a different treatment site, or a different profile of side activity or interaction with other drugs, and so on. Even comparing the cases for hernia repair can offer different opportunities for outpatient versus overnight surgery. In the case of the patient who stays overnight following the procedure, a general anesthetic can be used, but an ambulatory patient is given a local anesthetic. And, of course, the questions arise, Who will be more satisfied, and is this outcome worth the price?

Cost–Utility Analysis

In a cost–utility analysis, outcomes are evaluated in quality of life-years rather than simply in terms of dollars or prolonged lives of patients. If two therapies both are able to prolong life to the same extent, then costs may be compared, but so, too, may side effects or patient-perceived quality of life. Many rehabilitation services purchasers are now giving closer scrutiny to the "recoverability" of patients with strokes, brain or spine injuries, and the like. Large databases now make it possible to identify what a patient with a given rehabilitation-suited condition and with other specific medical and personal characteristics (such as age at the onset of the condition) is likely to achieve with physical therapy. If the capacity to ambulate or the capacity toward self-sufficiency or other improvements in the quality of life are very minimal, high expenditures for therapy may not be warranted. Quality of life measures are obtained from a number of standardized batteries now available to the researcher: the Sickness Impact Profile (SIP), the Quality of Well-Being (QWB) scale, the Patient Utility Measurement Set (PUMS), and a well-known scale, the Activities of Daily Living (ADL) index. Even with such measurement tools available, cost–utility decisions are difficult to make, to say the least. But the increasing availability of data helps providers make informed decisions about medical interventions and the relative return on investment for individuals faced with options at different prices. Given these parameters, cost–utility analysis most often is associated with choices in the management of chronic diseases.

Hypothetical Case Study 2-D: Turnaround Time and Reenrollment

Recall that cost–benefit analysis is differentiated from cost-effective analysis in that both inputs and outcomes can be measured in dollars. Suppose that XYZ Care HMO is a managed care plan on the group model with 150,000 enrolled lives. It has several hundred physicians operating in ten different facilities throughout a major metropolitan market and maintains a number of key services in a single, central location to minimize overhead and retain economies of scale. One of these services is laboratory testing of blood samples that may be drawn at any of the remote sites and transported by special courier to a central reference laboratory. There, samples are processed and results are transmitted to physicians' offices by the following morning. The laboratory testing process seems efficient and satisfactory—that is, efficient and satisfactory from management's point of view.

Management is informed that patient satisfaction scores are sufficiently low that "selling" the managed care plan to employers has become increasingly difficult and that disenrollment rates have grown to undesirable levels. Patient satisfaction research is conducted, with one of the results quite serendipitously offering feedback on laboratory testing. Patient satisfaction with turnaround time for laboratory testing is only 3.80 on a 5-point scale, where 5 equals "very satisfied," and this time dimension is statistically associated (indirectly through overall satisfaction with ancillary services) with overall likelihood to reenroll in the plan. Other important details of this research are the following:

- The average annual revenue per covered life is $1,300.
- Disenrollment this past year has been 22 percent of total patient base.
- Patient satisfaction surveys show reenrollment intentions are consistent with experience.
- Satisfaction with ancillary services is statistically associated with likely reenrollment.
- Satisfaction with time spent waiting for laboratory test results is statistically associated with satisfaction with ancillary services overall.
- For every hour of waiting time for "quick response" tests, such as strep testing, laboratory satisfaction declines 0.40.
- For every point by which laboratory satisfaction declines, likely reenrollment declines 0.5 percent.
- The average time wait for "quick response" tests is six hours.
- Each year, 50 percent of enrollees have a quick response test of some sort.

When these figures are put together, the annual cost of dissatisfaction with laboratory turnaround time, therefore, is $1,170,000. XYZ CARE HMO calculates that the normal health care and administrative charges associated with the 900 lives that this amount represents, plus the cost of placing desktop laboratory testing units at each of the ten practice sites and operating them for the requisite number of tests (labor costs, reagent costs, and overhead), will generate a total charge of approximately $850,000. Laboratory turnaround time for these tests should be reduced from the present six hours to less than one hour, with a consequent decrease in disenrollment losses of $195,000, for a net revenue gain of approximately $125,000. Enhancing patient satisfaction has a cost associated with hardware and staffing, but, as this case study shows, the return on this investment more than makes up for it.

Hypothetical Case Study 2-E: Hospitalizations versus Home Management

Cost–utility analysis recognizes that outcomes may be evaluated not just in dollars or quantity of life, but also in quality of life. Each year approximately 400,000 new cases of congestive heart failure (CHF) are diagnosed in the United States, giving rise to a running total CHF patient population of more than 3 million (Ghali and others, 1990; Parmley, 1989). This progressive disease typically moves the patient through a series of increasingly life-threatening hospitalization episodes to the point that only a heart transplant will save the patient. The composite profile of a CHF patient is of a 63-year-old man with fluid retention in the lungs and some type of cardiomyopathy and/or hypertension who is confined to bed virtually around the clock and is a candidate for a heart transplant. Following are two alternative treatment options:

- Treatment A consists of office-based care as feasible with numerous readmissions to the cardiac care unit through the emergency room during acute episodes, which typically are brought on by edema.
- Treatment B consists of telemetric home monitoring with continuous drug infusion to maintain fluid levels and cardiovascular functioning.

Both treatments are of comparable cost over the period of a year, but treatment B allows an increasing regimen of normal family and social activities. Based on quality of life considerations, treatment B is selected, with the following results:

- After a period of time on treatment B, vital signs have improved, the diagnosis is upgraded, and the patient is more self-sufficient and has a better psychological outlook, although he still relies somewhat on infusion therapy.

- Home infusion is increasingly administered by a member of the family, with commensurate reductions in charges for skilled nursing personnel.

Although the patient may ultimately lose the battle against this chronic condition, treatment B has afforded dramatic improvement in quality of life (patient satisfaction), improvement in the patient's ability to be a productive member of the household, and, ultimately, some reductions in health care costs by the minimization of nursing time required. Treatment A would have maintained the same charges into the future with no improvement in quality of life.

Summary

Most patients, by their own reports, are mostly satisfied with the health services they receive. Nevertheless, to inspire loyalty to a provider, patients must be more than mostly satisfied. They must be *very* satisfied — and very satisfied with the dimensions of service that are important to them. At its most fundamental level, satisfaction is a positive evaluation of specific service dimensions, based on patient expectations and provider performance. Patients' perceptions of quality and patient loyalty build on cumulative satisfactory experiences across salient service dimensions. For different provider settings, different variables will be important to the patient. Variables may also be different across providers within the same business. This chapter has outlined the many factors that help to form a patient's impressions of a service experience. The following chapter provides working models and case studies that illustrate how the perspective of this chapter can inform better patient satisfaction measurement and management at the provider level.

CHAPTER THREE

Service Encounters and Satisfaction Outcomes

Health care has devoted too much effort to measuring how a provider stacks up against an external frame of reference, such as the pooled average scores of a vendor's clients or a national average. No one would argue with the statement that high scores are cause for pride and are helpful when negotiating contracts with insurers or employers. But many providers use external comparisons to identify if they are better than the average, or "good enough," when the real question should be, Have I given the customer every good reason to return for future needs? Repeat business requires earning the highest scores possible on dimensions that are important to the *customer*.

How does one foster an environment that encourages events which will make positive impressions on patients? How does one build both an insightful measurement system for monitoring patient satisfaction and a proactive management system for creating ever higher levels of patient satisfaction? To accomplish these ends, the provider must use a measurement system that focuses management attention on what matters to the customer. Equally important, the provider must develop a corporate culture that trains and rewards managers for catching staff in the act of "doing things right."

This chapter extends the general model of patient satisfaction laid out in chapter 2 by looking at the categories of experience that define the patient's point of view and the associated attributions and valuations made. In this context, attributions are descriptive of an element of service such as "courteous," "timely," and "understandable". The associated valuations will be captured by whatever rating scale or response format is selected by the researcher. These categories tend to coincide with the departmental structure of most larger provider organizations or the geographic structure of others. To measure patient satisfaction, specific compartments of service are broken down into a series of service encounters that define the attributes or processes of that overall category within which the patient ultimately forms impressions.

Building on the foundation of this service delivery model and survey feedback, managers can use survey data to ask the right questions and learn how to enhance services from the customer's point of view. Survey results from any given question may not always offer a clear, unambiguous response to patient service needs, but the focus on what is important to the customer and how the provider is performing provide the *direction* for subsequent problem-solving or quality improvement efforts. Service managers must then look to the impact of specific service evaluations on outcomes such as global satisfaction or overall quality of service. Two statistical methods for assessing important dimensions of the service experience are presented both conceptually and in parallel case studies in this chapter. Both methods have the potential to turn patient satisfaction surveys into powerful measurement and management tools. The chapter then concludes with some observations and recommendations for integrating a patient satisfaction research and management system with organizational goals.

The Service Delivery System

To achieve an optimal delivery of service in a health care setting, the provider must balance unique clinical and operational needs with service satisfaction goals. This balancing act sets the health care provider apart from other service-oriented organizations. For example, a fast food restaurant chain may respond to Americans' dietary preferences with heaping helpings of salt in its menu, but a hospital must exercise restraint in such areas where there are contrary health indications. In other words, the mandate of health service providers is qualitatively different from the mandate of other service providers; and it is perhaps for this reason that health service delivery has few good role models in other sectors of the economy.

The balancing act in health care is further complicated by the complexity of delivery mechanisms in today's medical environments (Peterson, 1988). One need only look to the thick procedural manuals of most medical centers to recognize the tremendous number of constraints and demands placed on personnel in their day-to-day functions. Multiply these procedures by the variety of personnel and departments, and one begins to see a veritable web of interfaces for any single provider during even a short hospital inpatient stay or outpatient procedure.

Peterson's Model of Service Delivery

Kristine Peterson (1988, pp. 54–55) simplifies the service delivery system of a typical hospital in the components arrayed in figure 3-1. The following list shows how she compartmentalizes the entities that serve patients as they move through the medical system:

- *Entry:* The two most common points of entry into the system are the admitting department and the emergency department.

Figure 3-1. Service Delivery System

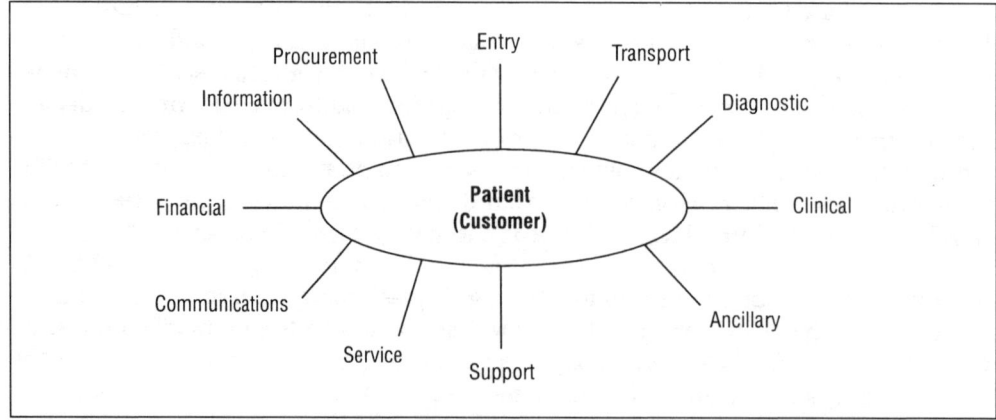

Source: Adapted from Peterson, K. *The Strategic Approach to Quality Service in Health Care.* Rockville, MD: Aspen Publishers, 1988, p. 54.

- *Transport:* This system moves the patients from one point of service delivery to another. It is facilitated by transporters, volunteers, and employees using wheelchairs and gurneys.
- *Diagnostic:* Laboratory, imaging, and radiology departments are found within the diagnostic system.
- *Clinical:* Clinical services are performed at the patient's bedside by nursing staff, physicians, and other allied health professionals.
- *Ancillary:* Cardiopulmonary and physical therapy are two examples of ancillary services.
- *Support:* This system supports the execution of business. Education and training and patient relations are examples of two departments within this system.
- *Service:* Food service, housekeeping, maintenance, laundry, and security are service departments. Services performed by social workers and discharge planners also belong within this category.
- *Communications:* The communication system relays information over telephones, computers, and pneumatic systems.
- *Financial:* The financial systems are created to ensure payment for services rendered.
- *Information:* Information pertaining to the patient, his or her diagnosis, and treatment is managed by the medical records department.
- *Procurement:* This category includes the central supply, pharmacy, and material management departments of the system, which acquire the supplies needed to perform services and support the staff in the execution of their jobs.

The patient is at the center of all these activities within the service delivery environment that Peterson proposes. Because Peterson's model logically organizes the complexities of the service delivery environment into clear categories, it is very useful for management purposes. It also offers a valuable perspective from which patient feedback may be conceptualized: the graphic can be applied to virtually any environment, from traditional acute care inpatient service to outpatient and physicians' office encounters and rehabilitation and long-term care settings.

Even though the model provides a useful picture of the patient experience, the model does not literally translate into questionnaire design, because the patient's experiences and ways of referring to the experiences are more concrete. For the patient, there is no "entry" experience—there is "admitting"; there is no "diagnostic" experience—there is "X ray"; there is no "clinical" experience—there is experience with "nurses"; there is no "financial" experience—there is "billing." This criticism does not denigrate the overall conceptualization Peterson offers; it simply points out the need to translate Peterson's model—or any other model—into the patient's own language and experience. This seemingly small point is very important in questionnaire design.

Discrete Service Encounters

Recall from chapter 2 that specific encounters experienced over the course of a health care visit or hospital stay are the building blocks of satisfaction or dissatisfaction. Patients form opinions of the overall encounter by first compiling the sum total of all experiences into relevant categories. Picture the typical patient entering an inpatient service delivery setting. The initial impressions begin with the patient's attempt to locate the appropriate entrance and/or a parking space. The patient creates a category, or "bucket," that he or she may call *facility*, and into this bucket are placed a number of discrete experiences for later reference as the overall experience is evaluated retrospectively.

After the patient enters the facility, the next category of experience is likely to be the bucket the patient calls *admitting*, which may include everything from the patient's first stop at the reception desk and impressions the patient forms of the person who greets him or her to the point at which the patient is offered transport to an assigned room. *Transport* becomes a bucket into which the patient eventually places all impressions of all personnel and equipment who helped navigate him or her to and from the assigned rooms for services and, ultimately, discharge.

The *room* becomes another bucket into which impressions of everything from the bed and television to the bathroom features are deposited. When a nurse first enters the room, this visit becomes the basis for lumping into another bucket all impressions and encounters associated with these caregivers by title. (In fact, other impressions that may not truly spring from nursing may end up in this bucket because the patient is unable to differentiate among ancillary, nursing, and other staff.) And so the experience unfolds, with buckets of categoric experience created as necessary and the buckets increasing in size to accommodate the scope of the patient's experiences.

In the end, this model affords a chance to measure and compare the volumes of the different buckets to assess the relative importance of larger categoric impressions. The model also allows measurement of the specific attributes or processes within each bucket to give definition to the salient elements of each categoric experience. For every encounter, the patient has the opportunity to evaluate the provider (or health plan or system) experience as a whole, as well as the specific encounter itself. An overall evaluation, then, will be the product of sorting through many specific experiences, such as those with the assigned nurse, the transport person, and other staff. The optimal patient survey captures feedback on all the service encounters that the patient ultimately uses to form a total opinion of the provider. Effective surveys provide this detailed prescriptive information so that provider management knows either precisely what to change or precisely where to look for elements of service warranting change.

To design a questionnaire from the patient's point of view, then, it is essential to begin with the larger categoric distinctions the patient makes, using the patient's own language. These buckets provide a foundation on which the details can be erected so that management has a reading not only of the big picture but also of the details that form it. Each of the units, or buckets, of experience can be given boundaries to help describe where one service element ends and another begins. The reference of a question should clearly point to where action can be taken that will enhance the patient experience. By "tracking," or walking in the patient's steps, the researcher can analyze the overall continuum that is the patient's service experience to pinpoint discrete components, each of which can be evaluated or scored by the patient in a survey. (Chapter 7 provides greater detail on how the researcher can track a patient's progress through the hospital system.)

Specific Outcomes and Global Satisfaction

An underlying assumption in Peterson's model is that superior performance on as many of the discrete service dimensions as possible—especially dimensions important to the patient—should create a positive experience. But what is the linkage between ratings of specific elements and the patient's overall ratings? To establish a link, the researcher must measure patient perception of the range of detailed service elements as well as the patient's overall perception of the service encounter. The first step toward this goal is to define the desirable outcomes (beyond the health outcomes) of the patient service encounter. Global outcome measures, or questions, most often asked include the following:

- Based on your recent experience at XYZ, how satisfied were you overall with the care you received?
- Based on your recent experience at XYZ, how would you evaluate the overall quality of care you received?

Examples of consequent, intended behavior questions are as follows:

- Based on your recent experience at XYZ, how likely is it that you will return if you have a medical need in the future?
- Based on your recent experience at XYZ, how likely is it that you would recommend us to a friend or relative should that person need medical care?

These questions exemplify the four major kinds of measures that many providers use in their patient satisfaction surveys. The underlying dimensions reflected in these questions are virtually universal, although the wording of questions and response codes may change in minor ways to reflect differences in settings. For instance, analysts assessing overall return likelihood within the context of a health plan would probably insert language reflecting "reenrollment" intentions. Analyzing responses to these questions and the detail indicators that form these lasting impressions can yield valuable information for improving service.

Linkage of Discrete Service Inputs to Satisfaction Outcomes

How does one move beyond simply regarding low scores as indicating areas for remedial action and high scores as indications of what is noteworthy? What do the scores actually mean? Certainly, higher scores are better than lower scores, and upward movement over time is a desirable track when one is monitoring patient satisfaction. But will one see movement in the overall, or global, measures of satisfaction when the discrete service encounters show improvement? How much improvement in the details is needed for measurable improvement in a global measure such as "overall satisfaction"?

A broad overview of two useful methods for linking discrete service measures with global outcomes is presented next. The two approaches are distinct; the goals of the specific research project will determine which method is to be preferred. At the same time, the two methods can yield complementary statistical insights into the customer experience. Both perspectives can refine a provider's method for measuring, and ultimately managing, patient satisfaction. Case studies for each method follow.

Attitude Scaling Approach

One way to evaluate the service being delivered in a health care environment is to aggregate responses from a group of items to produce an overall score for a service dimension. This is done most often as a practical consolidation because (1) a single question in a survey may not be as valid a measure of its reference point as several related items, or (2) a single question must move a great deal in order for the movement to be statistically significant. Historically, psychologists have the most successful track record in designing, refining, and aggregating survey responses to create summated scales. They have developed numerous methods that help evaluate and test the reliability and validity of question items. (Chapter 11 discusses in greater detail the issues of reliability and validity of question items or scales.)

For now, it is necessary to note only that *summated scales* represent the additive scores across a series of question items. For instance, if one measures satisfaction with each of 50 service attributes on 5-point scales, each item score will range somewhere between 1 and 5. If one creates a single, summated scale, one simply adds all items together to create a range for a 50-item scale with a low at 50 points (representing the lowest possible score of 1 on each of 50 attributes) and a high at 250 points (representing the highest possible score on each of 50 attributes).

More commonly, however, the items on a survey may actually reflect a number of relatively homogeneous underlying dimensions of the patient experience. This is because scales and the methods for constructing them are particularly well suited for identifying a subset of items within a larger grouping of items that have more in common among themselves as a subset than they do with all other items in the total grouping. Take the example of the 50 question items previously mentioned. It would be far more likely that there are two, three, four, or more relatively homogeneous subsets of question items than simply one within the total, which would then comprise as many summated scales. In chapter 2, factor analysis was applied to this end.

The construction and statistical refinement of summated scales have the distinct advantage of producing a series of items that can be used with measurable statistical confidence or reliability. By combining a number of items with statistically determined "scalability," one reduces the amount of error variance in the data, increases the variability of the summated score, and obtains a more normal distribution of scores. Scalability refers to statistical measures that quantify the extent to which items in a scale produce similar response distributions. Error variance refers to the dispersion of scores around a given response's statistical mean. The variability of a summated score is a product of numerous responses to multiple questions that offer greater dispersion of scores for respondents. For instance, a single question with a 5-point response code offers only five categories for respondents to be placed ("very satisfied," "somewhat satisfied," and so on), but ten questions afford 50 (10×5) places for respondents.

Because of the greater reliability of summated scores, one can be more confident that score changes actually reflect a change in the services to be measured instead of measurement error. Therefore, an increase in summated scores from one quarter to another should mean that satisfaction with the measured service dimension has improved. By extension, movement in the summated scale score should be related to movement in some independent overall outcome question such as satisfaction, quality perception, and so on. The relationship of scale score change to outcomes such as overall satisfaction, perceived quality, or likely repeat business can be assessed through tests of statistical association.

As with most statistical efforts, a price is paid in one area for an advantage in the other. Aggregating items into a single score from a number of individual item scores hampers testing the impact of specific service attributes within dimensions on desirable outcomes, such as overall satisfaction or quality. For instance, combining all nursing questions into a summated scale may show a dramatic impact on global satisfaction, but one may not know precisely how much impact comes from response to call buttons, empathy, or some other aspect of nursing care. In short, while this multi-item scale has desirable distributional and reliability traits, the aggregation can mask individual effects. For example, one may ask, What role does a specific facet of nursing care, such as response to call buttons, have on overall satisfaction?

Hypothetical Case Study 3-A: Factor Analysis

In chapter 2, factor analysis was used to identify the common groupings that form the basis for patient evaluations. Recall that the three case studies showed that patients in three different service settings—inpatient, outpatient, and physician's office—evaluated their experiences in a way that suggested an underlying structure to those experiences that hinged on categoric distinctions such as "nurse" and "physician." The categories that emerged from patients' responses to questionnaires about their experiences are shown again in figure 3-2, this time with the amount of variance each category explains. We can use factor analysis to decide what should be included in a summated scale that captures the essence of the inpatient experience.

But first, it is helpful to go a bit deeper into the statistical tools used in factor analysis to determine the efficacy of any scale of question items that grows out of such an effort. Factor analysis allows the researcher to determine common groupings by looking at all the variability in the original 38 questions on the inpatient questionnaire. In this case, 13 groupings (or factors) together explain 81.8 percent of the variance in all the patients' answers to all 38 questions. However, further examination shows that the first six factors explain 65.4 percent of all the variance, leaving only about 16.4 percent of the variance to be explained by the last seven factors (81.8 percent − 65.4 percent = 16.4 percent). Based on this analysis, one can see that the first six factors and their 28-question items are the best set of indicators for ongoing tracking of the overall inpatient experience. This insight allows the researcher to trim a time-consuming questionnaire to one that is likely to take less than ten minutes to answer, without compromising statistically important information.

The analysis also tells the researcher where to put the effort for the greatest impact on the patient's perceptions. In this case, the focus is nursing. Note that the six items

Figure 3-2. **Statistically Important Categories of Inpatient Questions**

Dimensions and Items	Explained Variance
1. Nursing	40.1%
• Skill of nursing staff assigned?	
• Nurses' communication with patient?	
• Care and concern shown by nurses?	
• Nursing staff ability to solve patient's problems?	
• Nurses' response to call buttons?	
• How well nurses did their jobs?	
2. Doctors and Staff	7.4%
• Physicians' willingness to listen to/answer patient's questions?	
• Physicians' ability to keep patient informed?	
• Physician care and concern?	
• Accessibility of patient's physician?	
• Courtesy of volunteer staff?	
• Coordination of testing and procedures?	
3. Meal Service	6.4%
• Timeliness of meals served?	
• Quality of patient's food?	
• Correctness of food patient ordered?	
• Variety of food patient ordered?	
• Temperature of food served?	
4. Parking and Signage	4.1%
• Security of parking lots?	
• Valet parking services?	
• Signs on how to get to main entrance?	
• Internal signs directing patient?	
5. Discharge and Billing	3.8%
• Discharge instructions from nurses?	
• Time it took patient to leave the hospital?	
• Information patient received about billing?	
6. Room Environment	3.6%
• Intercom system at patient's bedside?	
• Television in patient's room?	
• Quiet of patient's room?	
• Cleanliness of patient's room?	

under nursing explain 40.1 percent of the total variability in the 38 question item survey, approximately half of all that can be explained and nearly two-thirds of what can be explained in the short version (28 items) of the questionnaire.

Factor analysis does not afford the same level of detail at the next level, however. That next level asks what changes and investments in nursing would have the greatest impact on patient attitude. In fact, the six items that define nursing all tend to be statistically linked at roughly the same level of association. At this point, one may look to another method for help in sorting out the details that will give a total quality improvement (TQI) effort the direction it needs to move the needle.

Multiple Regression Approach

At the root of patient satisfaction research is a provider's desire to assess the extent to which the services a patient receives meet the patient's expectations. But high ratings on selected scores do not guarantee overall satisfaction, repeat business likelihood, or reenrollment. Conversely, low scores do not always mean that a patient is sufficiently dissatisfied to switch providers. Were this the case, then every hospital in America should focus its efforts on food services and hire a world-class chef.

What a provider most needs to know is how to direct management efforts to the specific elements of patient care that most significantly increase the following:

- Patients' *overall satisfaction* with the experience
- Patients' *perceptions of the quality of care* of the provider
- The *likelihood that a patient will return* for future health care needs
- The *likelihood that a patient will recommend the provider* to others

If one applies a statistical technique called multiple regression analysis to measure the impact of specific service experiences on overall quality, a quantifiable coefficient emerges for every significant, predictive association between the service input and the lasting impression conveyed to the patient. Recall that factor analysis affords no statistical and predictive linkage between the service inputs and the larger measure, such as "overall satisfaction." Note also that multiple regression is superior to simple correlation, which can only take into account the association between two variables.

Multiple regression analysis quantifies the extent to which specific patient perceptions can predict an outcome such as overall quality or repeat visit potential. Each aspect of patient care receives a *regression coefficient* that quantifies how much overall perceived quality or likely repeat business increases with an improvement in a specific care component. Larger coefficients, when significant, show where improvements in patient perceptions will result in a greater impact on a provider's bottom line, whether through repeat business, referral potential, overall satisfaction, or perception of the hospital's overall quality of care delivered.

Having praised the strengths of multiple regression, we must also point out a potential weakness. Recall that factor analysis looks to smaller subsets of questions that are sufficiently alike to be placed on a single scale, and the scores from the individual items on the scale can be summated. If the individual input items are too much alike in a multiple regression model, the "assumption of independence" is violated. Statisticians disagree about the level beyond which items are too similar and not sufficiently independent, but all agree that it is a consideration when one applies multivariate models. As a result, the reader should exercise caution in applying any multivariate software packages, because these packages alone cannot make judgment calls about the similarity of items.

Case Study 3-B: Multiple Regression

As an example of multiple regression modeling, take the data from Hospital X's inpatient study displayed in figure 3-3. The evaluations represented by the statistical

Figure 3-3. Overall Inpatient Experience: Mean Ratings in Rank Order

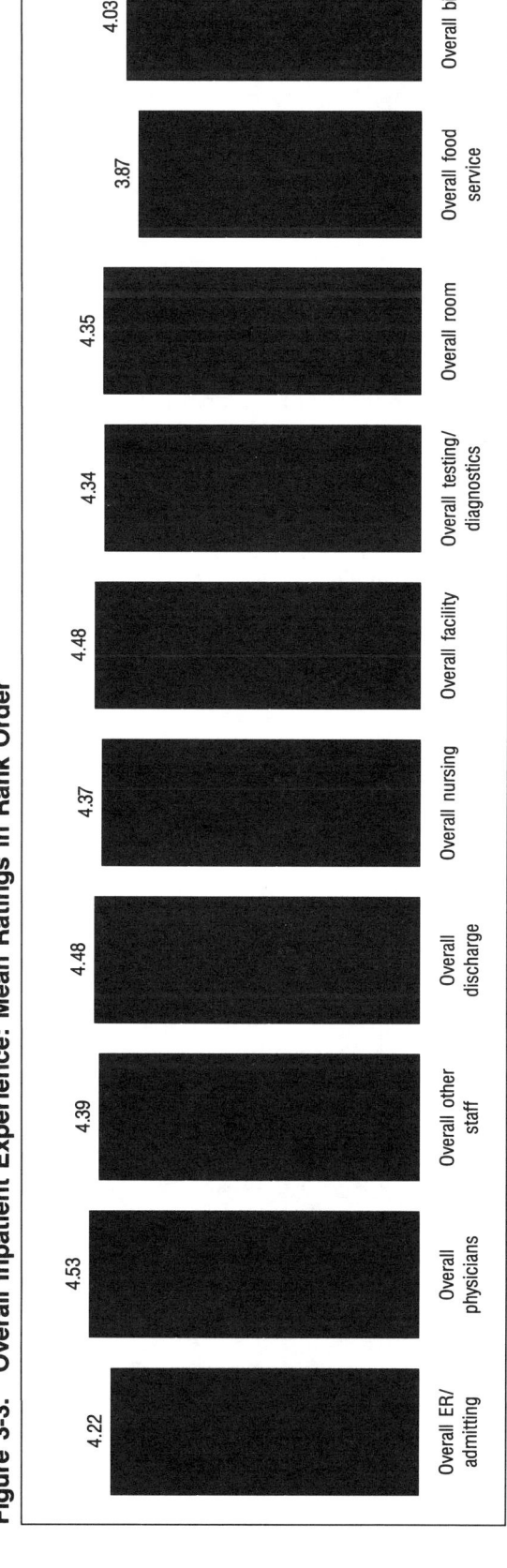

Note: Mean ratings based on a 5-point scale where 5 equals "very satisfied" and 1 equals "very dissatisfied."
Source: *National Health Care Consumer Survey*, Opinion Research Corp., 1996.

means in this figure are typical of scores that one would see from an inpatient experience in which the customer is asked to rate service on a 5-point scale in which 5 equals "very satisfied" and 1 equals "very dissatisfied." These data are from a telephone-administered questionnaire on recent inpatient experiences, but the example can be generalized to other care settings, such as outpatient, emergency room (ER), and primary care. Scores range from a low of 3.87 for "overall food service" to a high of 4.53 for "overall physicians."

From a management perspective, what can be said about these results? If you were managing the patient care process and concerned about getting these patients to return when they have their next medical need, where would your instincts tell you to devote your attention first—to billing procedures or food services, because they receive the lowest ratings?

Unfortunately, figure 3-3 shows you only where Hospital X has done well and where it has not. It does not tell you where your management efforts will deliver the greatest impact or how to prioritize those efforts. These shortcomings are typical of traditional analyses of survey results, which fail to give adequate direction for management decisions.

Determining what brings inpatients back does not necessarily require new questions, but rather a different way of statistically analyzing patient feedback. With this tool, a provider can develop a clearer picture of how satisfaction and improvements in targeted services will affect repeat business and the bottom line.

Figure 3-4 is a graphic representation of a model that shows the general categories of patient experience in the boxes in the left-hand column and the outcome perception on the right. (Although this model focuses on the inpatient experience, the insights it provides apply also to the outpatient, ER patient, acute care patient, and other

Figure 3-4. Structure of the Quality Perception Model

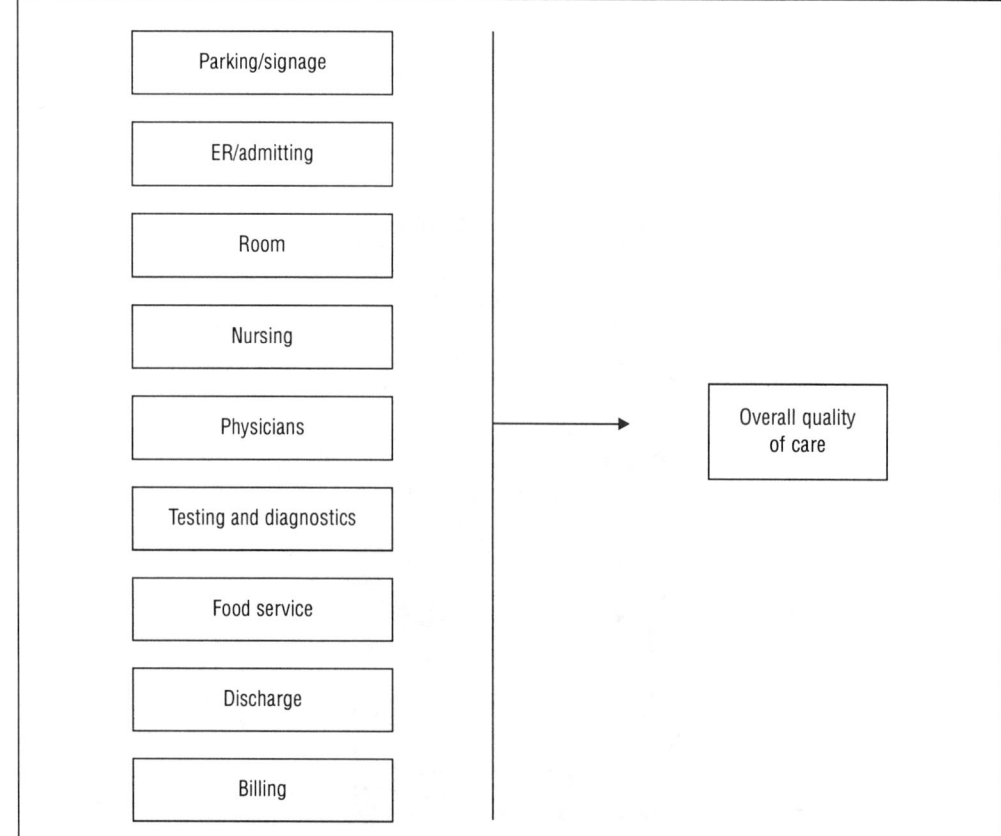

patient care experiences.) When everything operates smoothly in an inpatient experience from the beginning (experiences with parking and signage) to the end (impressions about services such as billing), then the patient will have a more favorable impression of the provider's quality of service. Of course, dimensions beyond those listed in the figure can affect a patient's ultimate evaluation of quality, but the listed categories are the core of a working model that can account for much of the variance in the overall outcome.

In figure 3-5, four of the boxed factors are highlighted and have coefficients. Each coefficient describes how much influence the box on the left has on the outcome, "overall quality of care." Take, for example, the largest coefficient—that associated with nursing. The coefficient provides a means to compare two patients, one of whose nursing evaluations are 1 point higher than the other's. Imagine that the first patient rates nursing a 5 on a 5-point scale, and the second patient rates nursing overall a 4. If enough patient responses are compared, a predictable pattern emerges in which the patient who rates nursing 1 point higher also predictably rates overall quality of service higher by 0.370 points.

Figure 3-6 shows how scores might distribute themselves as they describe the relationship between nursing (on the horizontal axis) and overall quality (on the vertical axis). There is a clear pattern in this scatter plot of scores among patients. The pattern is described by the coefficient, which in turn is visually represented by a regression line. As one follows overall nursing from left to right, the scatter plot shows a move from lower scores to higher scores. Because a statistically significant relationship between nursing and overall quality exists, however, one also sees higher scores for overall quality as one moves into higher nursing scores. This relationship is shown

Figure 3-5. Quality Perception Model (Inpatient)

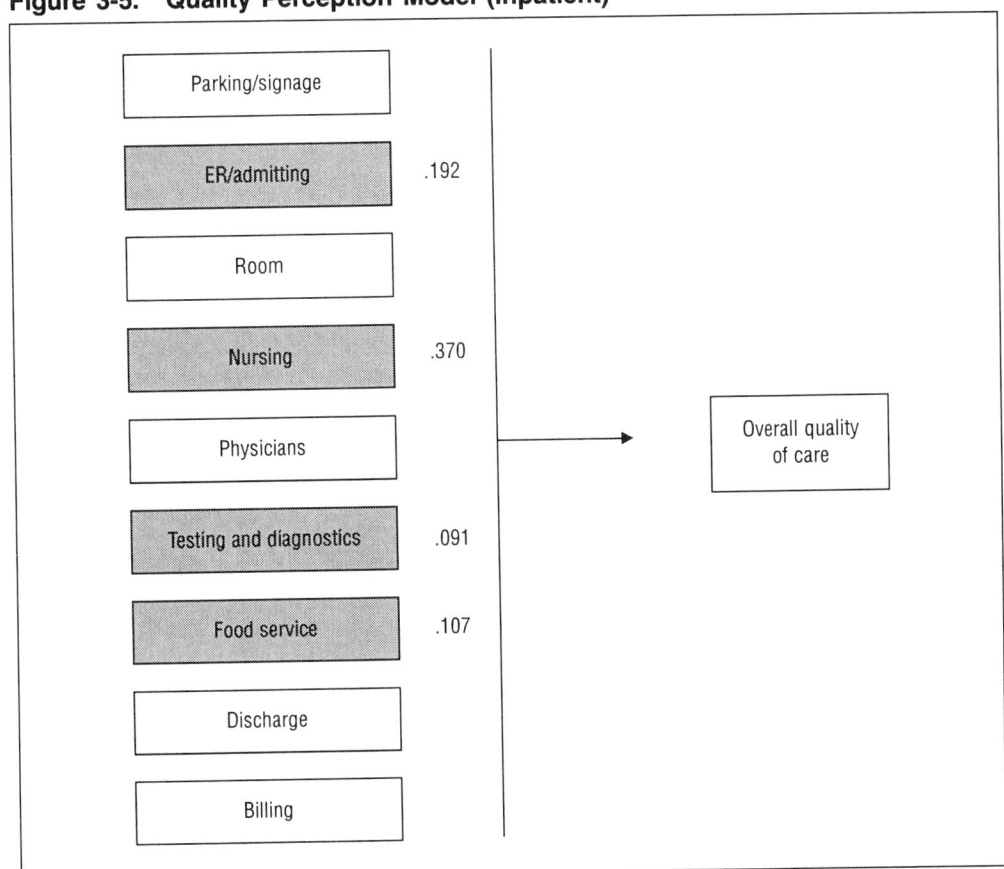

Figure 3-6. Scatter Plotting of Association between Nursing and Overall Quality

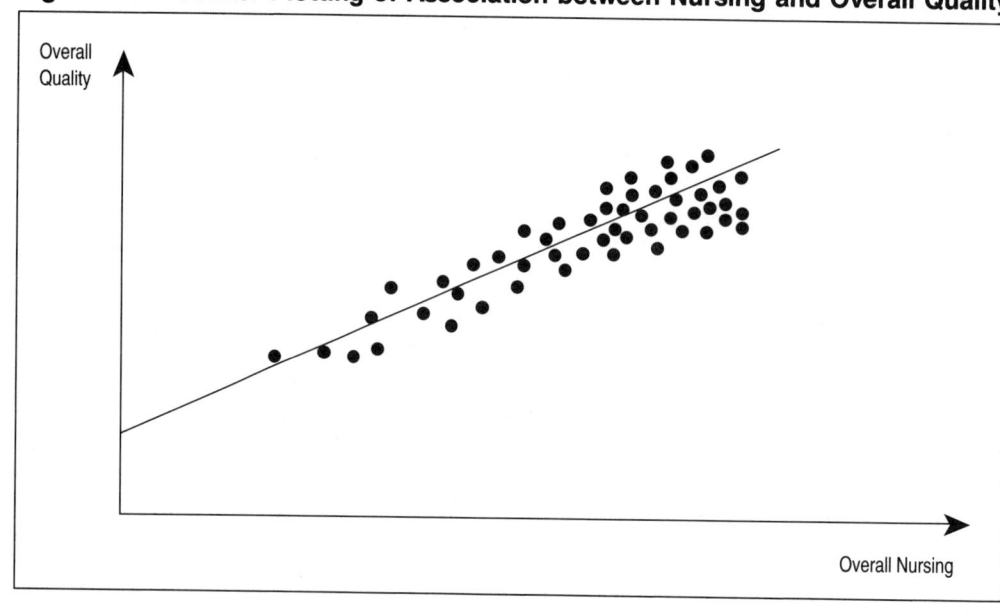

by the line. Notice also that there are more points clustered at the upper, right end of this line than at the lower, left end. This is typical of most providers' scores, which generally have a relatively greater number of higher scores than lower scores. The fact that the two performance indicators (nursing and overall quality) are significantly associated with one another is what allows one to include the line on the scatter plot.

It is appropriate at this point to offer a methodological note on the important distinction between regression and correlation. Regression helps explain how nursing and overall quality perceived are statistically related, or how changes in nursing evaluations are associated with changes (in the same direction) of overall quality perceived by the patient. Correlation explains how far the average point in this graph falls away from the regression line in figure 3-6.

The results provided by this kind of model are useful as a predictive tool that suggests improvements in the performance of nursing (the largest coefficient) will help begin to improve a patient's overall perception of service provided. And this information has revenue consequences that result in brand (provider) loyalty.

Looking back one last time at figure 3-5, note that the relationship to overall quality of each of the four factors is quantified. Nursing is the most important factor in this model, and larger coefficients suggest a greater influence on "overall quality" than smaller coefficients, but all are unique, *independent* effects. Thus, for the patient who offers a 1-point higher score than his or her counterpart for nursing, if there also is a favorable and concomitant 1-point difference in "ER/admitting," then "overall quality of care" is likely to be 0.370 + 0.192, or 0.562 higher. Here again, regression shows its superiority over correlation, which can only take into account the association between two variables. Multiple regression not only is a better predictive tool, it is also a means of capturing the influence of multiple inputs like "nursing" and "ER/admitting."

To better understand what should be done to improve nursing, one should look to other detail measures of nursing activities and their associated coefficients in a manner similar to that shown in figure 3-5. Likewise, the Hospital X case study further prioritizes the remaining dimensions. The model suggests that the next priorities after nursing ought to be, in order, ER/admitting, testing and diagnostics, and food service. The details that define these general service experiences offer insight into what changes will make the most difference to patients.

It may still be unclear about what steps should be taken to enhance nursing performance, to continue using this example, in order to move the needle on overall quality of care perceived by the patient. At this point, then, additional regression modeling of the detail processes that potentially drive nursing's overall evaluation can be undertaken. In our experience, it is generally a combination of factors that, in psychological terms, describes both the instrumental and the expressive aspects of nursing that define that experience for the patient. Instrumental aspects of nursing can include how much time elapsed before a response to a call button, whether the nurse called the patient by name, and how staff provided other services that reflected the simple act of doing what the patient required.

Expressive processes typically include dimensions such as caring and concern, communication, and other elements reflective of how nurses relate to the patient. It may still require further analysis through qualitative research or quality improvement team discussions to identify when a patient deems "care and concern" have been optimally demonstrated or when adequate communication has taken place.

The instrumental features may be substantially easier to analyze. For example, call button response time can be measured in number of minutes elapsed. In addition, some of these elements may be better managed by also focusing on expectations. Patients must be assured before any need arises that a nurse will be in instantaneous contact with them through two-way voice communication at times when the nurse is unable to come to a patient's room immediately.

Scaling and Modeling as Management Tools

We have looked at two unique statistical methods for analyzing the data derived from patient satisfaction research. The question remains, how does one choose one over another? Quite simply, the answer is that one need not necessarily choose, because the methods do not contradict one another so much as they offer complementary information to one another. Attitude scaling, facilitated by factor analysis, offers a broad-based tool for assessing the key elements that collectively define the patient experience and offers a means of testing the ultimate reliability of this aggregate measure. Factor analysis can be used to refine summated scales of patient satisfaction that offer a broad-based and sensitive measure of the patient's total experience. This is a big picture of what the patient experiences, but the details of what drives desirable outcomes such as repeat business, word-of-mouth recommendations, or overall satisfaction come from multiple regression models. In effect, the researcher gains measurement reliability from attitude scaling and management insights from multiple regression analysis.

One can also look for a consistent pattern of response across the two methods. Recall that nursing was the most important single factor in the factor analysis case study 3-A, and "overall nursing" also was the most important single variable within the multiple regression case study 3-B. In an analysis not reported in these case studies, the authors also applied regression modeling to the data in case study 3-A. Of the six variables that defined nursing—the most important factor of the data set in case study 3-A—five of these also were statistically significant drivers of a variable, "overall nursing," when multiple regression was used. In case study 3-A, the top three factors also were the top three drivers of overall quality perceived in the multiple regression model. And of the 17 question items that helped to define the top three factors in case study 3-A, multiple regression statistically identified 13 in its model. Of the 15 question items important in the relevant multiple regression models (those defining "overall nursing," "overall physicians," and "overall meal service"), 13 were also found in the factor analysis to define the top three factors.

Multiple regression analysis should always have a great deal in common with factor analysis when applied to the same data and when looking to the most important variables. Although there may be nominal departures from this kind of cross-method consistency, especially with smaller databases, the differences should not be so great as to suggest competing descriptions of the same patient experience.

Management Implications

Although it is essential to use measurement tools that afford insights into what satisfies the customer, it is just as important to build a management culture dedicated to meeting and exceeding customer expectations. However, one cannot force health care providers to deliver a more satisfactory service experience to the customer. Emphasizing the stick and not the carrot flies in the face of current management theory. Yet this is precisely the mistake some corporate cultures make, perhaps as a legacy of the early days in managing resource costs associated with diagnosis-related groups (DRGs). The early research that created a basis for compensation by category pointed to negative outliers ("bad apples") and then sought ways to bring these outliers back in line with the more common and less costly examples. Contemporary management theory seeks to model service behavior after the moments of truth demonstrated by the "good apples" within a service delivery environment. This philosophy helps provide the underpinnings for a better motivated and better directed management of the patient experience.

No patient satisfaction tool can be any more effective than management allows it to be. Equipped with reliable data derived from the powerful techniques described in this chapter, top-level management must still set a responsive tone and aggressive pace for change to occur. A sophisticated patient satisfaction management system requires top-down commitment and bottom-up action. How can this happen?

Management Commitment to Patient Satisfaction

First and most obvious, management must be committed to patient satisfaction and to continuous quality improvement. The kinds of models presented in this chapter do not encourage management to sit on its laurels. They encourage change wherever the patient's feedback presents an opportunity, and management must be energetic in implementing the change.

The most fundamental management rule in this context will be to reward desired behavior and remold less desirable behavior. The goal of satisfying customers must appear desirable to staff. If staff come to see the patient as the individual whose ratings adversely affect their standing with management, they can become patient adversaries. The whole patient satisfaction system also is at risk from staff who "game" the system to create artificial (and high) evaluations. The authors have seen conspicuously dissatisfied customers "conveniently" missing a satisfaction survey in their package of materials when they leave the facility in institutions in which patient care personnel are charged with satisfaction improvements and administration of surveys.

But if management shows in tangible ways that it values the satisfied customer and staff's efforts to create customer satisfaction, then the rest becomes easy. Committed management creates the kind of environment in which desirable staff behavior emerges and flourishes. Some providers have followed the lead from other service sectors by establishing an employee-of-the-month award based on the employee's contribution to superior service or patient satisfaction. Others have tied management compensation to satisfaction scores. In this case, however, it is important that the scores have sufficient statistical precision and sensitivity and that the goals be realistic and realizable. Some elements of patient satisfaction—satisfaction with waiting time, for example—may be relatively easy to see and change, while others, such as care and concern, may be less obvious or tangible and thus more difficult to change.

Customer-centered management need not be costly. A 5 percent increase in patient satisfaction need not equate with a 5 percent increase in expenses; recall the return on quality information presented earlier in the book. Instead, patient satisfaction should be the natural outgrowth of a truly market-driven organization. Rewards (monetary and otherwise) certainly can be in place, but the payoffs to management should be no less tangible. Greater care and concern need not represent new expenditures but, instead, embracing a new outlook. But even if some changes require disbursements, the investment should see a handsome return.

Satisfaction Measurement as a "Blunt Instrument"

Most of this chapter has focused on what is measured as the provider attempts to assess patient perceptions of the service experience. At this point it is appropriate to pause and offer a methodological perspective on the science of opinion measurement. All of the methods discussed to this point offer ways of measuring a patient's relative satisfaction with a health care service experience. But it is important to recognize that just because one can ask a question does not mean that the information one receives in return offers razor-sharp measurement precision of what one thinks one is asking. (Validity is addressed in detail in chapter 11.)

How much weight can one place on data once results from a survey are in? Rule one is that no single question should go to the bank; that is, one should never make large decisions based on small numbers of respondents or small numbers of questions. Real precision comes from very large databases or from aggregations of a number of question items that together begin to tell an important story. Even though detailed question items help health care management make decisions that have a bearing on TQI programs, management should beware that as movement is tracked, it is done so (1) with sufficient respondents in the database, (2) with sufficient time points to identify clear trends, and (3) with sufficient question items bearing on the issue under scrutiny so that management is truly able to identify meaningful change.

Summary

Successful patient satisfaction management depends on successful patient satisfaction measurement. This chapter has outlined elements that can be important in building a model of the patient experience that affords an opportunity for both measuring what the patient perceives and assessing what is important to the patient throughout this experience. Using two multivariate tools, factor analysis and multiple regression analysis, the chapter has offered examples of how to gain greater statistical insights into what factors support the patient's ultimate sense of provider quality and what will have the potential to affect purchasing decisions in the future. In this light, effective patient satisfaction measurement and management are as integral to ongoing quality improvement programs as any other clinical, operational, and financial issues.

CHAPTER FOUR

Potential Pitfalls in the Research Process

Virtually all health care facilities assess patient satisfaction in some manner—from complaint cards and suggestion boxes to computerized measurement feedback systems. Whether rudimentary, sophisticated, or somewhere in between, most providers' measurement systems suffer from one or more shortcomings. Some flaws can seriously bias research results, thereby misleading management. Management decision making may also be hampered by systems that offer incomplete or dated information.

Fortunately, most research problems can be remedied. To help readers recognize and avoid shortcomings in their own institutions' systems, the chapter begins with an overview of problems most often encountered in the two major approaches to research, qualitative research and quantitative research. The chapter then examines potential pitfalls in the major steps in the research process—survey administration, survey structure, survey sampling, and survey response and processing. An understanding of research flaws in these areas will help readers appreciate the merits of the research methods presented in later chapters.

Before we begin looking at the numerous pitfalls that can plague satisfaction research, readers should be aware of the nature of objectivity in research. At best, the results of a research study provide only a partial or incomplete view of reality. This is true regardless of how rigorous a study's design, how careful its implementation, or how complex and thorough the execution of the data analysis. Although there is no such thing as true objectivity in research, one should nonetheless try to reduce bias by understanding its nature and causes.

Pitfalls in Qualitative Research

Qualitative research attempts to understand the service experience as seen through the customer's eyes. It requires the researcher to suspend his or her view of the service and take on the patient's. Qualitative research is primarily conducted through three methods: observational techniques, in-depth interviews, and focus groups. Each of these methods is subject to pitfalls.

Lack of Objectivity

For all three methods of qualitative research, the most common pitfall is a lack of objectivity. Researchers' perceptions will be skewed if they have preconceived notions about what they will find or a vested interest in the study's outcome. The possibility of bias brings into question whether providers, clinicians, or management can objectively study their own services. To maintain objectivity, facilities are advised to draw research staff from the planning and research department. Smaller facilities without this resource may be well advised to contract with an external researcher.

Patient Reactivity

Patient reactivity—another form of bias—may occur if interviews are done while the patient is still receiving services. Once a patient knows that he or she is being studied, the individual may attempt to anticipate what the researcher wants to hear or see, and then provide it. Although patient reactivity cannot be eliminated, it can be lessened if the researcher assures the patient that constructive criticism is welcomed and if the researcher is a "disinterested party" rather than the health service provider.

Patient reactivity can also be a problem when focus groups are used to gather feedback about satisfaction. Just as groups can help members recall certain experiences or events, they also can influence or censor the expression of opinions. The danger, then, is that patients can become reactive to the expectations of the group. (Chapter 7 explains ways to differentiate between responses biased by group dynamics and responses that reflect patients' actual perceptions of the service experience.)

Overgeneralizations

The strength of qualitative research lies in its capacity to understand and describe a patient's unique experiences. Should researchers attempt to use qualitative data to estimate the proportion of service recipients that hold a certain opinion or the extent to which an opinion has changed from one time period to another, they are guilty of overgeneralizing from the data. At best, the researcher can describe the range of experiences held by service recipients but not the frequency or intensity of such experiences in the universe of all service recipients.

Pitfalls in Quantitative Research

Many researchers argue the preeminence of quantitative research over qualitative, claiming to have "real numbers" on which to base their view of reality. An antidote to this argument is provided by Albert Einstein's famous dictum, "Not everything that counts can be counted. Not everything that can be counted counts." It is worth remembering that both the qualitative and quantitative approaches have strengths and weaknesses in capturing some piece of reality.

Quantitative satisfaction research most often involves administering structured questionnaires, either in person (face to face), over the telephone, or through the mail. Each method of administration has its own potential pitfalls.

In-Person Surveys: Timing and Communication Problems

The major pitfalls of the in-person survey, or face-to-face interview, arise from the timing of the contact and the dynamics of interpersonal communication. It may not be reasonable to expect a patient to give a fair assessment of the delivery system while still, to some extent, a "hostage" of that system. When asked to complete patient satisfaction surveys while still hospitalized or in a situation in which they fear a breech of confidentiality, many patients stop short of being candid in their evaluations. They may either upwardly bias their performance evaluations or simply omit items that they perceive as too direct. As a result, even though the in-person survey may have a high rate of compliance, the quality of that response suffers.

The quality of responses to in-person surveys also may be affected by the dynamics of interpersonal communication. When a survey arrives in the mail, the respondent does not see or hear the surveyor. With a telephone call, the respondent only hears the interviewer's voice. But the very nature of in-person surveys brings into play a full array of personal and environmental factors that may influence the respondent. In public opinion methodological research, it has been documented that an interviewer's gender, age, ethnicity, or any other conspicuous characteristic may introduce a bias into responses. These effects are most pronounced when the characteristics tie in closely to the question (French, 1981). For example, a male respondent will tend to offer more "liberated" responses on the subject of women's rights when the interviewer is female. Also, bias may be introduced in responses to questions about civil rights when the interviewer is African-American. Even when the subject matter does not directly reflect the nature of the interviewer's characteristics, bias can result from lack of rapport between respondent and interviewer. Respondents form an impression of the institution and of the interviewer within the first moments of contact, and these impressions influence responses or willingness to respond.

Some influences can be balanced by randomly assigning interviewers to patients and maintaining a diverse interviewing staff. Another way to minimize response bias is to distribute but not administer the survey. For example, the hospital may give patients a survey card with a business response number or a postage-paid envelope, requesting that they complete and return the survey after discharge from the hospital. Although this method avoids bias stemming from interpersonal and environmental pressures, it also transforms the in-person survey into a mail survey. To avoid the problem of lower response rates associated with mail surveys, some facilities make follow-up telephone calls to discharged patients who have been given questionnaires.

Telephone Surveys: Timing and Communication Problems

Like the in-person interview, the telephone interview provides an opportunity for the researcher to interact with the patient and capture that individual's unique perspectives. However, the telephone survey also carries with it some of the same potential for bias because it, too, involves some of the dynamics of interpersonal communication, even though the interviewer and respondent do not meet face to face.

In addition, researchers must be sensitive to the length and timing of interviews, as well as to the number of contacts. Lengthy telephone interviews that tax the respondent's patience can lead to careless and inaccurate responses.

Survey efforts also may be compromised if telephone contacts are scheduled to occur only at times convenient to staff. For example, many volunteers prefer to be available during regular business hours. But interviewing only during business hours typically results in overrepresentation of homemakers, the unemployed, and retirees. These individuals, although important to the survey, cannot represent the balance of market, who may be at work or away from home. Typically, the most successful telephone interviews are those conducted during evening and weekend hours, when callers have the best chance of reaching a representative cross section of recent patients. In markets where there is a high percentage of second- or third-shift workers, the contact timetable should be modified to reach workers during off-hours.

Finally, telephone interviewing that does not employ repeat contacts runs the risk of contacting only households that are easy to reach, such as those headed by members out of the work force. In these cases, an age bias may be inadvertently introduced. Younger, more socially active individuals are less likely to be home and therefore could be underrepresented in a sample with only one contact effort per telephone number and name. Without several attempts over a period of days, the contacted sample will be biased.

Mail-Out Surveys: Administration and Design Problems

Mail-out surveys represent some of the same problems as unmanned space missions. Like the unmanned shuttle, the survey instrument must be flawlessly designed so that it reaches the appropriate target with little necessity for human intervention and returns home once the mission is complete. The comparison breaks down, of course, because even unmanned space missions are in contact with the sender throughout the flight.

What all this means in terms of patient satisfaction measurement is that a mail-out questionnaire must make a great first impression for the respondent to even consider answering the questions. Furthermore, the survey must be "user friendly." Questions must be easy to understand and answer, and the survey must be easy to return at no cost to the respondent, which means that return postage must be prepaid.

It is also important to remember that a weakness of mail-out surveys is that they do not provide the opportunity to probe for more information when a respondent gives incomplete or evasive responses. The authors recall an experience in which an in-person survey was conducted with a patient awaiting discharge. After answering a series of specific questions, the patient, whose spouse was present, was asked whether anything had *not* gone right during hospitalization. The initial response was a lukewarm "not really." After the interviewer probed for specific details or certainty of response, the patient turned to the spouse and asked, "Do you think we should tell her?" At this point, of course, the interviewer recognized that the patient's experiences had not been fully satisfactory, and the details of the negative experience were revealed. If not for the interviewer, who was trained to probe for more information when confronted with evasive responses ("not really"), the information would have been lost. To help compensate for the lack of an ability to probe, mail-out surveys might include questions that directly ask for feedback about any negative experiences the patient may have had.

Pitfalls in Survey Construction

Effective patient satisfaction research consists of asking the right questions, in the right way, of the right people. This process is not as simple as it may sound. People sometimes have the misconception that creating a questionnaire is as easy as completing one. But asking the right questions involves the painstaking work of drafting various forms of a question; grouping questions to create a thematic flow; pretesting the questionnaire; and revising and pretesting again until respondents seem to comprehend the questions, response options, and instructions as intended by the researcher. Then, to examine the instrument's psychometric properties, the questionnaire is pilot tested on a sample of respondents large enough to allow for multivariate statistical analysis. At each step in the construction process, the researcher can fall prey to various pitfalls.

Lengthy Surveys

A survey should be detailed enough to capture the desired information yet short enough to be completed in a reasonable amount of time. Recognizing when a survey is too long requires something of an empathetic eye. Respondents are doing researchers a favor by answering survey questions, and so the least researchers can do is not overstay their welcome. On rare occasions a survey actually is too short; that is, it cannot accomplish what it is charged to do because it does not ask all the relevant questions. More often, however, the opposite problem occurs, and the lengthy survey irritates the very people whose business the provider wants to retain.

Lengthy surveys also run the risk of truncated interviews, because respondents may hang up before completing all survey items. Also, the potential for less thoughtful responses or for response bias grows as weary respondents give less accurate responses or responses that begin to reflect their answers to earlier questions.

How can one gauge whether a survey is too lengthy? Typically, the critical watershed appears to be somewhere between 15 and 20 minutes for telephone surveys and between 45 and 75 questions for self-administered questionnaires. For a more precise measurement tailored to a particular survey, time barriers can be charted during the testing process. In the pretesting of face-to-face surveys, respondents can be asked for their reaction to the questionnaire length. Self-administered questionnaires can be examined after pilot testing for signs of "erosion," such as incomplete surveys or surveys in which the same response option to questions has been repeatedly selected in the later parts of the instrument. Telephone questionnaires can be monitored for hang-ups prior to completion.

Poorly Worded Questions

A second potential pitfall of survey construction involves the phrasing of questions. Researchers should be alert to the "double-barreled question," an apparently single question that, in fact, asks about two different things. Double-barreled questions are particularly troublesome when the answer to one subquestion may be at odds with the answer to the other. Suppose, for example, that a discharged patient is asked: "Did admission staff serve you *promptly* and *courteously?*" Clearly, the service could easily have been high on one dimension and not the other, the question thereby rendering responses ambiguous.

Researchers should also be careful to avoid unfamiliar, vague, and offensive wording. It is easy to overlook the fact that respondents may be unfamiliar with jargon and abbreviations that are well known to the provider. Unfamiliar vocabulary is problematic because it can lead to responses based on guesses—or no response at all. Equally problematic are vaguely worded questions, because they can be interpreted in a variety of ways. Finally, one should be alert to questions that may be perceived as threatening, offensive, or otherwise objectionable to respondents. Poorly worded questions produce biased and uninterpretable results. They also tend to frustrate respondents and drive up the number of incomplete questionnaires, as well as nonresponse rates.

Vexing Questions

Questionnaires should not burden the respondent by asking unnecessary follow-up questions, such as "If yes, why? If no, why not?" Many times, the follow-up question proves to be more of an irritant than an opportunity to explain. Although these questions may sound reasonable during instrument design, if they are not analyzed through pretesting, they may prove to be unreasonable, and the respondent may not give satisfactory answers.

Also counterproductive are questions that ask too much of the respondent, such as "What other services would you like to see offered at Hospital X?" Respondents are not often prepared to answer what arguably are management questions. Irritated with the interviewer who asks too much of them, their response is typically a resounding "don't know."

Inappropriate Response Formats

Questions may be worded correctly but still miss the mark if they are accompanied by an inappropriate response format. Suppose, for instance, that a question asks, "How satisfied were you with the care you received from the nurses?" If this question is followed by the scale "never, seldom, often, very often," patients will have a difficult time responding, because the question asks for the degree of satisfaction, while the scale offers a frequency response.

A different problem is created when an insufficient number of scale levels are included. Satisfaction with service exists along a continuum, from "extremely dissatisfied" to "extremely satisfied." Many people's satisfaction levels fall between these two extremes. If only two response options are offered, how can respondents answer the question?

A more technical scaling pitfall involves the use of the "excellent-good-fair-poor" response format. Although it provides respondents a continuum from positive to negative, the format offers only an *ordinal* scale; that is, the analyst can know only that excellent is higher than good, that good is higher than fair, and that fair is higher than poor. Nonetheless, these items should not be statistically scored to offer a mean, because they really are not equal intervals apart from one another. Alternative response formats can be used to offer intervals that appear equal, such as Likert-type scaling (for example, "very satisfied, somewhat satisfied, somewhat dissatisfied, very dissatisfied") or rating scales that explicitly attach numbers to performance (for example, "On a scale from 1 to 10 . . ."). (Scaling and response formats are discussed in greater detail in chapter 5.)

Pitfalls in Survey Sampling

Largely owing to cost considerations, providers seldom survey all patients who receive services from their facility. Instead, they elect to draw a sample. If all patients were identical to one another in all respects, and services across departments or floors were also identical, there would be no need for concern as to who was sampled. However, patients tend to be heterogenous and services diverse. As a result, carefully designed sampling procedures are required. If a sample is to provide a useful description of the population of patients from which it is drawn, then the sample must contain the same variability of characteristics (for example, age, gender, ethnicity, services received) as exists in the population. When this is achieved, it can be said that the sample is representative of the population. Probability sampling is the method of choice for selecting a representative sample. Insufficient sample sizes and unrepresentative samples are common pitfalls of the sampling process.

Inadequate Sample Size

Many providers attempt to get by with small samples to conserve research dollars. However, the smaller the sample, the larger the sampling error in the collected data. For example, if 50 out of 1,000 patients were randomly selected to complete a satisfaction questionnaire, the sampling error would be approximately plus or minus 13.5 percent; in a sample of 100, it would be plus or minus 9.3 percent; in a sample of 200, it would be plus or minus 6.2 percent. These sampling error ranges are "adjusted" for population size. For a research study that requires statistical precision, a sample of 50 or 100 would be grossly inadequate. (Chapter 6 will discuss how to estimate sampling error and the optimal sample size.)

It is common for researchers to compare satisfaction scores across service locations (for example, floors 1, 2, 3, 4, and 5) or segment respondents according to age, gender, ethnicity, or other characteristics. However, the more ways a sample is sliced, the smaller each subsample becomes. Although a sample of 100 past patients would be sufficient to draw general conclusions about satisfaction in the population, this sample size would be insufficient for subsample comparisons. It is essential for the researcher to anticipate the types of subsample analysis that will be required when sampling procedures are being designed.

Faulty Representativeness

There is a common misconception that a large sample is always better than a small one. It is true that sampling error decreases as sample size increases, but this fact alone does not guarantee a more representative sample. Representativeness comes from (1) a sampling design that provides all members of the population under study an equal chance of being selected, and (2) obtaining completed questionnaires from the vast majority (preferably 80 percent or more) of the sample. When the response rate falls short of this goal, the sample may fail to be representative because of systematic differences between respondents and nonrespondents. In such instances, the researcher should compare the obtained sample characteristics (for example, age, gender, race, diagnosis) with the population characteristics to determine their equivalence.

Inadequate Definition of Patient Population

The next pitfall to be discussed involves the potential for inadequately defining the patient population from which a sample is drawn. Simple random sampling is adequate if the population of service recipients is relatively homogeneous, but not when it is heterogeneous. In this case, additional safeguards should be introduced. In such instances, it is better to draw random subsamples from identifiable population segments (for example, hospital floors 1, 2, 3, and 4, facilities A, B, and C). The size of any given subsample ideally should be proportional to the size of this group within the total patient population. Within these defined population segments, random pools are then drawn for survey administration. Systematic bias now is countered at many levels rather than only one, thereby ensuring a more representative aggregate sample of patients.

Pseudonormative Samples

Some health care facilities look to external frames of reference to compare how well they are performing. Many times, however, the standard against which they are being measured is of questionable value. Research vendors often claim to have "normative data" to make such comparisons; however, the buyer should beware. A true normative database requires that all health facilities have an equal and random chance of being included in the sample of facilities. Of those selected, their patients must be randomly selected or a census surveyed, using a standardized instrument administered uniformly across all facilities. Alternatively, a random sample of patients from the consumer population at large also could approximate a "normative" frame of reference. In reality, what many research vendors actually offer for comparison are data from a convenience sample, namely an aggregate of their own clients' patient satisfaction data. It is vital that providers know to what other sample their facility is being compared.

Pitfalls in Survey Response and Processing

During the response and processing stages of a research effort, many pitfalls can be encountered. These problems include low response rates, data entry errors, and incorrect statistical analysis.

Poor Response Rates

To many health care providers, the satisfaction questionnaire is not only a measurement tool to gauge patient satisfaction but also a public relations vehicle. These providers mail every patient a satisfaction survey as a way of saying "we care." Not surprisingly, return rates are often abysmally low, typically in the range of 8 to 15 percent. Because so many questionnaires are sent, a reasonable sample size is achieved, creating an illusion of having a representative sample. Recall that sample size and representativeness are not one and the same. Poor response rates reflect a self-selection process that usually generates highly biased results. This pitfall can be avoided by encouraging survey participation prior to discharge, utilizing a personalized letter of transmittal, structuring the questionnaire to ensure that it is user friendly, and adhering to effective follow-up procedures.

Poor Processing of Data

A researcher can exert considerable effort to construct a top-notch questionnaire, design and implement a sound sampling plan, obtain an 80 percent response rate, and still produce unreliable data through shoddy processing of responses. Prior to data entry, each questionnaire must be edited, and open-ended responses must be carefully coded.

Although surveys should be designed first and foremost to make response as easy as possible for the patient, the layout should also take into account ease of data entry. Questionnaires should include data location indicators that specify the computer fields where responses are to be recorded (for example, "The response to question 6 belongs in column fields 10 through 12"). If data entry is done in-house without appropriate software, the researcher is inviting data entry errors. Quality data entry software is designed to mirror the questionnaire. Each question is provided a range of responses so that entries outside the range will not be accepted. Quality data entry software also provides for data being entered twice, typically by two different persons, so that entries can be compared for discrepancies. More recently, scanning technology has become available, which, when properly used, further reduces data entry errors. If in-house resources are unavailable for data entry, the alternative is to send questionnaires to an outside contractor who has the software to do the job correctly.

Poor Analysis of Data

Is "eyeballing" the data good enough? The answer is a resounding no! Even when all patients are sent a satisfaction questionnaire, only a portion will respond, in effect creating a sample. When the sample mean is taken at face value, this assumes that if all patients had responded to a certain question, the population mean would be identical to the sample mean. In terms of statistical analysis, such an assumption is on thin ice. Statistics allows researchers to make an educated guess concerning how accurately a sample mean or a given percentage represents the population mean. Statistics also allows researchers to determine the amount of sampling error within a given body of data. Larger samples yield narrower confidence intervals because they contain less sampling error.

Even researchers convinced that sample data should always be statistically analyzed still make mistakes. At times, they may use a parametric test without meeting the assumptions of a particular test, or they may inadvertently use the wrong parametric test. (Chapter 14 explores these issues in greater detail.)

Inappropriate Comparisons

Health care managers often are keenly interested in knowing how their facility's scores compare with other facilities' scores. Although some managers have the sophistication to ask how they compare with other hospitals of similar size, in similar markets, or with a similar case mix, the fact remains that very few comparisons of satisfaction scores across facilities actually make sense. Providers should remember that within every given category of service (such as hospital, emergency department, and ambulatory services), every provider is different—so are patients' demographic characteristics, acuity levels, expectations, and service experiences.

In our view, health care managers truly need to know what uniquely motivates their own patients and how to improve their own scores on the salient dimensions. If any comparisons between facilities are to be made, the comparisons should be motivated only by the need for "best practices" as an external frame of reference. By looking to the stellar providers of comparable services in similar community environments, a fair and known comparison is being made. Such a comparison offers a quality benchmark against which quality improvement efforts can be measured.

Summary

Most hospitals have some sort of patient survey system in place for assessing patient satisfaction. Most systems, however, have at least some shortcomings. The researcher who is aware of the pitfalls that can occur during the research process is in the best position to prevent or remedy them. Because patient satisfaction feedback systems are not static entities, they should be constantly adapting to better meet the information needs of providers and management so that services can be continuously improved.

CHAPTER FIVE

Research Design

This chapter provides an overview of the five steps in designing satisfaction research:

1. Identifying decision makers
2. Determining research objectives
3. Defining patient satisfaction
4. Selecting the methodology
5. Developing the research plan

Note that the first step in the planning stages of any research project is to identify and meet with key decision makers to determine what information they need. Once the information needs have been identified, the research objectives can be formulated, the methodology can be devised, and all of these elements can be documented in the research plan.

Identifying Decision Makers

Typically, key decision makers in a health care organization are senior managers, board members, physicians, and health care purchasers. Before collecting data, the researcher should meet with key players to answer these questions:

- What information is needed?
- What are the purposes of gathering the information?
- When is the information needed?

Unfortunately, some administrators prefer to absent themselves from the planning process, delegating patient satisfaction studies to junior staff, such as a planning associate, an office manager, or a practice administrator. The researcher should inform those involved that, at the very least, it is essential to secure decision makers' approval for the research and the use of the findings to influence management decisions. The researcher may also point out that waiting to involve key decision makers until study results are presented can be disastrous: If vital issues are overlooked, time and money will have been wasted.

Determining Research Objectives

Every study should be guided by explicitly stated objectives. During planning meetings with decision makers, the researcher should conduct a thorough analysis of objectives to help ensure that the proposed study fulfills the purposes that management intends.

It is not uncommon for management to initiate a research project with questions as vague as "How satisfied are our patients?" "How good a job are we doing?" "Is our guest relations program working?" Before attempting to answer such questions, the researcher should establish *which* patients, departments, or services management wishes to study and *why* management wants to study them. The researcher might ask, "What service-related decisions are pending, and what information will help management make those decisions?" In obtaining answers to these questions, it is likely that numerous issues will surface. For example, some administrators erroneously assume that one study can answer all management's questions. But because most health care organizations consist of an array of departments and services, several studies may be needed. Part of the researcher's job is to educate management about the need for specific research questions related to specific patient populations and services. When the researcher and decision makers work together, then well-defined research objectives can be formulated and used to guide the study.

Defining Patient Satisfaction

As a corollary to determining the objectives of the study, the researcher must also establish what management means by patient satisfaction. Some managers equate satisfaction with few patient complaints, believing that as the number of complaints decreases, satisfaction increases. Other managers believe that satisfaction is generated by meeting or exceeding patients' expectations, while still others may not be able to articulate what they mean by patient satisfaction. It also is common for managers to have multiple definitions of patient satisfaction and a variety of reasons for wanting to conduct a satisfaction study. Sometimes, underlying assumptions can be ascertained by asking what prompted management to conclude that a study was needed. The complexity of motives that may be uncovered is illustrated in the following case study, which is based on the authors' experiences.

Case Study: The Ambulatory Surgery Center

The first meeting with the center administrator and head nurse revealed that nursing staff were concerned with the waiting and reception areas because numerous complaints had been received from patients' families. Nurses also were concerned about crowding—and consequent noise—in the recovery room, conditions that were disturbing, particularly for patients recovering from general anesthesia. When nursing requested that these areas be renovated and expanded, the administrator requested "hard data" to support contentions that patients were indeed dissatisfied with the facility and that repeat business was being affected. Whereas nursing had conceptualized the satisfaction study as documenting patient complaints, the administration was interested in answering a cost–benefit question.

An additional concern was that a competitor hospital had recently announced its plan to build a freestanding ambulatory surgery center. The announcement prompted the administrator to ask whether patients preferred freestanding centers to hospital-based facilities. If so, he reasoned, then instead of pouring money into renovating the existing facility, an alternative facility should be constructed. In this case, the administrator was concerned with meeting patients' expectations.

After considerable discussion, a consensus was reached that the satisfaction study should address patient complaints and patient service expectations. In addition, it was agreed that the study should also address whether service expectations were being met and whether expectations would be better met at a freestanding facility.

The case study illustrates several key points—the complexity of identifying the key decision makers and what they mean by patient satisfaction, the need to pinpoint what decisions hinge on the research, and the importance of establishing what information will assist with those decisions. Once these questions are answered, the researcher can formulate the research objectives and begin designing the study.

As a side point, the researcher should bear in mind the importance of building rapport with staff. Health care professionals take considerable pride in their work, and if approached in a manner that implies "I'm here to find out what you're doing wrong," they may become guarded and defensive. On the other hand, they generally welcome assistance in obtaining patient feedback that will allow them to improve services and make effective management decisions. In short, if staff perceive the researcher as an ally, they will be more likely to share what they see as the strengths and weaknesses of their services—information that provides a sound foundation for a research project.

Selecting the Methodology

Once the research objectives have been formulated, attention can be turned to selecting the methodology best suited to a particular area of interest. At its most fundamental level, patient satisfaction research, like all social science research, can be divided into two general categories: qualitative and quantitative. Although neither method can be said to offer all the *right* answers to all questions, each body of tools offers specific strengths and weaknesses and is suited to answering specific types of questions. Selecting the right method or deciding whether to use a combination of the methods requires careful consideration of the research objectives.

Qualitative Methods

Recall from chapter 4 that *qualitative research* describes both the service received and the patient's experience of it. To obtain this information, the researcher must enter the patient's world and experience the service from the patient's perspective. To gain this viewpoint, the researcher immerses himself or herself in the service as if he or she were a patient. Further understanding can be gained by conducting informal and in-depth patient interviews as well as focus group discussions. To gain clinical staff's perspective of the patient experience, staff members, too, may be interviewed.

Quite often, qualitative research is the first stage in a research project because it affords an opportunity to explore the patient's world. However, qualitative research may also be conducted after quantitative research to give meaning to the numbers.

Appropriate Uses for Qualitative Methods

Qualitative methods are recommended in the following circumstances:

- Management's concerns and questions about a service are not well-defined.
- Management is primarily interested in obtaining information that will be helpful in understanding how to improve the service.
- The researcher does not fully understand the service, the characteristics of the patients, or patients' problems, language, expectations, and needs.
- It is unclear how to interpret quantitative patient satisfaction data.

(Chapter 7 provides more detailed information about qualitative research.)

Quantitative Methods

Quantitative research measures patient satisfaction by counting or by using scaled responses. For example, counts might be made of the number of patients who complained, the number who indicated that they were satisfied with the nursing or physician care, or the number who were willing to recommend the hospital or service to a friend. By asking respondents to score service attributes on an evaluative continuum (scale), a researcher can conduct a more sophisticated form of measurement, such as the following:

Rate the overall quality of care you received at the XYZ Baby Clinic. Was it:

1. Poor
2. Fair
3. Good
4. Very good
5. Excellent

Another continuum might range from "very dissatisfied" to "very satisfied," "not caring" to "very caring," or "incompetent" to "very competent." Scale anchor points are given numerical values (for example, excellent = 5), which become the respondent's score on an item. Better ratings typically are assigned higher numerical scores and poorer evaluations lower numerical scores.

An even more sophisticated form of measurement involves the creation of multi-item scales, on which individual item scores are combined to generate an aggregate, or summated, score.

Recall from chapter 4 that the response codes or scales the researcher chooses to use are as important as the phrasing of the questions. By convention, there are four general categories of scaling: nominal, ordinal, interval, and ratio. Each has its unique characteristics, and each offers unique opportunities for analysis once data have been collected.

Nominal Scales

As the name implies, nominal scales use "naming" conventions to assign responses to distinct categories based on characteristics of the respondent or the service rendered. One of the most obvious nominal scales assigns individuals to gender categories—male versus female. In health care delivery, another nominal scale is the assignment of a service unit or service experience—Unit 2-South versus Unit 2-North, or inpatient versus outpatient.

Nominal scales are used to classify patients or customers. They do not imply a better or worse score or any evaluative judgment.

Ordinal Scales

Whereas nominal scales allow the researcher to show that the responses of two patients may differ by service unit or a similar nonevaluative category, ordinal scales allow the researcher to go one step further by distinguishing a direction based on scores, that is, by showing that one score is clearly *higher* or *lower* than another. One common ordinal scale uses this continuum: excellent, very good, good, fair, and poor.

By introducing an evaluative component that can gauge relative performance, this kind of scale affords the analyst a new way to look at data. Some analysts also use ordinal scales to compute means or to conduct multivariate analysis, but these applications may overreach what such scores actually allow. By assigning numerical values to the categorical response of an ordinal scale (for example, excellent = 5, very good = 4, good = 3, fair = 2, poor = 1), measures of central tendency like the mean can be computed, and other sophisticated analyses can be performed. The assumption here is that an "excellent" score is the same distance from "very good" that "very good" is from "good," that "good" is from "fair," and that "fair" is from "poor." Many researchers make this assumption, but it is *only* an assumption about the scale. Nothing inherent in the scale states this numerical correspondence. Interval scales, on the other hand, *do* have these "numerical attributes."

Interval Scales

Technically, an ordinal scale can state only that a given score is higher, lower, or equal to another score. An interval scale allows the researcher to state explicitly how many measurable units separate two responses. Moreover, interval scaling means that all points on the scale are separated by *equal intervals*. The only point that does not appear in an interval scales is an absolute zero ("0").

One of the more common interval scales is the 5-point Likert scale. Developed more than 60 years ago by Rensis Likert (1932), this scale traditionally has used a semantic continuum ranging from "strongly agree" to "agree" to "neutral" to "disagree" to "strongly disagree." This same format has been extended to other semantic scales, such as "satisfaction" (that is, "very satisfied" to "very dissatisfied"), "quality" (that is, "very low quality" to "very high quality"), and others. Although in the strictest sense, the intervals between levels (for example, the interval between "strongly agree" and "agree" versus the interval between "agree" and "neutral") are not exactly equal, they nevertheless are comparable. As a result, many authors label them "equal-appearing intervals."

A principal advantage of interval scales is their ready translation into numerical values from semantic labels. If "strongly disagree" on a 5-point scale = 1, then "disagree" = 2, "neutral" = 3, and so on. With interval scales, measures of central tendency can be calculated without fear of "overreaching assumptions," as can be the case with ordinal scales. By extension, multivariate analyses also can be performed, although as with any scales, one must examine the distribution of scores on the scale. Ideal scales are those that offer something approaching a "normal" distribution of scores about a mean; that is, the scores array themselves so that approximately half are above the mean and half are below the mean.

Ratio Scales

Ratio scales introduce a meaningful zero-point, where zero represents a real *absence* of a characteristic. Although zeros typically are not meaningful in attitude scores, they can be useful in scoring other variables, such as income, age, time, and formal education. In all of these cases, the zero is real and can be assigned. (Of course, a zero *age* score would disqualify a respondent from any survey, and a zero length of residence also lacks utility.)

As its name suggests, the ratio scale allows the researcher to relate scores to one another not simply in their relative distance from one another (intervals), but in the *ratio* of one value to another. In the Likert scale, "neutral" (scored as 3) cannot be meaningfully interpreted as three times (3/1) the "strongly disagree" (scored as a 1); it is simply two intervals away. But a 40-year-old respondent clearly is twice as old as a 20-year-old respondent, and an income of $30,000 a year is twice an annual income of $15,000. For most statistical analyses, the distinction between ratio and interval scales is not crucial. Correlations, for instance, are insensitive to the difference, and so are many other more sophisticated statistics. For most satisfaction research, therefore, both interval-level and ratio-level scores are equally well suited.

Descriptive and Causal Quantitative Methods

Quantitative methods are used for both descriptive and causal purposes. Descriptive research answers questions such as these: How satisfied are patients? Are women more satisfied than men with a service? Causal relationships are illustrated in questions such as these: Why are patients dissatisfied with a service? Did the change in nursing staff improve patient satisfaction? Establishing causal relations typically requires gathering quantitative data under controlled conditions. (Chapter 13 examines the use of evaluation designs with quantitative data to establish causal relations.)

Appropriate Uses for Quantitative Methods

Quantitative methods are recommended for addressing the following types of research questions:

1. How satisfied are patients?
2. Will service changes (for example, increasing or decreasing the number of staff or improving facilities) affect patient satisfaction?
3. Are patients more or less satisfied on Unit 2-South as compared to Unit 3-North, or at Hospital A versus Hospital B?
4. Has patient satisfaction changed over the past two years?
5. With what service aspects are patients more satisfied or less satisfied?

(Chapter 8 addresses quantitative research in more detail.)

Combining Qualitative and Quantitative Methods

Patient satisfaction studies often require using a combination of qualitative and quantitative methods. Typically, the researcher begins with qualitative methods to explore the service and the aspects that appear to be creating satisfaction. Then quantitative methods are used to determine the proportion of patients who are satisfied, the intensity of their satisfaction, and the extent to which various aspects of the service are contributing to patient satisfaction. If the interpretation of quantitative data is unclear, the researcher once again may return to the service setting to collect more qualitative information that will give meaning to the quantitative results.

Although both approaches to conducting research are considerably different, a certain amount of common groundwork needs to be established, regardless of the research method used. The success of any research project depends on careful planning.

Developing the Research Plan

After the initial meeting with management and clinical directors has been conducted and research methodology has been discussed, a preliminary research plan should be created. Figure 5-1 illustrates the contents of a preliminary plan. It is useful to begin the plan with a brief statement of the background of the project, the reasons why the study was requested, and the names of the key decision makers. Next, the researcher should list the research objectives, describe the plan for conducting the research (the research design), and indicate the contents of the final product.

A study is not worth the paper on which it is written if management does not read it or believe the results are relevant and accurate. It is therefore essential for the researcher to discuss the research plan with decision makers once the document is drafted. A meeting should be called to ensure that consensus on the research objectives has been reached and to assess the feasibility and acceptability of the plan to

Figure 5-1. Preliminary Research Plan: XYZ Ambulatory Surgery Center Patient Satisfaction Study

Background Information and Decision Makers:

The nursing staff has requested that the reception and waiting area and the recovery room be renovated and expanded to better meet the needs of patients. They report that the reception and waiting area is frequently crowded and complaints have been received from patients' families. They also are concerned about the lack of space and noise in the recovery area, particularly for patients regaining consciousness from general anesthesia. In response to nursing's request, the center's administrator has requested that a study be conducted to determine patient satisfaction with the facility and whether conditions are affecting repeat business. Last, the administrator also wishes to know whether patients would prefer a freestanding ambulatory surgery center to a hospital-based one.

Research Objectives:

1. Determine whether patients are dissatisfied with the waiting and reception area and the recovery room.
2. Determine the level of patient satisfaction with care provided by nurses, physicians, and anesthesiologists.
3. Determine the level of patient satisfaction with the center's location, parking, and other amenities.
4. Determine whether a hospital-based or a freestanding ambulatory surgery center would best meet patients' service expectations.

Plan:

Before initiating a quantitative survey of patients, it is recommended that an assessment be conducted of the number of patient visits, the number and types of procedures performed over the past five years, the sociodemographic characteristics of patients served, and any changes that have been made to the facility during the past five years to accommodate volumes or patients' needs. Staff will be interviewed to determine their perceptions of the facility and patients' needs. The center will be observed by the researcher, and informal and in-depth patient interviews will be conducted. Interviews will also be conducted with a sample of the center's surgeons to obtain their perceptions of the facility and patients' needs.

Results:

A preliminary report will be presented to management based on this qualitative assessment. After review and discussion of the findings, this information will be used to guide the planning of a quantitative survey of patients.

---

achieve the objectives. The meeting will not only improve the plan, it will also encourage management to take ownership of the study and its ultimate results.

After the initial planning meeting, the researcher should revise and elaborate the plan so that it becomes a step-by-step guide to the research process. As shown in figure 5-2, the revised plan indicates what will be done, where it will be done, and when it will be done. Again, management should review and comment on the plan, and revisions should continue until consensus is reached and management signs off on the plan.

No matter how well the plan is conceived and specified, erroneous assumptions, oversights, unrealistic time frames, and other problems can arise during the implementation phase. When problems are uncovered, periodic plan modifications should be made. Although it is tempting just to "do what needs to be done" and tell management about it later, this can be a serious mistake. Management should be kept informed of any significant changes and approve them. If management does not accept the methodology, it is unlikely to give credence to the results.

Summary

It is vitally important for the researcher to have a clear understanding of what management wishes to know about a service and why. Although considerable up-front time can be consumed in establishing research objectives and a research plan, the time is well spent. If managers are to give credence to the research results, they must be included in developing and approving the research plan.

Figure 5-2. Revised Research Plan: XYZ Ambulatory Surgery Center Patient Satisfaction Study

Background Information:

The nursing staff has requested that the reception and waiting area and the recovery room be renovated and expanded to better meet the needs of patients. They report receiving frequent complaints from patients' families regarding the waiting and reception areas. Also, they are concerned about the lack of space and the noisiness of the recovery area, particularly for patients regaining consciousness from general anesthesia. In response to nursing's request, the center's administrator has requested that a patient satisfaction study be conducted to address these issues and overall satisfaction with services and to determine whether repeat business is being affected. Last, the administrator also wants to know whether patients' expectations regarding the service and facility would be better met in a freestanding ambulatory surgery center as opposed to the existing facility.

Research Objectives:

1. Determine patient satisfaction with the existing facility, including the waiting and reception areas, the recovery room, and other areas to which patients are exposed while receiving services.
2. Determine patient satisfaction with care provided by nurses, surgeons, and anesthesiologists.
3. Determine patient satisfaction with the center's location, parking, and other amenities.
4. Determine whether a hospital-based or a freestanding ambulatory surgery center will best meet patients' service and facility expectations.

Phase I Plan:

The study will be conducted in two phases. Activities to be conducted in phase I include:

1. Examining service census reports (for the past five years) to assess trends in the:
   a. number of patient visits
   b. number and types of procedures performed
   c. sociodemographic characteristics of patients
   d. patient origin by zip code
   Completion date—February 15.

2. Determining staff perceptions and assessments of:
   a. services provided
   b. changes in the number and types of patients served and procedures performed over the past five years
   c. facility changes that have occurred
   d. the activities staff members perform on behalf of patients as they are processed through the service
   e. patients' expectations, complaints, and satisfaction
   f. staff's recommendations for service and facility improvements that they believe would improve patient care and satisfaction

   Staff interviews will be conducted by the research consultants of the following personnel:
   a. the center administrator
   b. the director of nursing and all nurse supervisors
   c. a sample of staff nurses
   d. a sample of surgeons
   e. a sample of anesthesiologists
   f. one of the receptionists
   Completion date—March 10.

3. Observing the service and conducting informal patient interviews to:
   a. record the sequence of activities that patients experience while receiving the service
   b. determine the adequacy of the existing facility to meet patients' needs and expectations
   c. assess the quality of patient-staff interaction
   d. determine how well services are meeting patients' expectations
   Completion date—March 15.

4. Conducting in-depth patient interviews to assess:
   a. the adequacy of the existing facility to meet patients' needs and expectations
   b. the quality of patient-staff interaction
   c. how well services are meeting patients' expectations
   d. whether an alternative freestanding surgery center would better meet patients' expectations

   Interviews will be conducted with a representative sample of 20 patients within one week of discharge. Research consultants will conduct interviews at the patients' homes or, if patients prefer, at an off-site location.
   Completion date—April 15.

Figure 5-2. (Continued)

> 5. Data will be analyzed and summarized in a draft report to be delivered to management by May 5.
>
> 6. Consultants will review and discuss phase I study findings with the management team. Recommendations for the design of phase II will be presented at this time.
> Completion date—May 15.
>
> *Phase II Plan:*
>
> 1. Design and deliver a research plan for phase II.
> Completion date—May 23.

Tools available to the researcher for answering management questions include both qualitative and quantitative methods. Qualitative methods are particularly suited to describing the service and the patient's experience of it. In-depth information about patients' perceptions, reactions, and evaluation of the service is obtained from these methods. Quantitative methods are best suited to answering questions about the degree of satisfaction with various service attributes and in assessing change in satisfaction as services are modified. Most studies require that both methods be used.

CHAPTER SIX

Sampling

As stated in chapter 4, successful patient satisfaction research involves asking the right questions of the right people. This chapter explains how to find the "right people"—in short, how to collect a representative response base.

Ideally, every customer should be given an opportunity to offer feedback on service received. But research is not conducted in an ideal world. Limited budgets and time frames constrain the kind and amount of information that can be collected. Moreover, even the most effective survey methods fall short of a 100 percent response rate. Sampling, when properly executed, does not sacrifice the quality of information about patients' perceptions of service. However, it is essential that the sample surveyed be *representative* of the total population from which it is drawn. When satisfaction surveys are used as decision-making guides for management or as a basis for calculating rewards or bonuses, samples must be drawn using the most exacting methods. These methods ensure a scientific and defensible representation of the patient population of a facility. The basic guidelines in this chapter will help researchers ensure that they select samples that are scientifically representative as well as large enough for meaningful analysis.

History of Survey Sampling

Historians have documented instances of sampling methodologies as early as the 18th century, but these cases are few and far between. Although scientific sampling became widespread after 1920, the applications were primarily in agricultural research. Faced with the inevitable variabilities across observations, the natural sciences very early developed methods to "average out" any potential sources of bias associated with where, when, or how population samples were collected (Goode and Hatt, 1952, pp. 209-14; Parten, 1950, p. 106; Stephan, 1948).

In his forecasting of the electoral results of 1936, the late George Gallup, Sr., was one of the first and most widely known individuals to refine the science of sampling (Simon, 1969, pp. 109-17). His correct forecast of the 1936 presidential contest, which contradicted the call of *Literary Digest*, the leading source of the day, carved out a significant role for Gallup personally and opinion polling generally. In the contest between Franklin D. Roosevelt and Alf Landon, the *Digest* launched a mammoth straw poll of adult Americans, mailing out questionnaires to more than 10 million voters whose names were drawn from telephone directories and automobile registrations. By October 31, with 1,293,669 returned ballots for Landon and 972,897 for Roosevelt, the *Digest* felt confident enough to call Landon the winner. As everyone now knows, the poll was wrong. A short time later, the *Digest* went out of business owing, in part, to the negative public reaction to its poll.

What went wrong? The poll was based on a large sample, with more than one in every 20 voters in America responding, and it had a response rate of nearly 23 percent among those contacted. Despite its impressive size, the poll was doomed to fail because it was biased. Although it tapped a very large base of voters, the results were collected over several months. The aggregated base therefore masked shifts in opinion as the election date neared. In addition to biases introduced by timing, the sample itself was biased. The 1936 election brought increasing numbers of voters from lower socioeconomic strata to the polling booth. *Literary Digest,* with a sample drawn from telephone and automobile owners, entirely missed the "swing vote" of lower-class Americans. At the time, the majority of Americans did not have telephone service, and approximately 45 percent of families did not own an automobile. Gallup, whose sample size was less than one-tenth of 1 percent the size of the *Literary Digest* returns, demonstrated that size alone does not guarantee accuracy and generalizability of results. Rather, scrupulous attention to sample replications of key population parameters significantly ensured the Gallup sample's ultimate representativeness.

Not until 1940 did the U.S. Bureau of the Census apply sampling methods to the decennial census as a supplement to the larger canvass of the American population. Presently, the U.S. census extends significantly beyond a mere counting of residents, and sampling is the basis for many of the more detailed surveys of population, labor force, and other characteristics.

Randomness

Virtually every sample drawn from a population, or *universe,* as it is called by statisticians, relies at least in part on the element of randomness. This is not to say that samples are drawn in a purely accidental manner. *Randomness* means that every individual within a universe has an equal probability of being drawn, thereby eliminating any systematic tendencies to draw one kind of individual over another. Samples using randomness introduce as unbiased a method as is practical, affording the researcher a predictable and quantifiable chance to represent the universe of past customers. In this role, randomness is the great safeguard of representativeness.

Sampling Error

The predictability of the chance to draw a representative sample is expressed by sampling theory. This theory tells the researcher what level of confidence he or she can have in the results of a sample as compared to what the results of a survey of everyone in the population would show. Sampling theory further states that every sample of a known size randomly drawn from a population of a known size will offer a statistically quantifiable level of precision or confidence. Conversely, every sample has a known level of variation, or *sampling error,* associated with it. Sampling error is the potential amount by which any given response in a sample can vary from the "true" response the population would show if one were able to survey all members of the population. We are forced to live with at least some level of quantifiable sampling error because it is rarely possible to survey all members of a population.

For instance, if 50 percent of recent patients reportedly were "very satisfied" with the overall service received from an organization, then we would know that this 50 percent only estimates what a survey of everyone in the population would offer. However, if we knew how large the sample was, we could identify within a specified range what the "very satisfied" rate would be in the population a predictable percentage of the time.

The traditional confidence level at which researchers work is commonly referred to as the "95 percent level." When this level is used, we are saying that in 95 out of 100 samples drawn from the same population, our percentage response in the sample will vary by no more than plus or minus so many points — the *confidence interval* — from the true population value we are trying to estimate.

If we assume a large population relative to the sample, then the confidence interval is calculated by a straightforward formula. The formula for the 95 percent confidence interval is as follows:

$$\text{Confidence interval} = 1.96 \frac{p(1-p)}{N}$$

In this formula, p is the percentage of responses associated with our sample, 1.96 is the number of standard deviations on either side of our percentage that will encompass 95 percent of the normal distribution of expected responses, and N is the size of the sample. *Standard deviation* is a statistical term that refers to the dispersion about the mean in a distribution.

As an example, assume that we have a sample of 100 recently treated patients in our survey base. Our results have shown that 50 percent of them reportedly are "very satisfied" with the overall service experience. The confidence interval formula allows us to determine how well this sample represents the larger population of patients from which it is drawn. Inserting the values N equals 100 and p equals .50 (that is, 50 percent translated into a fraction), we can say that the experience of all patients suggests that 50 percent plus or minus 9.8 percent are "very satisfied" with the service at the 95 percent level of significance. Put another way, we can say that if we were to draw 100 samples of 100 patients, 95 of the 100 samples would show "very satisfied" scores within plus or minus 9.8 percent of the 50 percent.

As the percentage for which we are calculating the confidence interval becomes larger or smaller than 50 percent, the confidence interval begins to narrow. For instance, if p equals either 10 percent or 90 percent with our sample of 100, the confidence interval will be plus or minus 5.9 percent. This equivalence is a simple outgrowth of the mathematics, where $.10(1 - .10) = .90(1 - .90)$. The confidence interval also narrows as the size of the sample increases. For instance, the confidence interval for a sample of 400 patients, 50 percent of whom report a "very satisfactory experience," would be plus or minus 4.9 percent.

Although there is no ideal sample size per se, there are confidence intervals with which we will have greater or lesser comfort. How large a sample is large enough? If we increase our sample by a factor of four, we will have reduced our confidence interval by a factor of one-half. Using 50 percent as our response estimated from the sample, if we move from a sample of 100 to a sample of 400, we have reduced our confidence interval from plus or minus 9.8 percent to only plus or minus 4.9 percent. This a very reasonable trade-off between sample size and increased precision. If we increase our sample by another factor of four, the improved precision is calculated according to the same formula. Moving from 400 to 1,600 respondents, our confidence interval drops from plus or minus 4.9 percent to plus or minus 2.45 percent. In the first example, we increased our sample by only 300 interviews; in the second, an additional 1,200 interviews were needed to get the same proportional improvement. This latter effort might have been a costly exercise in improving survey precision.

In the experience of the authors, hospital patient satisfaction surveys range between 100 and 1,000 completed surveys. When sample sizes exceed the high end of this range, it typically is because the sample required substantial segmentation. For instance, while 400 interviews might be sufficient to offer insights into the overall patient experience at a hospital, to offer statements with reasonable precision for each of 20 units within this same facility, a substantially larger sample would be needed. For purposes of comparison, table 6-1 offers complete calculations of confidence intervals associated with 10 to 90 percent response distributions and with sample sizes of 100 to 1,000. The confidence interval formula may be used to calculate confidence intervals for alternative sample sizes or response percentages.

Correction Factor

Confidence intervals, largely a function of sample size and the percentage estimate in question, can also be affected by another significant factor: the size of the sample relative to the population from which it is drawn. When a sample is drawn from a very large number of patients, the confidence intervals are calculated by using the confidence interval formula. But when the sample comes to represent a larger proportion of the total population size, a correction factor must be introduced.

For all intents and purposes, unless the sample is larger than about one-tenth the size of the population from which it is drawn, the correction factor does not appreciably affect estimates of confidence intervals. The correction becomes increasingly relevant, however, as the sample exceeds one-tenth of the population, as the following formula shows:

$$\text{Correction factor} = 1 - (N \div M)$$

In this formula, N equals the size of the sample and M equals the size of the population. If the survey sample includes 100 patients and the population of discharged patients is 1,000, the formula tells us that the correction we would apply to the confidence intervals would be approximately 0.949. In other words, if our confidence interval at the 50 percent mark ordinarily is plus or minus 9.8 percent, then the correction factor reduces this interval to 0.949 of its original value, or plus or minus 9.3 percent—still not an overwhelming reduction in the confidence interval.

However, if a sample of 100 is drawn from a population of only 200, the correction factor changes dramatically. Using the same 50 percent response from the sample, the new confidence interval would be corrected by a factor of 0.707 to a range of plus or minus 6.9 percent. In short, confidence in even small samples is greatly enhanced if the populations those samples represent are also relatively small. Taken to its logical conclusion, if the sample size is equal to the population size, the correction factor

Table 6-1. Confidence Intervals for Market Samples of Various Sizes

Sample Size	Approximate Response Rate								
	10%	20%	30%	40%	50%	60%	70%	80%	90%
100	±5.9	±7.8	±9.0	±9.6	±9.8	±9.6	±9.0	±7.8	±5.9
200	±4.2	±5.5	±6.4	±6.8	±6.9	±6.8	±6.4	±5.5	±4.2
300	±3.4	±4.5	±5.2	±5.5	±5.7	±5.5	±5.2	±4.5	±3.4
400	±2.9	±3.9	±4.5	±4.8	±4.9	±4.8	±4.5	±3.9	±2.9
500	±2.6	±3.5	±4.0	±4.3	±4.4	±4.3	±4.0	±3.5	±2.6
600	±2.4	±3.2	±3.7	±3.9	±4.0	±3.9	±3.7	±3.2	±2.4
700	±2.2	±3.0	±3.4	±3.6	±3.7	±3.6	±3.4	±3.0	±2.2
800	±2.0	±2.8	±3.2	±3.4	±3.5	±3.4	±3.2	±2.8	±2.0
900	±2.0	±2.6	±3.0	±3.2	±3.3	±3.2	±3.0	±2.6	±2.0
1,000	±1.9	±2.5	±2.8	±3.0	±3.1	±3.0	±2.8	±2.5	±1.9

becomes 0.0, and multiplying this correction by any confidence interval will, in turn, produce zero. The real question facing the patient satisfaction researcher at any point, however, is how representative the sample is, a topic explored later in this chapter.

Goals and Sample Size

One final point should be made regarding the selection of a sample size for patient satisfaction surveys. In discussing research design in chapter 5, we suggested strongly that one should have a clear idea of the use of satisfaction data before initiating the survey effort. In the case of sample design, this issue becomes very important. For instance, to compare satisfaction scores across several hospital units, the researcher would need a total sample large enough to allow each individual unit to be examined with statistical confidence. A sample of 100 patients may offer a reasonable base in and of itself, but if we attempt to divide or segment this sample into the five or six acute care units it represents, we would have sufficient data for meaningful analysis.

Similarly, if the goal of a project were to break out specific payer groups for subsequent analysis, it would be very important to identify how large a total sample would be needed for this effort. For instance, in cases where the researcher knows in advance that only a small percentage of discharged patients are in a desirable payer class, it may be advisable to oversample these individuals. When we overrepresent or underrepresent any given group in our sampling plan, however, it is important to account for these differentials as data are aggregated for total patient sample analysis. This accounting will safeguard against attaching too little or too much weight to any group.

As a final note on "how much sample is enough," we remind readers that response rates affect final sample size. If we have a targeted final sample as our goal, it is important to test a method to identify how much effort will be needed to produce the given sample. After testing a method, we would look at the number of surveys mailed out, the number of past patients called, and so on. This simple preliminary step helps eliminate unnecessary delays or costs later in the survey process.

Representativeness

Because it is impractical in most cases to survey, much less analyze, the total population of past patients, it is critical that we have in place a mechanism for surveying a representative sample. Sampling theory assumes that we will never have a *perfectly* representative sample of a population (hence the notion of sampling error or confidence intervals). But how do we get to the point where we have a predictable level of precision that will assure us of a usable response base?

The answer lies in our ability to negate as much as possible any elements that could systematically bias our sample. For example, if we surveyed only individuals discharged from one unit of the hospital, we could not expect them to represent the total population of discharged patients. Patients who received care in only one of the many units will have had a particularized patient care experience and likely will represent a particularized medical classification or acuity level as well.

By the same token, we would not want to implement a survey of all individuals admitted through the emergency room. Any sample of these individuals cannot hope to be a cross section of patients throughout the hospital, many of whom will have been admitted under nonemergency circumstances.

Some patient care populations are relatively homogeneous, thereby reducing the elements that can distort sample responses. The more homogeneous a patient population is, the more the researcher can rely on random sampling alone to tap patient opinion. For the most part, however, hospital patient populations are significantly heterogeneous. This heterogeneity has significant implications for patient satisfaction researchers, who must avoid *systematic bias*, that is, any influence on the final sample that specifically favors the inclusion or exclusion of specific types of respondents. Surveying only one hospital unit, for instance, systematically biases a sample by excluding patients from other units. Conducting telephone surveys only during daylight hours taps only those underrepresented in the workforce, thereby also introducing systematic bias. Not all sources of systematic bias may be so obvious, however, and so measures must be introduced to guard against unforeseen sources.

Random Sampling

To mitigate systematic bias, sampling theory first assumes randomness. As with many scientific assumptions, however, the required conditions are hard to come by in the real world. Virtually every sampling method introduces some element of nonrandomness, even when we attempt random sampling. As a consequence, most methods safeguard against systematic bias by introducing measures whose sole function is to protect us from known sources of systematic error. We protect ourselves from the ever-present *unknown* sources of error by randomness.

Case Study 6-A: Computerized Random Sampling

Suppose that a physician's office wishes to randomly sample 500 names from a list of patients who have seen the doctor within the past two months. The questions to be asked are not considered time sensitive, as might be the case with questions on how long the patient waited in the reception room or the examination room, and so a sample spanning the entire two months will be acceptable. Because the office maintains a computerized database for billing and general correspondence, the researcher can simply call up a software routine that randomly draws, without replacement, 500 unique names from the list. (Drawing an initial list of 525 names, the researcher removes duplicates to result in the final sample of 500 names.) A software routine such as this typically uses a preexisting, unique identification number for each patient and then matches its randomly generated numbers with the preexisting numbers to create a sample. Such routines also may simply generate a sequential identification number for each patient name and draw according to these numbers.

Had the researcher for the physician's office not had access to this software solution, the only real recourse for creating a true random sample would have been to assign unique identification numbers to each patient and then randomly draw patients based on the unique identification numbers. (An example of a table of random numbers is provided in appendix A of this book. Most introductory statistics books also contain tables of random numbers.) The method for drawing random numbers in this latter, labor-intensive manner is described in the next case study.

Systematic Sampling

The term *systematic sampling* is so named not because it introduces systematic bias but because it typically works from a list of names of potential respondents and draws every nth individual for contact. Simply put, this means that each name drawn for the sample is a fixed interval (where the interval width equals n) from the name prior to it on the list. Randomness is introduced in this method because the researcher selects at random a starting point on the list and also a random interval for selecting subsequent potential respondents. When the researcher has a list of recently discharged inpatients or recently treated outpatients, then a random number generator may supply a point at which to begin—for example, the 24th name on the list. Assuming that the list is long enough to sample repeatedly individuals at fixed intervals, another random number—for instance, nine—is selected to be the selection interval. This means that in addition to the 24th person, we will also draw the person who appears nine names later than this, and repeat the exercise through the entire list. Therefore, following the 24th individual, we would also select the 33rd, the 42nd, the 51st individuals, and so on, to be in our sampling frame. These individuals will be contacted to respond to the survey, and the final database will include those who have consented to answer our questions. Systematic samples often include several randomly selected starting points and associated randomly selected intervals to offer more random elements guiding the ultimate sample.

Case Study 6-B: "Manual" Random Sampling

ABC Clinic sees approximately 100 patients per day, six days per week, 50 weeks per year. The researcher has been asked to sample and assess patients' perceptions of the new scheduling system just implemented four weeks ago. It is concluded that a sample of 200 patients will afford sufficient precision for the purposes of this assessment, and it is expected that approximately 50 percent of patients who receive the survey in the mail will ultimately complete the questionnaire and return it. Moreover, those patients who have received treatment within the past two weeks are considered to have a sufficiently fresh recollection of the scheduling system to offer useful feedback.

Two weeks' worth of patients will produce a starting base of 1,200 patient visits. After purging multiple visits per patient, the researcher is left with 1,100 actual patients. Fifty percent of 1,100 patients, or 550 respondents, seems to be overkill, so it is decided to draw a systematic sample of 400 patient names and addresses for solicitation. The researcher consults a table of random numbers with six fields of two-column random numbers. If you turn to appendix A of this book, you can draw your own random numbers with the help of some very inexpensive technology: a six-sided die and a coin.

The researcher has determined that the roll of the die will give a number that is to be the column indicator for starting to find "the random number." There are six columns, so any face that may appear will identify which column to start with, "1" indicating the first column on the left and "6" indicating the last column on the right. A roll of the die shows the number "3," which dictates starting at the third column from the left. Turning to the second piece of technology, the coin, the researcher decides that heads will dictate counting from the top of the column down, and tails counting from the bottom of the column up. A toss of the coin results in heads (counting from the top down). Finally, another roll of the die calls for selecting the fifth number from the top, number 23.

Although this may not sound like the science on which physics is based, it offers a truly random assignment of numbers. The more scientifically self-conscious reader may wish to use any of a number of computer routines available with most statistical packages that will draw a random number of a desired dimension at the press of a button. However, a computerized method is no more or less scientific than the example here.

Having drawn the first number, the researcher begins with the patient who is number 23 from the top of the list. After proceeding through the same randomizing process once again, the researcher randomly gets the number 38, which now becomes the skip interval for selecting the rest of the numbers. The next patient selected will therefore be number 61 (23 + 38), followed by 99, and so on. When the researcher reaches the end of the list, it is necessary to wrap around to the top and continue once again, until the 400 starting names and associated addresses are drawn. (Some researchers will take a short cut by simply using the first random number to count down each page and not resort to another skip interval.)

Sequential Sampling

Although not as desirable as random sampling from a scientific standpoint, sequential sampling offers a very cost-effective opportunity to take a "straw poll" of recent patients. The method simply draws a convenient succession of individuals who will make up a small sample of the population. If, for example, you wish to know whether a new program in guest relations has been noticed or appreciated by patients, you might not go to the expense of a large-scale random sample. Instead, you would simply have someone interview the first 100 patients processed to see whether, in fact, they have noticed the key elements of the program and, if they have, how they perceived them.

The sequential sample is the classic "quick-and-dirty" method for getting a "feeling" for the customer's perspective, although it does not offer a sample with calculable confidence intervals. Let's say that you sample the first 100 patients and find that all of them noticed the program and that all of them endorse it to some degree. This clearly does not tell you everything you may wish to know, but it may help you decide whether to move forward with the next steps, either programmatic or research.

Stratified Sampling

Stratified sampling is a method that allows us to use what we may already know about identifiable groups within our patient population to draw a sample. The strata (and their associated quotas) can be viewed as extra insurance beyond that supplied by randomness alone. Stratified sampling will break out the original database into a number of identifiable subgroups, or strata. Within each stratum a sample is drawn of a proportion that represents the stratum's overall part of the total population.

Let's say that you wish to draw a sample of 100 recently discharged patients that reasonably represents the population of all discharged patients. You also know that there are two distinct medical units from which these patients have been discharged, and about one half of the patients have been discharged from each. The most direct sampling method might encourage simply a random sample of all discharged patients to give us a final sample of 100. But what if the sample quite accidentally drew disproportionately more from one unit than the other? The result would be a sample biased toward that unit at the expense of the other. How do you avoid this potential source of bias?

Case Study 6-C: Stratified Sampling

The researcher presented with this challenge will introduce quotas by strata, rather than one overall quota or sample size. A reasonable safeguard against systematic bias in the case of 100 patients from two medical units would include sampling 50 patients from a list of each unit's discharged patients. First, the researcher divides the starting lists into two distinct groups representing medical unit 1 and medical unit 2. Within each of these units, the researcher then proceeds to draw two independent samples just as would have been drawn with either the random or the systematic methodologies for the single, overall sample.

This way, the researcher has taken a precaution that will help ensure (even with small numbers) that he or she has not introduced at least the one known potential source of systematic bias. This method also has the advantage of giving predictable subsamples that will allow later comparisons of one unit's patients against the other's.

Cluster Sampling

Stratified sampling is a method for collecting information by using a relatively small sample to represent the population. Cluster sampling attempts to minimize the logistics of gathering data by collecting surveys from individuals in a consolidated way. This consolidation typically is geographic, with sample clusters drawn from designated locations throughout a given setting so that the final sample is the aggregation of all these clusters into the final database.

Take the example of a hospital-based researcher using an in-person data collection method and planning to survey a sample of 100 patients on the day of their discharge. The counsel of perfection would encourage us to randomly identify a target number of individuals from across the entire hospital that would afford a representative cross section of all patients. Imagine the legwork—literally—involved in collecting these surveys from across a large medical center. Cluster sampling allows the interviewer to save time and wear and tear, yet still collect a reasonable sample.

Cluster sampling encourages us to cluster our surveys geographically within the hospital. For instance, the interviewer employing this method has chosen to select only half of the hospital units for surveying every other day. Although individuals on the omitted floors on any given day will be systematically left out of the sample, this omission should not introduce any profound distortion into the final sample. At the same time, this effort probably saves the hospital money while saving the interviewer time. Recall, however, that randomness saves us from unforeseen catastrophes. If there are systematic differences between included and excluded units, the unwitting researcher may introduce substantial bias into the final sample, thereby tainting any conclusions or recommendations.

Nonrandom Sampling

Some samples used by researchers have less or even no element of randomness. One such method involves simply "taking what is convenient." Using this truly quick-and-dirty method, the research simply takes a convenient sampling of patients at hand for interviewing. These interviews may be conducted among only the patients discharged from the most convenient unit or only on one day of each quarter. Both of these examples run the significant risk of surveying a group of individuals who do not represent the total population.

The single-hospital-unit approach is in danger of tapping into a group of patients who may be unique in their service needs (such as exclusively medical patients versus exclusively surgical patients) or in their relative levels of acuity. Neither these biases nor a whole host of others offer a desirable sample on which important administrative decisions may be made, but occasionally smaller decisions or those with too little time for more rigorous research can benefit from this feedback.

This kind of sampling is less common in patient satisfaction research, but some applications of nonrandom sampling have made their way into common usage. One of these methods is the "quota sampling" employed originally by Gallup. Although this method may have served political pollsters well, it is not useful in health care settings. On the surface, quota sampling resembles stratified sampling because it identifies unique subgroups within the patient population. The relative incidence of these subgroups in the population then provides the basis for specific quotas of the same individuals for the sample. The principal difference between stratified sampling and quota sampling is in the convenience that drives a quota sample. There is little pretense of random selection within quota sampling. Stratified sampling, by contrast, randomly selects individuals for initial contact within the constraints imposed by subgroup size. Quota sampling therefore can introduce a significant bias because it does not eliminate interviewer bias in selecting the qualified respondents.

An example of the bias introduced by quota sampling can be seen in a very early study by Yates (cited in Hansen and others, 1953, p. 72) in which subjects were presented with an array of 1,200 stones on a table. They were then asked to select a "representative sample" of 20 of these stones. In the majority of cases, subjects collected a sample of 20 stones whose average weight was significantly greater than the average weight of the 1,200 stones on the table. What implications does this have for patient satisfaction surveys?

Interviewers are not objective as they approach subjects for data collection. We have already discussed how patients themselves respond to the characteristics of the interviewer as they formulate their answers to specific questions. These same respondents also formulate some answers based on the rapport they experience with the interviewer. When given the opportunity, interviewers also systematically, if subtly, select certain subjects to interview over others. For example, they may gravitate toward individuals who are of the same or a preferred gender or who are of their same or approximate age. Or they may not approach patients who have significant disabilities or who may be recovering from a severe medical episode. All of these factors discourage against nonrandom sampling methodologies.

Summary

Although some health care providers poll all former patients to create a database for management purposes, many rely on sampling a percentage of the total patient population. The final sample may be drawn using a number of alternative methods, most of which incorporate some element of randomness to help ensure representativeness. A random, nonbiased sample then will provide a basis on which management can confidently build a patient care and feedback system.

CHAPTER SEVEN

Qualitative Research

Qualitative research seeks to provide a deeper understanding of a service experience from the patient's point of view. Using an inductive approach, the researcher attempts to grasp the patient's reality without imposing his or her expectations on the service. Through direct experience (for example, observing the clinical program in operation) and indirect experience (for example, interviewing patients after the fact), the researcher develops a written description of what *is* as it might be perceived by the patient.

This chapter identifies the major types of information that researchers collect and analyze in conducting qualitative patient satisfaction studies. It discusses methods for collecting this information, such as review of existing documents and records, observations of the clinical program, interviews with staff and patients, and focus group discussions. Methods for data analysis are reviewed, along with explanations and examples of report composition. The chapter ends with a discussion of some of the qualifications a researcher should have before attempting to conduct a qualitative satisfaction study.

The qualitative research team may consist of a single individual who conceives, structures, executes, and interprets the study, or it may consist of multiple individuals who contribute expertise during different stages. In particular, in a large qualitative research study many people may assist in data collection and sorting. Thus, when the chapter refers to an interviewer or a group discussion leader or moderator, that person may be the primary researcher or someone else, who is performing that specific function during the study. No matter how many people make up the team, however, the researcher who structured the study is generally also responsible for interpreting the results and writing the final report for the client.

Review of Existing Data Sources

"Assume nothing" when investigating, fictional detective Sherlock Holmes once advised. This is good counsel for researchers as well. Before interviewing or observing patients, the researcher should try to develop a thorough understanding of the department or service and the types of patients who use it. This measure guards against biasing research with faulty assumptions.

Service information can be gleaned from program descriptions and proposals, corporate brochures, policy and procedure manuals, or any descriptive documents that provide the researcher with an overview of the clinical service and what it is supposed to be. Information about patients can be gathered from patient records, which typically include personal and demographic information, such as the patient's age, gender, educational level achieved, and location of residence; clinical information, such as the diagnosis, procedures performed, types of care, and length of stay; and possibly clinical outcome information. Service volume trends can be gathered from census reports.

Although these sources of information help the researcher acquire some knowledge about the service, they have limitations. Program descriptions tend to be dated, reflecting how management wanted the program to be perceived when the description was written rather than how patients and staff actually perceive the program in the present. Moreover, brochures may be biased, reflecting management's intentions, or "corporate vision," rather than patients' reality. Patient records, although containing information useful to the researcher, similarly are not intended to reflect the patient's perception of the experience. Census reports are useful for assessing utilization and changes in utilization over time. However, they do not tell *why* changes have occurred.

Interviews with clinical staff help fill in the missing pieces, especially those having to do with program components and processes. The goal is to identify and describe, in writing, the sequence of interactions between staff and patients, beginning as early as the initial referral and ending with program follow-up. The document should also describe the physical facilities (for example, reception area, waiting rooms, changing areas, diagnostic and treatment rooms) and procedures performed. Guided tours conducted by staff can be helpful in describing and flowcharting this information. A walk-through during off-hours can allow an uninterrupted scrutiny of the physical structure of the delivery setting, while a tour during business hours will reveal the supporting service structure.

In addition to questioning staff about how the service is delivered, the researcher should ask about any limitations staff may have observed, including those discovered through patient complaints (for example, comments about amount of time spent waiting, noise levels, and uncomfortable room temperatures). Of course, praise from patients is equally noteworthy.

Observations

Before gathering feedback from participants, it is helpful to spend time observing the service. If possible, the researcher should recapitulate the steps of a clinical program as a patient would go through the same program. This process is more difficult than it sounds. As Katzer and others point out (1982, p. 23), one problem with observation is that researchers cannot possibly see everything they are trying to observe. A second difficulty inherent in observation as a research tool is that researchers must interpret and try to draw generally valid conclusions from what they do observe, and a third problem is that they almost always interact with the system under observation, which can skew the normal functioning of that system and potentially produce bias. The instruments and training of a researcher are not always able to resolve these problems.

When a researcher approaches a health service for an initial observation, the researcher may feel overwhelmed, especially if he or she lacks a clinical background and familiarity with the service. Most hospitals are veritable mazes of departments, services, support facilities, corridors, and connecting links spread across several buildings and floors. Just finding the way to a specific department without a personal escort can be difficult. Compounding this difficulty are the unfamiliar sights, sounds, and smells that vie for the attention of the uninitiated. Until someone is familiar with the setting, it is impossible to see it all; nor is the uninitiated likely to grasp everything the first time through. A couple of short visits before initiating formal observation can help acclimate the researcher to the environment so that distractions do not become the focus of attention. It is also useful to discuss personal reactions to the setting with a colleague. Observations can easily be influenced by selective perceptions, expectations, beliefs, values, and other subjective factors. A second opinion can help minimize the influence of these factors.

Before beginning formal observation, the researcher should decide on the extent of his or her participation in the clinical program; that is, will he or she participate as a patient or as an observer of patients? In addition, the researcher must decide which aspects of the service to focus on.

Participation

As Michael Patton (1980, p. 127) notes, participation can range from "complete immersion in the program as full participant to complete separation from the program as spectator...." The more immersed the researcher, the more he or she feels and sees what it is like to be a patient. Frequently, however, the nature of a program limits the extent of involvement. For example, it obviously is easier for a researcher to participate fully in primary care and preventive health programs, such as ones aimed at weight loss or stress reduction, than in surgical programs — undergoing surgery for the sake of research is above and beyond the call of duty!

Another consideration is how participation might affect the staff and patients in the program. The more socially sensitive the patient problem, the more likely it is that patients will minimize their problems to outsiders and put on their "game face" (Ross and Mirowsky, 1983). Imagine, for example, how a researcher's presence might influence a mental health program that treats parents who have sexually abused their children. It is likely that patients would not talk about their problems in front of a researcher out of fear of disapproval or breach of confidentiality. In turn, program staff may purposely not probe or encourage discussion so as to protect patients from embarrassment. Obviously, the researcher's participation could drastically alter what he or she has come to observe, thereby distorting and invalidating the findings.

In addition, the researcher should be sensitive to the fact that some illnesses, such as disorders of the reproductive system, may be a source of embarrassment to patients, because they must physically expose themselves in the course of diagnosis and treatment. The researcher should not only respect the right to privacy but also remember that if patients or staff alter their behavior while under observation, the data become biased.

One way to reduce the effects of observation is to make the observation less obtrusive through concealment. For example, to avoid having observers present during therapy, mental health professionals have long used rooms equipped with two-way mirrors. The researcher might also consider viewing videotapes of sessions rather than the actual sessions themselves. In cases where physical privacy is a concern to patients, the researcher can simply avoid being present during certain procedures. Of course, this all assumes that the researcher has obtained informed consent from patients.

Focus Areas

The time and resource constraints of most studies require focused observation, rather than perception of the "big picture." The primary goal of patient satisfaction research is to focus on the services patients receive and their personal evaluations of those services, including the setting and the sequence of experiences.

Setting

Attention should be paid to the physical environment in which services are offered, including size, furnishings, decor, and function. Equal attention should be paid to patients' perceptions and reactions to the setting. The following excerpt of a study conducted by one of the authors describes a reception area:

> The area measures 10 × 20 feet with a corridor bisecting the space. The receptionist's desk is located adjacent to the corridor. The area is brightly lit with aging fluorescent lights that hang from a 12-foot ceiling. There are no windows in the area, and the air has a slightly stagnant odor. The walls are a faded light green in color, while the doors and trim are an off-white, showing signs of dirt and wear. In addition to the receptionist's aging wooden desk and chair, there are 12 gray metal fold-up chairs where patients sit, and a small table covered with dated magazines that reflect their age.
>
> The floor covering is a speckled gray tile, with a few tiles missing. The only sign is on the receptionist's desk, and it reads "Receptionist." As patients enter the area they gaze around looking lost. Their first question usually is: "Is this the XYZ Baby Clinic?" Frequently, the receptionist is busy scheduling appointments on the phone, and patients stand restlessly in front of the desk. Discussions between the receptionist and new arrivals are frequently interrupted by the phone. By mid-morning the room is crowded, with 20 or more patients waiting. Mothers are pacing with babies in arms; some of the babies are crying. The room temperature is hot, around 75 to 80 degrees F. Occasionally, complaints are overheard: "What's taking them so long?"

As this excerpt illustrates, qualitative reports allow the reader to sense what it is like to be a patient and to visualize and experience the ambiance of the physical setting. Effective descriptions also note instances in which the physical setting does not protect the patient's privacy or right to confidentiality.

Sequence of Experiences

Although clinical staff tend to think about health care as the provision of discrete diagnostic and treatment procedures, the researcher should be mindful that numerous activities take place between procedures. Typically, inpatients spend less than 40 percent of their time receiving medical care; the balance is spent watching television, listening to the radio, eating meals, talking on the phone, visiting with family or friends, waiting for services, asking about services, sleeping, talking with the chaplain or social worker, and so on. To fully appreciate a patient's hospitalization experience, the researcher must focus on these activities as well as on the actual care procedures, because together they form the "gestalt" of the patient's experience.

Observation should begin when the patient first makes contact with the hospital or clinic staff. Thus, if a patient is admitted to the hospital through the emergency department, observation should begin as he or she passes through the department doors. For a routine admission, observation begins at preregistration or at the patient registration desk. On a psychiatric service, observation may begin when a patient shows up to schedule an appointment or for a first visit. These first contacts with the service providers affect a patient and play an important role in shaping patients' expectations of services. After the point-of-entry observation, the researcher follows the patient through the chain of activities, up to and including discharge.

To understand the observation process, consider the sequence of a routine hospital admission. The patient experience is likely to begin at registration. Therefore, the researcher should be present in the reception area to make observations by answering questions such as these:

- Who is present? Who greets the patient?
- How long does the patient wait before being greeted?

- What do the patient and staff say? In what manner? Does the interaction appear friendly and courteous? Distant and rude?
- How long does the registration process take?
- How is the patient informed of the next steps? Who informs the patient? When and where?
- Does the patient have difficulty following staff's directions?

Next, the patient is instructed to go to the laboratory to have a blood sample drawn. During this process, the researcher might answer these questions:

- How long does it take the patient to get from the registration area to the laboratory? Was the patient given clear directions?
- How far did the patient have to walk? Was the hospital signage clear?
- Are other patients or visitors who are in the hallways asking for directions?
- Are laboratory staff available when the patient arrives? How long was the wait?
- Are staff members courteous, respectful, and helpful?

After the laboratory work is completed, the researcher might ask:

- How long is it before the patient is escorted to his or her room?
- Do the nurses greet and orient the patient upon arrival?
- Is the room ready? Is it clean?
- How much time passes before the physician sees the patient?
- How does the physician interact with the patient?

The researcher continues to observe the patient and the setting until the patient is discharged, the whole while recording brief notes for later elaboration and analysis.

Informal Interviews

Another method of collecting qualitative research information is through informal and formal patient interviews. For informal interviews, the researcher does not have a preestablished list of questions or a schedule of whom to interview, and the patient does not answer questions by choosing from among predetermined responses, such as "true/false" or "agree/disagree." Rather, questions and responses about specific aspects of service arise from insights of the moment.

To understand how informal interviewing can emerge from a situation and its clinical context, consider this hypothetical situation: Upon noticing a mother at XYZ Baby Clinic wiping sweat from her brow, the researcher might comment, "It seems kind of warm in here." "Warm?" the mother might respond. "It's hot in here! You'd think they'd at least make the room decent if they're going to make us wait all morning. You know, I treat my dog better." Notice that the researcher's casual comment provided the woman with an opportunity to share her reaction to the setting. Not only does the woman validate the researcher's perception about the temperature and environment, she also reveals her reaction to the wait and the setting as well.

At other times, the researcher may ask specific open-ended questions, such as "How do you like the way the nurses treat patients around here?" "How was your physical therapy today?" "How do you like the appearance of this room?" "How difficult was it to find the X-ray department?" The choice between conversational comments and actual questions depends on the topic, the situation, and the skills of the interviewer. With experience, the researcher is likely to become more comfortable and skillful in the use of casual questions to elicit patients' perceptions and reactions. In either case, "leading questions"—those that direct the respondent to a certain answer—should be avoided. As a general rule, questions should be free of embedded value statements (for example, "Do you find that nurse as annoying as I do?") and, instead, be neutral and open-ended (for example, "How does the bedside manner of that nurse make you feel?"). Neutral, open-ended questions allow the patient to respond in his or her own terms—an essential characteristic of qualitative measurement.

Formal, or In-Depth, Interviews

After the observation phase of the study, the researcher should have the necessary background information to develop a formal interview guide. The purpose of the guide is to help focus the interaction between the interviewer and interviewee to ensure that key topics and issues are covered. Even so, the interviewer is free to generate spontaneous questions that build on a conversation about the specified topic or issue. An abridged interview guide that has been used to assess patient satisfaction with an ambulatory surgery service is presented in figure 7-1.

As the sample in figure 7-1 suggests, considerable work goes into constructing the guide. This particular guide begins with the patient's first contact with program staff and identifies specific activities as the patient progresses through the program of care. At each benchmark, the patient is asked questions to elicit information about the experience. Notice that activities are presented in chronological order to help the patient recall each experience more fully. For services that cannot be easily divided into serial, component parts, the interviewer may ask the patient to indicate the unique chronology of activities experienced.

To make the most of interviews and help ensure that they run smoothly, the interviewer must spend considerable time becoming familiar with the guide. Prior to patient contact, interviews should be role-played, and after each completed interview, the interviewer should compare the information obtained with that requested in the guide.

Sample Selection

How does the researcher decide how many patients (and which) to interview? Often, the nature of the service and the diversity of the patient base shape the sample selection. For example, picture a high-volume emergency department that treats a variety of patients—old and young, rich and poor, male and female—who may be suffering from something as minor as a sprained ankle to something as major as a heart attack. Patients may include rape victims, burn victims, and accident victims. Because the emergency department provides multiple services to several different populations, the interviewer may need to speak with as many as 40 to 50 patients to understand how well each service is meeting the needs and expectations of these different populations. Contrast this patient group with attendees at a prenatal clinic in an affluent middle-class suburb. Because the latter patient group is likely to be relatively homogeneous, the range of patient experiences may be captured by interviewing only 15 to 20 patients.

Unlike the situation in quantitative research, there are no formulas in qualitative research by which to calculate the "correct" number of interviews. The number and types of patients included in a sample depend on the depth and breadth of a project. Ultimately, the qualitative researcher wants to interview a sufficient number of patients to understand how each major segment of the patient population experiences the care received.

Although the researcher usually works with providers in recruiting a sample of patients to interview, the researcher still should exert control over the process by developing a sample selection protocol. This document specifies the sample attributes (for example, age, gender, race, diagnosis, procedure performed) according to the purpose of the study. Suppose, for example, that an outpatient rehabilitation center

Figure 7-1. Interview Guide

ABC Surgery Center

1. Determine the patient's reasons for having surgery performed at ABC instead of another facility.

2. What role did the patient's surgeon play in influencing the patient's decision to use ABC? Did anyone else influence the patient's choice? If so, in what way?

3. How convenient was the center's scheduling of the surgery for the patient?

4. Patients are to be called the day before surgery by a center nurse to confirm the appointment, provide preoperative instructions, and answer patient questions.
    a. Did this occur?
    b. How well prepared did the patient feel for the surgery?
    c. How helpful was the nurse's call?

5. Determine what difficulties the patient may have had in locating the center, parking at the center, and finding and getting to the reception desk.

6. Upon arrival at the reception desk, how long did the patient wait before being registered?

7. How was the patient treated by the receptionist?

8. How long did the patient have to wait before being called back for surgery?

9. What were the patient's impressions of the waiting area? Prompt about its cleanliness, noise, comfort, crowding, temperature, and decor.

10. When called back for surgery, what were the patient's impressions of the changing/instructional area? Prompt about its cleanliness, noise, comfort, crowding, temperature, and decor.

11. Next, the patient will have blood drawn, a detailed medical history taken, the surgical procedure explained, and questions answered by a nurse. What was the patient's evaluation and reaction to the nurse and the care provided? Prompt about courteousness, helpfulness, competence, availability, quality of care, privacy, and concern.

12. Next, the anesthesiologist meets with the patient and performs a physical examination. What was the patient's evaluation and reaction to the anesthesiologist and the examination? Prompt about courteousness, helpfulness, competence, availability, quality of care, privacy, and concern.

13. Next, the patient is taken to the holding area. The surgeon will briefly meet with the patient, answer any questions, explain the procedure to be performed and possible complications, and complete the consent form. When done, the patient remains in this area until taken to the operating room.
    a. What is the patient's evaluation and reaction to the surgeon? Prompt about courteousness, helpfulness, competence, availability, quality of care, privacy, and concern.
    b. What were the patient's reactions to the holding area? Prompt about its cleanliness, noise comfort, crowding, temperature, and decor.

14. Next, the patient is taken into the operating room and surgery is performed. If a general anesthesia is used, the patient will have minimal recollection of the operating suite or staff. If local anesthesia is used, then ask questions about staff and care provided. Prompt about courteousness, helpfulness, competence, availability, quality of care, privacy, and concern.

15. The patient is taken to the recovery area where a nurse monitors the patient's condition. Prompt about its cleanliness, noise, comfort, crowding, temperature, and decor.
    a. What were the patient's impressions of the recovery area?
    b. What were the patient's impressions of the nursing care?

16. During recovery, the nurse also talks with the patient's family, informing them of the patient's status, home care instructions, and so on. Did this occur? What were the patient's and family's reactions?

discovers through a mail survey that in comparison to other patients, older women offer lower scores on service satisfaction. Because management would like to know more about this dissatisfied market segment, the researcher develops the following sample selection protocol:

> The sampling frame will be derived from the patient registration database. Names will be selected if they meet the following criteria: female, 50 years of age or older, received services in the last three months, and resides within ten miles of the facility. Once the list is compiled, a random sample of 50 names will be drawn. It is assumed that only half of the original sample will agree to be interviewed, thereby generating a final sample of 25 individuals.

Note that the example uses random selection. Although this is desirable, it is not essential, because the goal of qualitative research is to provide insights into patients' perceptions and preferences, not to approximate population parameters through the use of statistics.

Interview Timing and Length

In contrast to informal interviews, which are conducted while the patient is still hospitalized or receiving care, formal interviews should be conducted after the patient is discharged. Although it is possible for the researcher to conduct interviews prior to discharge, the authors' experience indicates that this practice is inadvisable, for several reasons. First, many patients are reluctant to say anything negative while still dependent on staff to complete treatment. Second, patients recovering from serious injuries or illnesses tend to be preoccupied with their own well-being and recovery. Consequently, they are less willing or able to participate in service evaluation. Third, patients currently under care may not be able to provide a fully developed evaluation of the service because they have not yet experienced all aspects of it.

At the same time, interviews should be conducted relatively soon after discharge (within two to seven days), while the experience is still fresh in patients' minds. Consider the fact that most people, if asked what they ate for dinner yesterday, would be able to recall fairly accurately both the types and amounts of food consumed. But if the question were asked about a dinner three weeks ago, nearly everyone would have difficulty remembering unless it had been a special occasion. When people cannot remember what they did or how they felt, their responses are likely to be incomplete or biased.

Because qualitative research is concerned with gaining an in-depth understanding of a person's service experience, each interview typically requires at least one hour. Lengthier interviews may occur with persons of unusual perceptiveness and rich insights into themselves, other patients, or service providers. The researcher should be willing to sacrifice talking to large numbers of patients for the opportunity to gain an in-depth understanding of the patient experience from a more modest number of patients.

Interview Scheduling

Ideally, prospective interviewees should be informed before discharge that the hospital or clinic is evaluating its service and may contact them to participate in an interview. In addition, informed consent to participate in the study should be obtained from patients when they are contacted to schedule the interview. The following sample introduction illustrates how to procure consent to participate and orient the prospective interviewee to the project. The contact is in the form of a telephone call, which may be placed by the researcher or by someone else on the research team who is assigned this task.

> Hello. Is this *John Doe* [patient's name]? My name is *Sally Smith* [interviewer's name]. I'm with the *XYZ Research Group* [firm conducting the study]. The *ABC Ambulatory Surgery Center* [provider being studied], where you recently received services, has asked us to contact a sample of patients to obtain their reactions to the care provided. Your honest opinion will be very helpful to us in understanding how services might be improved. What you tell us will be kept strictly confidential. May I schedule a time when *Dr. Steiber* [interviewer] can come and interview you at your home? Or, if you prefer, he can interview you at our office, whichever is more convenient. The interview will take approximately one hour.

Note that the example contains several key facts: who is calling, whom the caller represents, how the respondent was selected, why it is important that the respondent participate, that honest opinions are expected, that confidentiality will be maintained, how long the interview will last, how a home or office interview can be scheduled, and who will conduct the interview.

It is extremely important to use this kind of introduction, particularly when patients have not been informed of the interview before discharge. In only a few words, the caller must persuade the respondent that by sharing his or her reactions to the service, shortcomings are likely to be improved and the respondent (or respondent's family) will reap the benefits in the future.

The caller must be prepared to answer questions about the study as well as to persuade the respondent of its importance and usefulness. Thus, the caller must be made aware of the nature of the study and briefed on how to answer questions. When a respondent asks a question that the caller cannot answer, the call should be forwarded to the supervisor.

After the respondent agrees to the interview, a follow-up letter should be sent confirming the interview time and purpose and thanking the person for agreeing to participate. The letter serves a dual purpose: it allays any fears regarding the call's legitimacy, and it serves as a reminder of the interview place and time.

Interview Process

Once the interview begins, it is important to maintain the interviewee's interest to ensure that the interview is completed. Both verbally and nonverbally, the interviewer must convey genuine interest in understanding the respondent's service experience.

During the initial moments of the interview, respondents are frequently anxious or fearful. The interviewer can detect respondents' uneasiness by noticing their facial expressions, eye movements, posture, and voice intonations. Part of this discomfort stems from not knowing what they will be asked and whether their answers will be accepted. To allay these concerns, the interviewer might preface the questions with a brief explanation of what will be asked. A few minutes of explanation affords interviewees a chance to focus and organize their thoughts. It also makes it clear that the interviewer is not randomly picking questions but that the questioning has a well-thought-out purpose.

To help ease anxiety, the interviewer must also convey empathy by perceiving, recognizing, and accepting the inner feelings and experiences of the respondent. The empathic interviewer refrains from imposing personal judgments on what is said and attempts to understand the private logic and meaning of the service experience to the interviewee. Once the experience is grasped, the interviewer conveys this understanding to the respondent. Empathic interviewing, a skill that must be modeled and practiced, is illustrated in figure 7-2, which also illustrates affirmation and appreciation.

Another technique that conveys the interviewer's interest and generates an orderly flow to the process is to summarize answers prior to introducing a new set of questions. Both the summarizing and the prefacing techniques are illustrated in figure 7-3. The

Figure 7-2. Empathic Interviewing

Interviewee: I was really tense before this interview started. I kept thinking, why do they want to talk to me?
Interviewer: It sounds like you were feeling pretty uncomfortable and unsure of why you were chosen.
Interviewee: Well, nobody ever asked me what I thought about the hospital before. I didn't think they cared.
Interviewer: This is a new and kind of strange experience for you. You didn't think the hospital cared what you thought.
Interviewee: That's right.
Interviewer: Well, I just want to assure you that the hospital does care. We value your opinion and appreciate your taking the time to talk with us today.

Figure 7-3. Summarizing and Prefacing Technique

Interviewer: Let me see if I got all of what you said. You found the waiting area to be hot, the receptionist to be rude, and the wait to be way too long. This, along with the fact that you were feeling sick, made you want to get up and leave. Right?
Interviewee: (Respondent nods head in agreement.)
Interviewer: But you stayed because you didn't know where else to go for care. Have I left anything out?
Interviewee: I think you pretty well got it.
Interviewer: OK. Now I'd like to move on and find out what happened when you were called back to the examination area. First, who took you back to the room, and how did that person treat you?

summarization technique also allows the interviewee to validate what has been said, to add anything that has been missed, and to correct any possible misinterpretations.

The interviewer should also be alert to the manner in which the interviewee frames responses. Through careful listening, the researcher comes to understand not only the feelings, thoughts, and experiences of the interviewee, but also the language in which they are expressed. Learning the interviewee's "language" is of critical importance, especially when middle-class interviewers attempt to communicate with other social groups. Weiss (1975) notes that specific groups have their own special vocabularies and patterns of speech. Not only do the meanings of words differ from group to group, but "differences in language reflect different patterns of perceiving and thinking" (p. 370). If the interviewer does not understand these differences, questions will be inappropriately worded, and responses will be misunderstood.

To illustrate this point an example is drawn from one of the author's experiences in evaluating a day treatment center for adolescent substance abusers. While interviewing a participant, the question was asked: "Tell me about your experience in the program?" The interviewee initially did not respond to the question and, after a moment, began talking about "not being there yet." Asking the interviewee about the meaning of the question was unproductive as well. Later, in questioning staff about the possible meaning of the "program" to participants, it was discovered to have an idiosyncratic meaning related to their treatment approach. Staff would encourage participants to drop their facade of anger or indifference and reveal their true feelings. A participant who had done so was referred to as being "with the program" or "working the program." As the author learned the language of staff and participants, interviews flowed more smoothly.

Because language usage varies from one service setting to another, across ethnic groups, life stages, and occupations, it is vitally important for the interviewer to take advantage of the unique opportunities qualitative interviewing affords for probing, asking, for example, "What did my question mean to you?" or "Why did you answer the question this particular way?" Not only can the interviewer correct any miscommunication, but he or she can also learn how to speak and interpret the language of the interviewee. Once the language is mastered, the interviewer can pose questions that are clear and understandable to the interviewee.

The manner in which the researcher has structured the questions that the interviewer will ask can also affect responses. Patton (1980) has noted that researchers sometimes unwittingly discourage respondents from talking by creating questions that imply a dichotomous response. For example, "Was the doctor courteous?" implicitly asks for a yes or no response. To encourage self-disclosure and discussion, a better wording might be, "What was your reaction to Dr. Smith's bedside manner?" or "How did you feel about the way Dr. Smith talked to you?" These questions invite respondents to describe their thoughts, feelings, and observations more fully.

Although most respondents react favorably to this open invitation to talk, some are hesitant or their answers are too general to be useful. In such instances, the interviewer will need to prompt respondents by asking more specific questions, as illustrated in figure 7-4. Notice that if the questioning had stopped with the initial answer ("pretty well"), the interviewer would have missed much of this person's experience. By probing, the interviewer gained detailed feedback about the availability of nurses and the respondent's reaction to waiting.

In asking questions, the interviewer must always guard against biasing responses by prefacing questions with personal opinions. Potential interviewers should be screened to eliminate those with strong opinions about either the service under study or its participants. (Chapter 10 addresses interviewer screening in more detail.)

Finally, the interviewer should remember that "if questions are demeaning, embarrassing, or upsetting, respondents may terminate the interview or falsify the answers" (Sudman and Bradburn, 1982, p. 5).

Focus Groups

Another method used to gather information in qualitative research is the focus group session. In the health service setting, focus groups bring together current or past patients to discuss their feelings, attitudes, and perceptions about a service. This method is similar to the formal, in-depth interview in that the researcher has prepared a guide (for use by the group moderator or leader) that outlines the topics to be discussed. Rather than a one-on-one situation, questions are posed to the group, and a group discussion of each topic is conducted.

A major advantage of focus group sessions over individual interviews is the interaction among the group's members, which tends to stimulate memories, thoughts, and evaluations of the service experience. When asked questions about the service experience, many people are not immediately aware of their own feelings and perceptions. When given an opportunity to hear others' experiences, their own memories are jogged, and their opinions are clarified or formed.

Figure 7-4. Prompting Technique

Interviewer: How would you describe the way the nurses treated you?
Interviewee: Oh . . . pretty well.
Interviewer: Do you feel the nurses could have done anything more for you that would have made your care better?
Interviewee: Well, I wish they would have come sooner when I pushed the call button.
Interviewer: How frequently did you have to wait for them to respond?
Interviewee: Most of the time.
Interviewer: It sounds like it happened fairly often.
Interviewee: Yeah.
Interviewer: How did it make you feel to have to wait?
Interviewee: Well, at first I got a little mad. But then I figured that they must be awfully busy, being short-staffed. So I just learned to wait my turn.
Interviewer: So at first it bothered you to wait, but after a while you just came to accept it.
Interviewee: Nothing else you can do.

In addition, focus groups can serve as perception checks for individuals who might be inclined to overgeneralize on a quantitative survey. For example, a patient who is asked only to rate global satisfaction with a service may give a very negative response based on a single unpleasant experience with a parking lot attendant or an aide. However, when part of a group, the same individual may examine his or her opinions and consider all aspects of the experience before rendering a judgment.

The open and accepting environment characteristic of well-run focus groups promotes self-disclosure. As a participant divulges sensitive information, others begin to feel less inhibited and follow suit. In response to skillful probing on the part of the moderator, individuals who normally would not talk about certain topics or reveal certain feelings or opinions in a one-on-one situation may do so in a group.

Another advantage of focus groups is that they are more efficient than individual interviews with respect to the amount of research time invested. In the course of a 1½- to 2-hour session, the researcher can obtain service perceptions from 8 to 12 patients, rather than one or two, as would be the case with one-on-one interviews. Focus groups also are less expensive to conduct, and yield results more quickly than surveys. When management urgently needs information, a focus group session can be arranged and convened in approximately two weeks. Typically, about two months elapse before data derived from surveys or one-on-one interviews are in hand.

Because of their special advantages, focus groups are particularly useful when management is looking for creative ideas for modifying existing services. A plethora of ideas can be generated for service improvement through group brainstorming. Once a list is compiled, the group can be asked to assess the strengths and weaknesses of each idea. As the discussion unfolds, concepts for service modification can be refined and their feasibility considered.

However, like all research methods, focus groups have disadvantages. In some circumstances, participants' lack of anonymity can be a problem. If participants are apprehensive about the provider's hearing what is said or are afraid of other participants' reactions to what is said, then responses may be distorted. Although the researcher can ask group participants to treat whatever they hear in the group as confidential, confidentiality is difficult to enforce. (In one-on-one interviews, patients tend to perceive the interviewer as a "professional" and therefore are less apprehensive about the interviewer's reaction to what they reveal.) In light of these disadvantages, focus groups should not be used when patients are deeply private or concerned about others finding out what they have to say about the service experience.

Focus groups also require a skilled moderator or facilitator. A poorly run group can stymie self-disclosure or exert pressure on the members to conform to a prevailing opinion. Such groups are likely to generate highly biased results that mislead decision makers.

Last, the massive volume of information generated from each focus group can be a time-consuming and daunting analytic challenge. When the researcher compares the findings across groups, the results may be vastly different. In that event, the researcher must determine whether the discrepancies reflect true differences in opinion or a methodological bias involving sampling, group dynamics, a change in group leadership or style, or other factors.

Group Size

The ideal group size ranges from 8 to 12 participants. With fewer participants, the group loses the mutual stimulation that makes focus groups unique. In addition, some members may feel pressured to speak before they are ready or on topics about which they have no opinion.

When the group exceeds 12 participants, it becomes difficult for the moderator to control the group process and include everyone in the discussion. The larger the group, the more likely it is to fragment into subgroups, with participants making side remarks to one another rather than addressing the group as a whole. Moreover, participants who wait too long to talk are apt to lose spontaneity and forget what they wanted to say. Another disadvantage of large groups is that they afford shy participants the opportunity to "hide in the crowd" while outgoing members assume center stage.

Setting

Because communication among individuals is affected by the setting in which it occurs, the researcher setting up the protocol should give careful consideration to the area in which focus groups are to be held. In general, it seems best to have a relaxed atmosphere to encourage informal discussion (Bellenger and others, 1979, p. 15). Therefore, very large rooms such as lecture halls and auditoriums should be avoided. Furnishings generally include a large rectangular or circular table with comfortable chairs. If the sessions are to be observed by other members of the research team, the room should have a two-way mirror. Audio or audiovisual equipment for recording sessions should be discreetly placed; microphones often are mounted in the ceiling, and cameras are placed on the viewing side of the two-way mirror. Although spontaneity can be maintained with conspicuous microphones, cameras and their operators should be avoided because they are distracting.

In addition, there should be a reception and waiting area outside the meeting room. As participants arrive, a receptionist should greet them and record their names. Coffee and snacks should be available to reduce tension and provide a pleasant distraction for those who arrive early and must wait.

Although many health care facilities have office and conference areas physically suited to focus groups, an off-campus site is usually preferable. Conducting focus group sessions on a neutral site tends to encourage members to express their honest feelings and perceptions about the service. Concerns about confidentiality are minimized, and participants appear to relax and open up more readily. For these same reasons, sessions should be conducted only with patients who have been discharged from the service. The reasons given earlier for conducting in-depth interviews after discharge are equally applicable to focus groups.

Sample Selection and Group Assignment

In selecting patients to participate in focus groups, the goal is to obtain the views of a representative cross section of recent patients. A sample selection protocol should be developed, and procedures similar to those outlined for in-depth interviews should be followed. An additional factor that should be considered is group assignment. Because the composition of a group can enhance or inhibit members' interaction, care should be taken to create homogeneity.

Ideally, there should be a separate group for each segment of the patient base. For example, in conducting research for an ambulatory surgery center that offers an array of services to a diverse market, one group might consist of middle-aged women who have undergone tubal ligations, while another might include senior citizens who have had cataracts removed. If these two diverse segments were combined in one group, they could not discuss a common service experience, nor would they necessarily share common needs and expectations.

It is important to recognize that focus groups, regardless of the number of participants, cannot be considered a statistically representative sample of the patient population. Despite diligent efforts to recruit participants, focus groups will not equally attract all individuals contacted. Members will self-select based on the availability of free time, willingness to participate in a group, and a variety of other factors.

Number of Sessions

Just as the number of market segments and services affects sample selection, so it also affects the number of sessions to be conducted. The more diverse the segments and services, the more sessions will be needed. (Cost-benefit considerations should, of course, be factored into the decision.) As a rule of thumb, enough groups should be conducted to ensure that 80 percent of the service volume is represented. Suppose, for example, that 45 percent of an ambulatory surgery center's business consists of tubal ligations and 35 percent consists of cataract removals. Assuming that no further segmentation of these two services is warranted, a total of four group sessions (that is, two for ligations and two for cataracts) may be sufficient. It is wise to have two groups per segment to determine whether the second group produces results similar to those of the first. If the second group's results are substantially different, then conducting a session with a third group may be advisable to avoid making spurious conclusions based on a particular group's nuances.

When is further segmentation necessary? The ambulatory surgery center provides a useful illustration. Because only women have tubal ligations and the patient group tends to be homogeneous with respect to age (that is, primarily between the ages of 30 and 45), this group does not warrant further segmentation. If the first and second focus groups produce generally the same results, then a third group is unnecessary. The researcher might, however, consider segmenting cataract patients into two groups based on gender. If the two groups produce similar results, the researcher need not conduct further sessions. If differences emerge based on gender, then at least two additional groups, one for males and one for females, should be conducted.

Participant Recruitment

As with in-depth interviews, patients should be informed prior to discharge that the provider is evaluating the service and that they may be contacted to participate in a focus group. Most focus group participants are recruited by telephone after they have been discharged (patients of long-term care facilities are an exception). The initial part of the telephone introduction, explaining who is calling and why, is generally the same as for in-depth interviews. The caller explains when and where the session will take place, how long it will last, who will moderate the discussion, and what to expect. If participants are to receive an honorarium for participating, this, too, is mentioned. (Honoraria typically range from $20 to $50 for nonprofessionals.)

Cash incentives motivate participation. Because focus groups can consume a considerable amount of participants' time (approximately two hours of discussion, plus travel time), recruiting participants without an incentive can be difficult.

In some cases, incentives other than money may be offered. For example, the authors know of a dental practice that offered a free dental examination, and of a women's health facility that offered a free therapeutic massage. However, before using such incentives, the researcher should consider whether the incentive might bias the sample. For example, if the goal of a study is to understand why some patients are dissatisfied, a free examination is likely to attract only satisfied patients who are predisposed to return. Under such conditions, the information obtained would have marginal relevance to the research question. Cash incentives prevent this type of problem.

When a candidate agrees to participate, a follow-up letter of confirmation should be sent. The letter should specify the time, location, sponsorship, incentive, and other details of the agreement. Letters serve not only as reminders but also as formal invitations that legitimize the transaction and allay the fears of people who are leery of phone solicitations. To help ensure that participants attend, the researcher might also arrange for follow-up telephone confirmations the day before or the day of a focus group.

Focus Group Guide

Similar to the in-depth interview guide, the focus group guide keeps the leader on track to ensure that key topics and issues are covered. However, the leader determines when and how to introduce each topic and how to phrase questions. Because the leader is facilitating a group discussion, as opposed to conducting individual interviews within a group, the leader must allow the group process to influence the order and range of topics discussed. At the same time, discussion of topics that are clearly unrelated to the participants' service experience must be minimized, and the group's attention must be refocused on the service experience.

Opening Remarks

The leader's opening remarks play a crucial role in determining the success of the focus group because they define the purpose, the topics to be discussed, and the ground rules.

As figure 7-5 illustrates, the opening statement ties together the explanation given over the telephone with an introductory comment on focus groups. The leader provides an overview of what will be discussed to focus interaction around the service experience and to define other topics as off limits. Because some individuals are reluctant to be critical in group discussions, the leader encourages members to express both negative and positive opinions about service, noting that criticism will be used for constructive purposes.

By asking respondents to speak one at a time, the leader prevents the formation of splinter groups. The importance of each person's comments is emphasized by the leader's noting that the session is being taped and that the recording will be reviewed later. (Of course, the leader has an ethical responsibility to inform each person of the taping as well.)

To reduce the group's concern that health care staff may learn which participants offered negative comments, the leader promises that confidentiality will be maintained. The leader attempts to develop an empathic group atmosphere by noting that there are no right or wrong answers and that each person is entitled to an opinion. If any concerns remain about the group's purpose, the leader's inquiry—"Any questions?"—allows them to be addressed.

Figure 7-5. Focus Group Leader's Opening Remarks

Hello, my name is _____. As you know from our phone conversation, you've been invited here today to talk about your impressions and reactions to the services you received at the XYZ Baby Clinic. During the session, I'll be asking questions as to how you decided to use the XYZ Baby Clinic, questions about the services you received, how the staff treated you, the physical facilities, and so on. It's important that each of you share with us the things that you liked and disliked about the clinic. I know that sometimes people are reluctant to be critical. However, if the people who run the center don't know about the problems that might exist, they can't fix them. Right?

Before we get started, I have a few requests. One is that only one person speak at a time and that you speak up. This session is being tape-recorded so that later on I can review what was said, just in case I missed something. What you say will be kept confidential by me. I would also ask that if you talk to anyone about what was said in this group that you not mention any names.

Second, I would ask that each of you listen carefully to the person talking, and keep in mind that each of us sees the world a little differently. Each of us has a right to our opinion. That's what makes us all individuals. What is most important here is that we try to understand why each of us feels the way we do.

Are there any questions before we get started? Let's start by getting to know one another. Why don't we go around the table and introduce ourselves. Also tell the group a little bit about your family—number of children you have, their ages, maybe something about your spouse.

Finally, the leader uses a round-robin technique to break the ice and give each person an opportunity to speak and get to know the others. If a member's introduction is excessively brief, the leader should attempt to draw the person out by gently probing (for example, "Could you tell us a little more about your family, such as how old your children are?"). When a person remains reluctant to talk, the leader should ease the pressure with an empathic response and refocus the group's attention on the next member to speak (for example, "Why don't we go on to the next person? After a while we'll all feel a little bit more comfortable and it will be easier to talk. OK?").

Techniques for Leading Discussions

After the opening remarks have been presented and members have introduced themselves, the leader introduces the first topic by indicating that the group should begin by discussing a certain point (for example, "I would like you to share with one another your first impression when you enter the XYZ Baby Clinic"). Early in the session, members are inclined to speak to the leader instead of one another. It is important that the leader redirect responses in a manner that facilitates a discussion, as opposed to question-answer interactions. When a member directs a response to the leader, one approach is to ask, "Did any one else have this experience?" Observing other members nodding their heads "yes," the leader can respond, "It seems that several of you may have had a similar impression. Why don't you share your experiences with one another?" A slightly different response would be, "Why don't you ask if anyone else in the group had a similar experience?" Before long, members become conditioned to talking to each other.

As the leader becomes aware that several members have had a similar experience, it will be useful to comment on this observation (for example, "It seems that several of you had to wait a long time"). The nodding or shaking of heads provides the leader with feedback about the generalization. However, it is also important for the leader to elicit divergent views. Groups can exert considerable pressures on members to conform to a prevailing sentiment, and some members may agree with a prevailing opinion simply to avoid being seen as different. To prevent "groupthink" from occurring, the leader should invite a range of perceptions (by asking, for instance, "Is there anyone in the group who didn't have to wait?" or "Would you share with us your experience?").

As in in-depth interviews, the group leader asks open-ended questions that invite explanations, as opposed to those leading to simple yes or no responses. As the group discussion progresses, the leader learns the participants' language and incorporates it into his or her own phraseology. The summarizing and prefacing technique suggested for in-depth interviews should also be used in focus groups. By summarizing commonly shared service experiences, the group develops a clearer understanding of its stated purpose. Like the summary paragraph at the end of a chapter, it brings closure to one topic and prepares the group for the introduction of a new one.

The leader is a role model for the group. His or her behavior tends to shape how members will conduct themselves. When strong emotions are expressed in the group, the leader should model an accepting and empathic response. For example, an irate participant may say, "Do you think it's right that they kept me waiting with a sick baby all afternoon?" The leader might respond with, "It must have been really frustrating for you to have to wait that long." This response demonstrates the leader's sensitivity to the person's feelings, thereby implicitly illustrating how group members are expected to respond. Again, to redirect the dialogue back to the group, a follow-up comment would be, "Has anyone else had a similar experience?"

Focus group discussions must be kept on track so that all the relevant topics are addressed. Directive leadership should be exercised without confronting or offending group members. If the group discussion does stray, the leader might respond by saying, "This is an interesting point, and I'm sure we could spend a whole hour discussing it.

Unfortunately, we have limited time and a lot of ground to cover. Could we return to an earlier point about...." Once the group becomes familiar with the leader as director, briefer comments will suffice, such as, "Are we straying off the topic?" (*pause*) If we've got everyone's thoughts, maybe we should move on to the next topic. Next, I'd like the group to discuss..." or "Are we getting just a little off course?" (*pause*) "How about if we go back to Mary's point about... Was there something else you wanted to share with the group?"

At times, a leader must deal with a group monopolizer. Typically, these individuals are highly opinionated and like to hear themselves speak. If not kept in check by the leader, monopolizers can take over the group. If one participant is dominating the discussion, the leader might interrupt and say, "Excuse me. I hate to interrupt because you've made a number of important and valuable points. However, I'd like to find out if other group members have had similar or different experiences. It's important that we each have an equal opportunity to share our experiences." In extreme cases, the leader must remind the monopolizer to be brief and let others speak.

Group Observation

Group dynamics exert a substantial influence upon the participants as well as the leader. Consequently, it is common practice to utilize other research team members to observe the group process from behind a two-way mirror. Being outside of the group allows the observer greater objectivity and opportunity to analyze the communication process. If the observer notes a salient point in need of further exploration, detects an omission of relevant information, or perceives the group process as distorting individual contributions from members, a written message can be given to the leader, suggesting a mid-course correction. Observer feedback is also useful during the data analysis process.

Telephonic Focus Groups

One of the greatest obstacles to focus group attendance is the time and trouble it can take to travel to a facility. Picture the end of a long workday: It is raining (or, worse, snowing), and you have been invited to "share your opinions and perceptions" at a small group discussion with other former patients. If you are like most people who are recruited for a focus group session, the likelihood of your attending has now slipped to only about 66 percent. Similar problems can prevent interviewees from keeping their appointments for one-on-one interviews. Because of problems like these, telephonic focus groups are sometimes substituted for face-to-face interactions.

Given the wide geographic market served by some providers, a telephonic focus group ensures greater representation from among busy former patients who are unable or unwilling to travel to a group facility. Moreover, telephonic focus groups place another element of control within the researcher's hands. The research facility initiates the telephone call that will link all participants; the call is not dependent on the recruited participant's initiative.

Because telephonic group participants can be recruited from a wide geographic market, even tertiary care centers can gather representatives from select subspecialty services into one focus group. For certain services that may not see great volume over a given period of time for any given finite market area, telephonic groups can be used to overcome the travel obstacle. Picture the self-referral market for a Johns Hopkins University Medical Center, a Mayo Clinic, or a Cleveland Clinic: all of these can use telephonic groups across state boundaries, just as a community provider might bring together recently discharged patients from its six-zip-code market area.

Data Analysis

Once the raw data in the form of patients' perceptions have been gathered, the next major phase of the qualitative research process is data analysis. Ideally, the analysis of qualitative data should be done both formally and informally, with each method employed at a different stage in the data collection process.

An informal analysis should be conducted concurrently with patient data collection. During the course of interviewing respondents or conducting focus groups, the interviewer (or group leader) may repeatedly hear respondents indicating that a certain aspect of the service (for example, a rude receptionist or staff addressing patients by nicknames) is unacceptable or demeaning. Although this topic may not have been included in the interview or focus group guides, the interviewer should probe respondents to determine the pervasiveness of this experience and its impact on patients' expectations and satisfaction. Through careful listening, the interviewer has identified a theme or pattern of responses that is important in understanding how patients experience the service. The interviewer makes note of this theme and systematically questions respondents to determine its pervasiveness. The formal analysis of field notes and transcriptions is an extension and elaboration of this same process. These data are examined to determine what issues fit together and what patterns and themes emerge from the data.

When the researcher begins the formal analysis of data, a crosscurrent of feelings, impressions, and thoughts is likely to emerge. The reams of notes and transcripts may seem overwhelming, yet at the same time unasked questions may seem to call for one more interview, focus group session, or day of observation. The inexperienced researcher is frequently tempted to return to the field, hoping that one more piece of information will magically make the pieces fit together and the conclusions fall into place.

The best advice anyone can give the researcher is to *stop* at this point. The researcher should return to the original research plan, the notes that detail the goals and rationale of the study, and reflect on the insights and impressions gained while collecting and recording the data. Once the researcher realizes that each source of information (for example, observations, interviews of patients, program documents, staff interviews) has its own bias, then he or she can look for the common threads that are relevant to the research questions. The following example illustrates how data converge:

> In the study of the XYZ Baby Clinic, one research question that was investigated involved whether the clinic's reception and waiting area significantly detracted from patients' satisfaction with the service. Observational data indicated it to be frequently crowded, hot, and stuffy, with a threadbare appearance. Informal and in-depth interviews revealed that respondents perceived it in a similar manner. A review of program documents revealed that over the past five years, patient volume had increased by over 100 percent, while space had actually decreased by 15 percent. Program staff perceived the area as an embarrassment that detracted from what they considered an otherwise excellent clinical service. Having mentally gone through this analytic exercise, the researcher concluded that these data from multiple sources were sufficiently consistent and detailed to indicate that additional data collection was unnecessary.

When this level of convergence and detail exists for all of the research questions, then the researcher can be fairly confident that additional data will contribute only minimally to the findings. However, this tentative conclusion must be verified during the editing, coding, cutting, sorting, and compiling stages.

Coding and Editing

Qualitative research data are voluminous. As a first step toward finding a path through the data, the researcher should code the data according to each research question that was specified in the research plan. This generally involves making a hard copy of the field notes and transcriptions and assigning a code based on each section's relevance to a particular research question. For the XYZ Baby Clinic, the question regarding the reception and waiting area was abbreviated "RWA." As the field notes and transcriptions were read, relevant sections were bracketed and coded with this abbreviation.

A significant body of information that cannot be classified by the original questions usually remains. If the original questions were exhaustive and if all factors that influence patient satisfaction are accounted for, residual materials can be discarded. But this is seldom the case. One advantage of qualitative research is that it tends to unearth, by serendipity, issues that neither program staff nor the researcher anticipated at the study's outset. When these materials are carefully analyzed, they can offer valuable insights into a service.

Again, these residual materials are examined to determine how the pieces fit together. The researcher asks, "What themes are present that bear on patients' experience and satisfaction with the service?" Once additional themes are identified, the remaining field notes and transcriptions can be coded, cut, and sorted. For consistency's sake, the researcher may create a research question that each theme addresses (for example, "How does addressing patients by nicknames affect their satisfaction with the service?").

To facilitate data analysis, the researcher may edit the transcriptions of patient comments. Patients seldom express exactly what is on their minds in perfect prose. They repeat themselves, hem and haw, and use incomplete sentences. Omitting this material while retaining the essence of the respondents' own words enhances readability.

Cutting and Sorting

The next step in data analysis is to cut and sort the data so that each research question is followed only by relevant information. Each bracketed section is also coded so that the reader will know from which document it was cut (for example, notes on program records or a particular focus group or interview). The appendix at the end of this chapter illustrates coded and sorted data for one research question.

Perspectives

Focus group data offer the researcher multiple perspectives on participants' comments. Not only do different patient perspectives come to light through the patients' own descriptions, but the researcher himself or herself has multiple pathways into the material collected. As an example, the leader has an immediate and unique perspective that can come only from being face-to-face with participants and communicating interactively. Observers behind a two-way mirror are in a different position with respect to the unfolding session, and they therefore bring to the analysis an alternative point of view. Those who view a videotape or listen to an audiotape after the fact may bring an additional perspective to the analysis. Finally, those who read transcripts from a group discussion will see all the words that every other observer has heard, but the printed word does not offer inflection, decibel level, or other dynamics that recordings or real-time observations afford. On the other hand, nuances that may be lost during the full-sensory unfolding of a group session from, say, the leader's perspective may come to light later during a careful and unhurried scrutiny of the transcript or videotape. During the analytic phase, each perspective is considered in compiling a report.

It is also helpful to analyze the qualitative data with an eye to pinpointing the more important generalizations that may emerge from participants' comments. Four patterns to seek in fathoming the underlying "facts" in qualitative research are consensus, intensity, extent, and dissensus.

Consensus

When everyone agrees with a point of view, then that point of view becomes elevated to "fact." In focus groups, it is common for a participant to offer an observation that seems to sum up others' experience, such as "The nurses at Hospital XYZ really listen when you have a problem or a question." As the leader looks at everyone seated around the table nodding in agreement, it is clear that virtually everyone else has had an experience that affirms this observation. Probing to uncover just what this means or in what contexts such listening occurred can be revealing, but the simple fact that all participants concur is in itself meaningful.

Directed probing of consensus impressions sometimes leads to discovery of a particular service or transaction that respondents were involved in. As an example, in a research project that involved talking with physicians, one of the authors found that all the physicians seemed to concur that management at a particular medical center was very attentive to physicians' needs. On this dimension, the facility stood out among all the rest. On probing, it was discovered that the CEO of the facility routinely visited the surgical suites to personally meet, greet, and thank physicians for using the facility. The physicians saw in this extra effort a sign that management at that facility listened to physician concerns, and this became a distinguishing feature of the hospital about which all physicians could agree.

Intensity

In addition to noting points of consensus in a focus group, researchers are also interested in the intensity of participants' comments as a guide to salient points of service. For example, in a series of focus groups among emergency department patients, there was no consensus on nursing care overall, but a subset of participants consistently had nothing but rave reviews. Middle-aged and older men made extraordinarily positive comments about nursing care. Were these patients singled out for better treatment than their age or gender counterparts?

On further probing, it was discovered these patients had one condition in common—a myocardial infarction. Although a heart attack alone did not define their unique experience, the nursing care on the cardiac intensive care unit where they were transferred from the emergency department did afford a uniquely positive experience. Patients treated and released from the emergency department or patients admitted to other units simply had not shared in this experience. But the heightened interest, louder speech, and superlative adjectives used by this segment allowed the researchers to probe further and determine a salient point of service.

Extent

Often, a single service provider or a single event does not define the service experience for a patient. Instead, a recurring theme or an underlying corporate culture seems to permeate an organization and leave a lasting impression on patients or other customers. Within the context of in-depth interviews that the authors conducted among a number of patients, the same characterization was offered time and again about a number of different health care professionals across a number of settings within a given facility. Comments ranged from "They really cared" to "Someone took the time to ask how I was doing" and "I felt they were looking out for me." Whether the reference point was the outpatient registration person, the laboratory technician, a nurse, or some other professional, the entire corporate culture seemed to encourage the staff to make a connection with the patient in an ambulatory care setting. It was a different pattern from the intensity of the cardiac care unit experience, and it served to underscore an important finding for the provider.

Dissensus

It is important to look beyond a variety of opinions offered in a group to determine if, in fact, the diversity says something. In a series of focus groups conducted by one of the authors, again among recently treated emergency department patients seen at a single facility, women reported that the attendant at the door was their first encounter with the provider, younger respondents of either sex claimed it was the reception desk professional, and older participants talked about being helped from their cars to wheelchairs, if needed. Even with these relatively clear distinctions, which suggested different perceptions or different experiences according to age or sex, not all patients reported experiences that would neatly fit into their appropriate age or sex categories. Did all these individuals simply enter the facility from different access points?

From the service descriptions in the focus groups, it became clear that the security guard was the only employee consistently stationed close enough to the door to intervene. It also became clear that not all security guards were equally attentive. Finally, further probing revealed that one security guard in particular was attentive to women as he opened the door for them, tended to ignore young (apparently capable) men altogether, and left his post in the building to greet older patients and assist them out of their cars. Further quality improvement activities sought to elevate all guards' behavior across all patient types to that attentive behavior manifested for older patients.

Report Compilation

After the editing, coding, and reorganization of the raw data are complete, a first-draft summary of this material should be constructed. A useful way of organizing the summary is to list each research question and theme as a section heading and then condense what was said, commenting on the consistency or inconsistency of the multiple data sources. Before the report is finalized, it is recommended that the researcher schedule a meeting to share these preliminary findings with program management and clinical directors to elicit their assistance in interpreting the data. By presenting a first-pass summary to this group, the researcher can gain their insights and hear their further questions and concerns. Frequently, staff comments may suggest alternative perspectives from which to view the data, with alternative explanations as to how the data could be interpreted. The researcher may find that more than one such working meeting is necessary to reach consensus on the results. Nevertheless, the time is well spent, because the more that staff members wrestle with interpreting the data, the more likely they are to accept the final results and recommendations.

The final report should contain the following elements:

1. The purpose of the patient satisfaction study
2. The research questions that were to be answered
3. An explanation of why a particular research method was used (for example, the advantages and disadvantages of qualitative research relative to quantitative research)
4. The types of data that were collected, and when and how they were collected
5. The steps that were taken to verify the accuracy of the data
6. The methods by which the data were analyzed

7. The study results, organized by each research question
8. The limitation of the data in answering the research questions
9. Recommendations for service modifications
10. Recommendations for additional or follow-up research
11. An appendix containing the edited data organized by research question or theme

Researcher Qualifications

What training and experience are required to conduct qualitative patient satisfaction studies? To the best of our knowledge, no graduate schools offer courses that specialize in this area. We will attempt to answer this question by describing the type of person and the knowledge and skills that seem important in the authors' experience.

The researcher who plans to conduct interviews and function as a group moderator should like people and be intrigued by the many ways the world can be perceived. Cultural differences among people should be a source of fascination rather than a cause for alienation. In addition to being comfortable around people of diverse backgrounds, the researcher-interviewer should have a knack for striking up and carrying on conversation. While interacting with people, he or she should be able to enter the world of those being interviewed, see it as they see it, and yet remain sufficiently detached to reflect on alternative ways the situation might be perceived. In addition to having these insights into people and situations, the researcher must be able to describe and record what is seen in a coherent and readable document.

Thus, academic preparation might include course work in sociology, psychology, social psychology, human motivation, organizational dynamics, social anthropology, human growth and development, and related subjects, all of which can provide useful conceptual models for understanding human behavior. Counseling courses, clinical interviewing, and empathy training provide valuable skills for conducting in-depth interviews, while courses in group dynamics are particularly relevant to leading focus groups. Finally, courses that focus on qualitative research methods and program evaluation provide the researcher with important analytic models to guide his or her thinking.

Typically, individuals with this blend of personal characteristics and academic training are not available in health care settings. Hospitals with mental health departments occasionally have a psychologist or social worker with training and interest in qualitative research that can be adapted to conducting patient satisfaction studies. Colleges and universities are another potential source of qualitative researchers. Departments where these individuals are most likely to be found include psychology, sociology, social work, and sometimes business. Some research firms also specialize in qualitative research.

Summary

The primary goal of patient satisfaction research is to focus on what services patients receive and their personal evaluations of these services. Although researchers can gain a basic understanding of services by reviewing existing data and observing the clinical program from the patients' point of view, the most useful qualitative information is obtained from interviews and focus groups. Data must be analyzed, edited, coded, and sorted before they are compiled into a report.

Appendix. Data Coded and Sorted by Research Question

Research Question:

How satisfied are patients with the reception and waiting area of the XYZ Baby Clinic?

a. Is the space sufficient to handle patient volume?
b. Are the furnishings adequate and acceptable to patients?
c. Upon arrival, are patients promptly greeted by the receptionist, and are questions answered in a considerate and helpful manner?
d. Is the receptionist courteous, polite, and friendly toward patients?

Results

Observational Data

The area measures 10 feet × 20 feet with a corridor bisecting the space. The receptionist's desk is located adjacent to the corridor. The area is brightly lit with aging fluorescent lights that hang from a 12-foot ceiling. There are no windows in the area, and the air has a slightly stagnant odor. The walls are a faded light green in color, while the doors and trim are an off-white, showing signs of dirt and wear. In addition to the receptionist's aging wooden desk and chair, there are 12 gray metal fold-up chairs where patients sit, and a small table covered with outdated magazines that reflect their age.

The floor covering is a speckled gray tile, with a few tiles missing. The only sign is on the receptionist's desk, and it reads "Receptionist." As patients enter the area they gaze around looking lost. Their first question usually is: "Is this the XYZ Baby Clinic?" Frequently, the receptionist is busy scheduling appointments on the phone, and patients stand restlessly in front of the desk. Discussions between the receptionist and new arrivals are frequently interrupted by the phone. By midmorning the room is crowded, with 20 or more patients waiting. Mothers are pacing with babies in arms; some of the babies are crying. The room temperature is hot, around 75 to 80 degrees F. Occasionally, complaints are overheard: "What's taking them so long?"

Informal Interview Responses

Interviewer: It seems kind of warm in here.
Interviewee 1: Warm? It's hot in here! You'd think they'd at least make the room decent if they're going to make us wait all morning. You know, I treat my dog better.
Interviewer: How long have you been waiting?
Interviewee 1: Oh, seems like most of the morning. I got here before 9 a.m. and I'll probably be here until noon.
Interviewer: Have you been here before?
Interviewee 1: Oh, yeah. It's always like this. Nothing changes. Hurry up and get here, then wait.
Interviewer: These chairs seem a little hard on the old bottom.
Interviewee 1: You bet. Especially when you've got to sit here forever.
Interviewer: How long have you been waiting?
Interviewee 2: Oh, almost an hour.
Interviewer: Seems a little warm.
Interviewee 2: They need some windows in the place. Better yet, they ought to just level this old building. Put up something new.
Interviewer: That phone seems to ring a lot.
Interviewee 3: That poor girl [referring to the receptionist], she ain't got time to go to the bathroom. She could use some help.

In-Depth Interview: Patient

Interviewer: When you arrived at the reception area, how long was it before the receptionist checked you in?
Interviewee: Oh, about 5 to 10 minutes.
Interviewer: Did you mind waiting?
Interviewee: Well, she was busy on the phone. I know what that's like. Too much to do.
Interviewer: The receptionist seemed overworked to you? In what way?
Interviewee: Well, she's the only one there. She's got to answer the phone, check people in, answer questions. Too much. She needs some help.
Interviewer: When she finally got a chance to check you in, how did she treat you?
Interviewee: Oh, real nice. That girl's great. She always has a smile on her face. She even remembers my name every time I come here.
Interviewer: What's your impression of the waiting area? You know—is it large enough, comfortable enough?
Interviewee: Well, some days it seems big enough, but most days it's too small. People stepping on each other's toes. Babies crying. No place to sit.
Interviewer: Sounds like it's crowded on most days.

(Continued on next page)

Interviewee: Yeah. Most days it ain't too good.
Interviewer: How do you like the furnishings?
Interviewee: Well, if they're gonna make us wait, they should at least have soft chairs, and a TV to watch or at least music. You know the place could use some painting, too, and carpets.
Interviewer: It sounds a little run-down.
Interviewee: You bet.

In-Depth Interview: Receptionist

Interviewer: So you've worked here for over seven years.
Interviewee: Yeah, I'm the old-timer around here.
Interviewer: What kind of changes have occurred in your job over the years?
Interviewee: Well, the first five or six years were pretty much the same. I just greeted patients when they arrived, answered their questions, checked them in, and sometimes even held their babies.
Interviewer: Then what happened?
Interviewee: Well, then I guess money started to get tight and they put me in charge of the phones. I gotta answer all these calls, schedule new appointments, and do my old job, too.
Interviewer: Sounds pretty busy.
Interviewee: Too busy. They could use two people for the job, but it comes down to no money.
Interviewer: How has this affected your ability to take care of patients when they arrive?
Interviewee: I just can't keep up. Before, if they had questions or needed a hand with one of the kids, I was right there. I used to feel real good at the end of the day. Like I'd made somebody's life a little easier. Now I could use the help. Some days I get such a headache. Too much work to keep up.
Interviewer: Any other changes?
Interviewee: Well, the clinic's a lot busier. I bet we've at least doubled the number of patients.
Interviewer: Tell me, what's your opinion about the space and furnishings of your area?
Interviewee: Oh, it's too small and run-down. The area should be twice the size. It would be nice to have carpets, fresh paint, nice couches, better lighting, and all that kind of stuff. Could also use a play area for the kids.
Interviewer: Sounds like some improvements are needed.
Interviewee: How about a major overhaul.

Program Documents

The XYZ Baby Clinic was first opened in July 1969. Its intended capacity was to serve 100 patients a day, Monday through Friday. Over the years the demand for services has grown, and it now serves over 250 patients a day. Hours have been expanded from 9 a.m. until 4 p.m. to 9 a.m. until 8 p.m. The size of the reception/waiting area has remained approximately the same.

Originally the receptionist's duties were restricted to greeting arriving patients, answering their questions, and logging their arrival. One year ago, the responsibility of answering the phone and scheduling appointments was shifted to the receptionist.

CHAPTER EIGHT

Quantitative Research

After qualitative methods have been used to identify specific service areas and attributes of interest in a patient satisfaction study, quantitative methods are used to measure them. The principal quantitative method that will be discussed in this chapter is the standardized questionnaire. Standardized questionnaires ask all respondents the same questions in the same sequence and using exactly the same words; the instructions and response formats are also the same for all respondents. Although some open-ended questions may be included in a standardized questionnaire, most questions are closed-ended, with predetermined response options. The purpose of this structure is to ensure the comparability of responses, which is essential to quantitative data.

Standardized questionnaires may be designed as self-report surveys or as interviewer-administered surveys (typically conducted by telephone or in person). This chapter will focus on the principles of questionnaire construction that are applicable to both interviewer-administered and self-report questionnaires. We will discuss the types of information that can be collected through standardized patient satisfaction questionnaires, the wording of questions, the structuring of response formats, and the creation of multi-item scales. Although questionnaire wording and the structuring of response formats are presented in separate sections for ease of reading, there is considerable overlap between these two topics. The chapter ends with a discussion of methods for pretesting and revising questionnaires.

Categories of Quantitative Information

Before writing questions, the researcher must consider the kinds of quantitative information desired from respondents. Occasionally, researchers become so immersed in the details of constructing survey questions that they lose sight of the three types of information that can be obtained from patients: (1) reports of facts, (2) evaluations or ratings of providers and service settings, and (3) reports of intended behavior.

Reports of Facts

Questions that ask for a report of facts seek information that is objective and verifiable. These questions ask for factual information about (1) the respondent or provider,

(2) the service setting, or (3) attributive characteristics (that is, personal attributes) of the patient. The following questions illustrate these three categories of information:

- Do you have a family doctor?
- Did you have an X-ray study done?
- How many minutes did you have to wait to see the doctor?
- How often did the nurses stop by your room to check on you?
- Where is the hospital located?
- How many patient beds were in your room?
- How often was your room cleaned?
- What is your age?
- Are you male or female?

Reports of facts are frequently utilized to aggregate data according to patient characteristics. For example, aggregating data by gender allows the researcher to compare satisfaction ratings among males and females. Aggregating data by service location (for example, east side clinics versus west side clinics) allows for satisfaction comparisons by location. Similar comparisons can be made based on age, ethnic origin, socioeconomic status, physicians, and so on. Another use of these data involves comparing sample and population characteristics to determine their equivalence. Time reports can be used to compare how long patients are waiting for service relative to benchmark standards that the institution has established. Frequency reports such as how often nurses stopped by your room can be used in a similar fashion.

Evaluations or Ratings

In contrast to reports of facts, evaluative or rating questions are subjective. They ask how the patient *evaluates,* or feels about, (1) the provider's behavior (for example, "I had to wait too long for the doctor," "Nurses were seldom available," "The doctors were always courteous") and (2) the service setting (for example, "The waiting room was crowded," "My room was very clean," "The clinic was difficult to find"). Usually patient satisfaction questionnaires include both reports of facts and ratings of various elements. However, rating questions are better measures of patient satisfaction than questions that report facts (Ware, Snyder, and Wright, 1976).

Reports of Intended Behavior

Questions about intended behavior ask patients about the future use of services. These questions do not measure patient satisfaction directly, as rating questions do. However, they may be considered satisfaction outcome measures in that if patients are dissatisfied with a provider's behavior, they may not return.

Figure 8-1 illustrates how all three types of questions are used in combination. Assume a researcher is conducting a study to determine community residents' satisfaction with primary care physician services. Question A asks whether respondents have a family physician. If they indicate yes, then question B asks how frequently they see their physician. Questions A and B are both reports of facts. Questions C, D, and E ask for ratings. Evaluative questions typically try to determine whether the respondent considers the provider's behavior or the service setting desirable or undesirable, excellent or poor, satisfying or dissatisfying, sufficient or insufficient, acceptable or unacceptable, and so on.

Questions F and G tap respondents' intended behavior with respect to their future use of services. Questions H, I, and J are further examples of reports of facts based on personal attributes—in this case, personal and demographic characteristics of respondents. As mentioned before, such questions often are used to group and study

Figure 8-1. Types of Quantitative Research Questions

Reports of Facts:

A. When you are sick or injured, do you have a regular family physician whom you go to for care? (Please circle your answer.)
   1. Yes
   2. No (If "No," please skip to Question F)

B. How many times have you seen your family doctor in the past 12 months, that is, since ___-___ (month-year), for any health problems? _____ (number of visits)

Ratings:

C. Do you feel there are too few, about the right number, or too many physicians in your community?
   1. Too many
   2. Just the right number
   3. Too few
   4. Don't know

D. How available is your family physician when you need an appointment? Would you say:
   1. Never available
   2. Sometimes available
   3. Usually available
   4. Always available

E. How satisfied are you with the care you receive from your family physician? Are you:
   1. Completely satisfied
   2. Somewhat satisfied
   3. Neutral
   4. Somewhat dissatisfied
   5. Completely dissatisfied

Reports of Intended Behavior:

F. How likely are you to see your family physician during the next year? Are you:
   1. Very likely
   2. Somewhat likely
   3. Somewhat unlikely
   4. Very unlikely
   5. Don't know

G. How likely are you to change family physicians during the next year? Are you:
   1. Very likely
   2. Somewhat likely
   3. Somewhat unlikely
   4. Very unlikely
   5. Don't know

Reports of Facts:

H. What age group are you in? (Place an X in the box next to your answer.)
   ☐ Under 18   ☐ 45 to 54
   ☐ 18 to 24   ☐ 55 to 64
   ☐ 25 to 34   ☐ 65 to 74
   ☐ 35 to 44   ☐ 75 or older

I. What is the highest level of education that you have completed?
   1. Less than high school diploma
   2. High school graduate
   3. Associate's degree (two-year degree)
   4. Bachelor's degree
   5. Some graduate school or more

J. What gender are you?
   1. Male
   2. Female

responses according to respondent characteristics. For example, the researcher may be interested in answering questions such as the following: Are male patients more satisfied with services than female patients? Are younger patients more satisfied than older patients? Are highly educated patients more satisfied than less educated patients? Questions about personal attributes are also useful in determining whether the sample is representative of the population from which it is drawn (discussed in chapter 6). By asking attributive questions that have the same response formats as patient registration data, one can make these types of comparisons.

Question Construction

Although it might seem fairly easy to construct a patient satisfaction questionnaire, the experienced researcher realizes that it frequently takes considerable time, with numerous pretestings and revisions, before an instrument is ready for pilot testing. One of the most difficult tasks in questionnaire construction is writing questions. A questionnaire must use clear and precise questions that are specific without being too specific, easy to understand but not insulting to the respondent's intelligence, precise yet not too narrow, direct but not objectionable. Stanley L. Payne, in his classic text *The Art of Asking Questions* (1951), provides a list of 100 elements to consider in writing questions.

It is not uncommon for a question to be rewritten five or ten times before the wording captures what the researcher wants to know in a form and phrasing that are understandable and acceptable to the respondent. Frequently, the researcher does not fully appreciate what a question is asking until patients actually respond to it. When a question misses the mark, it must be revised and pretested again. This trial-and-error process leads to well-structured questions.

In addition to reading books on how to structure questions, it is also helpful to examine the mistakes often made in constructing patient satisfaction questionnaires. In preparing to write the first edition of this book, the authors solicited patient satisfaction questionnaires from hospitals across the country. The basic pitfalls in question design were discussed in chapter 4. The following section considers how to write questions correctly and avoid common mistakes.

Double Negatives

Frequently, questions are written that contain a negative adverb (for example, "not competent," "not good," "never") instead of a contrasting word (for example, "incompetent," "bad," "rarely"). When the response options also contain a negative, double negatives can occur ("He is not a not good doctor"). The following example suggests the problems that can arise when respondents are asked to make an evaluative choice in this situation:

The medical care I received was not excellent.

1. Strongly agree
2. Somewhat agree
3. Neutral
4. Somewhat disagree
5. Strongly disagree

For respondents to indicate that the care received was good, they must disagree with the statement that the care was "not excellent." This can be very confusing, particularly to the person who cannot interpret a question with a double negative.

The following revision illustrates the solution, which is to substitute the appropriate adjective:

The medical care I received was poor.

1. Strongly agree
2. Somewhat agree
3. Neutral
4. Somewhat disagree
5. Strongly disagree

Double-Barreled Questions

A double-barreled question asks about two disparate service attributes. In figure 8-2, for example, the original question asked if nurses were "friendly and competent." Note that if nurses were equally friendly and competent or equally unfriendly and incompetent, only one response would be needed. However, it is possible for nurses to be friendly but incompetent or unfriendly and competent. Thus, two responses are needed. As figure 8-2 shows, the solution is to ask two separate questions, each with its own response options.

Jargon and Abbreviations

Sometimes, patient satisfaction questions contain professional jargon, titles, names, and abbreviations. The assumption is that the respondent knows the language of the health care worker and can identify by technical name or abbreviation various departments, health professionals, and diagnostic and treatment procedures. This erroneous assumption can produce unreliable survey results. When respondents do not understand a question, they are likely to skip it or guess at the answer. Figure 8-3 shows both an original question and a revision, in which a brief explanation or example is given to help respondents understand unfamiliar terminology.

Irrelevant Questions

Because questionnaires can be designed to cover a wide range of experiences, they may contain questions that are irrelevant to a particular patient's experience. Hospitals offer an array of services based on what physicians prescribe. Seldom, if ever, would

Figure 8-2. Double-Barreled Questions

Original Question:	Revised Question:
The nurses were friendly and competent.	The nurses were friendly.
1. Strongly agree	1. Strongly agree
2. Somewhat agree	2. Somewhat agree
3. Neutral	3. Neutral
4. Somewhat disagree	4. Somewhat disagree
5. Strongly disagree	5. Strongly disagree
	The nurses were competent.
	1. Strongly agree
	2. Somewhat agree
	3. Neutral
	4. Somewhat disagree
	5. Strongly disagree

Figure 8-3. Use of Jargon and Abbreviations

Original Question:

Hospital Services

Please rate if you were satisfied or dissatisfied with the following services during your hospital stay. (Circle "1" if you were satisfied and "2" if you were dissatisfied.)

Services	Satisfied	Dissatisfied
Physical therapy	1	2
Social work	1	2
Respiratory therapy	1	2
Radiology	1	2

Revised Question:

Hospital Services

Please rate if you were satisfied or dissatisfied with the following services during your hospital stay. A brief description of each service is provided. Please circle "1" if you were satisfied and "2" if you were dissatisfied.

Physical therapy—(You were taken to the rehabilitation department, where a physical therapist helped you exercise an arm, leg, or other joint.)
   1. Satisfied
   2. Dissatisfied

Social work—(A social worker saw you just prior to discharge to help you apply for home health services, admission to a nursing home, medical assistance, or a similar service.)
   1. Satisfied
   2. Dissatisfied

Respiratory therapy—(You were given therapy to expand your lungs and help you breathe.)
   1. Satisfied
   2. Dissatisfied

Radiology services—(You were taken to the radiology department where one of the following tests was performed: X-ray, CT scan, Mammogram, Ultrasound, or MRI.)
   1. Satisfied
   2. Dissatisfied

a patient receive all or even most of the services a hospital has to offer. Nevertheless, numerous questionnaires are constructed as though every patient received every service offered. Consider the questionnaire that asks respondents to indicate whether they were satisfied or dissatisfied with a list of services. What answer can be given by the respondent who did not receive one or more of the services? Frequently, the respondent leaves such questions unanswered. Unanswered questions are problematic, because the researcher cannot distinguish between intentional nonresponses (that is, "does not apply") and unintentional nonresponses (that is, overlooked questions). The same dilemma occurs when a questionnaire lists a number of services and asks the respondent to place a check beside each service that he or she received. If respondents do not check a service, the researcher is left to ponder whether the omission means that they did not receive the service or whether they inadvertently skipped the question.

Figure 8-4 illustrates branching, an effective way to structure such questions. First, respondents are asked whether the service was received. If they respond "yes," they are then asked to rate how satisfied they were with the service. If the response is "no" or "unsure," they are instructed to skip to the next service. The "unsure" option is included for those who remain uncertain about actual services received.

Figure 8-5 illustrates an alternative to branching, where "does not apply" is included as a response alternative. Using this format requires less space than the branching method. However, the authors' experience in pilot testing these questions suggests that some respondents are frustrated by being asked to rate services they did not receive, even if "does not apply" is offered as an alternative. The authors also have found that this response format generates a slightly higher proportion of nonresponses than the branching format.

Figure 8-4. Branching Question

Hospital Services

Please indicate which of the following services you received during your hospitalization. If you received a service, please circle "Yes" and indicate how satisfied you were with the service. If you did not receive the service, circle "No." If you are unsure whether you received the service, circle "Unsure."

Physical therapy—(You were taken to the rehabilitation department, where a physical therapist helped you exercise an arm, leg, or other joint.)
  1. Yes ─────────┐
  2. No
  3. Unsure   ↓
      How satisfied were you with the service?
        1. Completely satisfied
        2. Somewhat satisfied
        3. Neutral
        4. Somewhat dissatisfied
        5. Completely dissatisfied

Social work—(A social worker saw you just prior to discharge to help you apply for home health services, admission to a nursing home, medical assistance, or a similar service.)
  1. Yes ─────────┐
  2. No
  3. Unsure   ↓
      How satisfied were you with the service?
        1. Completely satisfied
        2. Somewhat satisfied
        3. Neutral
        4. Somewhat dissatisfied
        5. Completely dissatisfied

Figure 8-5. "Does Not Apply" Response Alternative

Hospital Services

Please rate how satisfied you were with the following services during your hospital stay. A brief description of each service is provided. If you did not receive a service, please circle "Does not apply."

Physical therapy—(You were taken to the rehabilitation department, where a physical therapist helped you exercise an arm, leg, or other joint.)
  1. Completely satisfied
  2. Somewhat satisfied
  3. Neutral
  4. Somewhat dissatisfied
  5. Completely dissatisfied
  6. Does not apply

Global Questions

In an effort to keep a questionnaire short, researchers may construct global questions about services. A typical item found in many surveys is "Please rate how satisfied you were with hospital meals." Assume that this item produces the following response distribution: 15 percent of respondents said that they were "completely satisfied," 40 percent were "somewhat satisfied," 20 percent were "neutral," 15 percent were "somewhat dissatisfied," and 10 percent were "completely dissatisfied."

The director of nutritional services, on receiving these results, may respond with a note asking, "What does this mean?" The researcher proceeds to explain that 25 percent of the respondents were "somewhat or completely dissatisfied." Now the director asks, "Why were 25 percent dissatisfied?" The researcher responds, "I don't know." The fact is that some respondents may have been dissatisfied because the food had no taste, others may not have liked the selection, some may have wanted meals served at different times, some may have been satisfied with supper but not with lunch, and the remainder may have been too sick to enjoy eating.

Whenever a global item is being considered for use in measuring satisfaction, one should apply the "so what" test by asking, what can one do with the results? If no one cares about the answer, why ask the question? But if someone is going to ask, "What do the results mean?" the researcher should make sure that the global question is useful.

Another concern about global satisfaction questions is that they tend to yield disproportionately positive ratings (for example, completely or somewhat satisfied). This occurs even when other questions show that respondents are dissatisfied with various aspects of the service being measured (Ware, Snyder, and Wright, 1976).

Some researchers attempt to get specific information from global questions by using them as a screen for follow-up questions regarding what dissatisfied the respondent (see figure 8-6). The limitation to using open-ended follow-up questions, particularly on self-report questionnaires, is that some respondents fail to answer follow-up questions. For those who do respond, responses vary in length and legibility. When readable responses are provided, they require coding, which is a time-consuming task. Follow-up questions appear to work better in telephone surveys, where interviewers can probe for more detailed answers or clarifications.

The recommended alternative to global questions is to ask specific questions about specific, relevant service attributes. In the previous example, the researcher could have asked about the temperature of the food, the selection on the menu, the taste and quantity of food, and so on. These questions would more likely satisfy the needs of decision makers.

Figure 8-6. Global Question with Open-Ended Follow-Up

Please rate how satisfied you were with the hospital meals on the scale below. If you were either "Somewhat dissatisfied" or "Completely dissatisfied," please tell us what dissatisfied you.
1. Completely satisfied
2. Somewhat satisfied
3. Neutral
4. Somewhat dissatisfied
5. Completely dissatisfied

What dissatisfied you about the meals?

_____
_____
_____

All of this notwithstanding, global satisfaction questions can be useful. When time or space constraints limit the number of questions, it is better to ask global questions about support services (for example, dietary, X ray, social services) than no questions at all. Global questions can provide a rough indicator of patient satisfaction and alert the researcher to the need for a more extensive study of a particular service. When trend data from these measures suggest a consistent decline in satisfaction scores for at least three time periods, a focused study should be conducted. Once the problem is assessed, changes can be made and global scores improved, at which time the special study can be terminated. Global questions also can provide the dependent variables for regression models such as those discussed in chapter 3.

Vague Questions

Figure 8-7 illustrates another type of poorly structured question—the vague question. After reading the original question, one might ask: What is consistent nursing? Is it consistent when the same number of nurses are on day and evening shifts? When nurses check on patients with the same frequency throughout the day? When all nurses address patients as Mr., Ms., or Mrs.? Assume that 50 percent of respondents did say, "Yes, nursing was consistent." How should the researcher or manager interpret this result? Obviously, vague questions generate vague (and uninterpretable) answers. If the researcher considers nursing consistency to mean availability to answer patients' questions, then the question should be so worded.

A commonly used vague word is *efficient*. What are efficient admissions staff—or, for that matter, efficient nurses, physicians, or researchers? The revision in figure 8-7 shows how to rephrase a question that contains a vague word like *efficient* for greater clarity.

Objectionable Questions

When patients find questions to be objectionable, they may skip them and disregard other questions. Typically, objectionable questions are those that seem unrelated to the stated purpose of the survey or that ask personal questions without explaining their purpose. The questions that follow illustrate these problems:

- Why were you hospitalized?
- At what other hospitals have you been hospitalized?

Figure 8-7. Vague Questions

Original Question:	Revised Question:
The nursing was consistent.	Nurses were always available to answer my questions.
1. Strongly agree	1. Strongly agree
2. Somewhat agree	2. Somewhat agree
3. Neutral	3. Neutral
4. Somewhat disagree	4. Somewhat disagree
5. Strongly disagree	5. Strongly disagree
Original Question:	**Revised Question:**
The admissions staff were efficient.	Upon arriving at the hospital, I was promptly admitted.
1. Strongly agree	1. Strongly agree
2. Somewhat agree	2. Somewhat agree
3. Neutral	3. Neutral
4. Somewhat disagree	4. Somewhat disagree
5. Strongly disagree	5. Strongly disagree

- What is your address?
- How many years of education did you complete?
- How old are you?

After reading these questions, the respondent is likely to mutter, "What is this survey about?" It is important that questionnaires be constructed so that the first few questions the respondent reads or hears are consistent with the stated purpose of the survey. Moreover, questions about respondents' demographic or other personal characteristics should be near the end of the questionnaire and prefaced by an explanation of why this information is requested.

Figure 8-8 illustrates how age, education, and address questions can be modified and accompanied by an explanation of purpose. Note also that the example indicates that a particular question can be skipped if it is objectionable. In this way, the researcher helps ensure that respondents will answer the remaining items as directed instead of skipping the entire section.

Biased Questions

Questions can bias or unduly influence respondents by suggesting a "right way" to answer or by providing inappropriate response options. Instead of obtaining an accurate account of how the person actually feels or evaluates the service, the question influences the responses by the way it is asked.

Figure 8-9 illustrates how, through the question's preface, respondents can be led to believe that there is a right or expected response. If "most people" believe that health care costs too much, does the respondent dare go against what most people think? Many respondents will feel they should be in step with the majority, although some will take the opposite point of view to prove they are different. In either case, the respondent's answer is influenced by the wording of the question. The revision in figure 8-9 shows that when prefaces are used, they should provide both sides of the issue (revision 1) or be worded neutrally (revision 2).

Questions with unbalanced response categories can also bias results. A common mistake is to give respondents more options for positive responses than for negative responses, which biases them to check a positive option (see figure 8-10). Notice that the revision of this question offers an equal number of categories for "satisfied" and

Figure 8-8. Explaining the Purpose of Personal Questions

Personal Questions—The following questions are for statistical purposes only. They are used to help us understand how different groups of people feel about our services. If you object to answering a specific question, please skip it and go on to the next question.

1. What age group are you in?
   - ☐ Under 18
   - ☐ 18 to 24
   - ☐ 25 to 34
   - ☐ 35 to 44
   - ☐ 45 to 54
   - ☐ 55 to 64
   - ☐ 65 to 74
   - ☐ 75 or older

2. What is the highest level of education that you have achieved?
   a. Less than high school diploma
   b. High school graduate
   c. Associate's degree (two-year degree)
   d. Bachelor's degree
   e. Some graduate school or more

3. What is your zip code? ___ ___ ___ ___ ___

Figure 8-9. Biased Questions

Original Question:
Most people feel that health care costs are too high. Do you consider the cost of your hospitalization to be too high?
1. Yes
2. No
3. Don't know

(Revision 1)
Some people feel that health care costs are too high, while others consider the costs to be reasonable. Do you consider the cost of your hospitalization to be too high or reasonable?
1. Too high
2. Reasonable
3. Don't know

(Revision 2)
Next, I would like to ask a question about the cost of your hospitalization. Do you consider the cost to be too high, about right, or too low?
1. Too high
2. About right
3. Too low
4. Don't know

Figure 8-10. Biased Response Categories

Original Question:
Please rate how satisfied you were with hospital food using the following scale.
1. Completely satisfied
2. Mostly satisfied
3. Dissatisfied

Revised Question:
Please rate how satisfied you were with hospital food using the following scale.
1. Very satisfied
2. Somewhat satisfied
3. Neutral
4. Somewhat dissatisfied
5. Very dissatisfied

"dissatisfied" responses. In conjunction with the use of identical adverbs for both negative and positive responses (that is, "very" and "somewhat"), this creates a balanced scale with equal-appearing intervals. (This also has implications for scale construction, which will be addressed later in this chapter.)

Variations in Wording

Frequently, questionnaires are administered to assess changes in patient satisfaction over a period of time. At times, the researcher may be tempted to alter question wording or make other changes, hoping to improve the questionnaire. Unfortunately, although the changes improve the questionnaire, they also may dramatically influence responses, thereby invalidating comparisons with earlier surveys.

This point is illustrated in the following case of a primary care practice's open-ended global satisfaction question. On examining the responses to question 1 (see figure 8-11), the physicians in the practice were disappointed that they could not identify the sources of patient dissatisfaction. As a result, they asked the researcher to modify the question to pinpoint what was dissatisfying to patients (question 2). The responses indicated that patients were unhappy with the parking, billing, waiting, and so on. After several organizational changes were made to address patients' concerns, the physicians wanted to know whether patients were more satisfied than when the questionnaire was first administered. Unfortunately, because the satisfaction question had been altered, this comparison could not be made. The problem could have been prevented had the researcher and the physicians thought through the objectives of the satisfaction study before collecting the initial data.

Figure 8-11. Changing Question Wording

1. How satisfied are you with the care you received from the physician?

   Typical responses:
   I like my physician.
   I'm real satisfied.
   I'm very satisfied.
   He's so nice.
   His care is the best.
   He's usually pretty good.

2. What dissatisfied you with the care you received from the physician?

   Typical responses:
   He's frequently late.
   I can never find parking.
   Can't think of anything.
   He charges too much.
   He's always in a hurry.
   His office is sometimes cold.
   I can never reach him by phone.
   I can't understand the bill.

The pilot-test phase is the time to examine results and ask whether the type of information being obtained will address the objectives of the study. When a time-series or trend study is being conducted, questionnaire modifications should only be made prior to the first baseline measurement. When one wishes to compare two or more services (for example, Hospital A with Hospital B), the identical instrument must be used for both. (Of course, comparisons between Hospital A and Hospital B can introduce other problems, as discussed earlier in this book.)

Other changes that may invalidate comparisons include (1) altering response formats (for example, changing from open-ended to closed-ended response formats or vice versa), (2) switching response categories (for example, changing from satisfaction to quality scale ratings), (3) modifying the number of response levels in the rating scales, (4) changing the order of questions, (5) adopting new sampling procedures, and (6) altering the method of administration (for example, changing from a self-administered written survey to a telephone survey). (See chapter 12 for a further discussion of these evaluation design issues.)

Response Construction

Properly constructed response formats ensure that the data gathered from standardized questionnaires are usable. For open-ended questions, responses often need to be categorized consistently before they can be tabulated. For closed-ended questions, responses need to be specified so that relevant response options are included.

Open-Ended Questions

In open-ended questions, respondents are asked structured questions but are allowed to answer in their own words. When open-ended questions are used in "other-administered" satisfaction interviews, answers are recorded verbatim by the interviewer. In self-report questionnaires, blank spaces are left after each question for respondents to record their own answers.

Open-ended questions are often employed during the early phases of questionnaire development, when the researcher is exploring the appropriate wording and scaling of response options. By allowing the respondent to answer in his or her own words, the researcher gains an appreciation for how the person thinks about the issue, the language that is used in verbalizing an answer, and the range of possible responses. Open-ended questions may also be used when the qualitative phase of a study is omitted. In such instances, the researcher may attempt to utilize both open-ended and closed-ended questions in a survey instrument to obtain both qualitative and quantitative data. The danger in employing both methods simultaneously is that neither will be done well.

Answers to open-ended questions vary considerably in length and detail from person to person. Some respondents will provide an elaborate answer, while others will be terse in their reply. When respondents provide brief or sketchy answers to such questions in administered interviews, the interviewer can always probe for additional information. However, in self-report questionnaires, the researcher must accept whatever is written, regardless of its length or content. As a result, it is recommended that open-ended questions be used primarily in other-administered questionnaires.

Usually, open-ended questions also generate a wider range of answers than closed-ended questions. In part, this is due to the fact that open-ended questions allow the respondent the freedom to qualify answers. These qualifications, which occur frequently, provide the researcher with a deeper understanding of the respondent's feelings and thoughts about the issue.

Unfortunately, this richness of response has certain well-defined drawbacks when it comes time to analyze and summarize data. Categories must be created and responses coded if this information is to be statistically analyzed. In large surveys, coding manuals have to be created, and coders must be trained and coordinated to process responses. In addition to being time-consuming, this coding process can introduce errors in the data. Frequently, researchers will have two or more persons independently code the data and then compare the results to determine intercoder reliability. When coders do not achieve at least 80 percent agreement, the categorization system may need revision, coders may need additional training, or both.

Closed-Ended Questions

Closed-ended questions provide respondents with predetermined answers from which to choose. For some questions, response options may be dichotomous (for example, "yes" or "no"); others may contain a frequency scale (for example, "very often," "often," "sometimes," "never") or an intensity scale (for example, "strongly agree," "somewhat agree," "neutral," "somewhat disagree," "strongly disagree"); and yet others may consist of a variety of discrete categorical replies (for example, "single," "married," "separated," "divorced," "widowed").

An advantage to closed-end questions is that the response options help clarify the meaning of the question as well as indicate the dimension along which answers are sought. Recall the variety of answers given in response to the question, "How satisfied are you with the care you received from the physician?" (see figure 8-11). For some respondents, the meaning they attributed to the question evoked an affective response (for example, "I like my physician" or "He's so nice"), others responded along a quality dimension (for example, "His care is the best" or "He's usually pretty good"), and yet others responded along a satisfaction dimension (for example, "I'm real satisfied" or "I'm very satisfied"). Had this question provided response options, such as an intensity scale ranging from "very satisfied" to "very dissatisfied," more respondents would have known that the relevant response dimension was "satisfaction with care." The scale also would have provided a standardized intensity continuum on which respondents could rate their satisfaction.

Closed-ended questions also have the advantage of allowing responses to be precoded with numerical values (for example, 5 = "very satisfied" through 1 = "very dissatisfied"). Such responses can be entered directly into the computer file without being transcribed to coding sheets. Closed-ended questions are also easier and faster for respondents to answer. Instead of the respondent struggling with the meaning of each question, trying to recall exactly what transpired during the service experience, and so on, the respondent's memory is aided by the response options provided. However, this aid can become a disadvantage if respondents do not exert any effort to think through their answers.

Another disadvantage of closed-ended questions is that they take considerably more time to construct than open-ended questions. Not only must the researcher labor at developing clear, unambiguous, and precise questions, but he or she must ensure that relevant response options are included. Closed-ended questions also tend to force an opinion, even when the respondent may not have one. For this reason, closed-ended questions should include "don't know" or "neutral" response options unless there is clear justification for forcing an opinion.

Despite the uniform wording in closed-ended questions, interpretation can differ, particularly when respondents differ in education and ethnicity. Weiss (1975) suggests that individuals vary in how they think about the services they receive. For this reason, qualitative pretesting of questions among a range of respondent groups is important. (Pretesting is discussed more fully at the end of this chapter.) Once questions have passed qualitative assessment criteria, they should be administered to a sample of patients and be statistically analyzed for response distributions and response variation associated with the attributive characteristics of the respondent (for example, age, gender, education, ethnicity). (This point is discussed more fully in chapter 11, which covers reliability and validity.)

In summary, closed-ended questions have several advantages over open-ended questions when the researcher is conducting a quantitative assessment of patient satisfaction. If the researcher understands the satisfaction dimension under study, the way patients think about the dimension, the language they use to express their thoughts and feelings, and the range of expected responses, then closed-ended questions should be used. If these conditions are not met, then the researcher should begin with a qualitative research approach (see chapter 7). Open-ended structured questions may provide information that is needed before closed-ended questions can be developed.

Exhaustive Categories

In closed-ended questions, the response options should always be both *exhaustive* and *mutually exclusive*. Exhaustive categories include the range of possible responses that might be expected. For example, assume that a female respondent, separated but not divorced from her husband, is asked to indicate her marital status by the question in figure 8-12. Because the response options do not include "separated," how should she respond? Some would leave the question unanswered, others would write in "separated," and still others would check "divorced." This problem is avoided by including the option "separated," which then makes the options exhaustive.

Occasionally, the researcher encounters a situation in which several response options apply only to a very small portion of the population under study. If every conceivable reply were listed, considerable space would be required. A good example is religious preference. In most areas of the United States, the overwhelming majority of individuals are Protestant, Catholic, or Jewish. Rather than list every conceivable religion (for example, Hindu, Islam, Ancestor Worship, and so forth), it is better to offer an "other" category. Figure 8-13 illustrates two ways that the "other" category can be used. If the researcher is not interested in why the respondent selected "other," version 1 should be used. Version 2 illustrates that by providing a blank with the instruction "please specify," additional information can be obtained.

Figure 8-12. Exhaustive Response Options

Original Question:	Revised Question:
What is your marital status?	What is your marital status?
1. Single	1. Single
2. Married	2. Married
3. Divorced	3. Separated
4. Widowed	4. Divorced
	5. Widowed

When "other" is used as a response option, the authors generally recommend version 2; the researcher can always ignore the explanation given and use the precoded value for "other." However, should the need arise, detailed responses can always be coded and the data analyzed. Also, monitoring the distribution of responses will alert the researcher when the precoded response options need to be expanded.

Mutually Exclusive Categories

Mutually exclusive response categories do not overlap. To determine if responses are mutually exclusive, a researcher might ask: Could a respondent select more than one accurate answer? Figure 8-14 illustrates overlapping response categories regarding religious preference. Lutheran and Methodist are denominations of the Protestant religion; that is, Lutheran and Methodist are subsets of the response Protestant. The revised question illustrates that if the researcher is interested in knowing both the type of religion and (for Protestants) their denomination, then a branching question should be used.

Another common mistake is providing numerical response groupings that overlap, typically in questions about age, income, or days hospitalized. As shown in figure 8-15, if a person were hospitalized for two, four, six, eight, or ten days, two answers would be possible. In the revision, only one answer is possible, because the grouped numbers do not overlap.

Figure 8-13. "Other" as a Response Option

(Version 1)
What is your religion?
1. Catholic
2. Jewish
3. Protestant
4. Other

(Version 2)
What is your religion?
1. Catholic
2. Jewish
3. Protestant
4. Other _____
       (Please Specify)

Figure 8-14. Mutually Exclusive Response Categories

Original Question:
What is your religion?
1. Catholic
2. Jewish
3. Lutheran
4. Methodist
5. Protestant
6. Other

Revised Question:
What is your religion?
1. Catholic
2. Jewish
3. Protestant ─┐
4. Other   │
               ▼
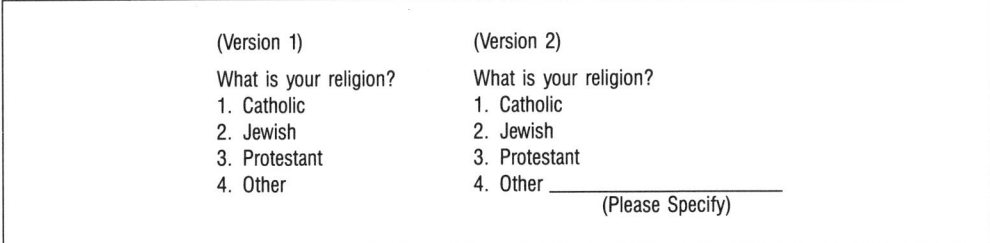
If your religion is Protestant, what denomination is it?
1. Adventist
2. Baptist
3. Congregationalist
4. Episcopalian
5. Lutheran
6. Methodist
7. Mormon
8. Pentecostal
9. Presbyterian
10. Unitarian
11. United Church of Christ
12. Other _____
         (Please Specify)

Figure 8-15. Mutually Exclusive Response Grouping

Original Question:	Revised Question:
How many days did you remain in the hospital?	How many days did you remain in the hospital?
1. 1–2 days	1. 1–2 days
2. 2–4 days	2. 3–4 days
3. 4–6 days	3. 5–6 days
4. 6–8 days	4. 7–8 days
5. 8–10 days	5. 9–10 days
6. 10 or more days	6. 11 or more days

Rating Scales

In assessing patient satisfaction, the researcher usually wishes to measure the intensity or strength of the feelings the patient has about various service dimensions. Closed-ended questions that provide a gradation of responses along a single dimension are ideally suited to this task. These questions are described as having scaled-response formats, frequently referred to as rating scales. Although there are several ways to construct rating scales, they all share a common characteristic: The respondent places a service dimension on some point along a graded continuum, and each point has a numerical value.

Satisfaction Scales

Many survey instruments ask a series of questions that begin "How satisfied were you with," and then specify the service attribute (for example, friendliness of nurses or availability of physicians) for rating on a satisfaction scale. Some questionnaires offer scales with only two levels (that is, "satisfied" or "dissatisfied"), but most use four or five levels. Two-level scales are generally considered too coarse and lose a significant amount of information.

Figure 8-16 illustrates a typical two-level satisfaction scale and a five-level satisfaction scale, where respondents are asked to indicate whether they were satisfied or dissatisfied with the availability of nurses. The two-level scale divides respondents into satisfied and dissatisfied groups. This grouping assumes that respondents at the same level (for example, all persons checking "satisfied") are equally satisfied or dissatisfied—typically an erroneous assumption, as the following example illustrates.

Hospital A had been using a two-level scale format for two years in its self-report, mail-out satisfaction survey. When the researcher suggested that considerable information was being lost because the scale was too coarse, the hospital's administration wanted data to support this assertion. Management agreed to conduct a split-ballot experiment in which each of two samples of recently discharged inpatients would receive different versions of the questionnaire. Four hundred patients were randomly assigned, 200 patients to each questionnaire. Patients in sample 1 received the questionnaire with a two-level scale format and those in sample 2 received the one with a five-level scale format. Of 400 questionnaires that were mailed, 218 were returned.

The two samples were found to be comparable with respect to age, educational level, gender, and rate of return of the questionnaire. Table 8-1 provides the distribution of responses for each sample on one representative question regarding the availability of nurses. In comparing the results, one can see that 90.8 percent of sample 1 rated themselves as "satisfied," whereas in sample 2, 41.3 percent and 42.2 percent rated themselves as "very satisfied" and "somewhat satisfied," respectively. Similarly, the 9.2 percent "dissatisfied" respondents in sample 1 would not seem all to be equally dissatisfied, in that in sample 2, 6.4 percent of respondents were "somewhat dissatisfied"

Figure 8-16. Two- and Five-Level Satisfaction Scales

Original Scale (given to sample 1):	Revised Scale (given to sample 2):
How satisfied were you with the availability of nurses? 1. Satisfied 2. Dissatisfied	How satisfied were you with the availability of nurses? 1. Very satisfied 2. Somewhat satisfied 3. Neutral 4. Somewhat dissatisfied 5. Very dissatisfied

Table 8-1. Distribution of Responses for Satisfaction Question Using Two- and Five-Level Scales

Sample 1		Sample 2	
Satisfied	90.8%	Very satisfied	41.3%
Dissatisfied	9.2	Somewhat satisfied	42.2
		Neutral	7.3
		Somewhat dissatisfied	6.4
		Very dissatisfied	2.8

and 2.8 percent were "very dissatisfied." These data support the assertion that satisfaction is a continuous, as opposed to a dichotomous, variable. When two-level scales are used, considerable information *is* lost, owing to the coarseness of the scaling.

Two-level scales also produce less variability in the data, making it difficult to detect differences between groups (for example, Hospital A versus Hospital B), changes over time (for example, quarter 1 versus quarter 2), and association between measures. Returning to the case illustration, Hospital A had been tracking patient satisfaction for more than eight calendar quarters. On a 12-item instrument, using a two-level scale format, staff compared the results of each quarter with the results of the immediately preceding quarter over the two-year period. This generated 84 comparisons (12 items × 7 quarterly comparisons). Over this period, only 4 comparisons revealed differences large enough to achieve statistical significance. Using the traditional .05 level of statistical significance, one would expect at least 4 out of 84 comparisons to achieve significance due to random fluctuations in the data. The difference between quarterly scores would have been easier to detect had the hospital used five-level scales. There simply would have been greater variability in the data.

Quality Scales

Many patient satisfaction questionnaires use a four- or five-level quality scaling instead of the satisfaction scales mentioned in the previous section. Typically, the respondent is asked to rate a service dimension on a scale ranging from "poor" to "excellent." As shown in table 8-2, this type of scaling logically follows when the question is concerned with quality. However, it tends to be somewhat cumbersome when applied to other types of questions.

In addition, some researchers have confused the use of Likert-type scaling (in which respondents are asked for their agreement or disagreement with statements) with quality scaling. Statements such as "Staff were courteous," "Nurses were available," and "My room was always clean" do not lend themselves to "poor, fair, ... excellent" responses. The revised version has better wording. Another solution is to leave the items worded in the original form and use an agree/disagree scale.

Service Attribute Scales

Another type of scaling does not mention the word *satisfaction* or *quality* but assumes that a particular service attribute contributes to patient satisfaction. Instead of respondents being asked to indicate their levels of satisfaction, they are provided with gradations of the service attribute itself. Figure 8-17 shows that these types of questions typically start with the word *how,* and then indicate the attribute to be rated. This type of scaling requires that each item have its own uniquely worded scale.

When questionnaire length is a concern, particularly in self-report questionnaires, this type of scaling is inefficient because of the considerable space required. Responses typically must be listed vertically under the item, because responses are different for each question. When scaling is uniform across questions, response categories can be placed to the right of questions and arranged in a column (see table 8-2). Because service attribute scaling has a more conversational quality, this format is often used in

Table 8-2. Quality Scaling

Please rate the following items on the scale provided. Circle the number that corresponds to your answers (for example, Poor = 1, Fair = 2, Good = 3, and so on).

Items:	Poor	Fair	Good	Very Good	Excellent
The quality of nurses.	1	2	3	4	5
The quality of physicians.	1	2	3	4	5
(Problems)					
Staff were courteous.	1	2	3	4	5
Nurses were available whenever I called.	1	2	3	4	5
My room was always clean.	1	2	3	4	5
(Revised)					
The courteousness of staff was	1	2	3	4	5
The availability of nurses was	1	2	3	4	5
The cleanliness of my room was	1	2	3	4	5

Figure 8-17. Service Attribute Scaling

How available were nurses when you needed one? Were they:
1. Never available
2. Seldom available
3. Usually available
4. Almost always available
5. Always available

How concerned were nurses about your comfort? Were they:
1. Not concerned
2. Somewhat concerned
3. Moderately concerned
4. Very concerned
5. Extremely concerned

How knowledgeable were nurses about your care? Were they:
1. Not knowledgeable
2. Somewhat knowledgeable
3. Moderately knowledgeable
4. Very knowledgeable
5. Extremely knowledgeable

telephone questionnaires. As will be discussed in chapter 10, on telephone surveys, questions can be worded so that the service attribute scale is actually embedded in the question, giving a distinct conversational quality to the question.

Frequency Scales

Frequency scales ask respondents to indicate how often a particular service attribute occurred. This type of scaling logically follows when the service attribute involves a behavior; however, this is not always the case with many service attributes. Table 8-3 illustrates that two out of three questions from the previous example can be reworded to ask how often nurses were available or showed concern. On the other hand, knowledge is an attribute characteristic of the person, not a behavior whose execution can be measured. When a person is asked how often nurses were knowledgeable, a non sequitur is created. Obviously, frequency scaling is not appropriate to all service attributes.

Another limitation of frequency scaling is that it lacks a subjective evaluative component, which is the essence of satisfaction ratings. Indicating how often something occurred is not the same as saying how it is perceived. Frequency scaling also assumes that more of a given behavior leads to greater satisfaction. However, the relationship between patient satisfaction and the frequency of a performed service is not always linear. To illustrate this point, assume that a particular patient is a stoic who dislikes nurses being "too available" or showing "too much concern." For this patient, satisfaction may initially increase as availability and concern increase, but it may level off and diminish with greater frequency.

Graphic Scales

Graphic scales provide the respondent with two bipolar characteristics such as extremely dissatisfied to extremely satisfied, very poor to very good, very incompetent to very competent, very unfriendly to very friendly, and so on. Sometimes also referred to as visual analogue scales, they typically provide a horizontal line between these two extremes suggesting a linear continuum. Respondents are instructed to place a vertical line through that point on the line that best represents their answer. Some researchers provide numerical values along the continuum, typically 7-, 9-, or 10-point scales. Others omit numerical values and provide a midpoint anchor labeled "neutral." Table 8-4 shows examples of both scaling options. When numerical values are omitted, the scale is scored by using a ruler to measure where the vertical line crosses the horizontal axis. One of the advantages of omitting numerical values is that it allows for greater discrimination among scores. A 5-inch line can easily be scored at ⅛-inch intervals, generating a 40-point scale. With this greater precision also comes the opportunity to attain statistical significance with smaller relative differences in scores between sample groups or over time.

Table 8-3. Frequency Scaling

How Often:	Never	Seldom	Often	Very Often	All the Time
Inappropriate Question:					
Were nurses knowledgeable about your care?	0	1	2	3	4
Appropriate Question:					
Were nurses available when you needed one?	0	1	2	3	4
Did nurses show concern for your comfort?	0	1	2	3	4

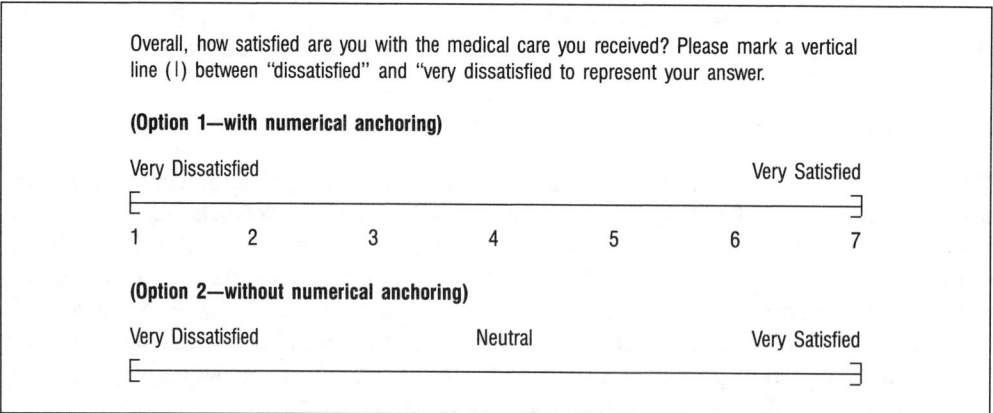

Table 8-4. Graphic Scaling

Likert-Type Scales

With Likert-type scaling, the researcher generates a number of statements, instead of questions, about various service attributes. As table 8-5 shows, these statements can be either positive (for example, "Nurses treated me with respect") or negative (for example, "Nurses were frequently rude"). Each statement is then rated on a scale ranging from "strongly agree" to "strongly disagree." To capture the continuous nature of the underlying attribute, most researchers use either a four- or five-level scale. The five-level scale with a neutral midpoint is recommended because respondents are not forced to give an opinion if they do not have one.

Summated Scales

Summated scales provide distinct advantages over some other scaling methods. To understand these advantages, it is helpful to look at how scores from individual items are used. Many researchers assess patient satisfaction with a service dimension using scores from an individual question or item. For example, they may report that 65 percent of respondents indicated that the quality of nursing was "excellent," 25 percent said it was "very good," and the remainder said it was "good." This distribution of scores may be compared to scores from previous time periods to determine whether the quality of nursing care has changed; or a comparison may be made between hospitals, floors, or units to see which locations provide better services.

Unfortunately, these comparisons can be misleading because individual scores tend to have considerable measurement error. Ware and others (1976) have found that when a questionnaire is readministered at brief intervals (for example, six weeks), individual item scores can produce inconsistent or unreliable results. Therefore, what appears to be a significant change in scores may very well reflect measurement error. The solution to this problem is to create a multi-item scale to measure a service dimension. When items are internally consistent and combined into a summated score, the results are considerably more reliable. (This point will be discussed in depth in chapter 11.)

Another advantage of summated scales is that finer distinctions can be made among respondents, and scores have greater variability. Take, for example, a ten-item Likert-type summated scale with a five-level scale format, where "strongly agree" = 5 and "strongly disagree" = 1. A respondent who strongly agrees with all items would obtain a score of 50 (10 × 5), while another respondent might strongly disagree with all items, generating a score of 10 (10 × 1). On any single item, the range of scores is only 1 to 5, whereas it is 10 to 50 on a ten-item summated scale.

Table 8-5. Likert-Type Scaling

Please rate the extent to which you agree or disagree with the following statements about the care you received.

Statement:	Strongly Disagree	Disagree	Neutral	Agree	Strongly Agree
Nurses treated me with respect.	1	2	3	4	5
Nurses were always available.	1	2	3	4	5
Nurses were frequently rude.*	1	2	3	4	5
Doctors answered my questions.	1	2	3	4	5
Doctors were always in a hurry.*	1	2	3	4	5
Doctors were always available.	1	2	3	4	5
Meals were frequently late.*	1	2	3	4	5
The food was delicious.	1	2	3	4	5

Note: The asterisk indicates negatively worded items requiring recoding for summated scales.

Although it is possible to combine scores from questions that use many of the previously mentioned types of rating scales (for example, quality scaling, frequency scaling, satisfaction scaling), we recommend Likert-type summated scales for the same reason given by Ware and others (1983). The Likert-type approach allows for a uniform questionnaire response format, with choices listed to the right of items in an array, which requires considerably fewer pages of questionnaire space. Second, identical response scales for all items make it easier for respondents to complete the survey. After listening to or reading the first few statements with responses, the respondent has memorized the scale. From this point on, the respondent need only concentrate on the statement and select a scale level. Third, the wording of statements can easily be modified to obtain fairly normal response distributions. When satisfaction or quality scaling is used with questions, the distribution of responses tends to be highly skewed, with an excessive endorsement of favorable responses (that is, "excellent/very good" or "very satisfied/somewhat satisfied").

Scale Creation

The first step in creating Likert-type summated scales is to specify the service dimension (for example, satisfaction with nursing care) and what specific attributes of the dimension are likely to contribute to satisfaction. Qualitative research is helpful in identifying these attributes. Assume that the researcher is developing a satisfaction questionnaire for inpatient care and begins with the nursing care dimension. Based on qualitative interviews and focus group results, the researcher concludes that patients expect nurses (1) to be available when needed, (2) to show concern and caring toward patients, and (3) to be technically competent and thorough. Next, the researcher generates a pool of approximately 30 items, 10 for each of the above-mentioned areas. To control for acquiescent response set effects (that is, a tendency to agree with statements regardless of content), half of the items are positively worded (for example, "Nurses always treated me with respect") and the others are negatively worded (for example, "Nurses were frequently rude") (Ware, 1978).

As illustrated in table 8-5, these items are listed to the left, with the agree/disagree scaling to the right. Once the questionnaire is constructed, it should be pretested on a small sample of patients, about 15 to 20, for readability, clarity, meaning, and so on. After the necessary changes in wording have been made, the scale is pilot tested on a larger sample (100–150), and the results are statistically analyzed to determine which items are most strongly correlated with the selected service dimension. Items that are poorly correlated are assumed to be measuring a different dimension and therefore unreliable. Items with the highest interitem correlations are retained, and the remainder are discarded. (The reasons for doing so are explained in greater depth in chapter 11.)

Negatively worded items require that the scale coding for these items be recoded so that higher scores reflect more favorable ratings on that service attribute. Take, for example, the item "Nurses were frequently rude" in table 8-5. To disagree with this item produces a better rating of nurses than to agree, yet the existing coding gives agreement a higher numerical value than disagreement. To recode the scale values on negatively worded items in table 8-5, "strongly agree" would be recoded from 5 to 1, "agree" from 4 to 2, "disagree" from 2 to 4, and "strongly disagree" from 5 to 1. "Neutral" would remain 3.

Once scores on negatively worded items have been recoded, individual item scores for a particular service dimension (for example, nursing) are added together, generating a summation score for that dimension. On a ten-item summated scale with five-level item scaling, scores could range from 10 to 50. Some researchers prefer to convert the summated score to the original scaling metric by dividing it by the total number of individual items composing the summated score. This in no way affects the important statistical characteristics of the scale; it merely moves the decimal point.

Pretesting Questionnaires

The past two decades have witnessed a growing interest in the cognitive processes that underlie how respondents understand and answer survey questions. (Sudman and others [1996] have written about the application of cognitive processes to survey methodology.) Two common methods of determining what respondents think a question means are (1) asking them to think aloud as they complete the questionnaire, with the researcher listening to their thoughts (concurrent method), and (2) asking them to complete the questionnaire and then review their thinking about each question with the researcher (retrospective method). (See Ericsson and Simon [1984] for a detailed discussion of these and other verbal protocols methods.)

The use of these pretest methods will be illustrated with examples taken from a pretest of a satisfaction questionnaire conducted by one of the authors. After ten respondents had completed a self-administered questionnaire, each was interviewed and asked to "put in your own words what you think each question is asking." One item found to be particularly ambiguous was "Nurses were very efficient." (Respondents were asked to rate the item using a Likert-type scale.) Two respondents indicated that the item was a statement about how hard nurses worked, three thought it was about nurses' competence, two thought it was about productiveness, one thought it had to do with not being wasteful, and the remainder indicated being unsure of what it was about. The feedback resulted in this question being revised to "Nurses were very competent and skilled."

Although in this particular example, respondents were asked the meaning of the entire statement, they could have been asked what the word *efficient* meant to them in the context of the statement. As mentioned earlier in this chapter, certain words, such as *efficient*, mean different things to different people.

When questions ask a person to recall a specific behavior or its frequency (doctor visits, X rays received), the researcher wants to understand both what the question means to the respondent and how he or she arrived at the answer. In this case, the researcher might ask the respondent, "How did you come up with your answer?" or "Help me understand how you answered that question." In pretesting the question, "How many times did you see your family doctor this past year?" it was found that seven respondents counted only their own health care visits, while three included times when they took children to the doctor. Time frame can also be a problem. Most people assumed the question to imply "the past twelve months." However, two people answered it for the calendar year, and one person reported answering without precisely defining a time parameter. This feedback led the question to be revised as follows: "Have you had any health problems during the past twelve months, that is, since (Month-Year), for which you went to see your family doctor?" "How many times have you seen your family doctor, since (Month-Year), for these health problems?" Subsequent pretesting indicated that this version of the question was far superior to the original.

With the concurrent think-aloud method, respondents are told that the researcher is interested in both their answers and how they arrive at them. The researcher prompts them to "think aloud as you answer each question and tell me whatever comes to mind." As the researcher listens to the spontaneous comments, the respondent may need to be reminded to "think aloud" several times. When a person appears perplexed by a question, he or she may be asked to paraphrase a question to help the researcher understand how respondents are thinking and retrieving information. Some researchers record respondents' comments by taking notes; others use a tape recorder and then analyze comments later.

A variety of coding systems to classify think-aloud responses have been developed. (For an example of a coding system, see Bickart and Felcher, 1996.) However, it is the authors' contention that developing a coding system for satisfaction questionnaires would have limited returns, relative to the time invested. The authors have found that listening to a tape recording of comments and taking notes is generally sufficient to make substantive revisions. As the researcher reflects on what he or she thought the question was asking, and how respondents actually understood it, alternative phrasing becomes apparent.

Overall, the concurrent think-aloud method and the retrospective approach provide similar information. However, the concurrent approach has an advantage in that it allows the researcher to better capture the respondent's natural reaction to and processing of the questionnaire in toto. The researcher can assess the clarity of instructions that explain how to respond to questions and skip patterns, natural reactions to questions about sensitive issues, and the thematic flow of the instrument. Last, pretesting is not simply a "once-and-done" effort. After questions, response options, and instructions have been revised in light of the pretest results, a subsequent pretest should always be performed. Revising a questionnaire, in and of itself, does not ensure that the next version is error free. Frequently, revisions are just as problematic as the original wording; the errors are just of a different kind. Revisions should continue until the overwhelming majority of respondents understand questions, response options, and instructions as they were intended.

Summary

Constructing standardized questionnaires requires considerable time, thought, and work. The researcher must be clear about the objectives of the study and the nature of the service before instrument development begins. Next, he or she must understand how patients think about the service and know their language and the range of possible answers that might be given to a question before closed-ended questions can be constructed. To reach this level of understanding about the service and its patients usually requires conducting qualitative research prior to quantitative research. The decision on which type of scaling to use for specific questions is based on several factors, including the nature of the service attribute, the degree of measurement error that is acceptable, the length of the questionnaire, the objectives of the study, the type of statistical analysis that the researcher wants to conduct, and related factors. The choice of scaling frequently requires making some compromises once all of these factors are taken into consideration. Pretesting is an essential component of questionnaire development prior to collecting pilot data for statistical analysis.

CHAPTER NINE

Self-Report Questionnaires

In the previous chapter, questionnaire design was addressed from a microperspective, that is, how to construct specific questions along with various response options. This chapter approaches questionnaire design from a macroperspective. The chapter examines the layout of self-administered questionnaires, including appearance, formatting, and ordering and grouping of questions. Next, the chapter discusses methods for distributing written questionnaires that maximize the rate of return. By paying careful attention to the questionnaire's appearance and packaging and to prenotification and follow-up letters, the authors have achieved a return rate as high as 70 percent. Without such attention to detail, mail questionnaires are likely to produce response rates in the single digits. The chapter concludes with a look at the use of electronic technology in administering satisfaction questionnaires, examining both its strengths and its weaknesses.

Questionnaire Construction

The construction of questionnaires involves many elements—appearance, formatting, and question sequence and grouping. When the questionnaire is well executed, each of these elements has the potential to enhance the questionnaire's rate of return.

Appearance

Many researchers invest tremendous effort in designing, pretesting, and revising individual items but delegate layout to an assistant or printer. One might very well ask, what good are perfectly worded items if the survey is unattractive and the layout confusing? Appearance is what the respondent notices first. And appearance conveys a strong message. For example, imagine receiving a questionnaire from your physician with the print so smudged that some questions are barely legible. Regardless of how well each question is constructed, you would be likely to toss the questionnaire into the recycling bin before reading the first question. If you are like many people, you would be insulted, viewing the poor quality as a lack of personal regard. Other recipients might perceive the request as insignificant, reasoning that if the study were of any consequence, the provider would have put more effort into constructing a quality instrument. Still other recipients might refuse to make the extra effort to read and complete a marginally legible questionnaire. Simply put, appearance is crucial to obtaining respondent participation.

What creates a professional appearance? High-quality paper is the first ingredient. Some researchers may reason that lightweight paper should be used to minimize postage and stationery costs. However, when the respondent removes a questionnaire from the envelope, he or she first feels the quality of the paper before reading a single word. Economy paper feels cheap. Second, ink tends to bleed through to the reverse side of economy paper, which also creates an impression of cheapness.

Print quality also affects appearance. The original questionnaire should be printed with a high-quality laser (or comparable) printer and reproduced in a manner that renders copies virtually indistinguishable from the original.

Garish colors and gimmicky logos should be avoided. They tend to create the appearance of an advertising brochure or a solicitation for money. However, a logo can have a positive impact if it is commonly associated with the provider institution and strategically placed on the cover page.

Many feel that the booklet format creates an especially favorable impression. The cover page is reserved for a brief message (40–60 words) and the institution's logo. Because the booklet format allows questions to be printed on both sides of a page, questions can be presented over several pages, thereby disguising the questionnaire's length. An additional advantage of a booklet is that the back cover can be used for the return address and postage metering, thus making a return envelope unnecessary. At the end of the questionnaire, the respondent is instructed to tape the questionnaire closed and drop it in the mail.

Question–Response Formatting

Questionnaires should be user-friendly; that is, completion should require as little time and effort of the respondent as possible. Just as poorly worded questions take their toll on the respondent's patience and willingness to complete a questionnaire, so do poorly formatted instruments. The authors subscribe to many of Dillman's (1978) suggestions for formatting mail surveys and have applied them to satisfaction questionnaires. One of the first suggestions is to create a vertical flow, that is, to list response options down the page instead of across it. Many questionnaire designers are inclined to list response options across the page to minimize the questionnaire's length, thereby reducing postage and stationery expenses. As shown in figure 9-1, this approach requires respondents to move back and forth across the page to select answers and up and down the page to find questions. Moreover, questionnaires formatted horizontally tend to appear crowded. They make distinguishing questions and response options more difficult and increase the likelihood of inadvertent omissions. When the formatting is changed to vertical and response options are indented, a respondent can readily distinguish questions from response options from the layout alone. Another important feature, also illustrated in figure 9-1, is to number each response option one space to the left of each option. This allows the numbers and responses to be aligned vertically, one beneath another, creating a uniform appearance. The researcher also should strive for consistency in numbering response options. Numerical values tend to become associated with certain response options (for example, 1 = yes, 2 = no). Therefore, once a numerical value is assigned to a certain response option, it should be maintained throughout the questionnaire. (An additional advantage is numbering precoded responses, thereby facilitating the processing of data by key entry staff.)

An exception to the vertical flow principle occurs when several questions in series have identical response options, such as a numerical scale of 1 to 5. Identical response options are common with satisfaction evaluations (for example, very satisfied to very dissatisfied) and Likert-type scaling (for example, strongly agree to strongly disagree).

The authors recommend placing the statement to the left (for example, "Nurses were very courteous") and the response codes—1 to 5—in a linear array to the right. At the top of each column in the array is the heading for that particular scale anchor point description (see table 9-1). When there is considerable distance between the item and the response codes, a series of dots, called leaders, can be used as a visual aid to make the connection between the question and the response code.

To help readers distinguish between questions and answers, response options might be printed in all caps or boldface. To ensure that instructions are not confused with response options or questions, they should be placed in parentheses. No matter what format is selected, it should remain consistent throughout the questionnaire.

Question Ordering and Grouping

The first question is of vital importance because many respondents read it to determine what the questionnaire is about. It should always be relevant to the stated purpose of the survey, nonthreatening, and easy to answer. If the first question creates

Figure 9-1. Horizontal versus Vertical Format

Horizontal Format

Overall, how satisfied were you with the care received?
_____ Very satisfied, _____ Somewhat satisfied, _____ Neutral,
_____ Somewhat dissatisfied, _____ Very dissatisfied

What gender are you?
_____ Male   _____ Female

What is the highest level of education that you have achieved?
_____ Less than high school, _____ High school graduate,
_____ Associate's degree, _____ Bachelor's degree,
_____ Graduate degree

Vertical Format

Overall, how satisfied were you with the care received?
1. Very satisfied
2. Somewhat satisfied
3. Neutral
4. Somewhat dissatisfied
5. Very dissatisfied

What gender are you?
1. Male
2. Female

What is the highest level of education that you have achieved?
1. Less than high school
2. High school graduate
3. Associate's degree
4. Bachelor's degree
5. Graduate degree
6. Other _____ (specify)

Table 9-1. Likert-Type Scaling

Please rate the extent to which you agree or disagree with the following statements about the care you received.

Statement:	Strongly Disagree	Disagree	Neutral	Agree	Strongly Agree
Nurses treated me with respect.	1	2	3	4	5
Nurses were always available.	1	2	3	4	5
Nurses were frequently rude.*	1	2	3	4	5
Doctors answered my questions.	1	2	3	4	5
Doctors were always in a hurry.*	1	2	3	4	5
Doctors were always available.	1	2	3	4	5
Meals were frequently late.*	1	2	3	4	5
The food was delicious.	1	2	3	4	5

Note: The asterisk indicates negatively worded items requiring recoding for summated scales.

a favorable impression, respondents are more likely to continue on to subsequent questions instead of discarding the instrument.

Questions should attempt to follow the temporal order of the service experience, beginning with the service recipient's first encounter with the provider and following through to discharge. For an inpatient experience, the researcher should begin with the admission and registration process, followed by transport to the room, orientation to the unit, and so on. In addition to chronological sequencing, questions concerning the same service attributes should be grouped together. This provides continuity to the questionnaire. Moreover, when related questions are asked in a series, they tend to trigger associated memories of that experience. The inclusion of headings or transitional statements between groups of items helps break up repetitive questioning and alerts the respondent to retrieve a different set of memories and evaluations.

Questionnaire Administration

Some health care providers administer patient satisfaction questionnaires before discharge. Others distribute them to patients as they leave, asking that the questionnaire be completed at home and returned through the mail. A third alternative is to mail questionnaires to the patient after discharge.

Predischarge Questionnaire Administration

There are several disadvantages to administering questionnaires while patients are still in a health care setting. The authors' experience suggests that most patients tend to minimize their dissatisfaction while they are still facing their caregivers. Despite assurances of confidentiality, patients fear that a staff person will see their responses. Moreover, those still recovering from serious injuries or illnesses tend to be preoccupied with their own recovery and are not particularly interested in completing a survey. Finally, on the day of discharge, most patients are eager to leave the hospital and do not want to be bothered with filling out another form.

Take-Home Questionnaire Administration

Sending questionnaires home with patients would appear to sidestep the abovementioned disadvantages; however, another problem emerges. It is easy for the questionnaire to get mixed up with discharge papers, misplaced, or simply forgotten. As a result, only 5 to 10 percent are completed and returned – an unacceptably low return rate.

Mail Questionnaire Administration

The best method to administer self-report questionnaires is through the mail, shortly after patient discharge. Even this method, however, will produce an unacceptably low response rate if it is not carried out properly. To achieve an initial response rate of at least 40 percent, the following conditions must be met:

1. A personalized letter of transmittal, with an appropriate message to the recipient, must accompany the questionnaire.
2. The recipient's mailing envelope must be individually typed (no mailing labels) and first-class stamps must be used.
3. The questionnaire must be well constructed and of reasonable length.
4. A preaddressed, stamped or business-return envelope must be included (unless using a booklet format that has the return address and postal metering on the pack page).
5. The survey must be mailed within four to seven days after discharge.

To ensure a high response rate, special attention must be paid to the letter of transmittal and the mailing envelope that will be sent with the questionnaire. Even better results can be achieved when patients are notified beforehand that they will be receiving a questionnaire and when nonrespondents are tracked through follow-up methods and encouraged to return their questionnaires. If, in addition to the itemized conditions noted above, prenotification and follow-up mailings are also used, a response rate of 70 to 80 percent can be expected in most instances. Each of these response-enhancing mechanisms will now be discussed in detail.

Letter of Transmittal

The letter of transmittal is critically important in motivating the recipient to complete and return the patient satisfaction questionnaire by mail. In lieu of a separate letter, many hospitals use the face side of the survey to communicate its purpose. A typical letter begins, "Dear Former Patient." The problem with this approach is that it lacks personalization. Upon receiving the survey, the respondent frequently will reason that "If the hospital doesn't take the time to communicate directly with me, why should I bother responding?" or, "Everyone gets one of these surveys, so if I don't fill it out, nobody will miss it or care."

The letter of transmittal should make each respondent feel as if the provider were personally contacting him or her for feedback about services provided. Obviously, mass-produced letters addressed to "Dear Former Patient" fail to convey this message. Figure 9-2 shows a model letter.

Figure 9-2. Letter of Transmittal

XYZ Medical Center
2233 Dover Street
Smithville, Maine 10000

August 26, 1996

Dear Mr. Browne:

(1) I hope that you have continued to recover from the condition that resulted in your admission to our medical center. At XYZ Medical Center our goal is to provide the best possible medical care to everyone, and make each person's stay as comfortable as possible. However, we realize that at times our efforts may fall short of achieving that goal. Through carefully listening to what patients have to say about our services, we continuously strive to improve.

(2) It's very important for me to know your honest opinion of our services. I would like to know both what we did right, and where improvements may be needed. Let me assure you that your responses will be kept strictly confidential. You will notice that there is an identification number stamped on the questionnaire. It is solely used to check your name off our mailing list once we've received your completed questionnaire.

(3) Please take a few minutes of your valuable time to complete and return the enclosed survey. If you would like to make any additional comments about the services you received, please do so in the space provided.

(4) I appreciate your time and efforts in helping XYZ Medical Center improve services for you, your family, and the Smithville community. Thank you.

Sincerely,

George F. Smith
President

Before reading the body of the letter, the addressee should get the impression that the hospital president or another senior manager has written a personal letter to him or her. This impression is conveyed by:

1. Using business letterhead stationery
2. Typing the recipient's name and address and a personalized salutation on the letter
3. Dating the letter as of the day it is to be mailed
4. Signing each letter individually
5. Printing each letter separately

Just a few years ago, when letters had to be typed individually on a typewriter, such personalization was prohibitively expensive. Today, with the availability of personal computers, word-processing programs, and laser jet printers, personalized letters are very affordable and well worth the investment.

Typically, the first sentence of the letter acknowledges that the recipient was a patient at the health facility and conveys a concern for the person's continued recovery and well-being. The letter illustrated in figure 9-2 could be personalized further by mentioning the reason for care. If the recipient delivered a baby, for example, the sentence might read: "I hope that you and your baby have done well since your discharge from our hospital." If the facility specializes in a particular area of care, such as sports medicine, the letter might read: "I hope you have fully recovered from the sports injury that you were treated for at our center." When the personalization is on target, the recipient is usually impressed that the facility took the time to write specifically to him or her. However, if the personalization is inaccurate (for example, a woman who delivered a baby receives a letter about her sports injury), the recipient is likely to be offended. Instead of getting back a completed survey, the president may get a nasty letter or phone call pointing out the error.

The second paragraph is particularly important to individuals who are dissatisfied with the care that was provided. It informs them that the institution's philosophy is to provide the best medical care possible. When this goal is not met and there are problems, management wants to hear about them so that the situation can be corrected. It also appeals directly to the addressee by stressing that what he or she has to say is important. Recognizing that some respondents may fear offending clinical staff with negative reports, management states that both negative and positive comments are expected and assures recipients of confidentiality. However, because each questionnaire is visibly coded with an identification number, respondents are given an honest explanation as to the purpose of the number, which in this case is to check the individual's name off the list once the completed survey has been returned.

The third paragraph acknowledges that the recipient's time is valuable and that his or her efforts are appreciated. It encourages the respondent to make additional comments. The fourth paragraph tells the respondent how completing the questionnaire benefits him or her. Finally, the letter thanks the respondent.

Mailing Envelope

The mailing envelope for the questionnaire can convey to the addressee that the item is junk mail or that it is a personal communication of some importance. To create the image of personalization and importance, the envelope should be of high-quality paper, with the institution's logo and address printed on it. Instead of using mailing labels or an addressing machine—both of which indicate a mass mailing—each envelope should be individually addressed, as if a typewriter had been used. Each name and address should be checked for correctness and completeness; full names with appropriate titles are recommended. In essence, the envelope should meet the same standards as a business letter from one executive to another.

Postage should be first class and stamped, not metered. Not only does this contribute to the image of personalization and importance, it also has the highest handling priority with the U.S. Postal Service. If the addressee has moved, the mail will be forwarded; if the address is wrong or incomplete, it will be returned to the sender so that address corrections can be made and surveys remailed. If the addressee cannot be located, then the response rate can be corrected to reflect the true population base.

The envelope should be large enough to accommodate the questionnaire and a return envelope. Of course, the actual size will vary depending on the size of the questionnaire sheet and how it is folded.

Prenotification of Survey

Several opinion-polling studies have shown that questionnaires are more likely to be returned when recipients are given advance notice of the survey (Fox, Crash, and Kim, 1988; Herberlein and Baumgartner, 1978). With respect to patient satisfaction surveys, several oral and written methods can be used to notify patients. One oral method that the authors have found to work well is having nurses inform patients just prior to discharge that they will be receiving a satisfaction survey at home. A good time to mention it is at the end of a discharge planning session. The nurse might say to the patient:

> Before we end our discussion, I just want you to know that you may be receiving a letter from the hospital president asking for your impressions of the care you received while at XYZ Medical Center. If you are selected to be part of the sample, I would encourage you to reply and give your honest thoughts. We are always looking for ways to improve the services offered to our patients, and your thoughts would be most helpful.

Occasionally, a patient will ask to be sent such a letter as a vehicle for providing feedback. To accommodate the patient, the nurse notes the person's name and informs the department responsible for conducting the survey. Although these persons are sent surveys, their responses are kept separate unless their name is drawn through probability sampling.

Two cautions must be practiced in using oral prenotification. First, the message needs to be provided to *all* patients. When patients on one unit are notified but those on another unit are not, the response rate may be differentially affected. Second, the message needs to be the *same* for all patients. Imagine the effect on patients' responses if patients on one floor were led to believe that staff could lose their jobs if results were unfavorable, while patients on another floor were given a less ominous message. It seems reasonable to expect that responses on the questionnaire would reflect these different staff inputs.

Another opportunity for oral notification is at the end of the billing process at the time of discharge. After the paperwork is complete, the billing clerk informs patients that the institution may be contacting them to participate in a survey. The explanation is essentially the same as previously illustrated for nurses. Typically, this method works best in outpatient settings, where the person paying the bill (or authorizing the billing of the insurance company) is the same person who received services. In inpatient settings, this method of notification is not as effective because frequently a family member, instead of the patient, will go through the discharge billing process, particularly when the patient is debilitated. When this happens, the family member may forget to inform the patient or may not clearly convey the point of the survey.

Written notification can include either handouts or mailings. Figure 9-3 illustrates a typical handout. For inpatients, the handout can be included in their discharge packet or given to the patient at the conclusion of the discharge planning session. An alternative is to have billing clerks hand them out with receipts. Handouts are desirable because the message given to patients is uniform, there are no mailing costs, and if someone other than the patient goes through the billing process and receives the handout, the patient still has an opportunity to read it. All of this notwithstanding, the notice still may not be read.

A final prenotification method involves mailing either postcards or letters to notify recipients of the questionnaire they will be receiving in the mail. If a postcard is used, it should be imprinted with the institution's logo and address. Again, personalization is important to avoid the appearance of a mass mailing. The recipient's name and address and a salutation should be individually typed on each postcard. Figure 9-4 illustrates the format and content of a typical postcard.

A slightly expanded version of the postcard message can be sent via letter. A letter is more private and personal, but also more expensive. Research reported to date on mail surveys suggests that postcards and letters are equally effective in stimulating responses. Therefore, the prenotification postcard would be the method of choice when cost is a consideration.

Respondents should receive mail survey notification within three to five days after services are rendered so that questionnaires can be received shortly thereafter. This time frame places significant pressure on the service's registration system to generate a daily list of all discharged patients or clinic visits. Some institutions may not have the capability to meet this tight time frame. In such cases, predischarge oral or handout notification may have to suffice.

Follow-Up Methods

One of the most effective ways to increase response rates to mail surveys is through follow-up mailings. Herberlein and Baumgartner (1978, pp. 455–58), in reviewing 98 mailed questionnaire response rate experiments, found that questionnaires mailed without follow-up had an average response rate of 46.1 percent, whereas those with

Figure 9-3. Notification Handout

XYZ Medical Center
2233 Dover Street
Smithville, Maine 10000

August 26, 1996

Dear Patient:

We periodically contact a sample of recently discharged patients to ask them about the care they received while at XYZ Medical Center. When this information is received, it is used to improve the services we provide to future patients.

In the next few days you may receive a letter in the mail asking you to participate in this study. If selected, I would appreciate your taking a few minutes to respond to the questionnaire. Please be honest and tell us both what you liked and disliked about the care we provided. Thank you.

Sincerely,

George F. Smith
President

three follow-up mailings averaged 80.6 percent. This increase of over 30 percentage points is consistent with the authors' experience in conducting patient satisfaction surveys.

The first follow-up mailing is usually a postcard reminder sent to the entire sample within two to four days after the questionnaire mailing. Name, address, and salutation should be individually typed. As shown in figure 9-5, the message thanks early responders and encourages nonresponders to complete the questionnaire. By sending a message to both respondents and nonrespondents, the researcher does not have to wait for returns, thereby hastening the process. If the researcher waits to see who returns the questionnaire, he or she would need to wait approximately two weeks after it was mailed for most of the returns to arrive.

Figure 9-4. Prenotification Postcard

```
XYZ Medical Center
2233 Dover Street
Smithville, Maine 10000

August 26, 1996

Dear Mr. Browne:

In the next few days you will receive a letter asking you to complete a questionnaire about the services you
received at XYZ Medical Center. I would appreciate your taking a few minutes to respond to the questionnaire.
Please be honest and tell us both what you liked and disliked about the care you received.

This information will be used to improve our services. Thank you.

Sincerely,


George F. Smith
President
```

Figure 9-5. Postcard Follow-Up

```
XYZ Medical Center
2233 Dover Street
Smithville, Maine 10000

August 26, 1996

Dear Mr. Browne:

A few days ago a questionnaire about the services at XYZ Medical Center was mailed to you.

If you have already returned it, please accept our thanks. If you haven't had an opportunity to complete the
questionnaire, please do so today. We are very interested in your thoughts.

If you did not receive the questionnaire or if you have misplaced it, please call 555-4567 and one of my staff
will send you another one immediately. Thank you.

Sincerely,


George F. Smith
President
```

The message on the follow-up postcard is similar to, but briefer than, the letter of transmittal. One major difference is in the last paragraph of the postcard, where recipients are told what they should do if a questionnaire was not received or was misplaced. Occasionally, mail does not arrive at the addressee's residence or is discarded when received. In either case, the postcard informs the addressee that a questionnaire was sent and how to obtain another copy.

The second follow-up communication is sent only to nonrespondents and consists of a personalized letter and another copy of the questionnaire. As shown in figure 9-6, the letter restates that a questionnaire was sent, the purpose of the study, and why it is important that each recipient complete the questionnaire. The salutation includes the recipient's name, and the letter is individually addressed and signed, just as the transmittal letter was. In case the questionnaire has been completed by the respondent but is in transit, the recipient is thanked for completing it and told that it is not necessary to complete another one.

An additional follow-up letter that contains the same message as the previous letter can be sent. However, the extensive time that has elapsed between the time when the service was received and the time when this third follow-up occurs offers results of questionable value. By this time, most patients' memories of the service have begun to grow dim, and their responses are more subject to recall error. A more expeditious approach is to use a telephone follow-up to encourage responses; essentially the same message contained in the follow-up letter is conveyed orally. Although telephone follow-up is effective in increasing the rate of return of mail surveys, it is expensive.

Figure 9-6. Follow-Up Letter

XYZ Medical Center
2233 Dover Street
Smithville, Maine 10000

September 15, 1996

Dear Mr. Browne:

A couple of weeks ago a questionnaire was sent to you regarding the services you received at XYZ Medical Center. As of today, I have not received your completed questionnaire.

In case you've been too busy or forgot to complete it, may I ask that you take a few minutes and do so now? In case the questionnaire was misplaced, I've enclosed another copy. If you've completed the questionnaire and it's in the mail, then I thank you.

As I've said in my previous letters, at XYZ our goal is to provide the best possible medical care to everyone and make each person's stay as comfortable as possible. However, we realize that at times our efforts may fall short of achieving that goal. Only through hearing from you, Mr. Browne, will we ever know if our services have met your needs and expectations.

It's very important for me to know your honest opinion of our services. I would like to know both what we did right and where improvements may be needed. Again, let me assure you that your responses will be kept in strict confidence. You will notice that there is an identification number stamped on the questionnaire. It is solely used to check your name off our mailing list once we've received your completed questionnaire.

Please take a few minutes to complete and return the enclosed survey. I appreciate your time and efforts in helping XYZ Medical Center improve services for you, your family, and the Smithville community. Thank you.

Sincerely,

George F. Smith
President

By the time the researcher completes both the mail and telephone follow-ups, he or she could have conducted the survey by telephone at nearly the same cost but with a quicker response and a higher rate of return.

Coding

In order to know who responds and who does not, all questionnaires should be coded. This not only reduces the cost of follow-up mailings, it also allows the researcher to make sure that only one questionnaire per respondent is entered into the database. With second questionnaires mailed to nonrespondents, occasionally the recipient will complete and return both.

Coding should consist of a unique identification number prominently marked at the bottom of the first or last page of the questionnaire. Respondents have been told in the cover letter that questionnaires are coded. If for some reason they are uncomfortable with the coding, placing it at the bottom of the page allows it to be physically removed without destroying the questionnaire. In our experience fewer than 1 percent of respondents remove the coding. Furthermore, whenever identical questionnaires have been sent, with and without coding, the response rate has been virtually equivalent.

Another potential use of coding is that it allows questionnaire data to be merged with patient registration and service data. During registration, patients answer a variety of questions about their age, religion, marital status, address, educational level achieved, and so on. If this information can be retrieved, it eliminates the need to ask these same questions on the questionnaire. Likewise, retrieving information about admission and discharge dates, floor or unit where services were provided, the types of services provided, and so forth allows the respondent's questionnaire ratings to be linked to an objective record. When respondents are asked to provide this information on questionnaires, it sometimes is inaccurate or incomplete. When coding is used to merge patient registration and service data with satisfaction data, the cover letter explaining the coding must be modified accordingly.

Electronic versus Written Questionnaires

Televisions and computers have become an integral part of the health care environment. Beyond its use for entertainment purposes, television is being utilized by many hospitals to offer educational programming in the patient's room. Surgical patients receive both preoperative and postoperative instructions, maternity patients receive postpartum instructions, obese patients are taught about nutrition and exercise, and so on. This technology also has two-way information transmission capabilities: providers can receive information from patients as well as give information to them. For example, patients can select food choices from a menu presented on the monitor. More recently, this interactive capability has been employed to obtain patient satisfaction feedback both during hospital stays and just prior to discharge. Patients are presented with satisfaction questions on the room television monitor along with response options. The remote control keypad is used to provide answers by selecting a number that corresponds to their answer.

At first glance, in-room, electronically administered surveys appear to be an excellent method of obtaining rapid feedback on care with a minimal expenditure of staff time and resources. Because the patient is still under care, dissatisfaction could be remedied before discharge. Although the logic is appealing, a fundamental question remains: How accurate are the data so obtained? For example, Mr. Smith may honestly give his opinion about the room temperature or satisfaction with a particular meal, but will he indicate dissatisfaction with the nurses or doctors while he is still under their care? To examine this concern, the authors searched the professional literature and contacted vendors of this technology, but were unable to find relevant methodological studies. Until such studies are available, we can only consider this issue in light of related research and principles of sound measurement. Those principles and research suggest a somewhat negative picture.

First, are hospitalized patients in sufficiently good health to complete a satisfaction questionnaire? Many patients are too ill or in too much discomfort to participate in a survey during the majority of their stay. Even if the patient does participate, what effect will the patient's health status have on responses? Patrick, Scrivens, and Charlton (1983) have found that persons in poor health tend to be more dissatisfied with their health care than those in good health. This suggests that surveying hospitalized patients who are still acutely ill is likely to produce lower satisfaction scores because the results have been confounded by the patients' health status.

Second, will hospitalized patients feel free to criticize providers while they are still a captive of the hospital? Some have referred to this as "biting the hand that heals." We might speculate that satisfied patients may positively bias their responses, hoping to ingratiate themselves with providers, while dissatisfied patients may also positively bias responses to avoid feared reprisals.

Third, is it premature to survey patients either during or near the end of a health care experience, before they have had an opportunity to complete the experience and form an opinion? With today's short inpatient stays, many patients continue their treatment at home through the hospital's home care services. Therefore, general questions about the service ("How satisfied are you with the care you received at XYZ Hospital?" "How would you rate the quality of care at XYZ Hospital?") should not be asked until the service experience is complete and sufficient time has passed to allow the patient to form an opinion. On the other hand, it would seem appropriate to ask in-service patients about physical accommodations or the hospital environment, such as room temperature, hospital noise, or satisfaction with a particular meal, because those are discrete experiences and somewhat tangential to the treatment received. Respondents may be less likely to worry about offending someone when the criticism is of a thing or the environment as opposed to a person.

Fourth, is there a self-selection bias associated with electronic survey administration? We know that telephone surveys tend to underrepresent individuals who are seldom at home, who screen calls with answering machines, or who don't own a telephone. Mail surveys underrepresent the illiterate, blind, homeless, and transient populations as well as those who are generally more satisfied. The sampling bias associated with interactive television technology might include difficulty with, or apprehension over, operating a remote control. Persons who have never operated a remote control might be intimidated and decline participation. Another potential bias would involve the elderly and those with vision impairments, who may have difficulty reading the monitor. The illiterate could participate in the survey only if someone read the items to them. However, they may be embarrassed to ask, not wanting to reveal their illiteracy.

Until methodological studies address the above issues, we recommend that caution be exercised in drawing conclusions based solely on data gathered through this new technology. Having expressed this reservation, we also suggest that the jury is still out, and that time will tell what role these technologies will play in gathering patient satisfaction information in the future.

Summary

The success of a patient satisfaction survey depends not only on question and response wording but also on the layout, formatting, and appearance of the questionnaire. A vertical format has a clean, uncluttered appearance and facilitates distinguishing questions from response options. A horizontal format can be used when questions are constructed in a manner that allows identical scaling to be used in answering a series of questions.

The best method for administering self-report questionnaires is through the mail. To achieve an optimal response rate, personalized letters of prenotification and follow-up are necessary. These efforts can produce response rates in excess of 70 percent. The use of interactive television technology to administer questionnaires may provide rapid feedback from patients, but the accuracy of the information may be limited. Patients may give honest appraisals of the environment or service amenities but withhold criticism of their providers.

CHAPTER TEN

Telephone Questionnaires

Although telephone interviews may seem fairly easy to conduct—just pick up the phone and ask a few questions—they actually require detailed preparation and skilled execution. Because these interviews consist solely of oral communication, the interviewer cannot *see* when a respondent is confused by the wording of a question or by instructions that are unclear. The interviewer cannot emphasize key words or phrases through hand gestures or other nonverbal communication. No visual aids help respondents understand questions or response categories. In short, the nature of telephone interviewing places special demands on the interviewer and restrictions on the types of questions and response rating scales that can be used.

This chapter provides an overview of interviewer qualifications, training needs and supervision, and facility and equipment requirements for conducting telephone interviews. The chapter also explains how to adapt standardized questionnaires for telephone interviewing, including the construction of questions and response scales and questionnaire formatting. The chapter concludes with a discussion of pretest methods and an example of a telephone questionnaire.

Selecting Interviewers

What qualities should one look for in a telephone interviewer? One of the most important qualifications is a pleasing voice that carries well over the telephone. Consider that the first thing a respondent hears is the interviewer's voice; it sets the tone for the interview to follow. It is also known that respondents make judgments about the personal characteristics of the interviewer based on vocal cues (for example, pitch, volume, intonation, rate of speech, pronunciation, and fluency). If the interviewer creates a positive first impression, the respondent is more likely to participate in the interview (Oksenberg and others, 1986).

A good way to assess the quality of a person's telephone voice is to screen potential interviewers on the phone. Ask yourself: Is this person's voice clear, easy to hear, and pleasing? Deep, burly voices and high-pitched, squeaky voices are difficult to listen to and often hard to understand. How good is the enunciation? Is it easy to understand what is being said? People who slur words or talk through their teeth are poor candidates.

Second, interviewers should have a verbal demeanor that conveys friendliness with self-confidence. Upbeat, confident interviewers can persuade respondents to complete the interview and have demonstrably higher response rates than those with less optimism (Singer and others, 1983). If interviewers do not believe in the importance of conducting patient satisfaction surveys or if they feel hesitant about their ability to conduct interviews, these reservations are likely to be reflected in their voices.

Third, interviewers should have the ability to read questions fluently without sounding as though they were reading. On the other hand, although questions should sound conversational, the interviewer must be willing to stick to the script and not improvise.

Fourth, interviewers must be adept at addressing objections such as "Who told you my phone number?" or "Why are you asking me these questions?" without becoming defensive or flustered.

Finally, interviewers should have good hearing. It is not uncommon for interviewers to encounter respondents who speak softly or have poor phone connections. If an interviewer does not have excellent hearing, these interviews may be lost or responses may be heard and recorded inaccurately.

Choosing between Professionals and Nonprofessionals

Who makes the best patient satisfaction interviewer? Clinical staff? Clerical workers? Volunteers or professional interviewers? Some researchers argue that clinical personnel are the best qualified because they are knowledgeable about patient care and can more readily establish rapport with patients. Other researchers argue that regardless of the merits of using clinicians, they are too expensive and in too short supply to be used for interviewing. Clerical staff or volunteers, they argue, are sufficiently qualified for the task. On the other hand, some research vendors claim that only professional interviewers can conduct high-quality interviews.

This issue has not been empirically addressed through controlled research studies. However, based on experience, the authors feel that clerical and volunteer interviewers are the best choice, provided that they are well trained. Although we agree that clinical personnel have a better understanding of patient care and services than do the other groups mentioned, we also feel that clinicians may lack objectivity because they have a vested interest in what patients say about the services they have received. Even if clinicians read the questionnaire exactly as written, they can inadvertently transmit biases through vocal cues or selective probing. That these cues affect responses has been supported by the research of Robert Rosenthal (1966), who demonstrated the powerful effects that researchers' expectations can have on the outcome of animal laboratory studies. Rosenthal and Jacobson (1968) also have demonstrated the effects of teachers' expectations on student performance. Besides, we believe that if the questionnaire has been appropriately developed, with the input of clinical staff, and its content validity has been established, then it is unnecessary to use clinical personnel as interviewers.

Clerical staff or volunteers are probably more objective than clinicians, but this assumption should be tested through interviewer screening. If a potential interviewer has strong beliefs—positive or negative—about health care providers, then that person would have a difficult time being objective. A question worth posing to candidates is, "How often do you think physicians make mistakes in treating patients?" Beware if the answer is "never" or "all the time." Similar questions can be asked about other health care professionals and health facilities.

Whether clerical staff and volunteers have the skills to be telephone interviewers is largely a matter of training. As long as they meet the qualifications regarding quality of voice, verbal demeanor, ability to read questions fluently, and the like, formal education is not a prerequisite to effective interviewing. However, studies of public opinion surveys have shown that training interviewers improves interview cooperation rates, item response rates, and response quality (Billiet and Loosveldt, 1988). Several hours of training are needed to master interviewing skills, and these skills can be maintained only through regular use. Therefore, before deciding to use volunteers, one must be sure they are willing to devote the time required to complete the training and to work a minimum number of hours a week. Unless volunteers can work at least four hours a week, they will have difficulty maintaining their skills.

If neither volunteers nor clerical staff are available to conduct interviews, then the alternative is to contract with a research firm to conduct interviews. This alternative may be most appealing to smaller institutions where the number of interviews to be conducted each year may not be sufficient to warrant the investment of time and effort to train interviewers.

Training Interviewers

Once qualified interviewers have been selected, the next step is training. Interviewers need training in four distinct aspects of their job: (1) answering respondents' questions, (2) conducting telephone interviews, (3) recording responses, and (4) editing completed questionnaires.

Answering Respondents' Questions

No matter how clearly a researcher wrote the introduction to a telephone survey or how clearly the interviewer states it, some respondents will still have questions they want answered before agreeing to an interview. Others will interrupt the interview as questions or objections come to mind. Typical questions include:

- "Who did you say you were?"
- "How did you get my phone number?"
- "How do I know you represent XYZ Hospital?"
- "Why are you calling me?"

Other respondents take the call as an opportunity to express their concerns about topics or issues not included in the questionnaire (for example, "You're not treating any AIDS patients there, are you?" or "I think hospitals should pay their share of taxes"). Interviewers must know which questions they should answer and which questions should be referred to their supervisor.

When interviewers are initially recruited, they should be informed about why the hospital is conducting patient satisfaction surveys, how the data are used, who has access to this information, what the provider's policies on confidentiality are, and so on. This orientation helps trainees understand the importance of their job and provides background information for anticipating and answering respondents' questions. It is also important that interviewers give consistent responses to questions so that they do not inadvertently affect responses to the questionnaire items.

There are several routine questions that respondents are likely to ask. To help interviewers, these questions—and appropriate responses—should be listed on a question-and-answer sheet. Figure 10-1 lists some typical questions that the authors have encountered, along with answers that might be given. Placing this sheet near each phone gives interviewers an immediate and consistent reference for answering questions. If a respondent asks difficult or unusual questions that are not listed on the sheet, the interviewer probably should transfer the respondent to a supervisor for an answer.

Figure 10-1. Question-and-Answer Sheet

> **How did you get my name?**
>
> Your name was randomly selected from a list of persons who received services at the XYZ Baby Clinic during the last two weeks. Every person on the list had an equal chance of being interviewed.
>
> **Will the staff at XYZ Baby Clinic find out what I said about them?**
>
> No one other than me will know what you said. Your answers will be kept strictly confidential. The questionnaire on which I am recording your answers does not contain your name. Clinic staff will only see the statistical averages of answers to questions.
>
> **How do I know you are who you say you are?**
>
> I would be happy to give you our phone number so you can call me back. Or if you'd like, I will give you my supervisor's name and phone number so you can verify what I've told you.
>
> **Why doesn't the clinic pay taxes?**
>
> Sir/Madam, I don't know the answer to that question, but I'd be more than happy to give you the name and phone number of the clinic's public relations director. I'm sure he/she would be more than happy to discuss that question with you.

Conducting Telephone Interviews

When interviewers understand both the interviewer's and the interviewee's roles, they are able to conduct interviews more effectively. Before trainees actually begin the interviewing process, they should learn these roles through modeling. Dillman (1978, pp. 263–72) has suggested that trainees go through four types of practice interviews. During the first interview, the trainee observes experienced interviewers role-playing an interview. Through observing, the novice comes to understand each role and appropriate techniques for handling a variety of questions that the respondent might ask.

Second, after studying the questionnaire, trainees should practice interviewing each other to experience both roles. In this way, the interviewer learns the sequence of questions and the rhythm and pace of the questionnaire as the supervisor observes and critiques the process. When the trainee-interviewer fails to read questions as written, fails to probe for additional information or probes in a leading manner, does not follow instructions to skip certain questions, and so on, the supervisor steps in and tutors the interviewer. The trainee-respondent experiences what it is like to be asked questions and why certain questions may need to be read more slowly and certain words emphasized or repeated. At this point, the trainee also practices introducing the interview. As with all types of interviews, an effective introduction is critically important, particularly when patients have not been informed of the interview prior to discharge. In a few words, the interviewer must persuade the respondent that sharing reactions to the service will improve shortcomings. The benefit to the respondent is that problems that may have been experienced are likely to be changed. If the service is used again by the respondent, family, or friends, then they will reap the benefits of the respondent's participation in the study.

The third type of practice interview involves the trainee interviewing the supervisor. The supervisor plays the role of the difficult respondent, thereby testing the interviewer's capabilities. Through this simulation, the supervisor learns each interviewer's strengths and weaknesses. Identifying weaknesses allows the supervisor to know which interviewers will need additional training and close monitoring during actual interviews.

The final practice interviews are conducted during the pretest of the questionnaire, at which time interviews are administered to a small sample of actual patients to work out any remaining bugs in the questionnaire. During this interview process the trainee finds out what it is like to interview actual patients, and also discovers that most respondents are cooperative, friendly, and willing to answer questions about the services they have received. These last practice interviews help build the trainees' confidence that they can be successful telephone interviewers.

Recording Responses

Trainees learning how to record responses should first be instructed in the importance of carefully circling or checking responses. Also, they must learn to write accurate responses to open-ended questions with some sort of shorthand notation. During all practice interviews, trainees are required to record answers on the questionnaires, which teaches them how to record answers while preparing to ask the next question. For open-ended questions, they must learn how to capture the essence of the response without missing or biasing what was said.

Editing Completed Questionnaires

After each practice interview is completed, the trainee immediately edits the questionnaire to see that all answers have been circled and that written responses are sufficiently elaborate and legibly written. After editing is completed, the questionnaire is reviewed and critiqued by the practice interviewee. Particular attention should be paid to open-ended question responses. The interviewee informs the interviewer whether the essence of the response was captured. Last, the supervisor examines the questionnaires on the same dimensions.

Even after training is complete, questionnaires, including those of seasoned interviewers, should be edited. Although it is tempting to let editing wait until several interviews have been conducted, experience shows that the ability to distinguish among responses diminishes with each subsequent interview. Consequently, editing should always occur immediately after each interview is completed.

Scheduling Interviews

The best time to call respondents is when they are at home and awake and when the call will not interrupt important activities such as meals or social gatherings. Of course, the problem is knowing when these conditions can be met. Typically, the best times to call are weekday evenings (6 to 9 p.m.) and midday Saturday (10:30 a.m. to 4 p.m.) (Weeks and others, 1987). Although some households have finished dinner by 6 p.m., if the dinner has been interrupted, the interviewer should offer to call back. If early evening calls repeatedly find respondents at dinner, calling should be postponed until 7:00 p.m. or later. Calls should never be scheduled on holidays.

When studies are conducted for specific programs that serve distinct market segments, calling times may be tailored to these segments. For example, when interviewing mothers with newborn infants or the retired elderly, midday calls are likely to be very successful. In contrast, persons using an occupational health program are unlikely to be home during the day unless the local labor force works shifts around the clock. In cities where service industry jobs prevail, evening calls may be as successful in finding respondents at home as afternoon calls.

If careful records are kept of call attempts and completions and if callbacks are attempted on different days and at different times of day, these data can be used to guide the scheduling of future telephone-based studies. It is recommended that three to five callbacks be made before the potential respondent's name is dropped from the list and another substituted. When respondents are contacted but refuse to complete the interview, it is important that this information be captured as well, including the reason for the refusal.

Timing Interviews

Telephone interviews for discharged inpatients should be conducted between two days and two weeks after discharge. The authors' experience indicates that during the first day or two after discharge, many people are recovering from the hospital experience and trying to get resettled at home. Often during these first days, family or friends stay with the person to help out around the house, take care of children, or offer emotional support. Being asked to participate in a phone survey is likely to be considered an intrusion. In addition, if the patient has undergone surgery, he or she typically is still experiencing considerable discomfort and may not wish to come to the telephone.

At the same time, it is important to speak to patients reasonably soon after discharge, while the experience is still fresh in their minds. Because inpatient care is a significant life event, the authors' experience has shown that as long as surveys are conducted within two weeks of discharge, recall error appears to be minimal. An exception to this time frame is if detailed questions are asked about specific services (for example, rating the quality of food at specific meals) or staff members (for example, rating the care of nurses on day versus evening versus night shifts). The more time that elapses between the specific experience and the questioning, the higher is the probability of recall error. For these types of detailed questions, the interview optimally should be conducted within a week of discharge.

When studies are conducted of ambulatory care services (for example, minor emergency centers, preventive health screenings, health promotion programs, or physical rehabilitation services), calls can be made on the day the service was delivered or within a week of the visit. Because these services are generally brief in duration and less traumatic than acute care services, waiting longer than one week will increase the likelihood of recall error.

Interviewing Facilities and Supervision

Although most health care facilities have all the phones necessary to conduct telephone surveys, the phones tend to be dispersed throughout numerous unconnected offices. If telephone interviews are to be administered with any degree of uniformity, the phones must be centrally located. A centralized facility allows a supervisor to be immediately available to guide, monitor, and support interview staff. It also affords interviewers enough initial training to administer the telephone questionnaires to routine respondents while deferring unusual cases to the supervisor. As a result, each interviewer need not know how to handle every situation, because atypical respondents are handled by the supervisor.

When the facility is equipped with phone-monitoring devices, the supervisor can randomly listen to interviews. If an interviewer begins misreading questions, asks questions too quickly, or deviates from the questionnaire structure, the supervisor can correct the situation before numerous interviews are affected. Such a facility also allows the supervisor to review each questionnaire immediately upon completion of the call. By immediately scanning questionnaires for completeness and legibility, the supervisor can obtain clarification from the interviewer while the experience is still fresh. In addition, when interviewers know that calls are monitored and questionnaires checked, they are more conscientious and careful in their work, thereby reducing data errors.

Adapting Questionnaires for Telephone Administration

Although standardized self-report questionnaires may form the basis for telephone interviews, they cannot simply be read over the phone. Instead, modifications are necessary, both in the way the questions are constructed for presentation to the respondent and in the way they are formatted on the page for the interviewer. Although many principles of questionnaire construction are equally applicable to telephone and self-report surveys, there are some significant differences. An important difference is that with telephone interviews, respondents do not have visual aids to help them understand the questions or response options. The interviewer must depend on the respondent's ability to listen, comprehend, and retain what is said. Thus, questions that are too complex are likely to be misunderstood. On self-report questionnaires, respondents read questions at their own pace and reread them if necessary. Obviously, this is not the case with telephone questionnaires. Consequently, some types of questions and response formats that work well in self-report surveys may not be suited to the telephone questionnaire.

Adapting Response Scaling

As noted in chapter 8, well-constructed standardized questionnaires use rating scales with at least five or more levels to capture the variability inherent in various service attributes. On self-report questionnaires, respondents can see the ordering of anchor points between two extremes, but in answering telephone questionnaires, they must create an internal visual image. Although some individuals have no difficulty visualizing these scales, others do. Virtually all respondents can choose among three alternatives and most can choose among four, but five or more alternatives may be too many. The solution is to reduce the number of levels used in rating scales. Figure 10-2 illustrates a seven-level satisfaction scale that is truncated to four levels.

One point to consider in deciding how many levels to use is whether the same scale will be used with a series of questions or just once. For example, Likert-type scales have respondents rate the extent of their agreement or disagreement over multiple items. In such instances, most respondents quickly memorize the response options. The researcher can also instruct the person to write the scale anchor point descriptions ("strongly agree," "somewhat agree," "neutral," "somewhat disagree," "strongly disagree") on a piece of paper and look at it while items are read.

Another point to consider is how familiar the person is with the scaling. For example, quality scaling ("excellent," "very good," "good," "fair," or "poor") has been used to such an extent in consumer research that the general public is quite familiar with it. When respondents are familiar with the continuum of choices or when the same scaling is used frequently throughout the questionnaire, good results are obtained with scales having four or five levels (Miller, 1984).

One disadvantage of truncating scales is the loss of information. Using fewer levels tends to produce skewed response distributions (scores piling up at one end of the scale). An alternative to truncating is to divide questions into two parts. Figure 10-3 shows a solution to the problem. Note that respondents are first asked whether they

Figure 10-2. Reducing Scale Levels for Telephone Surveys

Overall, how satisfied were you with the quality of nursing care you received?

(Original Scale)	(Revision)	
1. Very satisfied	Very satisfied	1
2. Moderately satisfied	Somewhat satisfied	2
3. Somewhat satisfied	Somewhat dissatisfied	3
4. Neutral	Very dissatisfied	4
5. Somewhat dissatisfied		
6. Moderately dissatisfied		
7. Very dissatisfied		

Figure 10-3. Alternative to Truncating Scales

```
Overall, how satisfied were you with the quality of nursing care you received? Were you:

                                                    Satisfied              1
                                                    Dissatisfied           2

        Then would you say you were:

                                                    Very dissatisfied      1
                                                    Moderately dissatisfied 2
                                                    Somewhat dissatisfied   3

        Then would you say you were:

                                                    Very satisfied         1
                                                    Moderately satisfied   2
                                                    Somewhat satisfied     3
```

are satisfied or dissatisfied, and then the intensity of the satisfaction (or dissatisfaction) is probed. The negatives are that this method doubles the number of questions, increases interview time, drives up data collection costs, and limits the topics that can be covered in the survey.

Adapting Ranking Questions

Self-report surveys frequently use a laundry list of options from which respondents pick the most important reason or are asked to rank items from most to least important (see figure 10-4). Getting answers to ranking questions on the telephone is difficult because it requires the respondent to remember all mentioned items, compare each item to all others, and then order the items on the specified dimension. Most have difficulty completing this assignment unless there are four or fewer items. The shortcoming of using only a few items is that relevant items are frequently omitted. An alternative method suggested by Seymour Sudman and Norman Bradburn (1982, pp. 267–72) is to transform the question into a two-step process, as shown in figure 10-5. Each reason is first rated on a 3-point scale of importance. After this step is completed, the items rated most important are then ranked. Although the example shows only the top three reasons being ranked, it is possible to rank all items in a similar manner.

Ordering and Grouping Questions

The ordering of questions and their wording affect the flow of the interview. Interviewers cannot sound as though they are carrying on a natural conversation with the respondent unless the questionnaire is constructed to facilitate this natural flow. Like self-report surveys and in-depth interviews, telephone questionnaires should "start from the beginning" and follow the patient through the sequence of events that he or she experienced at the facility. Well-constructed questionnaires begin by asking why the person chose a particular facility for his or her care, then proceed to ask about the admission and registration process, and so on, concluding with issues associated with discharge and follow-up.

Questions should be grouped by topic. Imagine talking to a friend who asks you about your vacation, then work, then goes back to your vacation, then work, and continues in this manner. After a while, this shifting back and forth would begin to annoy most people. Imagine, on the other hand, that this conversation began with: "Hey, how was your vacation?" and continued to focus on the vacation until you finished

Figure 10-4. Ranking Question

Please indicate the *most* important reason why you chose to be admitted at XYZ Hospital. (Check one answer only.)

_____ Your doctor recommended XYZ.
_____ Your doctor is affiliated with XYZ.
_____ XYZ has the best doctors.
_____ XYZ has the latest medical equipment.
_____ XYZ provides the best medical care.
_____ XYZ was recommended by a friend or relative.
_____ XYZ is near your home.
_____ XYZ employees are concerned about their patients' well-being.
_____ Your insurance plan or employer requires that you use XYZ Hospital.

Figure 10-5. Telephone Ranking Question

People have a variety of reasons why they chose to be admitted to XYZ Hospital instead of to some other hospital. Some of these reasons are more important than others. After I read each reason, please indicate if that reason was very important, somewhat important, or not important in your choosing XYZ.

	Very Important	Somewhat Important	Not Important
1. Your doctor recommended XYZ.	1	2	3
2. Your doctor is affiliated with XYZ.	1	2	3
3. XYZ has the best doctors.	1	2	3
4. XYZ has the latest medical equipment.	1	2	3
5. XYZ provides the best medical care.	1	2	3
6. XYZ was recommended by a friend or relative.	1	2	3
7. XYZ is near your home.	1	2	3
8. XYZ employees are concerned about patients' well-being.	1	2	3
9. Your insurance plan or employer requires that you use XYZ Hospital.	1	2	3

Now, I will read back the reasons you indicated were "very important." *(Read items rated "very important")*

Which of these reasons do you consider the *most* important reason for your choice? _____ Most important

Which is the next most important? _____ Second most important

Which is the next most important? _____ Third most important

highlighting the more notable experiences. At that time, the friend says, "So now you're back to work. How is it going?" Telephone questionnaires should allow the interview to flow in a similar manner. Questions concerning respondent characteristics (for example, age, education, race) should be last, because it is not apparent to most respondents how these questions pertain to the stated purpose of the interview. It is helpful to explain briefly why these questions are asked (for example, "Now I'm going to ask you just a few final questions about yourself so we can classify answers").

Using Transitional Statements

It is also helpful to use transitional statements when shifting from one topic to another. For example, the interviewer might say, "Next, I'd like to know about the nursing care you received. When you arrived at your room, how soon did the nurses do X?" Notice that the transitional statement gives the interview a conversational flow while allowing respondents to focus their thoughts on the next topic. Research has shown that when respondents are given more details about a question, they tend to provide more detailed responses (Blair and others, 1972).

Incorporating Responses Mentioned within Questions

To facilitate recall of the appropriate response, some questions incorporate the response categories within the questions. This is not necessary in self-report questionnaires, where response categories occur after the question is asked and the layout of the survey makes it apparent to the reader that response options are either below or adjacent to the question. Telephone questionnaires, however, must convey this same information verbally, as this can break the flow of the interview. Dillman (1978) suggests incorporating response categories into the wording of the questions as a way around this problem. This technique is illustrated in figure 10-6. This works well when no more than three response alternatives are used. With more alternatives, respondents at times become confused, particularly when the alternatives are presented in the middle of the question. The trade-off for truncating the scaling to a manageable three levels is the loss of information that more levels would provide.

The reader will note that although response categories are contained in the question, they also are listed after the question to the right of the page in vertical format. This dual listing makes it easier for the interviewer to circle the response and for the data entry staff to identify what to enter.

Asking Income Questions

Asking for specific household income can offend respondents and result in refusal to respond. Offering income ranges, such as less than $10,000, $10,000 to $19,999, and so on, increases respondent cooperation. Another alternative in telephone questionnaires is the split-point income question shown in figure 10-7. The respondent is asked to indicate if his or her household income is above $25,000 or below. Once this is answered, respondents will typically answer follow-up questions. The results of William B. Locander and John P. Burton's (1976) study of four types of telephone income questions suggest that the split-point question has the highest completion rate and is least biased in estimating household income.

Formatting Telephone Questionnaires

Although the formatting of telephone questionnaires has much in common with the formatting of self-report surveys, there are several important differences. Here we will focus primarily on how questionnaires should be adapted to the needs of the interviewer. Remember that telephone questionnaires should facilitate a conversational mode of interaction. For example, if interviewers have difficulty reading questions, determining which questions to skip, or knowing where to record answers, the interview

Figure 10-6. Incorporating Response Categories into Questions

A. Did the nurses seem very knowledgeable, somewhat knowledgeable, or not at all knowledgeable about your treatment?	B. Did you find the nurses on your floor to be very courteous, somewhat courteous, or not at all courteous?
Very knowledgeable 1 Somewhat 2 Not at all 3	Very courteous 1 Somewhat 2 Not at all 3

Figure 10-7. Telephone Income Question

What was your approximate household income before taxes last year? Was it $25,000 or more, or was it less than that?

(If less than $25,000) Was it over $20,000 or under $20,000	$20,000–$24,999	3
(If under $20,000) Was it over $15,000 or under $15,000	$15,000–$19,999 $14,999 or less	2 1
(If $25,000 or more) Was it under $30,000 or over $30,000	$25,000–$29,999	4
(If over $30,000) Was it under $35,000 or over $35,000	$30,000–$34,999	5
(If over $35,000) Was it under $40,000 or over $40,000	$35,000–$39,999 $40,000 or more	6 7

will suffer. Equally important, the questionnaire must be administered in exactly the same manner to each respondent to minimize data errors and maximize consistency.

Obviously, the visual attractiveness and number of pages are minimal concerns in telephone surveys. The booklet format often found useful for self-report surveys is not necessary or even advisable for the telephone questionnaire. We recommend that the questionnaire be printed on standard legal-size paper. Printing on the reverse side saves paper, but one-sided printing helps the interviewer avoid flipping back and forth. If two sides are used, then page numbers proceed in the order of first front to last front side of the page and, reversing, from last back side to first back side of the page. Legal-size paper allows serial questions with numerous items to be contained on a single page. Whenever possible, these types of questions should *not* be split; if they are, scale headings are repeated at the top of the next page.

In telephone questionnaires, answer categories are aligned on the right side of the page, with the number assigned to each answer placed to the right of the answer (see figure 10-8). This format allows interviewer instructions to consistently appear to the left of answers, while the right-side numbering of answers facilitates key entry of data. Parentheses are used only to enclose interviewer instructions and indicate that whatever is contained therein is *not* read to respondents. Instructions are typed in uppercase or italic letters and placed in parentheses. The consistent use of uppercase or italic letters for instructions allows the interviewer to distinguish between the text of the questionnaire and directions without reading the contents. Answer options "(Don't know)" and "(Was not served)" in the first question also are not read. However, they are provided as responses so as to capture this information should the respondent spontaneously provide either answer.

Skip instructions can be provided by arrows that point to the next question, by written instruction, or both. In figure 10-8, if the answer chosen is either "very dissatisfied" or "somewhat dissatisfied," the arrow indicates that question 2 should be asked next. If "very satisfied" or "somewhat satisfied" is selected, the instructions indicate "Skip to question 3."

Consistent with Dillman's (1978) suggestion, the second question in this example is indented because it is only asked of a subset of the sample (that is, those respondents

Figure 10-8. Questionnaire Format

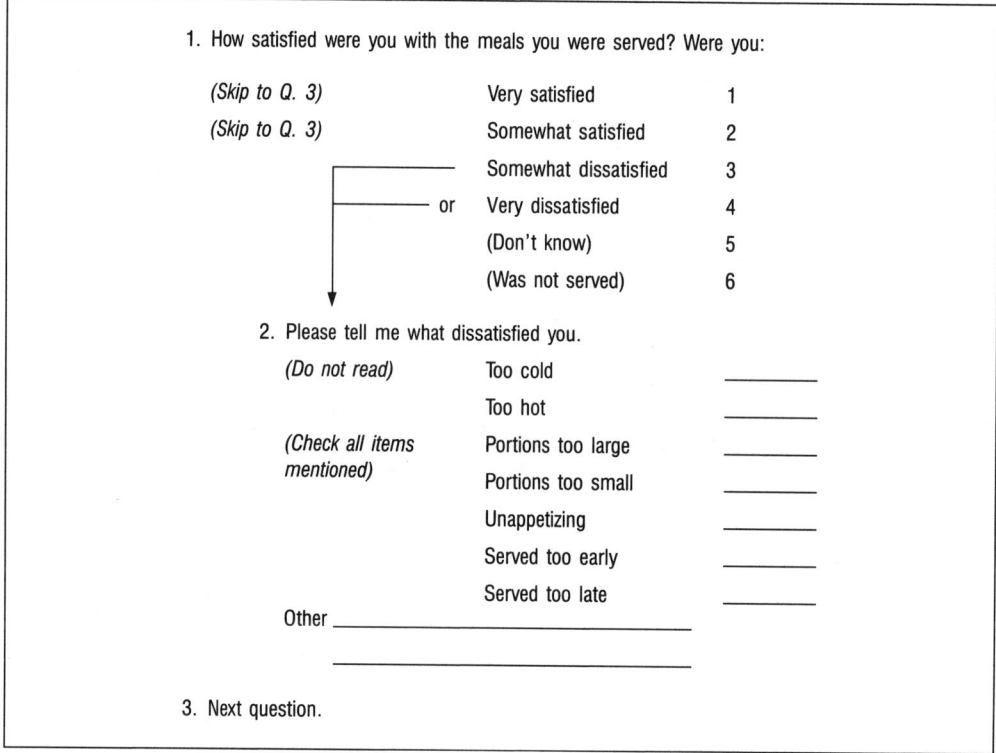

indicating "somewhat dissatisfied" or "very dissatisfied"). Questions applying to everyone begin at the left margin. This indented format alerts the interviewer that a question is conditioned by the answer to the previous question without the interviewer reading this information.

Pretesting Telephone Questionnaires

Telephone-administered questionnaires require more rigorous pretesting than self-administered instruments. The need for this additional effort is evident when telephone- and self-administered questionnaires are compared. When a self-administered questionnaire is executed, the respondent is interacting with a written document that is identical for each survey participant. The respondent has the opportunity to read and reread an item, taking as much time as necessary. When in doubt, he or she can scan ahead or review previous items to help comprehend the question under consideration. In contrast, telephone-administered questionnaires are completed through an intermediary. The respondent must comprehend instructions, questions, and response options through interaction with the interviewer. Although the questionnaire is standardized, the interviewer potentially can modify questions by paraphrasing or even more subtly by voice intonation. When the respondent is unclear about the meaning of a question, he or she must rely on the interviewer for clarification.

What influence, if any, does the interviewer's gender, age, nationality, or ethnicity have on the respondents? Methodological analyses of public opinion interview studies have shown that the interviewer's characteristics may introduce a bias into responses (French, 1981). Although similar studies have not been conducted of telephone patient satisfaction studies specifically, the researcher is well advised to anticipate this potential problem. Recognizing all these factors, it should be apparent that pretesting of telephone questionnaires involves not only the written document but the interview process as well. Telephone surveys place unique demands on the respondent and introduce another variable, that is, the interviewer as a potential source of bias.

Ideally, pretesting should be conducted in two phases. Initially, the satisfaction questionnaire should be constructed as if it were to be self-administered. This allows for pretesting of the questionnaire independent of the interview process. In this phase, the researcher follows the pretest procedures outlined in chapter 8. In the second phase, the instrument is adapted for telephone administration and pretested over the phone. It is important that the same interviewers who will eventually administer the survey be utilized during pretesting.

As with the pretesting of the self-administered version, a small (15–20) representative sample of patients is contacted and asked to participate in the survey. The patients are told that, in addition to soliciting feedback about their service experiences, their assistance is requested in making sure that the right questions are being asked and that the questions are asked in a clear manner. Assuming that the person agrees to participate, permission is requested to tape-record the call, and the interview then proceeds.

Once the last question has been answered, the interviewer announces, "We are done with the actual interview. Now I would like your help in examining each question. Let's go back to the first question, and I will read it again." The interviewer reads the question and then asks, "What does this question mean to you?" or "If you were to put this question in your own words, what would you say it is asking?" Another approach would be to allow the person to answer the question a second time, so that first and second responses can be compared. The interviewer might comment about the similarity or difference in response and then inquire, "Why did you answer by indicating...?"

Being attentive to emotional reactions to questions also is important. For example, if there is a hesitation followed by a tentative response, the interviewer might consider whether this reflects a problem in comprehension or a negative emotional reaction. In this case, the interviewer might ask, "How do you feel about being asked this question?" People are sometimes hesitant to reveal personal information or give an unfavorable review of a particular provider. Such tentativeness and hesitation may suggest the need for alternative wording or prefacing the question with an explanation of its relevance to the study's purpose. (The wording of potentially objectionable questions was discussed in chapter 8.) These and other retrospective "think-aloud" methods are aimed at determining if respondents are inferring the intended meaning of a question as asked by the interviewer, if response options are appropriate to the question, if the question is objectionable, or if the personal characteristics of the interviewer are influencing response.

While respondents are providing feedback about a questionnaire, the interviewer takes notes, especially on questions that may pose difficulties. Once the entire interview is completed, the researcher should flesh out his or her notes while the information is still fresh. Next, the audio recording of the interview is analyzed as a check on any difficulties the respondent may have had in comprehending questions, response options, or instructions. One indicator of a potential problem is the time it takes from when the question is asked until the respondent begins to answer the question. An undue pause may suggest excessive effort by the respondent to answer a question. Respondents may also answer a question with a question. Examples of such responses are "Could you repeat the question?" or "What do you want to know?" Needless to say, such responses are signs that the respondent is having difficulty comprehending the question. Another red flag is reflected in tentative responses, such as, "Let's see (*pause*) you want to know (*pause*) about the nurses. (*pause*) Well, I guess...," or "I guess what you're asking is...."

The relevance of a response to a question also may reflect on comprehension. For instance, a problem exists if a question is concerned with the availability of nurses but the reply is concerned with their friendliness. Or a problem exists if a person is asked to rate the quality of care on a quality scale ("excellent," "very good," "good," "fair," "poor") but responds using a different scale ("very satisfied"). Such a problem frequently reflects the inadequacy of instructions on how to respond.

To assess the possible effects of interviewer characteristics on responses, the researcher should compare responses across interviewers. For example, to assess gender effects, responses obtained from male interviewers would be compared with responses obtained from female interviewers. If it is found that responses are consistently and significantly different across interviewer gender, a potential problem exists. When such effects are discovered, the researcher must pay close attention to the composition of interview staff and the influences of the data given the research design. For instance, if monthly satisfaction scores are being compared over a one-year period and the composition of interviewers changes over this time period, differences in scores may be the result of the change in interviewer characteristics.

Once the pretesting and revision phase is completed, the questionnaire is pilot tested. This involves conducting as many as 50 to 100 interviews, followed by a statistical analysis of the data. Here the researcher is concerned about response distributions and the reliability and validity of the data. (Testing for reliability and validity is discussed in chapter 11.) A telephone-administered questionnaire is presented in the appendix to this chapter and discussed in the next section to illustrate the unique construction of this type of survey instrument.

Analyzing a Telephone Questionnaire

The appendix to this chapter provides a sample of a telephone questionnaire to measure patient satisfaction with inpatient services. To help readers better understand the various components of a well-designed telephone questionnaire, we will analyze the strengths of this survey instrument.

The questionnaire is designed to be user-friendly for both the respondent and the interviewer. To this end, there are detailed interviewer instructions identifying precisely how the survey questions are to be asked and how responses are to be encoded. With the respondent in mind, many questions have a conversational structure, using a three-level "service attribute scaling" format. This structure gives the questionnaire a comfortable flow and helps a rapport develop quickly between the interviewer and the interviewee.

Although the questionnaire may appear lengthy, the ample use of branching questions means that it takes only about 20 minutes to complete. Branching allows questions to be skipped when they are irrelevant to the respondent's service experience. For example, question 2 instructs the interviewer to skip questions 3 and 4, unless the individual was admitted through the emergency department. When question 3 is answered with either "excellent" or "very good," question 4 is skipped. Not only do the branching questions reduce interviewing time, they also prevent the kind of respondent frustration that may occur when irrelevant questions are repeatedly asked. Interview time also is reduced by obtaining sociodemographic and service information from hospital records (that is, questions 46 to 59), rather than asking the respondent for this information. These demographic questions are included to compare the representativeness of the sample relative to the patient population as well as for segmentation analysis.

Notice also that the interviewer is instructed to probe for detailed responses when the patient is dissatisfied with a service dimension or rates it less than "very good." Question 6, for example, asks what aspect of the registration procedure dissatisfied patients. The interviewer is provided with a list of the more common complaints to check. If a complaint not on the list is reported, an "other" response option is provided.

Because respondents must comprehend questions by listening to the interviewer, questions are constructed to be singular in focus, easy to understand, and short. For many questions, scaling is only three-level. For example, in question 11, responses include (1) always available, (2) sometimes available, or (3) not available, to minimize problems with response visualization and memory. The trade-off is that some information is lost because of the truncating of these scales. Most other rating questions use either four-level satisfaction scaling or five-level quality scaling response formats.

The order of questions attempts to follow the natural chronology of the service experience. Following an introduction, questioning begins with why the respondent chose XYZ Hospital for care, which department he or she was admitted to, and so on, through discharge. Questions also are grouped by topic (for example, all nursing questions appear together) so that the interview does not jump back and forth between topics. When the interviewer is changing topics, transitional statements are interjected.

This questionnaire also contains a "bottom-line" question for linking specific service attribute ratings with intent to use the hospital again (question 41). This item, along with the global quality question (question 42), allows for the application of the regression analysis described in chapter 3.

All items in this instrument have been pretested on a sample of 30 patients to determine that, in fact, they are perceived by patients to ask what they were designed to ask. Two groups of questions—the nursing questions, 7 to 14, and the physician care questions, 18 to 25—were used to create summated scales of these dimensions; each was statistically analyzed and found to be internally consistent (Cronbach's alpha greater than .80). These summated scales also were found to be stable (that is, they exhibit test–retest reliability correlations greater than .60).

This questionnaire is coded for easy data entry as responses are completed. Note the number values associated with each response category. These are road maps for the data entry personnel so that they can see at a glance the numerical value for easy data entry. This method has been demonstrated to greatly reduce incorrectly entered or omitted information. It also reduces the actual data entry time, thereby expediting turnaround on data processing and even saving dollars where data entry personnel are paid by the hour.

Summary

Although telephone questionnaires share many similarities with self-report questionnaires, adaptations are required. Because respondents cannot see the survey instrument, special demands are placed on ensuring that question wording is kept simple, fixed-response scales have fewer levels, and similar considerations. Equally important are the selection and training of interviewers. If interviews are to be administered with the uniformity required to produce reliable results, then a centralized facility and close supervision must be available.

Telephone questionnaires require pretesting of both the question and response options, along with the telephone administration process. Finally, the formatting of telephone questionnaires should take into consideration the needs of both the interviewer and the interviewee.

Appendix. Inpatient Telephone Satisfaction Questionnaire

Introduction

Hello. This is _____ with the XYZ Research firm. May I speak with _____ ?

I.D. (___ ___ ___ ___ ___ ___) (1–6)

(If person not available, make appointment to call back.)

(If person answering the phone is not the same person to be interviewed, then repeat introduction.)

XYZ MEDICAL CENTER has asked us to call a sample of recently discharged patients to see how satisfied they are with their care.

Your honest opinion will help to improve hospital care. However, only a profile of all patients' responses will be shown to XYZ staff, so your answers will remain strictly confidential.

1. May I begin by asking: What was your main reason for choosing XYZ Medical Center for your admission, instead of another hospital?

		Yes	No	
(DO NOT READ)	Have always gone there.............	1	2	(7)
	Good medical care	1	2	(8)
(CIRCLE ALL MENTIONED)	Close to home	1	2	(9)
	Doctor's recommendation	1	2	(10)
	Doctor's affiliation	1	2	(11)
	Best doctors	1	2	(12)
	Personalized care	1	2	(13)
	Self/relative works there	1	2	(14)
	New equipment and technology	1	2	(15)
	Employer recommended	1	2	(16)
	Employer requires..................	1	2	(17)

Other _____ (code) _____ (18)
(Specify)

2. Were you admitted to the hospital through:

(Skip to Q. 5)	The admitting office	1	
(Skip to Q. 5)	Outpatient registration	2	
(Skip to Q. 7)	The surgery center	3	(19)
(Skip to Q. 7)	Maternity department	4	
	or emergency department	5	
(Skip to Q. 7)	(Don't know)	6	

3. Would you rate the care you received in the emergency department as:

(Skip to Q. 7)	Excellent	1	
(Skip to Q. 7)	Very good	2	
	Good	3	(20)
	Fair or	4	
	Poor	5	

4. Please tell me what displeased you?

		Yes	No	
(DO NOT READ)	Unfriendly/discourteous staff	1	2	(21)
	Understaffed/lack of attention	1	2	(22)
	Staff not helpful	1	2	(23)
	Waited too long	1	2	(24)
	Procedures not explained.............	1	2	(25)

Other _____ (code) _____ (26)
(Specify)

_____ (Skip to Q. 7) _____

5. How satisfied were you with the admission registration procedure?

(Skip to Q. 7)	Very satisfied	1
(Skip to Q. 7)	Somewhat satisfied	2 (27)
	Somewhat dissatisfied	3
	Very dissatisfied	4

6. Please tell me what dissatisfied you.

		Yes	No	
(DO NOT READ)	Unfriendly/discourteous staff	1	2	(28)
	Understaffed/lack of attention	1	2	(29)
	Handled roughly	1	2	(30)
	Waited for admission tests	1	2	(31)
	Waited for room	1	2	(32)
	Procedures not explained	1	2	(33)
	Too many questions	1	2	(34)

Other _____ (code) _____ (35)
            (Specify)

Concerning the nursing care you received:

7. How fully did nurses explain to you the various medical procedures you received while hospitalized? Did they explain them:

Completely	1
Somewhat or	2 (36)
Not at all	3

8. Did you find the nurses to be very courteous, somewhat courteous, or not at all courteous?

Very courteous	1
Somewhat	2 (37)
Not at all courteous	3

9. How often did the nurses stop by your room to check on you? Would you say:

Very often	1
Often	2 (38)
Sometimes or	3
Never	4

10. How concerned were nurses about your comfort? Would you say:

Very concerned	1
Somewhat or	2 (39)
Not at all concerned	3

11. When you had a question or concern, were nurses always available, sometimes available, or not available to talk with you?

Always available	1
Sometimes	2 (40)
Not available	

12. Did you find the nurses to be very helpful, somewhat helpful, or not at all helpful in preparing you for hospital discharge?

Very helpful	1
Somewhat	2 (41)
Not at all	3

13. Did you find the nurses to be very skilled, somewhat skilled, or not skilled in caring for you?

Very skilled	1
Somewhat or	2 (42)
Not skilled	3

(Continued on next page)

14. Overall, would you rate the quality of the nursing care you received as:

Excellent	1	
Very good	2	(43)
Good	3	
Fair	4	
Poor	5	

15. Concerning your hospital room, did you find it to be:

    (A)

Too warm	1	
Just right	2	(44)
Too cold	3	

    (B)

Very clean	1	
Somewhat or	2	(45)
Not clean	3	

    (C)

Very noisy	1	
Somewhat or	2	(46)
Not noisy	3	

    (D)

Very comfortable	1	
Somewhat or	2	(47)
Not comfortable	3	

16. Did you find the bathroom to be:

Very clean	1	
Somewhat or	2	(48)
Not clean	3	

17. Were the cleaning staff:

Very friendly	1	
Somewhat or	2	(49)
Not friendly	3	

Concerning the physicians who treated you:

18. How fully did the doctors explain to you the various medical procedures they ordered for you? Did they explain them:

Completely	1	
Somewhat or	2	(50)
Not at all	3	

19. Did you find the doctors to be very courteous, somewhat courteous, or not at all courteous?

Very courteous	1	
Somewhat	2	(51)
Not at all courteous	3	

20. How often did the doctors stop by your room to see you? Would you say:

Very often	1	
Often	2	(52)
Sometimes or	3	
Never	4	

21. How concerned were doctors about your comfort? Would you say:

Very concerned	1	
Somewhat or	2	(53)
Not concerned	3	

22. When you had a question or concern, were doctors always available, sometimes available, or not available to talk with you?

Always available	1	
Sometimes	2	(54)
Not available	3	

23. How fully did doctors explain to you the nature of your illness or injury?

Completely	1
Somewhat	2 (55)
Not at all	3
(Does not apply)	4

24. Did you find the doctors to be very skilled, somewhat skilled, or not skilled in treating you?

Very skilled	1
Somewhat or	2 (56)
Not skilled	3

25. Overall, would you rate the quality of the doctors' care as:

Excellent	1
Very good	2 (57)
Good	3
Fair or	4
Poor	5

Concerning meals:

26. What type of diet were you *primarily* on in the hospital? Was it:

	A regular diet	1
	A calorie-restricted	2 (58)
	A low-salt diet	3
	A low cholesterol, or	4
(Skip to Q. 29)	A liquid diet	5
	(Don't know)	6

27. How satisfied were you with the meals you were served? Would you say:

(Skip to Q. 29)	Very satisfied	1
(Skip to Q. 29)	Somewhat satisfied	2 (59)
	Somewhat dissatisfied	3
	Very dissatisfied	4

  28. Please tell me what you were dissatisfied with?

		Yes	No	
(DO NOT READ)	Too cold	1	2	(60)
	Too hot	1	2	(61)
	Portions too large	1	2	(62)
	Portions too small	1	2	(63)
	Unappetizing	1	2	(64)
	Served too early	1	2	(65)
	Served too late	1	2	(66)

Other _____ (code) _____ (67)
(Specify)

Concerning other services that you may have received:

29. Did you receive *X-ray* services?

	Yes	1
(Skip to Q. 32)	No	2 (68)
	(Don't know)	3

  30. How satisfied were you with this service? Would you say:

(Skip to Q. 32)	Very satisfied	1
(Skip to Q. 32)	Somewhat satisfied	2 (69)
	Somewhat dissatisfied	3
	Very dissatisfied	4

(Continued on next page)

31. Please tell me what dissatisfied you?

    (CIRCLE ALL MENTIONED)   **Yes**   **No**

    (DO NOT READ)
    - Unfriendly/discourteous staff 1   2   (70)
    - Understaffed/lack of attention 1   2   (71)
    - Handled roughly 1   2   (72)
    - Waited too long 1   2   (73)
    - Procedure not explained 1   2   (74)

    Other _____ (code) _____ (75)
                 (Specify)

32. Were you visited by the hospital chaplain?

                         Yes   1
    (Skip to Q. 35)   No   2   (76)

33. How satisfied were you with the chaplain service? Would you say:

    (Skip to Q. 35)   Very satisfied   1
    (Skip to Q. 35)   Somewhat satisfied   2   (77)
                   Somewhat dissatisfied   3
                   Very dissatisfied   4

34. Please tell me why you feel this way?

    (CIRCLE ALL MENTIONED)   **Yes**   **No**

    (DO NOT READ)
    - Unfriendly/discourteous 1   2   (78)
    - Not understanding 1   2   (79)
    - Unavailable 1   2   (80)

    Other _____ (code) _____ (81)
                 (Specify)

35. Did you receive *physical therapy*?

                   Yes   1
    (Skip to Q. 38)   No   2   (82)
                   (Don't know)   3

36. How satisfied were you with this service? Would you say:

    (Skip to Q. 38)   Very satisfied   1
    (Skip to Q. 38)   Somewhat satisfied   2   (83)
                   Somewhat dissatisfied   3
                   Very dissatisfied   4

37. Please tell me what dissatisfied you?

    (CIRCLE ALL MENTIONED)   **Yes**   **No**

    (DO NOT READ)
    - Unfriendly/discourteous staff 1   2   (84)
    - Understaffed/lack of attention 1   2   (85)
    - Handled roughly 1   2   (86)
    - Waited too long 1   2   (87)
    - Procedure not explained 1   2   (88)

    Other _____ (code) _____ (89)
                 (Specify)

38. After your hospital discharge, were you in need of any further treatment or care?

                   Yes   1
    (Skip to Q. 41)   No   2   (90)

39. What type of care did you require?

    _____ (91–92)

    _____

40. How helpful were hospital staff in assisting you arrange for this care?

Very helpful	1	
Somewhat helpful	2	(93)
Not at all helpful	3	

41. If you ever needed to be hospitalized again, how likely would you be to return to XYZ Medical Center? Would you be:

Very likely	1	
Somewhat likely	2	(94)
Somewhat unlikely	3	
Very unlikely	4	

42. Overall, would you rate the care you received at XYZ Medical Center as:

Excellent	1	
Very good	2	(95)
Good	3	
Fair or	4	
Poor	5	

43. Have you received your hospital bill yet?

	Yes	1	
(Skip to Q. 45)	No	2	(96)

    44. Do you consider the cost of your hospitalization to be "higher than," "the same as," or "less than" you would have paid at other area hospitals?

Higher than	1	
The same as or	2	(97)
Less than	3	
(Don't know)	4	

45. Before ending this interview, are there any other comments or suggestions you would like to make about the services you received?

_____ (98–99)

_____

I've enjoyed talking with you. Thank you for your time. Good bye.

Name of interviewer: _____ (100)

Date of interview: _____ _____ / _____ _____ / _____ _____ (101–6)

(RECORD THE FOLLOWING CODES FROM THE PATIENT REGISTRATION DATABASE)

46. Patient ID# _____ _____ _____ _____ _____ _____ (1–6)
47. Age _____ _____ (7–8)
48. Marital status _____ (9)
49. Sex _____ (10)
50. Race _____ (11)
51. Religion _____ _____ (12–13)
52. Financial class _____ _____ (14–15)
53. Zip code _____ _____ _____ _____ _____ (16–20)
54. Nurse station _____ _____ (21–22)
55. Admission date _____ _____ / _____ _____ / _____ _____ (23–28)
56. Admission time _____ _____ _____ _____ (29–32)
57. Attending MD _____ _____ _____ _____ _____ _____ (33–38)
58. Discharge date _____ _____ / _____ _____ / _____ _____ (39–44)
59. Days stay _____ _____ _____ (45–47)

CHAPTER ELEVEN

Reliability and Validity

Reliability estimates the extent to which an instrument produces consistent or stable results. *Validity* estimates the extent to which an instrument measures what it is intended to measure. This chapter looks at the major factors that can influence patient satisfaction scores and explains how random and constant measurement errors can affect the results. In addition, several methods of estimating the reliability and validity of satisfaction scales are presented. For a more complete discussion of methods, readers are referred to Carmines and Zellar (1979), Nunnally (1978), Nunnally and Durham (1975), and Nunnally and Wilson (1975).

The Need for Reliability and Validity Assessment

When health care providers create their own patient satisfaction surveys, they often overlook reliability and validity assessment. Typically, the drafting process begins with a request for each major department to submit a list of questions it would like included in the instrument. Because the total number of questions submitted frequently exceeds what can be incorporated in a questionnaire, the number of questions is reduced through discussion, negotiation, and compromise. The revised draft is then sent to management for review and comment. A subsequent revision is pretested among a small number of recent patients (typically 10 to 20), revised on the basis of the pretest results, and sent to a printer for multiple copies. Finally, the questionnaire is field-tested among a representative sample of discharged patients while management awaits the results.

When results of the survey appear to show the service in a favorable light, seldom does anyone ask, "What was really measured?" or "How accurate are these results?" Generally, the assumption is that the instrument is measuring what it was intended to measure and that the results accurately reflect reality (Kerlinger, 1973, p. 430).

To understand why reliability and validity assessment is important, it is helpful to assume that there is an omniscient being who can tell us how satisfied each patient really is with services. If the questionnaire results are isomorphic to reality, then there is a one-to-one correspondence between the measured scores and the "real" scores, as revealed by the omniscient being. For example, if the omniscient being indicated that a certain patient was "completely satisfied," the satisfaction questionnaire would indicate the same thing.

To assess the accuracy of a hypothetical patient satisfaction questionnaire, imagine that the questionnaire was administered to ten recently discharged patients. Table 11-1 shows each respondent's measured and true hypothetical scores on a seven-level satisfaction scale. The omniscient being has been so kind as to provide their "true scores." An examination of the paired measured and true scores for each respondent (that is, respondents 7 and 10) reveals that only two pairs of scores are identical, indicating that in only two out of the ten cases are the measured results isomorphic to reality. Six respondents indicated a higher satisfaction level and two indicated a lower level than their true scores revealed. When scores are summed and divided by 10, the average measured score is 5.5, whereas the average true score is 4.3. These results indicate that the measured scores have substantial measurement error.

Of course, this example is unrealistic in that one can never know the true scores of respondents. Nevertheless, it illustrates a crucial question that is often overlooked in developing patient satisfaction questionnaires: How can one know what is truly being measured? Should one take questionnaire results at face value, or are there methods of estimating the accuracy and consistency of measurements? Indeed, such methods do exist, but they require that multi-item scales be used. With single-item measures, the researcher rarely has sufficient information to estimate measurement error (McIver and Carmines, 1981). Before looking at these methods, however, it is helpful to review the major factors that can affect patient satisfaction scores.

Sources of Error

Sources of measurement error are classified as either random or constant in nature. *Random errors* are caused by transient aspects of the respondent, of the measurement procedures, or of the environment in which the measurement is taking place. They are likely to change from one measurement to the next, even though the person's degree of satisfaction has not changed. This type of error reveals itself in a lack of consistency across repeated or equivalent measurements of the same respondent. *Constant errors* systematically influence the process of measurement or the characteristic being measured. For example, the tendency to agree with statements regardless of their content or to present oneself favorably influences a satisfaction score in the same manner over repeated measurements, thus creating systematic error.

Selltiz and others (1976) have found six major random and constant errors that can influence questionnaire scores: those due to attribute characteristics of the respondent,

Table 11-1. Paired Measured and True Satisfaction Scores

Respondent	Scores		
	Measured	True	Difference
1	7	4	3
2	7	5	2
3	6	4	2
4	6	5	1
5	6	2	4
6	6	3	3
7	5 =	5	0
8	5	6	−1
9	4	6	−2
10	3 =	3	0
Total	55	43	
Mean	5.5	4.3	

those due to transient personal factors, those due to situational factors, those due to variation in administration, those due to lack of clarity, and those due to biased sampling of the questions. Each source of measurement error is discussed below.

Attribute Characteristics of the Respondent

Attribute characteristics include such factors as intelligence, education, social status, gender, and personality characteristics. These factors can influence how respondents answer questions. For example, less educated individuals are likely to have difficulty reading and understanding complex questions or questions that use technical jargon or abstract language. As a result, these individuals are likely to guess at answers or not respond, thereby introducing error into the data. Individuals who want others to think highly of them tend to answer questions in a manner that gives a favorable impression of themselves. Answers reflective of this tendency are said to be affected by a social desirability response set (Edwards, 1953). Other individuals are prone to agree with Likert-type statements about services, regardless of the item content. Thus, if a summated scale does not contain an equal number of favorably and unfavorably worded items, scores will tend to be inflated. Answers which are biased by this tendency are said to be affected by an acquiescent response set. Ware (1978) has found that this response set effect is most prevalent among the less educated.

Transient Personal Factors

Transient personal factors such as a person's mood, health, attention span, and fatigue at the time the questionnaire is completed also affect responses. For example, Patrick and others (1983) have found that persons in poor health are more likely to be dissatisfied with services than those in good health, and LeVois and others (1981) have found that life satisfaction and level of psychiatric symptoms influence satisfaction scores. When respondents are tired, they are more likely to "just do it and get it over with," instead of providing thoughtful responses. Once respondents are feeling better or are less fatigued, their scores tend to reflect these changes. Thus, transient personal factors have obvious implications depending on when questionnaires are administered.

Situational Factors

Situational factors are distractions that can prevent the interviewer or interviewee from communicating accurately. For example, noise may cause the interviewee to have difficulty hearing questions or the interviewer to have difficulty hearing responses. Respondents may also be distracted by children crying, food burning on the stove, visitors calling, and the like. These distractions and competing demands for respondents' attention can cause scores to vary from one administration of a questionnaire to another.

Variations in Administration

A variation in how or where questionnaires are administered can influence results. Studies have shown that respondents tend to offer a greater number of favorable responses when questions are administered orally rather than through a written questionnaire (LeVois and others, 1981; Walker and Restuccia, 1984). Stewart and Wanklin (1978) have demonstrated that the setting (that is, the patient's home versus the physician's office) can influence results. Variations in the time of administration of the questionnaire relative to the time elapsed since discharge (for example, within one week of discharge to one month after discharge) also may affect questionnaire responses, owing to recall error. Last, varying explanations regarding the study's purpose, how respondents should answer, and anonymity may also bias results.

Lack of Clarity

When questions are ambiguous or vague or the logic of response categories is inconsistent with the question asked, respondents are likely to become confused. Variations in scores may reflect how the question is understood or misunderstood, instead of true variations in the dimension the researcher is trying to measure.

Biased Sampling of Questions

Recall from chapter 2 that patient satisfaction is a multidimensional construct reflecting several service dimensions (for example, quality of care, interpersonal style of providers, effectiveness of treatment, service availability and convenience, cost). When a questionnaire omits one or more of these dimensions, the results will only partially reflect the satisfaction construct. When questionnaires differ with respect to the dimensions measured, satisfaction scores will differ as well and therefore will not be comparable.

Most service dimensions represent complex service attributes, and therefore several questions are needed to adequately tap each dimension. For example, the dimension involving the provider's interpersonal style ideally should be tapped through several questions asking about the provider's courteousness, friendliness, concern, politeness, respectfulness, and thoughtfulness. If a single question is used to tap such a complex service dimension, it can hardly be expected to provide a reliable and valid score.

Assessment of Reliability

Reasoning about measurement and types of errors can be represented in the following simple equation:

$$Xm = Xt + Xc + Xr$$

where:
Xm = measured score,
Xt = true score,
Xc = constant sources of error, and
Xr = random sources of error.

The researcher's goal is to have measured scores be equal to true scores (that is, $Xm = Xt$). In the absence of an omniscient being, however, one never knows what the true scores are. Consequently, the researcher must find alternative methods with which to infer the accuracy and consistency of measures. These methods involve estimating a questionnaire's reliability and validity.

To understand internal consistency reliability, it is helpful to review a theoretical model of domain sampling. After examining this model, we will discuss three methods of assessing reliability—internal consistency, test-retest, and interrater reliability.

Model of Domain Sampling

The *domain sampling* model holds that the purpose of any measurement is to estimate the score that would be obtained if all items in the domain were used. Nunnally (1978, p. 193) indicates that "the most useful model for the discussion of measurement error is that which considers any particular measure as being composed of a random sample of items from a hypothetical domain of items." An example might be an arithmetic test that could be thought of as a random sample of problems from all possible problems that could be asked. If it were possible to ask all possible questions contained in the domain, one would measure a person's true score (Xt). However, in practice, a researcher typically uses a sample of items that are composed for a specific instrument. If it was found that scores from a sample of items were highly correlated with true scores, the sample would be considered very reliable. Conversely, a weak correlation would suggest that the sampling of the domain was inadequate, thereby producing measurement error. Because true scores are never known, they cannot be correlated with measured scores. Although the absence of true scores would seem to lead to an impasse, this measurement model does allow certain inferences to be made about a sample of items drawn from a domain of interrelated items.

The conceptual basis of the model is that there exists some infinitely large correlation matrix that shows all possible correlations among items in the domain (Nunnally, 1978, p. 195). All items are related, and yet they are also somewhat distinct. As our earlier example suggests, a single arithmetic problem would not be considered an adequate test of ability, but a combination of several addition, subtraction, multiplication, and division problems would adequately represent the domain. Although each problem is unique, all share a common core.

Applying this model to the measurement of patient satisfaction leads to the following conclusions: (1) a single item cannot adequately represent the domain from which it was drawn; (2) items that are drawn from the same domain are more highly and consistently correlated with one another than are items drawn from different domains; (3) the higher the average correlation among a sample of items, the more common core the items share; and (4) the reliability of a measure is directly related to the average correlation among the items that compose the measure.

Internal Consistency Reliability

The most important question to be asked about the reliability of a measure is to what extent all items in a particular scale are measuring the same construct. When items do measure the same thing, they are said to be *internally consistent*, or homogeneous. The best and most commonly used statistical formula for assessing the internal consistency of a multi-item scale is Cronbach's coefficient alpha (1951). A high coefficient alpha (that is, .80 or greater) indicates that the items are capturing a common core. Coefficient alpha is affected by the number of items in the scale and the correlation of scores for all possible combinations of items. Either too few items or one or more items that are poorly correlated with the remaining items will weaken the coefficient. (The formula for calculating alpha coefficients can also be found in Carmines and Zellar [1979] and Nunnally [1978].)

When the coefficient is found to be low (that is, less than .70), each item should be examined to assess its effect. Items found to bring the coefficient down should be discarded. (See the section on summated scales in chapter 8.) However, if all correlations are found to be weak, then additional items will need to be added to the scale to increase the coefficient alpha.

When a satisfaction scale has several dimensions (that is, subscales), coefficient alpha should be computed separately for each dimension. Each subscale is treated as though it were a separate scale. The process of deleting items from, and adding items to, subscales follows the same rationale as for a full scale. When the researcher intends to generate a total score for the full scale, a reliability estimate should be computed for it as well. Instead of using individual item scores and coefficient alpha, subscale scores are used to estimate the reliability of linear combinations. (Nunnally [1978] explains why coefficient alpha may be inappropriate and how to compute this type of reliability.)

Upon completion of this initial assessment and revision of the scale, the revised instrument should be assessed on a new sample of patients. The process follows the same logic and methods as described for the initial internal consistency assessment. If a high coefficient alpha is found with the new sample, the researcher can conclude that the items are tapping the same underlying concept or service dimension.

Test–Retest Reliability

Determining the internal consistency or homogeneity of items is necessary but not sufficient to demonstrate the reliability of a satisfaction scale. Reliability is not a property of the scale alone; rather, it is a property of the scale when administered to a specific sample under certain conditions. *Test–retest* reliability procedures are used to determine how susceptible a scale is to extraneous factors from one administration to the next. The stability of a scale refers to the extent to which the same scores are obtained on repeated administrations of the scale. Ideally, the answer a respondent gives to a question asked today will be the same if it is asked again tomorrow, next week, or a month from now, assuming no changes have occurred in the actual variable being measured. The researcher assesses the stability of the results by administering a questionnaire twice to the same group of respondents, at a four- to six-week interval, and comparing scores.

A correlation coefficient is computed to determine the strength of association between scale scores obtained at each administration. The stronger the correlation coefficient, the less susceptible the scores are considered to be to transient personal and situational factors affecting respondents. Helmstadter (1964) considers a test–retest reliability coefficient of .50 or greater to be acceptable for making group comparisons.

The major limitation of the test–retest procedure involves coefficients being inflated because respondents remember previous answers and try to appear consistent by providing the same answers on the second administration. For obvious reasons, long questionnaires (for example, those exceeding 100 questions) are less susceptible to this method artifact than shorter ones.

One solution to this memory problem is to administer an alternative but equivalent form of the questionnaire on the second trial; however, this requires developing two instruments. Not only does this require twice the effort, time, and expense, but seldom is it possible to develop two truly equivalent questionnaires. Therefore, the utility of this solution is somewhat questionable.

Another solution is to wait a longer period of time between administrations to lessen the recall of previous answers. But recall of the service experience fades as well, resulting in more frequent guessing or "don't know" responses. Experience suggests that a six-week interval between administering the first and second questionnaires is optimal for balancing recall of previous survey answers and recall of the service experience when attempting to assess the stability of scale scores.

Demonstrating test–retest reliability is not a substitute for assessing the internal consistency of a measure. Consistency of scores over time is not equivalent to demonstrating the homogeneity of items that compose a scale. If the researcher does not have the time or resources to assess both types of reliability, the authors would recommend testing for internal consistency.

Interrater Reliability

When satisfaction is assessed through telephone questionnaires, it is important to determine the equivalence of information obtained by different interviewers. In chapter 10, it was noted that interviewers can differ with respect to how they sound on the phone (for example, enthusiastic, bored, rushed), how they ask questions and record responses, how they probe for additional information, and so on. Despite training efforts to standardize how interviews are conducted, differences among interviewers remain. The only way to determine the extent of these differences and what effect they have on the data is to conduct an *interrater reliability* study.

This method requires that each respondent be interviewed twice within a brief period (that is, less than a week), using the same form of the questionnaire but different interviewers. Scale scores are correlated from the first and second interviews, with stronger correlations indicating greater agreement between interviewers. Here it is expected that the correlation coefficient should reach at least .80.

The reader may wonder whether these coefficients might also be inflated because the respondent remembers the questions and responses from the first interview and provides the same responses so as to appear consistent. This problem occurs only if the respondent hears the same question and response options being asked on both occasions. If the interviewer alters the question by changing the wording or voice inflections, for instance, the respondent will hear a different question. If the respondent hears the same question and response options on both occasions and replies consistently, this is the purest indicator of interrater agreement.

The reader should not confuse the time interval of four to six weeks required for test–retest assessment with the shorter period required for interrater reliability assessment. If the researcher waits a longer period of time to readminister the interview, then the results of interrater reliability testing become confounded by issues of stability. A low correlation coefficient might be found because the instrument lacks either stability or interrater reliability, and it would be difficult to determine which factor was responsible.

Assessment of Validity

A questionnaire will produce valid data if it measures what it was designed to measure. There are four different types of validity: face validity, content validity, criterion validity, and construct validity. Criterion validity and construct validity can be further broken down into more specific categories, which will be described in subsequent sections.

Face Validity

Face validity is concerned with whether the questionnaire appears on the surface to be a measure of patient satisfaction. It asks the question: Does the measure "look valid" to patients completing it and to management reviewing the results? Although face validity is superficial in a technical sense, it is important. If patients do not believe the questionnaire is about satisfaction, they hesitate to complete it; if managers believe the questionnaire is measuring something other than satisfaction, they will treat the results with skepticism or dismiss them altogether. The bottom line is that face validity, although not a substitute for other types of validity, creates an impression in other people's minds and cannot be ignored.

Content Validity

Content validity refers to the representativeness or the sampling adequacy of the questions (or items) used to measure satisfaction. At the theoretical level, an infinite number of questions could potentially be asked about satisfaction. Yet in reality, only a sampling of questions can be included in the instrument. Consequently, a decision must be made by the researcher about how many and what kinds of questions need to be included in the questionnaire to ensure that sampling adequacy has been achieved.

In that patient satisfaction is multidimensional, the sampling of items should also be proportional to the contribution of each dimension to the whole construct. For example, assume that a satisfaction questionnaire designed for use with inpatients contains ten questions about the cleanliness of the hospital, eight about the chaplain service, and only four questions about nursing care. If individual item scores were added together to generate a summated scale score, one could argue that the number of items devoted to each item is not proportionate to the relative importance of that item to the whole. Most researchers would agree that nursing care is more important than either the chaplain service or the cleanliness of the hospital. As it stands, the summated score would not be proportionately weighted to the relative importance of these dimensions.

Initially, content validation is a judgmental process whereby each item is examined for its relevance to how the satisfaction construct has been defined and relationships specified. Therefore, before this type of validation can occur, the researcher must first define the satisfaction construct. Although content validity is presented here as a separate type of validity, it could also be subsumed under construct validity. The content validation procedure essentially determines whether the items in a given set represent "the universe of possible questions that truly reflect a construct" (Koeske, 1994, p. 49). This point will become clear when construct validation is discussed further on.

Criterion Validity

Criterion validity can be subclassified into *concurrent validity* and *predictive validity*. Concurrent validity asks whether a newly developed satisfaction scale is strongly correlated with an existing criterion that itself has been demonstrated to be a highly reliable and valid measure. The second measure is used as a criterion to validate the new scale. When the second measure is administered at the same time as the first, researchers refer to this as concurrent validity, whereas when the second measure is administered at a future time, it is called predictive validity.

The example of the omniscient being comparing measured and real scores illustrates an effort to establish concurrent validity. Unfortunately, finding a criterion in the "real world" that is a pure measure of patient satisfaction is difficult, if not impossible. Because satisfaction is an internal state of the patient, it cannot be directly observed or measured. Although it may be tempting to use an existing satisfaction instrument as a criterion to validate a newly developed measure, doing so seems premature and inadvisable. Patient satisfaction research is far too embryonic to have developed a pure measure of the construct.

Another method of establishing concurrent validity uses the *known group technique*. If it is known that a certain group of patients is dissatisfied while another group is satisfied, these two groups can be used to validate a new scale. One would expect the satisfied group to score higher on a satisfaction scale than the dissatisfied group. The question is, what criteria should one use to assign patients to satisfied and dissatisfied groups? The authors are unaware of anyone to date who has successfully used this approach to validate a patient satisfaction questionnaire.

Predictive validity is of concern to the researcher when the intended use of the satisfaction scale is to predict some future behavior (for example, repeat use of a service or compliance with follow-up treatment). Establishing predictive validity requires that the predicted behavior be measured at some future time; hence, a longitudinal study must be conducted. For example, if a researcher wished to determine the extent to which satisfaction scores predicted repeat use of a service, a sample of patients would have to be followed over a period of time (for example, several months for outpatient services and several years for inpatient care) to determine whether they returned or went elsewhere for care when needed. The strength of association between the satisfaction scores and the later behavior scores would indicate the predictive power of the satisfaction scale. (See Ware and Davies [1983] and Marquis, Davies, and Ware [1983] for examples of predictive validity studies.)

Some researchers are hesitant to conduct such studies because of the time and expense involved. Instead, they approximate a longitudinal study by asking respondents, at the same time that the satisfaction scale is completed, to indicate their intended behavior (for example, "If you should become ill again, how likely are you to use XYZ Hospital?"). Of course, the limitation of this approach is that all too often, what we say and what we actually do are not the same.

In the current climate of concern over patient loyalty and retention, predictive validity has considerable practical importance. Numerous guest relations programs have been established in hospitals across the nation based on the assumption that improving satisfaction will lead to patient retention. Typically, the effectiveness of these programs is being assessed by changes in patient satisfaction scores. Ironically, very few hospitals have determined the predictive validity of their satisfaction questionnaires. In most instances, they have assumed that face validity (that is, "it looks good") is sufficient to infer predictive validity. Needless to say, this is a questionable practice. Last, it should be noted that predictive validity needs to be demonstrated only when the intended use of the scale is to predict future behavior or when the behavior is considered inherently part of the satisfaction construct. However, in the latter instance predictive validity would be subsumed under construct validation.

Construct Validity

Construct validation is a fairly complex process, but it is an important part of instrument development. Although many applied researchers tend to shy away from theoretical research, measurement is always based on theoretical assumptions about human behavior. In fact, it is difficult to talk about human behavior without using concepts that have been borrowed from one or more theories. Experience suggests that making one's assumptions about patient satisfaction explicit and clearly delineating the concepts that underlie assumptions result in better measurement.

Construct validity refers to the extent to which a scale measures the theoretical framework or construct it is designed to measure. As it applies to patient satisfaction, construct validation requires defining what one means by patient satisfaction, including (1) providing a description of how satisfied and dissatisfied patients differ with respect to their thinking, feelings, and behaviors; (2) specifying those factors that influence satisfaction (for example, patients' expectations, providers' behaviors, attributes of the health care setting); and (3) specifying consequent patient behaviors that result from satisfaction or dissatisfaction (for example, care-seeking behavior, adherence to medical regimens, compliance with referral or follow-up visits). Constructs, by their very nature, are always tentative and are revised on the basis of the accretion of new knowledge.

With this theoretical formulation, the researcher deduces hypotheses that predict relationships. For example, patients receiving high-quality nursing care will be more satisfied than those receiving low-quality nursing care. Patients who must wait to see their physician will be less satisfied than those who are seen immediately. Dissatisfied patients are more likely to change service providers than are satisfied patients. If the theory is correct and the measuring instrument is reliable and valid, then most of the predicted relationships will be empirically supported.

In determining the construct validity of an instrument, the researcher specifies two types of hypotheses: (1) the relationship of individual items that measure the construct to one another and (2) the relationship of the satisfaction construct to other constructs, including both relationships that should and should not exist. The first hypothesis involves the homogeneity of items that are supposed to tap the satisfaction construct. If one or more items in a summated scale are found to be weakly correlated or not correlated with the remaining items, then the hypothesized relationship of these items to the whole is not supported. If the satisfaction construct is hypothesized to be multidimensional, then the satisfaction scale should be found to have dimensions (that is, subscales) that correspond to the construct. Each subscale should also be found to be related to the others as specified by the theory. Typically, the researcher uses factor analysis, a multivariate statistical technique, to assess a scale's dimensionality. (Studies reported on by Cryns and others [1989], Ware and Snyder [1975], and Linder-Pelz and Struening [1985] are excellent illustrations of how factor analysis can be used in instrument development.)

Hypotheses about the relationship of the satisfaction construct to other constructs are frequently established through correlational analysis. Although this is similar to the approach used to establish criterion validity, the major difference involves the size of the correlations. With criterion validation, one expects a sizable correlation (that is, at least .60) between the new scale and an existing, fully validated scale of the same construct. However, with construct validation, somewhat weaker correlations (that is, .20 to .40) are expected between the satisfaction scale and measures of other constructs that are hypothesized to be related, and very weak or no correlation with measures of unrelated constructs. When scores on a satisfaction scale are found to correlate as predicted with other related constructs, the researcher has demonstrated that the scale has *convergent validity*. *Discriminant validity* is demonstrated when scale scores do not correlate with unrelated constructs (for example, intelligence, depression, life satisfaction). Convergent validity and discriminant validity are two subclasses of construct validity.

Campbell and Fiske (1959) devised a very useful method for assessing the convergent and discriminant validity of a measure through the multitrait/multimethod matrix. The procedure requires assessing at least two traits or constructs (for example, patient satisfaction, care-seeking behavior, life satisfaction) by at least two different methods of measurement (for example, a standardized self-report questionnaire versus open-ended interview questions). Correlations between each method of measurement and each trait (or construct) are placed in a matrix. A satisfaction scale is shown to have good convergent validity when the scale and other methods of measuring satisfaction are highly correlated, with somewhat weaker correlations found between satisfaction and related but distinct constructs (for example, satisfaction and changing providers). Discriminant validity is demonstrated by very weak or no correlation between satisfaction and measures of unrelated constructs (for example, satisfaction and depression).

Summary

Surveys used to assess patient satisfaction are imperfect instruments. As a result, the scores obtained by these tools always contain some measurement error, which can be classified as either random or constant in nature. Unless the researcher evaluates the satisfaction survey for reliability and validity, it is impossible to know to what extent the results reflect "true scores" as opposed to measurement error. Measurement error can be caused by situational factors at the time of measurement, variations in administering the survey, how questions and response categories are constructed, characteristics of the respondents, and a variety of other factors.

Reliability refers to the degree of consistency with which the survey measures a particular construct—in this case, patient satisfaction. The more reliable the instrument, the less random error is present in the scores. Validity refers to the degree to which the survey actually measures the satisfaction construct. Determining both reliability and validity can help to ensure that questionnaire results are accurate.

CHAPTER TWELVE

Evaluation Designs

Most health care providers conduct patient satisfaction surveys to obtain general estimates of how satisfied patients are with their health care experience and to identify specific service elements that influence overall satisfaction. Armed with these insights, the provider sets out to modify those service elements found to fall short of some expected standard. Once the service element is modified, the provider anticipates improvements in overall satisfaction as well as in specific satisfaction where changes were introduced. When scores move in the desired direction, providers are likely to assume that modifications were successful and the problem solved. However, if scores remain the same or worsen, providers are likely to take further actions in an attempt to produce the desired outcome. The reasoning underlying this behavior assumes that *all* variables that can influence patient satisfaction have remained constant, with the exception of those that were modified. However, this reasoning is based on questionable assumptions regarding causal inferences.

This chapter outlines some of the analytic and research tools that can assist providers in systematically evaluating their patient satisfaction improvement efforts. It begins by discussing the three requirements of causal inference, and some threats to the internal and external validity of studies. The chapter then reviews six experimental and quasi-experimental evaluation designs with respect to issues of internal and external validity.

Principles of Causal Inference

Patient satisfaction research encompasses both descriptive and causal elements. When researchers report the proportion of male respondents to female respondents or the average satisfaction scores for hospital food or nursing care, they are engaged in descriptive research. Statements such as "the results show that the crowded waiting room results in patients being less satisfied with their health care" are causal inferences. Waiting room crowding is the causal, or independent, variable (X), while satisfaction is the effect, or dependent, variable (Y). Another causal inference is that providing patients with presurgical training (X) results in greater overall satisfaction with care (Y). For this statement, X is the causal, or independent variable, and Y is the effect, or dependent variable.

Three Conditions of Causality

How does one know for certain that X does, in fact, cause Y? Blalock (1964), in his seminal work *Causal Inferences in Non-Experimental Research*, argues that three conditions are necessary to infer causality in empirical research. First, changes in the independent variable (X) must co-vary with changes in the dependent variable (Y). Second, changes in the independent variable (X) must precede changes in the dependent variable (Y). Third, the observed variations in X and Y cannot be attributable to some other third variable (Z) effects. In other words, the researcher must rule out alternative explanations for the association of X and Y.

To understand the three conditions of causality, we can consider the statement, "The crowded waiting room results in patients being less satisfied with their health care." To prove the cause-and-effect relationship, it is necessary to show that (1) as the waiting room becomes more crowded, patient satisfaction changes (covariation of X and Y), (2) the variation in crowding preceded the change in satisfaction (X preceded Y), and (3) no other factor (Z) can account for the observed association between crowding and satisfaction, thereby ruling out alternative possible explanations. In the presurgical training example, it would be necessary to show that patients receiving training are more satisfied than patients without such training (covariation of X and Y), that the training occurred prior to the change in satisfaction (X preceded Y), and that no other factor or third variable can account for the observed association between training and satisfaction.

Generally, the easiest of the three conditions to satisfy is demonstrating the covariation of X and Y. Often, covariation is demonstrated by showing a statistical relationship between questionnaire scores measuring X (for example, nursing care) and Y (for example, overall satisfaction). However, showing that a change in X preceded a change in Y is more difficult. For example, one can logically reason that satisfaction with nursing care should occur before a general impression of the health care experience is formed. However, when both variables are measured at the same time through a questionnaire, the researcher cannot provide empirical support that X precedes Y.

The most difficult requirement to satisfy is ruling out third-variable effects. Studies have shown that patient satisfaction is associated with a variety of service factors and sociodemographic characteristics of the patient (Hall and Dornan, 1990). Isolating specific service effects, exclusive of all others, is a difficult task in the typical provider environment, where many elements are in a state of flux. Suppose, for example, that Hospital A designs a new surgical patient education program that is expected to improve patient recovery and satisfaction with care. Before instituting a full-scale program, the staff managers decide to pilot test it. They inform a sample of patients of the study and its purpose, asking for volunteers to participate. Participants are compared with nonparticipants one week after discharge to assess both their health status and satisfaction with care. In comparison to nonparticipants, participants are found to have more fully recovered from surgery and are more satisfied with care. As a result, the managers conclude that the program is a success. What they don't realize is that a third variable may have influenced both X and Y. In this hypothetical study, patients who volunteered to participate in the program were less educated than nonparticipants, and educational level is statistically correlated with satisfaction. Hence, the association of educational level with participation and satisfaction likely accounted for the covariation of training (X) and satisfaction (Y).

Third Variables

Third variables, often referred to as either spurious or confounding variables, can account for the covariation between X and Y. Figure 12-1 shows a simple three-variable model. When a third variable (Z) completely accounts for the covariation of X and

Y, it is said to be *spurious*. If it only partially accounts for the covariation of X and Y, it is said to be *confounding*. In the surgical patient training example shown in figure 12-2, if the training had no actual effect on satisfaction and the covariation of X and Y was completely due to the subjects' education, this would be a spurious effect leading to a false conclusion. On the other hand, if training had an effect but the association due to education appeared stronger, this would be a confounding effect leading to an overestimate of the X–Y relationship (see figure 12-3). Confounding effects can either artificially amplify or suppress the magnitude of association between the independent and dependent variables in a study, thereby leading the researcher to overestimate or underestimate the influence of X. To determine the true effect of X (for example, training) on Y (satisfaction), the researcher must remove the effect of Z (educational level). This can be done using multivariate statistical methods, to be discussed in chapter 14.

Figure 12-1. Third Variables

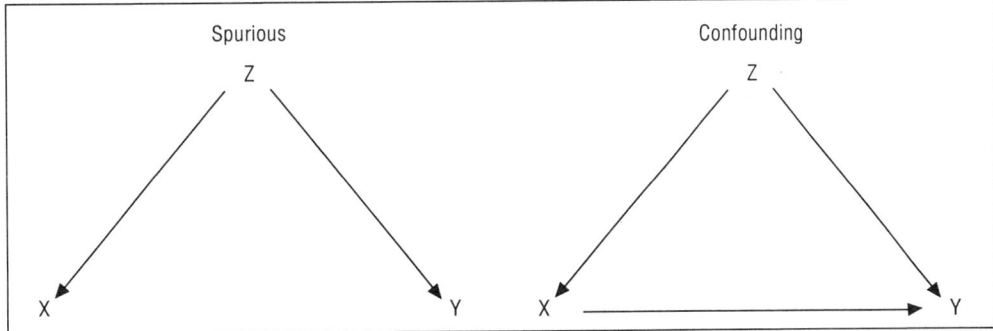

Figure 12-2. Education as a Spurious Variable

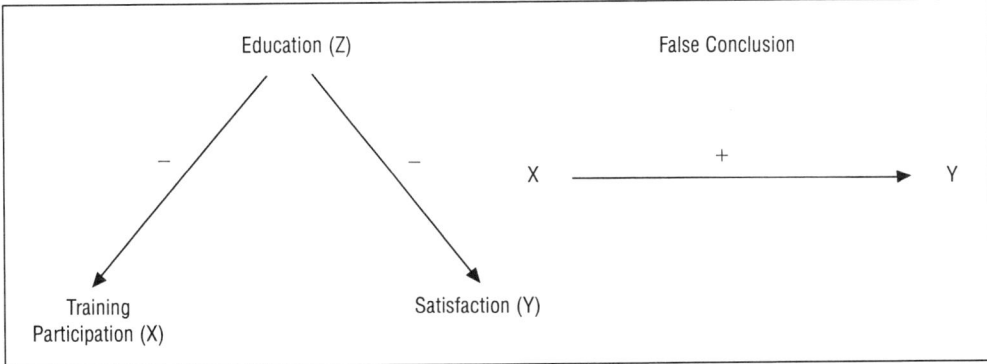

Figure 12-3. Education as a Confounding Variable

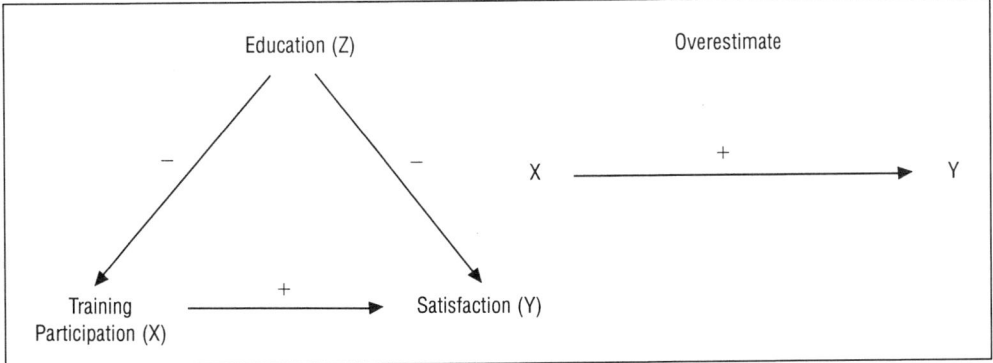

Third variables that influence X but not Y, or Y but not X, are called *extraneous variables*. Suppose that Hospital B notices that patients are dissatisfied with the availability of nurses. To address this problem, they modify the nurse staffing pattern. Patient satisfaction is routinely tracked by the hospital planning department, utilizing a mailed questionnaire. Not content with a 12 percent return rate, the planning staff modifies how it is administered, thereby increasing the return rate to 55 percent. By chance, this change coincides with the modification in nurse staffing. When the nursing department planners compare monthly satisfaction scores (time 1 versus time 2), they notice an improvement in scores that corresponds with the staffing change. They therefore conclude that patients are more satisfied because of the nursing change. But this conclusion may be premature until the change in response rate from 12 to 55 percent is carefully considered. In reality, under the old survey administration method, mostly dissatisfied patients completed the questionnaire, whereas the new method captures those who are more satisfied. Therefore, a sampling bias (that is, a third or extraneous variable) is responsible for the change of satisfaction. This example illustrates a very real research challenge: When a methodology has a low response rate, less satisfied respondents tend to be disproportionately represented.

Another variable could be added to this example. Suppose that changes in nursing and method of administering the survey occur during the first week of an unusually snowy December. As a result of treacherous driving conditions, a larger proportion of patients are admitted with broken bones sustained in automobile accidents. The demographic characteristics of admitted patients change, with a sizable increase in the number of young men admitted. Should one attribute a fluctuation in satisfaction scores to the change in nursing, the change in survey administration, or the change in patient characteristics? Given the available information, the answer is, we don't know. Several third-variable effects are possible.

No change or a negative change can also occur through extraneous variables affecting Y. Figure 12-4 illustrates a case in which the service modification does, in fact, have a positive effect, but multiple third variables suppress satisfaction scores, leading to a false conclusion of no effect.

As another example, consider an outpatient surgery department that begins a guest relations program. Staff members anticipate that the program will result in improvements in satisfaction scores. However, concurrent with the program's launch, Dr. Smith, who performs 25 percent of the surgical procedures, leaves for a two-month vacation. Dr. Smith is notorious for his acerbic interactions with patients. If scores change during his absence, should the researcher attribute it to the guest relations program or the absence of Dr. Smith? The answer once again is, we don't know. As these examples illustrate, researchers should always hesitate to draw causal inferences until third-variable effects have been considered and eliminated.

Threats to Validity

As the preceding examples have shown, merely monitoring changes in patient satisfaction scores (time 1 versus time 2) while assuming a covariation of X and Y can

Figure 12-4. Potential Effects of Extraneous Variables

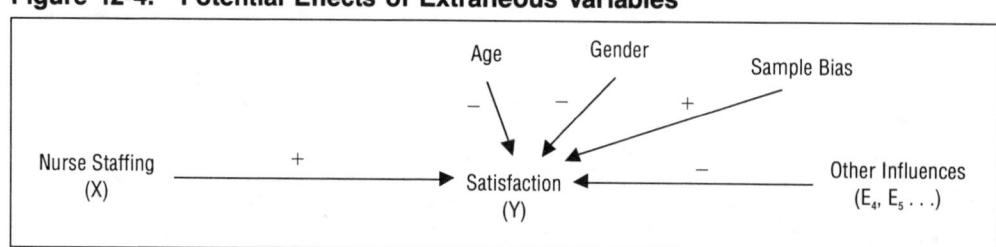

be dangerous. Numerous extraneous variables can affect satisfaction scores, leading to erroneous conclusions. These effects of variables are also known as "threats to validity." Donald Campbell and Julian Stanley (1963) established a framework that identifies threats to both the internal and external validity of an evaluation.

Threats to Internal Validity

Adapting Campbell and Stanley's (1963) framework to patient satisfaction studies, one finds seven threats to the internal validity of an evaluation: historical threats, maturation effects, testing threats, instrumentation threats, the threat of statistical regression, selection threat, and mortality threat. Each of these effects can produce false causal inferences.

Historical Threat

Events and circumstances occurring simultaneously with planned service modification may influence satisfaction scores. The outpatient surgery center example, in which Dr. Smith took a two-month vacation that coincided with the introduction of the guest relations program, illustrates a historical threat to validity. His absence could have been the sole or contributing factor that improved scores. Other potential historical threats are changes in nursing staff, changes in the characteristics of patients, and changes in postoperative recovery room procedures.

Maturation Threat

Study participants experience psychological and biological changes that can affect their satisfaction with service. This threat is more likely to occur in long-term settings (for example, nursing homes and rehabilitation centers) that repeatedly measure satisfaction of the same patients. A change in satisfaction from time 1 to time 2 may be due to service modification, but it may also spring from patients' getting older, improvements or declines in patients' health, changes in patients' interest in being part of the study, and so on.

Testing Threat

This threat refers to the effects of testing on the subject. In studies in which the same patient is studied both before and after a service modification, pretesting may influence posttest scores. For example, if patients are asked, shortly after admission, to evaluate hospital food on dimensions of quality, quantity, timeliness, appearance, and so on, they are likely to become more alert to these attributes. Posttest scores may reflect the interaction of pretest sensitization and food service modifications that would not have occurred in the absence of pretesting. Because the subjects' attention has been drawn to a particular aspect of a service, subjects become more cognizant of any subsequent changes.

Instrumentation Threat

Changes in the measurement of satisfaction during the course of a study are an instrumentation threat. For example, if telephone interviews are used to measure satisfaction, interviewer fatigue or growing disinterest in the task can produce changes in scores. Scores may also be influenced and produce misleading results if interviewer training or monitoring varies; if modifications occur in question wording, scaling, or ordering of items in a questionnaire; if instructions for completing a questionnaire are changed; or if there is a change in the method of administering a questionnaire (for example, from mail questionnaire to telephone interview) from time 1 to time 2.

Statistical Regression Threat

Extreme satisfaction or dissatisfaction scores tend to drift toward the mean, independent of service modification. When patients are selected to participate in a study because they report extreme dissatisfaction, their later scores are likely to improve, even if no service modification occurs. Statistical regression is attributable to measurement error.

Selection Threat

When a control or comparison group is created by means other than random assignment to condition, a potential selection threat is present. Only through random assignment can the researcher be confident that the experimental group (that is, those patients receiving the modified service) is equivalent to the control or comparison group (that is, those patients receiving the unmodified service). Unfortunately, random assignment is not always possible or feasible. Therefore, researchers will often attempt to create a comparison group that is equivalent to the experimental group. When a nonequivalent group is used, posttest scores are likely to differ between groups as a function of this initial dissimilarity. However, even when pretest satisfaction scores are the same, other personal characteristics (age, gender, health status) may interact with selection and affect level of satisfaction, independent of the service modification. Because all possible third variables may not be known, and even the known variables may not be measured, a comparison group is seldom identical to the treatment group. Hence, when the researcher detects significant differences between groups during posttesting, these differences may reflect the threat of selection.

Mortality Threat

Once an evaluation is under way, if a particular type of subject (for example, more dissatisfied) drops out of one of the groups before posttesting is complete, this attrition is considered to be a mortality threat. Suppose, for example, that a home health care agency conducts an experiment to determine the effect of worker degree (that is, a bachelor's of science in nursing versus a master's of science in nursing) on patient satisfaction. Although all patients initially agree to participate in the study, only 76 percent of the BSN group and 96 percent of the MSW group complete the questionnaire at posttest. This differential attrition may influence the average posttest score for each condition, especially if dissatisfaction is the main reason for terminating study participation. The missing posttest scores prevent the researcher from determining how missing scores might have influenced each group's average score.

Threats to External Validity

Even if the researcher has reasonable certainty that X, and not Z, causes Y, the question of generalizability of findings needs to be considered. Experimental controls tend to create their own set of potential problems or threats to the external validity of a study. The major concern is with the ultimate representativeness of results. The researcher should check for the following four threats to representativeness: the interaction effects of selection bias, the reactive effects of experimental procedures, interference from use of multiple services, and the reactive effects of pretesting. These are discussed next.

Interaction Effects of Selection Bias

The sample characteristics of study participants determine to whom results can be generalized. For example, a guest relations program may be shown to improve patient satisfaction at a geriatric clinic but have no effect at a well-baby clinic because of the difference in age, gender, service needs, and so on. Likewise, changing the decor of birthing rooms may improve women's satisfaction with care, while changing the decor of a sports injury center may have no effect on men's satisfaction with a sports injury center. As a rule, results should be generalized only to the population from which the sample was drawn.

Reactive Effects of Experimental Procedures

Participation in a study generates its own excitement for participants, regardless of the actual service changes. As a result of participating in a study, patients may rate the service better just because extra attention is given to them. Innovation also tends to generate enthusiasm among staff personnel who are part of the experimental service. However, once the innovation becomes routine and enthusiasm wanes, the service may produce no greater satisfaction than the traditional service.

Multiple-Service Interference

Some providers use a shotgun approach to service improvement, serially or simultaneously changing staff composition and training, modifying the physical facility, instituting guest relations programs, and so on. If satisfaction improves during the course of an evaluation, the researcher will not know which service attribute, combination of attributes, or sequence of attribute changes has influenced satisfaction. Without this knowledge, generalizing beyond the study setting is difficult, if not impossible.

Reactive Effects of Pretesting

Pretesting may interact with the service modification, creating an effect that requires both in order for satisfaction to change. In the food service example, pretesting sensitized patients to their meals, and that sensitization interacted with subsequent changes in the meals. It was the interaction that improved satisfaction scores, not just the change in the meals. Therefore, these findings can be generalized only if pretesting becomes a routine part of the meal service.

Evaluation Designs

The researcher has available a variety of evaluation designs to assist in answering the question: Did the service modification improve patient satisfaction, or did some other third or extraneous variable produce the effect? This section analyzes six experimental and quasi-experimental designs. Understanding the strengths and weaknesses of each design will help the researcher develop a better patient satisfaction measurement system.

One Group Pretest Posttest Design

In figure 12-5, design 1 offers a symbolic representation of the One Group Pretest Posttest design. According to the notation, O stands for the measurement of the dependent variable, with the subscripts 1 and 2 representing time 1 and time 2 measurements, respectively. X stands for the experimental treatment or service modification. With design 1, satisfaction is measured early in the care episode (pretest, or O_1) and again after the service has been modified (posttest, or O_2), often after discharge. Pretest and posttest scores are compared (time 1 versus time 2) to determine if a change in satisfaction has occurred.

Figure 12-5. Six Evaluation Designs

Design 1	One Group Pretest Posttest
	O_1 X O_2

Design 2	Randomized Control Group Pretest Posttest
	R O_1 X O_2
	R O_1 O_2

Design 3	Randomized Control Group Posttest Only
	R X O_2
	R O_2

Design 4	Control Group Pretest Posttest
	O_1 X O_2
	O_1 O_2

Design 5	One Group Interrupted Time Series
	O_1 O_2 O_3 O_4 X O_5 O_6 O_7 O_8

Design 6	Control Group Interrupted Time Series
	O_1 O_2 O_3 O_4 X O_5 O_6 O_7 O_8
	O_1 O_2 O_3 O_4 O_5 O_6 O_7 O_8

Although this design is frequently used in satisfaction research, it has several weaknesses that serve to illustrate how third variables can produce misleading conclusions. Suppose that the researcher detects a significant difference in satisfaction between O_1 and O_2. How can he or she be sure that the effect was produced by X rather than by other service changes or even by circumstances external to the service setting (threat of history)? Could it be that patients' health and psychological status changed from pretest to posttest, thereby affecting satisfaction scores (threat of maturation)? Did pretesting sensitize patients' responses to X (threat of testing)? Was there a change in the measurement instrument or procedures from O_1 to O_2 that produced the difference (threat of instrumentation)? Did patients who refused to complete O_2 testing drop out because they were dissatisfied with services, which would have positively influenced the group's average score (threat of mortality)?

Design 1 is often used because of its simplicity. In contrast to a true experimental design, which requires random assignment of patients to conditions, this design does not require the service to be substantially altered to accommodate the evaluation. Therefore, the researcher need not be concerned about the reactive effects of experimental procedures. As long as study participants are randomly selected from the service population and the evaluation results are only generalized to the population that utilizes the service, the researcher need not worry about the interaction effect of selection bias threat. The main external validity threat involves the reactive effects of pretesting on X (that is, in the absence of pretesting, will X alone affect satisfaction?). Multiple-service interference can be eliminated by modifying only one aspect of a service at a time during the duration of the evaluation.

Although patient satisfaction researchers are not always able to conduct true experiments, it is nevertheless useful to examine how an experiment controls for threats

Randomized Control Group Pretest Posttest Design

In design 2 in figure 12-5, R indicates that subjects have been randomly assigned to separate groups. O stands for the measurement of the dependent variable, with the subscripts 1 and 2 representing time 1 and time 2 measurements, respectively. X stands for the experimental treatment or service modification. According to this figure, a sample of patients is randomly assigned to either the service modification or the control group condition. Measurement of the dependent variable took place for both groups at the same time, both before and after the service was modified.

Design 2 is illustrated in the case of a psychiatric residential rehabilitation center that plans to implement a social skills training program for its residents. The program designers indicate that this training will help improve patients' interactions with each other and the center's staff. Overall, they predict a positive influence on patient satisfaction. To test this hypothesis, they randomly select a sample of 80 residents to participate in the study. A research consultant is hired to interview each subject (pretest, or O_1), utilizing a structured patient satisfaction interview guide. Next, subjects are randomly (R) assigned to either social skills training (X) or routine care conditions (absence of X). A week after the conclusion of the social skills training, both groups are interviewed again (posttest, or O_2).

The most important aspect of an experiment is the random assignment of subjects to condition (social skills training or routine care groups). Randomization ensures that all subjects have an equal probability of being assigned to each condition by distributing participants without regard to gender, income, age, diagnosis, and so on. With a reasonably large sample, random assignment will produce two statistically equivalent groups with regard to subject characteristics, effectively eliminating the internal validity threat of selection.

Historical threat is controlled insofar as events (other than the intended service modification) will equally influence both groups. For example, if there is a change in the center's staffing (due to vacations or turnover) during the evaluation, both groups, the experimental group and the control group, will be affected equally. The effects of training can still be determined by comparing the average posttest satisfaction score for each group, which allows the unique effects of training to be determined.

Because patient age, health status, and psychological condition are equivalent at pretest for both groups, changes in these attributes will be the same for both groups, eliminating the maturation threat. If pretesting influences the posttest scores, both groups will be equally affected, which eliminates the testing threat.

As long as measurement is identical for both groups, any change in instrumentation (alteration of the questionnaire or a change in the method of administration) will have an equal effect on both groups, eliminating instrumentation threat. Should the study sample be selected for its extreme dissatisfaction scores (or, in the unlikely case, for extreme satisfaction), statistical regression will occur equally in both groups, thereby eliminating this threat. If there is a differential loss of subjects between groups prior to posttesting (mortality threat), the availability of pretest scores allows the researcher to analyze them for nonrandom patterns. Should there be differences, they can be statistically controlled in performing between-group comparisons of posttest scores. (External validity issues will be discussed after design 3 is presented.)

Randomized Control Group Posttest Only Design

The symbolic representation of design 3 in figure 12-5 indicates that subjects are randomly assigned to condition, exposed to X, and posttested. Pretesting can be omitted with randomization, as long as the sample is large enough to create equivalent groups. Design 3 is particularly useful whenever pretesting may not be feasible, which is often the case in applied settings. Design 3 effectively controls for all internal validity threats without pretesting.

One limitation of design 3 is the absence of pretest data. The researcher cannot compare the groups for their equivalence at O_1. However, this does not pose a problem as long as the initial sample was sufficiently large to capitalize on the probability of random distribution. Second, although the effects of history and maturation are controlled in design 3, the absence of O_1 data prevents the researcher from estimating their potential contribution to O_2 scores.

Designs 2 and 3 both suffer from potential problems regarding external validity or the generalizability of findings. Both require modification of the service delivery environment, thereby introducing some degree of artificiality. Patient and staff awareness of their participation in the study will also contribute to the reactive effects of experimental procedures.

The reactive effects of pretesting are a potential problem in generalizing findings from design 2, but not design 3. In this respect, the Randomized Control Group Posttest Only design has greater external validity, in addition to being less costly and disruptive to patient care. In acute care settings with short stays, design 2 may not be possible, because there is insufficient time for both pretesting and posttesting of the same subjects, leaving design 3 as the only alternative.

Both designs are equally susceptible to the interaction effects of selection bias. With the inconvenience of experimental procedures in naturalistic settings, providers are inclined to conduct these studies where they will be least disruptive to patient care and most acceptable to participants. When such selection criteria are used to determine the setting and the participants, it introduces a potential limitation to the generalizability of findings.

Last, in naturalistic settings, it is impossible to hold everything, except for the planned service modification, truly constant while a study is under way. In both design 2 and design 3, there may be interactions of the planned service modification with some other unplanned service changes. Should that occur, a multiple-service interference threat would be present.

In short, through random assignment, designs 2 and 3 control for spurious and confounding variables that threaten internal validity. Experiments also allow the researcher to be certain of, if not control for, the time ordering of X and Y. Because the two groups are equivalent and only one variable is manipulated, the researcher can establish the precedence of X over Y. However, there is a trade-off with experimental designs, in that the greater the internal validity, the more likely external validity is to suffer. An alternative to experimental designs is the quasi-experimental design, to be discussed next.

Control Group Pretest Posttest Designs

When random assignment is not feasible, the researcher will often look for a comparison or control group. Ideally, this group should be equivalent to the treatment group on all potentially spurious, confounding, and extraneous variables. Design 4 in figure 12-5 provides the symbolic representation of the Control Group Pretest Posttest design. In comparing designs 2 and 4, the reader can see that they are virtually equivalent, except for the absence of randomization in design 4.

This design is illustrated in the following example of a nursing home chain. Management wishes to pilot test a new staffing matrix that it thinks will better meet the needs of residents and improve satisfaction. Before instituting this change across all 22 homes, they decide to evaluate it at two sites, one rural and the other urban. They then examine the characteristics of the remaining 20 homes to find two suitable comparison homes. The homes match on the basis of the location and size of the nursing home, residents' personal characteristics, and comparable initial satisfaction scores. A sample of residents from each of the four homes is administered a satisfaction questionnaire (O_1). Next, staffing changes are made at each test site. One month later, satisfaction is measured again (O_2). The O_1 scores are compared to O_2 to assess any changes in each of the four homes. Next, between-group comparisons are made for the two rural sites that have been matched and for two urban sites.

Although at first design 4 would seem easy to implement, it presents the researcher with a difficult task. In the authors' experience, finding a comparison group equivalent to the treatment group on "known" confounding and spurious variables is nearly impossible. Seldom are *all* potential confounding and spurious variables on which groups should be matched known to the researcher. Even if all variables are known, they may not be measurable within the confines of the study. (This is particularly true of psychological variables.) As a result, the internal validity of design 4 pales in comparison to true experiments (designs 2 and 3), where random assignment equally distributes both known and unknown spurious and confounding variables between conditions.

In those rare cases where an equivalent comparison group is available, design 4 is as effective as design 2 in eliminating the threats to the internal validity of a study. When the comparison group is found to be dissimilar, the researcher should pay close attention to the possible interaction of selection and maturation, selection and history, or selection and testing, all of which may severely threaten the internal validity of the study. When a comparison group is selected because of extreme scores, statistical regression becomes a significant threat. These scores will drift toward the mean even in the absence of service modification.

Design 4 has some practical advantages over designs 2 and 3 as far as external validity is concerned. This design is usually less disruptive to the service environment than a true experiment, thereby reducing the reactive effects of experimental procedures. But the reactive effects of pretesting with service modification may be as problematic for design 4 as they are for design 2. The interaction effect of selection bias with the service is always present, because results can only be generalized to the service setting and those who utilize it. As with all designs, multiple-service interference can be eliminated by modifying only one aspect of a service at a time during the duration of the evaluation.

One Group Interrupted Time Series Design

When providers continuously survey patients who are utilizing a service, they are employing a One Group Interrupted Time Series design. Design 5 involves repeated measurement of satisfaction over time, both before and after a service modification. The measurement can be of the same patients or of different patients, as when discharged patient scores are used.

The advantages of design 5 over the One Group Pretest Posttest design are illustrated in figure 12-6, where five trend lines are presented. Although each line has the same slope between O_4 and O_5, different inferences can be drawn about the effects of service modification (X). Line A indicates that satisfaction was improving until the introduction of X, which slowed the existing trend, thereby suggesting a negative effect. For lines B and C, X has no effect, whereas a short-term positive effect is noted for line E. Only line D shows a sustained positive effect, which is what service managers desire when service modifications are introduced.

Unfortunately, many satisfaction trend lines have unstable slopes, particularly when there are seasonal changes in the personal characteristics of service recipients. Figure 12-7 illustrates monthly satisfaction scores plotted for the ADZ Urgent Care Centers. The reader will notice considerable variation in monthly scores, ranging from

Figure 12-6. Five Trend Lines with Different Patterns

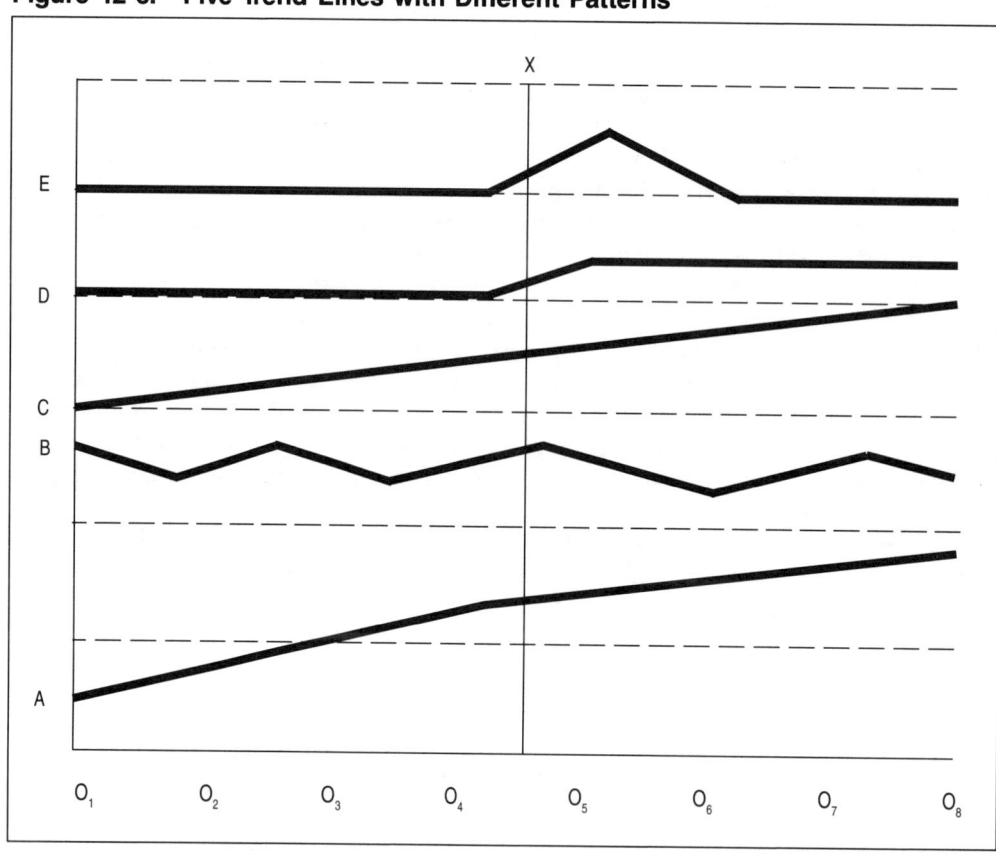

Figure 12-7. One Group Interrupted Time Series Design (ADZ Urgent Care Centers)

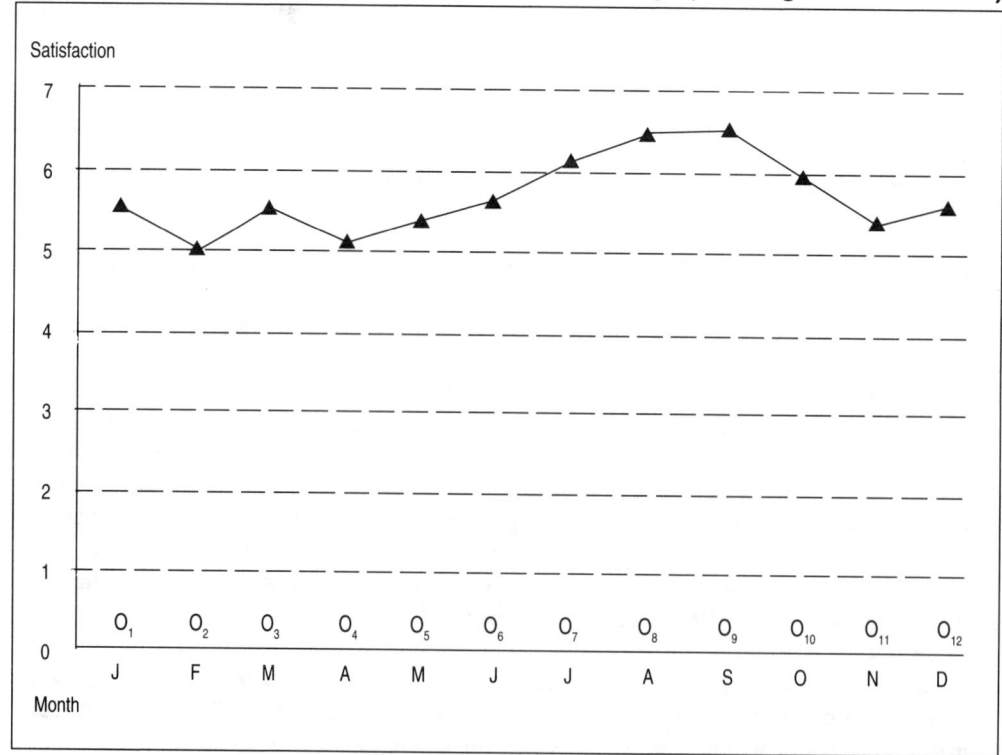

a high of 6.5 for August and September to a low of 5.0 for February. If we examine the months with extreme scores, it appears that satisfaction is generally higher during the summer and lower during the winter.

It is useful to consider what inferences may be drawn from these data if the researcher were using a simple pretest posttest design (design 1, figure 12-5). Assume that we know (but the researcher does not) that the planned service modification has no effect on actual satisfaction. If the service had been modified during January and only O_1 and O_2 scores were compared, the researcher would observe a negative slope and infer that patients were less satisfied as a result of changes than they had been with routine care. The same conclusion could be drawn had the service modification occurred in March, September, or October. Had the service modification occurred in August, no change would be observed between O_8 and O_9. The remaining months had positive slopes, which leads to the conclusion of a positive effect. This figure illustrates the importance of multiple measurements to determine the variation scores that are independent of planned modifications. In classic geometry, it may take only two points to define a line, but in evaluation research, several points are necessary to establish a trend.

When the researcher detects that satisfaction scores are varying in the absence of intended program modification, it is important to determine what variables account for the slope(s) in the trend line. In primary care settings, for example, there are significant seasonal changes in patient characteristics. During the winter months, a higher proportion of patients with colds, the flu, bronchitis, and other respiratory ailments are seen, whereas accidents, allergic reactions, burns, and bee stings are more common during the warmer months. These variations in ailments also are associated with variations in patient age and gender. Moreover, primary care facilities located in areas with transient populations (resort areas) are likely to see seasonal variations in patient characteristics. All these factors are likely to affect satisfaction scores.

Design 5 in figure 12-5 is best suited for service evaluation if (1) the service is invariant (with the exception of the intended service modification), (2) the same sample is repeatedly measured over time, or the personal characteristics of the samples (age, gender, education, health status) are consistent over time with different samples, and (3) the trend line has a fairly stable slope over several consecutive time periods (at a minimum, three periods).

In the event that these conditions are met, design 5 controls for the threats of maturation, testing, and regression. When there is serial measurement of the same sample, particularly at close intervals where subjects grow tired of repeated testing and refuse continued participation, mortality can pose a threat. In this case, the researcher may wish to widen the measurement interval (monthly to every other month) to reduce patient attrition. At the same time, the interval should not be too long or attrition may occur due to loss of interest in participating in the study. One of the advantages of using separate samples (assuming they are equivalent) is that it eliminates the effects of testing and mortality associated with serial measurement of one sample.

As long as the measurement instrument or method of administration remains unchanged, instrumentation should not pose a threat. Selection does not pose a threat as long as the same subjects or equivalent subjects are serially measured. However, even when the three specified conditions are met, history is a significant threat to internal validity of design 5. Other circumstances and events that temporally coincide with service modifications may produce a change in satisfaction.

The reactive effect of experimental procedures is of greater concern when serial measurement heightens subjects' awareness of participation in the study. Also, measurement may interact with the service modification to produce a reactive effect of pretesting. These two threats can be minimized by using separate but equivalent samples for each measurement. The interaction effect of selection biases and X determines to whom the results can be generalized. The multiple-service interference threat can be controlled by focusing service modification on one attribute.

One last caveat: When scores are obtained from different samples at each consecutive time point, the researcher should carefully examine sample characteristics to determine their equivalence. Numerous published studies have reported on the association of age and education with satisfaction. (See Hall and Dornan, 1990, for a meta-analysis of relevant studies.) With nonequivalent samples, changes in satisfaction may reflect variance in sample characteristics independent of the service. In such cases, the researcher would be advised to add an equivalent comparison group (design 6, to be discussed next) or statistically remove these third-variable effects. (Chapter 14 discusses statistical adjustments.)

Control Group Interrupted Time Series Design

When design 5 is supplemented with a control group, it creates design 6 (see figure 12-5). One advantage of the Control Group Interrupted Time Series design is in controlling for the main effects of history, that is, events and circumstances, other than the service modification, that affect satisfaction. Second, when satisfaction scores are unstable due to measurement error, seasonal variation in sample characteristics, or naturally occurring variances in the service, a comparison group will help to isolate these potentially confounding and extraneous effects from the effects of service modification.

To illustrate this point, we will return to ADZ Urgent Care Centers. The two locations of ADZ, on the east and west side, offer the same services to similar populations. The researcher ponders which design to use in evaluating the impact of a new guest relations program on patient satisfaction. She decides to compare the characteristics of service recipients at each location and finds no significant differences with respect to age, gender, education, ethnic status, payer mix, diagnosis, medical procedures, or satisfaction. Given the availability of an equivalent control group and wanting to minimize any disruption to the service, the researcher selects the Control Group Interrupted Time Series design.

The west side location is randomly selected through a coin toss to test the guest relations program, while the east side serves as a comparison group. The centers have been monitoring satisfaction for the past three years, using a mail questionnaire with a 60 percent return rate. To capitalize on the existing data and measurement mechanism already in place, the researcher uses this data source for the evaluation. The guest relations program is scheduled to begin the following month. She reasons that if the guest relations program affects satisfaction, then a significant increase in satisfaction scores will occur at the west side location beginning as early as May (O_5) and continuing, whereas this change will not occur at the east side facility. Data collection through December produces the trend lines shown in figure 12-8.

In reviewing figure 12-8, the reader will note that the trend lines run approximately parallel, with the exception of April to May scores (O_4 to O_5). Although both lines show an upward trend, west side scores improve more than east side scores at the expected time, and the improvement is sustained over the remainder of the year. Through the use of the comparison group, monthly fluctuations caused by third variables can be distinguished from the unique effect of service modification.

In reviewing possible threats to the internal validity of this evaluation, sample characteristics can be examined to ensure that between-group differences in May through December scores were not a function of nonequivalent samples, thereby ruling out selection threat. Assuming the samples are equivalent, the threats of history, maturation, and testing are eliminated because they would have an equivalent effect on both groups. Statistical regression threat is not applicable because neither sample was selected on the basis of pretest scores, nor were the same patients repeatedly tested.

Figure 12-8. Control Group Interrupted Time Series Design (Comparison of the West and East Side Urgent Care Centers)

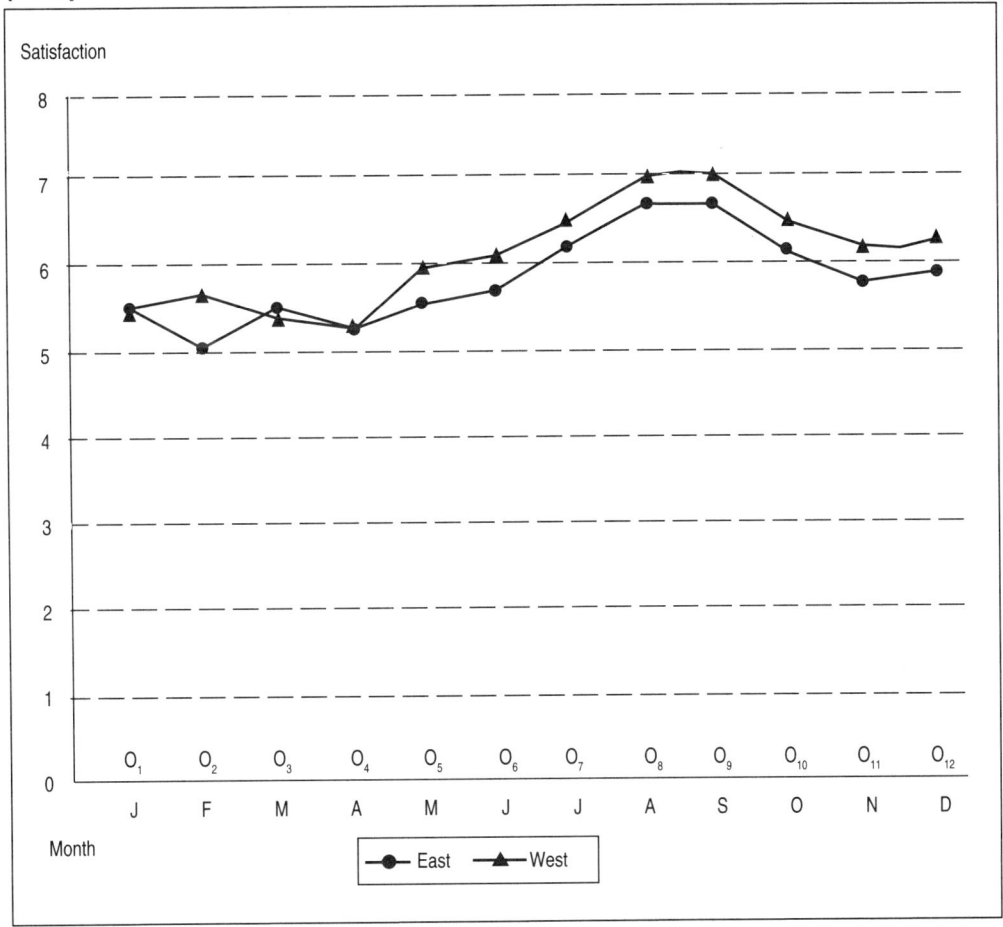

Instrumentation cannot account for the difference in that the measurement process remained constant for both groups across all time periods. The threat of differential mortality is irrelevant in that serial testing was not conducted and return rates at each time interval across conditions remained constant. External validity issues are essentially the same as for design 5. In conclusion, the researcher, having controlled for the threats to the validity of the evaluation, can be reasonably confident that the guest relations program caused the improvement in the west side Urgent Care Center's satisfaction scores.

Summary

The three requisite conditions of causality are that (1) changes in the independent variable (X) must co-vary with changes in the dependent variable (Y), (2) changes in the independent variable (X) must precede changes in the dependent variable (Y), and (3) the observed variations in X and Y cannot be attributable to some other third-variable (Z) effects. Three types of third variables — spurious, confounding, and extraneous — were discussed. Next, threats to the internal and external validity of a study were reviewed. A sample of six evaluation designs that are frequently used in applied settings were examined in light of their internal and external validity. The reader interested in a more comprehensive presentation of this topic is referred to Cook and Campbell (1979).

CHAPTER THIRTEEN

The Evaluation Plan

In a rush to "do better," providers sometimes treat the evaluation of the effects of service modification as an afterthought. The researcher is consulted either during or after implementation of the service change. Entering the picture this late in the game seriously limits the researcher's ability to select among research designs. As a result, the study's quality is jeopardized. Optimally, the researcher should be involved from the outset, and research should be conducted in sequential phases.

This chapter examines the major steps in creating an evaluation plan:

1. Describing the service and problem
2. Specifying the service modification
3. Establishing improvement objectives
4. Choosing an evaluation design
5. Collecting data
6. Analyzing data
7. Reporting results

To provide readers with a more detailed understanding of the process, a sample written evaluation plan is presented in the appendix to this chapter, and the text analyzes the behind-the-scenes decisions and activities that went into the plan.

Describing the Service and Its Problem

Every evaluation plan should begin by providing a brief description of the service, including the setting. Next, it should describe those aspects of the service with which patients are dissatisfied and provide supporting information. It is also helpful to elaborate on those circumstances that have contributed to the current problem. In this manner the problem is put into context, and the thinking of both the researcher and management is made explicit. For example, a primary care clinic may have originally been designed to treat families with young children but now finds itself primarily treating the elderly—a new patient base with very different needs from those of the original base. Or a sports medicine center that was originally designed to treat 50 patients a day may now find itself treating over 150.

To illustrate the development of an evaluation plan, the appendix to this chapter contains a sample evaluation plan based on the case of XYZ Ambulatory Surgery Center (presented in chapter 5). Recall that phase I results confirmed nurses' perceptions that patients were dissatisfied with the waiting room and the time spent waiting to register. The research also found that the overwhelming majority of patients preferred the current hospital-based site to an off-campus location. Based on these findings, management decided to renovate the existing facility and increase staffing. To determine if these changes alleviated the problems, management continued the research. The purpose of phase II was to evaluate the effects of service modifications on patient satisfaction. The appendix at the end of this chapter begins by describing the service, the problem, and the circumstances contributing to the problem, and summarizes the phase I research findings.

Specifying the Service Modification

Having described the service and problem, the plan should next specify those aspects of the service that will be modified and the rationale for the change. In essence, the plan should make explicit why management believes that the modification will solve the problem and improve satisfaction, that is, the assumed causal sequence. As shown in the plan for the XYZ Ambulatory Surgery Center patient satisfaction study, the belief is that there are too few registration staff and that this staffing problem produces a backlog of patients. This backlog, in turn, leads to patient dissatisfaction with the registration process. If staff are added, it is expected that less time will be spent by patients waiting to register, staff can spend more time with each patient, and patient satisfaction will improve.

It is worth noting that alternative explanations could have been equally valid. For instance, another person might argue that the registration procedure is too complex and lengthy, thereby causing a backlog and dissatisfaction or that staff are too slow in registering patients because they lack skill and knowledge of the registration procedure. These alternative explanations would lead to entirely different service modifications. In the first instance, the registration procedure itself would be modified; in the second, staff training would be instituted as an alternative.

In specifying the service modifications, the timing of the service modification should also be included so that the researcher knows when to anticipate the effects of change and can verify that the service modification actually took place as planned. Oftentimes what is planned on paper and what actually gets implemented are not one and the same. Intended service modification may not materialize as expected or when expected. The researcher should be certain what change is actually being evaluated so that the actual causal sequence can be specified.

Specifying times allows the researcher to interpret the outcome data at the conclusion of the evaluation. Should the data show no appreciable improvement in satisfaction, the researcher will have a better idea whether the lack of improvement is due to a failure in implementing the plan or to false assumptions regarding the causal sequence.

Establishing Improvement Objectives

It is tempting for service providers to assume that "good intentions produce good results." When questioning providers and service managers as to the objectives of service modification, the researcher may hear statements such as, "We're just trying to make patients happier and more comfortable," or "We all know what we're trying to accomplish here." Faced with "fuzzy thinking," the researcher may be tempted to read the provider's mind and formulate the objectives. However, such mind reading is hazardous, particularly if the evaluation outcome is not favorable to the provider. Providers may retort, "We never intended to accomplish that. Those were your objectives." When encountering fuzzy thinking or resistance, the researcher should patiently work with providers and service managers until a mutually agreed-upon set of usable objectives is reached. Only then will the researcher know what to measure.

Objectives should describe only the intended effect of service modification on patients, not the means to this end. Frequently, providers confuse the means to achieve an objective with the objective itself. Suppose, for example, that a hospital manager determines that patients are dissatisfied with the availability of nurses on a maternity unit. When asked to state the objective of modifying the service, she responds, "Our objective is to increase the number of nurses." In fact, the desired outcome is to improve patient satisfaction with nursing care. The means to this end involves increasing the number of available nurses.

Another way to conceptualize the distinction between means and objectives is to think in behavioristic stimulus–response terms. The stimulus is increasing the number of nurses and the response is the patient's satisfaction with nursing care. The stimulus is the action taken to bring about a response in the patient. The intended response of the patient is the objective.

Objectives should be stated in a clear, unambiguous, and measurable manner. The appendix illustrates objectives that meet these requirements. The first objective states that "from the point of arrival patients will wait, on average, less than five minutes before being registered." This statement clarifies what management intends to accomplish and what must be measured. The second and third objectives are less precise because they involve patients' perceptions and evaluations. Nevertheless, they are serviceable. The objectives specify the evaluative dimensions (for example, availability, helpfulness, crowding) and indicate that there will be an improvement, although without indicating a specific magnitude. The reason for this lack of specificity is that phase I of this research was qualitative, and at the time the plan was written, quantitative baseline data were not yet available. However, these data can be collected during pilot testing, allowing the objectives to be refined or quantified.

Choosing an Evaluation Design

Evaluation research is conducted to answer the question: Did the service modification "cause" the patient's perception of the service to improve? However, as noted in chapter 12, numerous variables other than the planned service modification can affect satisfaction during the course of a study. Evaluation designs help the researcher control these other variables so that the effects of the service modification can be determined. Although experimental designs offer the greatest internal validity to an evaluation, they are not always feasible or acceptable to providers or patients. In the case of the XYZ Ambulatory Surgery Center, for instance, it was not possible to randomly assign patients to either crowded or uncrowded waiting rooms, because only one room existed. Even if two rooms in close proximity were available, it would be difficult to convince patients to remain in a crowded room, with an uncrowded one readily available. Under such circumstances, it is difficult to secure patient compliance with assignment to condition. When experimental manipulation is not possible or acceptable, the researcher must select from several quasi-experimental designs, each having its strengths and weaknesses.

Once all factors have been considered and a design is selected, the next step is to summarize the reason for choosing the design in the evaluation plan. As shown in the appendix, the researcher documents which design is selected and why it was selected, as well as how threats to the internal and external validity of the evaluation will be addressed. This section of the plan should also describe the sampling design, type of sampling, sample size, and associated confidence interval. If the proposed sampling procedure is nonrandom, then an explanation should be provided as to how the sample's representativeness will be assessed.

Collecting Data

How will objectives be measured? The answer depends on the nature of each objective, the setting, provider and patient preferences, the characteristics of patients, available resources, and related factors. Behavioral objectives allow for several different methods of measurement. Consider the following behavioral objective: 90 percent of pregnant women using the prenatal clinic for the first time will return for continued care. This objective could be measured by (1) analyzing registration records to determine repeat use, (2) visually observing who returns for follow-up care, (3) calling clinic patients every two months and inquiring about their use of the clinic, and (4) asking each patient about her intent to return.

How does the researcher decide which method to use? We suggest that the researcher begin by considering first the relative accuracy of each method, then its expense, and then its feasibility. (Feasibility refers to factors that would impede the use of a method.) Applying these three criteria to the above example, assume that the clinic has an automated patient registration database that contains accurate utilization information. Table 13-1 provides a matrix comparing each method against the criteria of accuracy, expense, and feasibility. Using the registration database (method 1) would provide accurate utilization information at a minimal expense. Because the database is readily accessible to the researcher, the method is also very feasible.

Observing actual utilization (method 2) would require the researcher to intercept patients as they exit the facility and question each about current and previous clinic use. In addition, to verify the accuracy of patient self-reports, the researcher should check patients' historical records to determine if respondents had, indeed, previously utilized the clinic. Although this method is likely to produce accurate data, it is labor-intensive and expensive. Implementing such a study may also involve difficulties. For example, the researcher may not have enough time to conduct such a study, or the clinical staff may object to "bothering patients" or feel that conducting such a study on site is "unprofessional." If the researcher feels that these obstacles could be overcome with some effort, method 2 would be rated as "somewhat feasible."

Method 3 involves conducting a telephone survey of patients to retrospectively determine clinic use. However, these data will be less accurate than data obtained from method 1 or 2, and several hurdles must be overcome. Asking patients to remember past outpatient use inevitably introduces recall error. Research has shown that respondents tend to underestimate their outpatient utilization (Jobe and others, 1990). Second, telephone surveys suffer to some extent from sampling bias. Some patients either do not have a phone or have an unlisted number that they refuse to release. Other

Table 13-1. Comparison of Measurement Methods with Data Accuracy, Expense, and Feasibility Criteria

Method	Accuracy	Expense	Feasibility
1. Registration data	high	low	high
2. Intercept study	high	high	moderate
3. Telephone survey	moderate	moderate	moderate
4. Intent to return	low	low	high

households may use answering machines to screen calls. These constraints are likely to have a biasing effect on the data. The researcher could consider supplementing the phone survey with a mail questionnaire. However, mail surveys tend to have low response rates, introducing another set of potential biases. Clearly, this method will produce data of less accuracy than either method 1 or 2, and it involves considerable expense. However, because several obstacles can be overcome, this method should receive a "somewhat feasible" rating.

The least accurate information would be generated by questioning patients about their intent to return (method 4) as they are processed out of the clinic. Although it is feasible and inexpensive to have a billing clerk ask a patient a few questions, the data are likely to be unreliable and biased. Behavioral intentions are, at best, a weak predictor of actual behavior. (Consider how many people actually follow through on their New Year's resolutions.) Another accuracy limitation is that some patients will answer questions in a manner they believe will please the questioner, saying, "Oh yes, I'll definitely return." This bias is particularly present in face-to-face interviews and, to a lesser extent, telephone interviews. As shown in table 13-1, measurement method 1 will generate accurate data that are inexpensive and easy to obtain. Therefore, it is the method of choice.

A different type of behavioral objective can be found in the evaluation plan for the XYZ Ambulatory Surgery Center. Objective 1 shows that the researcher decides to measure time spent waiting by having patients, on arrival, sign in and record the time. The registration clerk then records the time as each patient begins the registration process. Waiting time is computed from these two data sources. An alternative measurement procedure that was considered involved observing each patient from the point of arrival to registration and using a stopwatch to determine the amount of elapsed time. This method was discarded because it was considered too expensive and unnecessarily precise.

The evaluation plan for the XYZ Ambulatory Surgery Center also illustrates the use of multiple measurements of objective 1. In addition to calculating the waiting time from registration and sign-in documents, patients were interviewed after discharge. They were asked to estimate how long they had to wait before being registered and how much the wait bothered them. Respondents were provided with the following 4-point scale to rate the latter question: "very bothered," "moderately bothered," "somewhat bothered," or "not at all bothered" by the wait. The purpose of using multiple divergent measures of the same objective was to determine the accuracy of patients' estimates of time spent waiting. Second, asking patients to rate the wait allowed the researcher to determine at what point patients became bothered by waiting. All three of these measures would also be used to measure the impact of adding registration staff.

This section of the evaluation plan should also address the reliability and validity of the instruments. If an established measure with known reliability and validity is being used, this information should be referenced. However, as in the case of the XYZ Ambulatory Surgery Center, the researcher described the procedures to be followed to determine the newly developed instrument's accuracy and consistency.

Analyzing Data

Next, the plan should specify what statistical techniques will be used to analyze the data, why each technique was selected, and what assumptions each technique requires. It is also suggested that graphs be used to display results, particularly when time series designs are employed in a study.

Reporting Results

All too often, research findings are underutilized by management in making decisions regarding service modification. One factor contributing to underutilization is that researchers often fail to recognize the research consumer's needs and level of sophistication. It is easy to lose sight of the fact that the way in which a message is delivered is at least as important as the message itself. Most providers are not well versed in research terminology and methods. If evaluation results are presented using an excessive amount of research jargon, the average reader will find the report daunting and respond by dismissing it. Yet it is important that the report document the relevant technical considerations so that the more sophisticated consumer can be informed of the various methodological considerations when interpreting findings. One way around this dilemma is to write an executive summary as well as a technical report. The technical report covers all of the topics addressed in the evaluation plan. It should conclude by indicating the degree of confidence the reader can have in the findings, the generalizability of the results, and the need for additional research. The executive summary provides only a brief statement of the problem, the service modification, and its effectiveness (or lack thereof) in bringing about the intended improvement in patient satisfaction.

In light of these considerations, we recommend that the evaluation plan indicate that the results will be presented both in a full technical report and in an abbreviated executive summary. The evaluation plan should indicate when the report will be available and that a meeting will be scheduled to review and discuss the findings. If a study is conducted in phases, it is useful to provide management with interim results at each step.

Summary

Although considerable time and effort are needed to develop an evaluation plan, in the long run, the effort is more than worthwhile. Once completed, the evaluation plan is to the researcher what a blueprint is to the builder. Ideally, the plan is developed long before service modifications take place. Planning for an evaluation requires the researcher, provider, and management to think through the various steps, agree on service modification objectives, calculate the necessary resources to conduct an evaluation, and understand the strengths and weaknesses of various evaluation designs that are available. The evaluation plan should describe the service and identified problem, the service modification and improvement objectives, the selected evaluation design with its strengths and weaknesses, data collection methods, statistical analysis techniques, and the manner in which results will be presented.

Appendix. Evaluation Plan: XYZ Ambulatory Surgery Center Patient Satisfaction Study

Service Description and Problem

The XYZ Ambulatory Surgery Center is hospital-based, with surgical procedures performed Monday through Friday, 7 a.m. to 3 p.m., and on Saturday from 7 a.m. until noon. Heaviest utilization occurs during the morning hours of operation. Service utilization data indicate that patient volume has increased by over 250 percent in the past five years. Staff frequently observe crowding in the waiting area and a backlog of patients at the registration desk. There has been an increase in patient complaints concerning the registration process and the space available in the waiting room.

A qualitative research study was undertaken to examine these concerns. The results corroborated staff concerns. Observation of waiting and reception areas, as well as in-depth patient interviews, confirmed that there is a problem. Patients perceive the waiting room as crowded, noisy, and uncomfortable. Registration staff are perceived as overburdened, hurried, and impatient.

Service Modification

To address the registration problem, an additional registration clerk will be assigned to the center. This change is expected to reduce the backlog and allow the staff to spend more time with each patient. This change will be implemented in approximately four months, on or about January 15.

Second, the waiting lounge will be expanded and renovated to reduce crowding and increase comfort. New and more comfortable furniture will be purchased to accommodate waiting room volumes. Noise will be reduced through the use of sound-absorbing materials and partitions. This modification will occur in approximately nine months, on or about June 15.

Outcome Objectives

The service modification objectives are as follows: (1) from the point of arrival patients will wait, on average, less than five minutes before being registered; (2) patients will perceive registration staff to be available, helpful, friendly, and courteous; and (3) patients and family members will perceive the waiting room to be comfortable, quiet, attractive, and spacious.

Evaluation Design

Each service modification will be evaluated separately (that is, staffing independently from facility) using a successive sample One Group Time Series design. Separate evaluations will allow for determining the unique cumulative effects of staff versus facility modifications on satisfaction. A quasi-experimental design was selected, because experimental manipulation was neither feasible in this setting nor acceptable to management.

First, the addition of the registration clerk will be evaluated, followed by evaluation of the waiting room expansion. At least four time periods before and after each service modification will be utilized to establish trend lines. Each time period will consist of aggregated monthly data. Because successive samples will be drawn for each time period, the personal characteristics will be compared across samples to detect any variations across time periods.

Internal Validity

With each time period utilizing successive random samples, pretesting, maturation, mortality, and regression will not pose threats to the evaluation's internal validity. As long as the samples do not differ with respect to personal attributes of subjects, then selection will not pose a threat. However, if there are significant variances, these effects will require statistical controls. The same identical measurement instrument and procedures will be used over the duration of the study, thereby eliminating the threat of testing. The major internal validity threat of this design is the threat of history; that is, other service changes or factors that temporally co-occur with the intended change could potentially affect satisfaction. To guard against this threat, the researcher will be alert to any events or service changes that may co-occur with the service modification. In the event that such circumstances do arise, the study may need to be repeated.

This design poses minimal external validity threat. Patient reactivity should be minimal with the use of successive samples and in the absence of experimental manipulation. Random sampling will ensure that study participants are representative of the population from which they were drawn. Changing one service aspect at a time will preclude the threat of multiple-service interferences.

Sample Selection

A daily list of service recipients will be used as the sampling frame. The center performs approximately 7,000 operations per year, for an average of approximately 583 per month or 135 per week or 22 per day. A confidence interval of plus or minus 10 percent is desired for each month's sample. Therefore, each day that the center is open, every fifth name will drawn from the daily list of surgical patients, using a random starting point. This will generate a monthly aggregate sample of approximately 117 names. Assuming that a minimum of 70 percent of the sample will be interviewed, the monthly database will consist of at least 82 subjects.

Collecting Data

Objective 1 will be measured through two different methods. First, on arriving at the center, patients will be instructed to sign in and record the time. The registration form completed by staff will have the following question added: "At what time did you begin to register the patient? Fill in the hour and minute in Box 4." Second, a structured telephone interview questionnaire will be administered between five and seven days after surgery. Two different questions will address the first objective. Patients will be asked, "After arriving at the center, how much time did you have to wait before being registered?" The interviewer will prompt, as necessary, to obtain the number of minutes. (All questionnaires will be coded so that actual and perceived waiting times can be compared.) Next, respondents will be asked: "How much did this wait bother you? Would you say: very much, moderately, somewhat, or not at all bothered?"

The second and third objectives will also be measured through the same telephone questionnaire. Service attribute scaling will be utilized to measure the registration staff's availability, helpfulness, friendliness, and courtesy and the waiting room's comfort, quiet, attractiveness, and spaciousness. The questionnaire will be pilot tested on a sample of 60 clinic patients to determine its validity. Construct validity will be assessed through factor analysis and estimation of the homogeneity of items. If two distinct factors with acceptable reliability coefficients (alpha > .70) are obtained, two summated scales will be constructed. Because the questionnaire will be administered by telephone interviewers, interrater reliability will be assessed. Thirty respondents will be interviewed twice, at a two-week interval, using the same questionnaire, but with different interviewers. Data from these two administrations will be correlated. The acceptable level of interrater reliability is set at .80.

The stability of each scale will be assessed through test–retest procedures. Thirty respondents (those not included in the interrater study) will be administered the same questionnaire twice, by the same interviewer, at a five-week interval. Data from these two administrations will be correlated. The acceptable level of scale stability is set at .60.

Analyzing Data

Data will be aggregated monthly and average scores will be computed for each measure. Summary scores will be plotted on graph paper, where the vertical axis represents scores on the outcome measures and the horizontal axis represents time. Trend lines will be estimated to visually determine if scores obtained after the service change are different from those obtained before. Because scores seldom, if ever, form a straight line, the line will be estimated both before and after the service change. The lines will be examined to determine if the slope of the line has changed or if there has been a jump in the line indicating a sudden increase or decrease score.

Next, data will be analyzed using autoregressive integrated moving average models and the associated modeling techniques developed by Box and Jenkins (1976).

Reporting Findings

Results of the study will be compiled in a detailed technical report and in an executive summary. The technical report will include a description of the service and the service problem, service modifications, improvement objectives, evaluation design utilized, data collection methods, statistical techniques used to analyze the data, and the analysis results. It will note if a significant change or jump in the trend lines occurred. The report will also describe any service changes or factors, other than the planned service modification, that could have influenced the study's outcome. Given the research design, statistical results, and possible confounding variables, the researcher will assess the degree of confidence the reader should have in the findings, the generalizability of the results, and the need for additional research. After management has had an opportunity to review the report, a meeting will be scheduled to present and discuss the findings.

CHAPTER FOURTEEN

Analysis of Research Data

Before data can be put to use, they must be analyzed and interpreted. Analysis can be a relatively straightforward process if basic guidelines are followed and appropriate tools are used. Moreover, if the analytic tools are anticipated at the beginning of the research planning process, greater insight will accrue during the research process and unpleasant surprises will be kept to a minimum.

This chapter details some of the basic tools that are used to interpret data. Building on information presented in earlier chapters, the chapter provides perspective on the meaning and use of qualitative and quantitative data. For quantitative data, some of the more straightforward statistics and their formulas are described and applications are worked out. More advanced statistical tests are demonstrated through case examples rather than algebraic formulas. Thus, the chapter provides a basic introduction to statistical analysis to help readers become better informed managers or consumers of customer satisfaction research.

A successful patient satisfaction research system does several things: (1) it provides insight into how to measurably enhance patient satisfaction, (2) it allows tracking of movement in patient satisfaction over time, and (3) it plays a role in a larger model of service management. The end goal of analysis, then, is to give meaning and direction to patient service efforts. Although the techniques for analyzing qualitative and quantitative research differ, the end goal is the same.

Qualitative Data

Qualitative research produces a mass of verbatim information whose function is to delve deeply into the customer experience—more so than a quantitative approach can. The guiding principle in qualitative research is to find out what perceptions patients as customers have of their service providers, and why. Qualitative research can be highly specific, plumbing and exhausting an individual's experience and assigning ratings (or descriptive words) to different dimensions of that experience. For that reason, qualitative research is often used to gain insight into the customer's experience and understand how providers' actions are interpreted. Those insights in turn can be taken to the provider to support change. But qualitative research is not an efficient tracking or trending tool once those changes have been introduced. If a service provider were to entirely remodel its service delivery environment, the provider should use qualitative research on its very first customers to learn, in the customers' own words, how the new design has been received. It would be less appropriate to use qualitative research to discern *changes* in satisfaction, or trends over time. For such comparisons across a time line, quantitative research is more appropriate.

Quantitative Data

Quantitative research is concerned with teasing out meaningful patterns in the wealth of perceptual data amassed through qualitative data. Although some people feel that quantitative data are more convincing because numbers are "more objective," it should be remembered at this point that all analysis is interpretive, and no data are so heroic that they will not confess to all sorts of crimes if subjected to sufficient statistical torture. The problem of misinterpreting data in the course of quantitative research has not abated with the introduction of statistical software packages, for the software itself does not deny the researcher the opportunity to violate important assumptions while putting the algorithms to work. Numbers lie as well as you or I.

The remainder of this chapter samples a variety of statistical methods that are commonly used in customer satisfaction research. The goal is not to create a treatise on statistics but to provide an appreciation of techniques well suited for many management demands. The net result should be a better understanding of what makes a difference to the customer, how to make the needle move on customer satisfaction, how to track results over time, and how to accomplish all of these goals within the real limitations of the data and the techniques.

Three dimensions define which statistical tools are most suitable for a given body of quantitative data: (1) the measurement level of the questions, (2) the number of respondents, and (3) the number of questions to be analyzed. The following discussion of quantitative statistical techniques begins with those methods that place the fewest demands on the data and are the simplest to apply. Then, more sophisticated techniques are presented. These techniques afford the researcher the opportunity to "model" the customer experience in its multiple dimensions. The goal of modeling, in turn, is to gain sufficient insight to make systemic changes in service delivery.

Measurement Levels

Some categorical and measurement terms discussed earlier in the book will reappear in this chapter; they are reviewed briefly here to help the reader be mindful of the limitations of any given measurement level and of the analytic tools appropriate to each. Previously we defined four levels of measurement in evaluation research: nominal, ordinal, interval, and ratio. Recall that each successive category introduces more information into the data. Nominal data, which name people or groupings, simply designate categories of responses that serve to distinguish one group or category of patients from another. For example, a question about gender notes only that men are one code and women another, or a question about a patient care group indicates that some respondents are on Unit 1-South and others are on Unit 2-North. Nominal measurement is like a marker, or a "namer." No evaluation is implied. No response category is better or worse than another, has more or less than another, or is anything but just different.

Ordinal data move beyond simple taxonomic distinctions to introduce direction and relative magnitude into the data. For instance, the classic ordinal scale used in satisfaction research ranks responses to a question of a specific service component from "excellent" to "poor." There may be four categories ("excellent," "good," "fair," "poor"), five categories ("excellent," "very good," "good," "fair," "poor"), or any number, but a respondent's answer to the question clearly defines less or more than a different response would.

Most often, these word responses are simply coded and entered into a database as 1, 2, 3, 4 or 1, 2, 3, 4, 5 for the four- and five-category question formats, respectively. Although this may be a convenient way to keep track of responses, it attributes more information, more precision, to the question than was initially there by converting word responses into numerical values, which we understand to be separated by equal intervals. This may violate the underlying assumptions of the statistical tools the researcher will later use on the data.

Interval data offer something more than the ranking of responses that ordinal data offer. They claim *equal magnitudes of difference* between any two adjacent response codes. (The word *claim* is used, because many question formats that purport to have interval status do not actually have it, but the violations in such cases typically can be overlooked.) True interval scales might ask a respondent to rate a dimension of service on a scale from 1 to 5, where 1 is "poor" and 5 is "excellent" (but with no positions between 1 and 5 labeled with word descriptors) or on a scale from F to A (again, with no positions in between those two termini labeled with word descriptors). By not labeling the responses 2 through 4, the researcher avoids introducing any semantics that would suggest anything other than equal distance between adjacent codes.

More commonly, however, interval scales use a Likert scale, with categories that range from "strongly disagree" to "strongly agree" or "very dissatisfied" to "very satisfied" or "strongly disapprove" to "strongly approve." This original scale and many adaptations using "satisfaction" instead of "agreement" possess "equal-appearing intervals" across responses. Translated, that means that one can confidently infer that the difference, or interval, between "strongly disagree" and "disagree" is equal to that between "strongly agree" and "agree." Other similar comparisons can be made, even though some of the semantic differences do not have the tidy comparability of these examples (for example, the interval between "agree" and "neutral" versus that between "strongly agree" and "agree").

Ratio-level data include a true zero point in the scale. Although it is possible for customers to say that they have a very low opinion of a service provider based on an unfavorable experience, it is conceptually difficult to imagine a true zero—*no* opinion. That is why most ratio-level data are found only in more tangible measures such as age, income, height, temperature, and the like. For all intents and purposes, however, interval-level questions can take advantage of the same statistical techniques as can ratio-level questions, so that the presence or absence of "zero attitude" is of little practical consequence.

Simple Tests of Differences

One of the principal management mandates in the competitive health care delivery environment is to "make something happen." To help management, it is important to actually measure whether or when change has occurred—in other words, to show that "something has happened." Management does not simply want to measure patient satisfaction. It wants to move patient satisfaction to higher levels or, in some cases, to prevent satisfaction from eroding from an existing level. At a basic level, management wants to know whether difference has occurred or has not occurred.

Therefore, in measuring satisfaction over time, it is important to have some statistical tools available that will quantify the extent to which favorable change, no change, or unfavorable change has occurred. The following tests do not necessarily offer insight into the relationships among the elements of service delivery that will help to manage toward favorable change, but they do show when change has, in fact, occurred.

Chi-Square Test

One of the long-standing statistical workhorses for analyzing nominal data is the *chi-square test*. A chi-square statistic (when significant) tells one if the responses captured from customers are significantly different from those one would expect if responses simply distributed themselves randomly. The chi-square test is referred to as a nonparametric test, because to use the test one need not make assumptions about a distribution of scores within a true population from which the sample is drawn. The only real restriction for appropriate use of the chi-square test is that each of the cells in the table being analyzed should possess a minimum of five respondents. Even this restriction, if not violated to the extreme, does no measurable harm to the statistic; it simply makes it more difficult to attain significance.

Hypothetical Case Study 14-A: Chi-Square Test

The following hypothetical situation references a study conducted among outpatients. Two questions are cross-classified by one another: "satisfaction with overall quality of care received" and "overall likelihood of returning for future health care needs." In the case of the former, satisfaction is measured on a Likert-format scale from "very satisfied" to "very dissatisfied." In the case of the latter, likelihood of returning has been reduced to a simple dichotomy: respondents are classified as either very likely to return or less than very likely. This dichotomy has been forced on what was originally a five-category variable because of extremely thinly populated cells – that is, few responses – in all the less than "very likely" categories. (See the data displayed in table 14-1.)

Chi-square is calculated according to the following formula:

$$\chi^2 = \sum \frac{(f_o - f_e)^2}{f_e}$$

where f_o = *observed* number of respondents in the category, and f_e = *expected* number if randomly distributed. Σ simply tells us to sum the arithmetic function for all "χ" cells or categories, counted from the letter $i = 1$ to $i = \chi$ (the largest number).

Where the observed and expected frequencies are close, the value of chi-square tends to be smaller; where the observed and expected frequencies are farther apart, the value of chi-square is larger. Calculating the chi-square statistic in this example offers a value of approximately 269.78 (approximately, because rounding error can enter the equation). A test to identify the extent to which the low cell frequencies in two of the cells

Table 14-1. Likelihood of Returning

	Total	Very Likely	Somewhat Likely
Total Responding	1,117	928	189
Very satisfied	895	823	72
Somewhat satisfied	179	93	86
Neutral	20	7	13
Somewhat dissatisfied	13	4	9
Very dissatisfied	10	1	9

introduced any spurious results found that no statistical problem was posed. Therefore, all that remains is to determine the degrees of freedom (*d.f.*) associated with this statistic, a value that is sensitive to the overall number of rows and columns in the table of appendix C at the end of this book. The more degrees of freedom (a function of the number of cells), the more opportunity for differences between the observed and expected frequencies. We counter the natural tendency for larger tables (more cells and degrees of freedom) to have larger chi-square values by making chi-square be larger in order to obtain statistical significance (see appendix C). The following formula is used:

$$d.f. = (r - 1)(c - 1),$$

where r = the number of rows (in this case, 5), and c = the number of columns (in this case, 2).

Refer to the distribution of the chi-square statistic and associated degrees of freedom in appendix C to this book to determine if this figure is, in fact, statistically significant with its 4 degrees of freedom. It is, in fact, significant beyond the 99.9 percent level of significance (sometimes referred to as $p > .001$ level). We can be certain that a distribution such as this would occur by random chance alone in less than one case in 1,000.

What can one then say about the relationship between expressed brand loyalty and overall satisfaction with quality of care? This is where chi-square and the nature of the data can be limiting. Chi-square tells only whether an event, such as an association between two variables (satisfaction and return likelihood, in this case), occurs nonrandomly or randomly. For this reason, it is useful to calculate chi-square very early, before one gets committed to exploring data that could represent chance associations alone. The chi-square statistic does not, however, say anything about the direction of the relationship (for example, when one variable goes up, the other goes down, or vice versa, or they both move in tandem, and so on), the magnitude of the relationship (for example, when one increases by 10 percent, the other increases by 5 percent), or the causality of the relationship (for example, perceived quality causes loyalty). We must content ourselves with saying simply that there is a statistically significant relationship between two variables. But that is where other statistical tools at our disposal can make better use of the data we have at hand.

Difference of Proportions Test

One can perform a simple arithmetic function on the data in table 14-1 and test the relationship between perceived quality and loyalty (return likelihood) in a different way than can be examined using just nominal data. The test is called a *difference of proportions* test, and it determines the statistical significance of the difference between two groups based on the percentage responding to a given question in one group versus the percentage responding to the same question in another group.

The difference of proportions test takes into account the differences between the two percentages reported; but to this, it adds a sensitivity to the sizes of the samples from which the two proportions are responding, as well as two factors to which chi-square was not sensitive: direction and magnitude. Being in one category over another will now have clear implications for the size and leaning of one's perspective.

Hypothetical Case Study 14-B: Difference of Proportions Test

In the case of the difference of proportions test, one can look at the percentage of outpatients who say they are "very satisfied with the quality of care" among those who also are "very likely to return for future needs" versus those who are less likely. Table 14-1 shows that of the 928 patients who are very likely to return, fully 823 (or 88.7 percent) also are "very satisfied" with the quality of care. Of the 189 who are less likely to return, only 72 (or 38.1 percent) reportedly are "very satisfied" with the quality of care. Are these proportions statistically significant?

The classic calculation of difference of proportion relies on a series of formulas that lead to what is termed a z score. This score is plotted along a normal curve to identify significant departures from what might be expected from random variation alone. Fortunately, there is a shortcut to identifying significant departures. Using confidence intervals (described in chapter 6), one can approximate the difference of proportions statistic without going to the trouble of performing all the arithmetic.

The confidence interval for the first sample of 928 patients is + or − 2 percent, and for the complementary sample of 189 patients it is + or − 6.9 percent. These two confidence intervals are brought together in a simple formula:

$$\text{D.P.} = (CI_1)^2 + (CI_2)^2,$$

where CI_1 is the confidence interval associated with the first sample, and CI_2 is the confidence interval associated with the second sample. Calculated, this offers a solution of approximately 7.2 percent as the magnitude by which the two proportions must differ for that difference to be statistically significant at the 95 percent level. (The critical figure, of course, gets larger for the 99 percent and 99.9 percent levels, but the operating principle is the same.) We now can say with confidence that those individuals who say they are "very likely" to return are, in fact, significantly more satisfied with the quality of care than their counterparts.

Difference of Means Test

Also known as Student's t-test or simply the t-test, this tool is useful in comparing the extent to which the averages, or statistical means, from two groups are significantly different. Whereas the difference of proportions test judges the distinction between two groups based on the proportion of respondents in a single response code, the t-test takes into account the entire distribution of responses along an interval or ratio scale.

Hypothetical Case Study 14-C: Difference of Means Test

The key input variables necessary for calculating this test statistic include the means for each of the two groups, the standard deviation of each mean, and the sample sizes from which these variables are derived. The equation looks like this:

$$t = \frac{X_1 - X_2}{\frac{s_1 + s_2}{(N_1 - 1)(N_2 - 1)}}$$

where X_1 equals the statistical average for the first group, X_2 equals the statistical average for the second group, s_1 is the standard deviation for the first group, s_2 is the standard deviation for the second group, N_1 is the sample size for the first group, and N_2 is the sample size for the second group.

Going into the details of the calculation of this statistic offers a value of 10.48, which is checked against the table in appendix B at the end of this book. Note that the appendix requests degrees of freedom and also distinguishes between what are termed one-tailed and two-tailed tests of significance. Where the sample sizes are relatively large, one can use the simple formula, $N_1 + N_2 - 2 = d.f.$ Where the samples are smaller, the formula for degrees of freedom gets a bit more complicated. The one-tailed test is appropriate if, before the data are even collected, the researcher can hypothesize that the difference will be a specific direction—not just that the samples will be different, but different in a specific way.

Intuitively, the reader will have anticipated in this particular case that those patients who are more likely to return to a provider for future needs ought also to have seen higher quality in the service. The one-tailed test, therefore, does not require as large a t statistic as the two-tailed test. In this case, the t-test reaffirms the same general nature of the relationship earlier defined by the difference of proportions test. With a value of 10.48, this test is significant beyond the .001 level. The average satisfaction with overall quality of those who reportedly are "very likely" to return to the outpatient facility for their future health care needs is significantly higher than among those who reportedly are less likely, beyond any reasonable doubt.

Measures of Association

A measure of association statistically describes the way in which variation in one item is consistently related to variation in another. A good measure of association allows the health services manager to describe, explain, understand, and ultimately manage the relationship between factors that the patient can perceive and evaluate. For instance, is there a statistical relationship between waiting time in a physician's office and overall satisfaction with care from that physician? In a noncompetitive service environment, the answer to this question may not matter a great deal, but in the competitive health care market, it may spell the difference between success and failure. However, one should not assume that more of some elements of service is better and that less of others (for example, waiting time) is better. One should quantify these associations to make informed service changes.

This section describes some of the fundamental measures that quantify the statistical linkage between two service elements and describes the insights that such measures can afford. Recall, however, that the customer's experience has multiple facets, with interrelations among the facets. In the example of the physician's office wait, it is not simply the waiting time that helps us understand how a patient arrives at a final evaluation of the service received. The physician also plays a pivotal role, as do other office personnel and the physical setting itself. This complexity requires more sophisticated statistical models to capture the associations of multiple elements that make up the customer's service experience. These models will be presented later in the chapter. For now, we will focus on the ways in which just two elements can be associated.

Correlation

Correlation is a very rudimentary although somewhat useful measure of association that ranges between a maximum of +1.0 and a minimum of −1.0. Correlation is the measure of the association between two intervals or ratio-level variables. By "measure of association" we mean that its magnitude and direction (that is, positive or negative) characterize the extent to which two service dimensions generally move in concert with one another. If one looks at how the correlation between two variables is calculated, a better appreciation of its true meaning and inherent limitations is possible.

Figure 14-1 shows an idealized adaptation of a *scatter plot* of two variables, or the simultaneous plotting, on the same graph, of all the actual scores that recent patients have reported for two specific questions. Patients' ratings of satisfaction with

Chapter 14

Figure 14-1. Scatter Plot of x and y

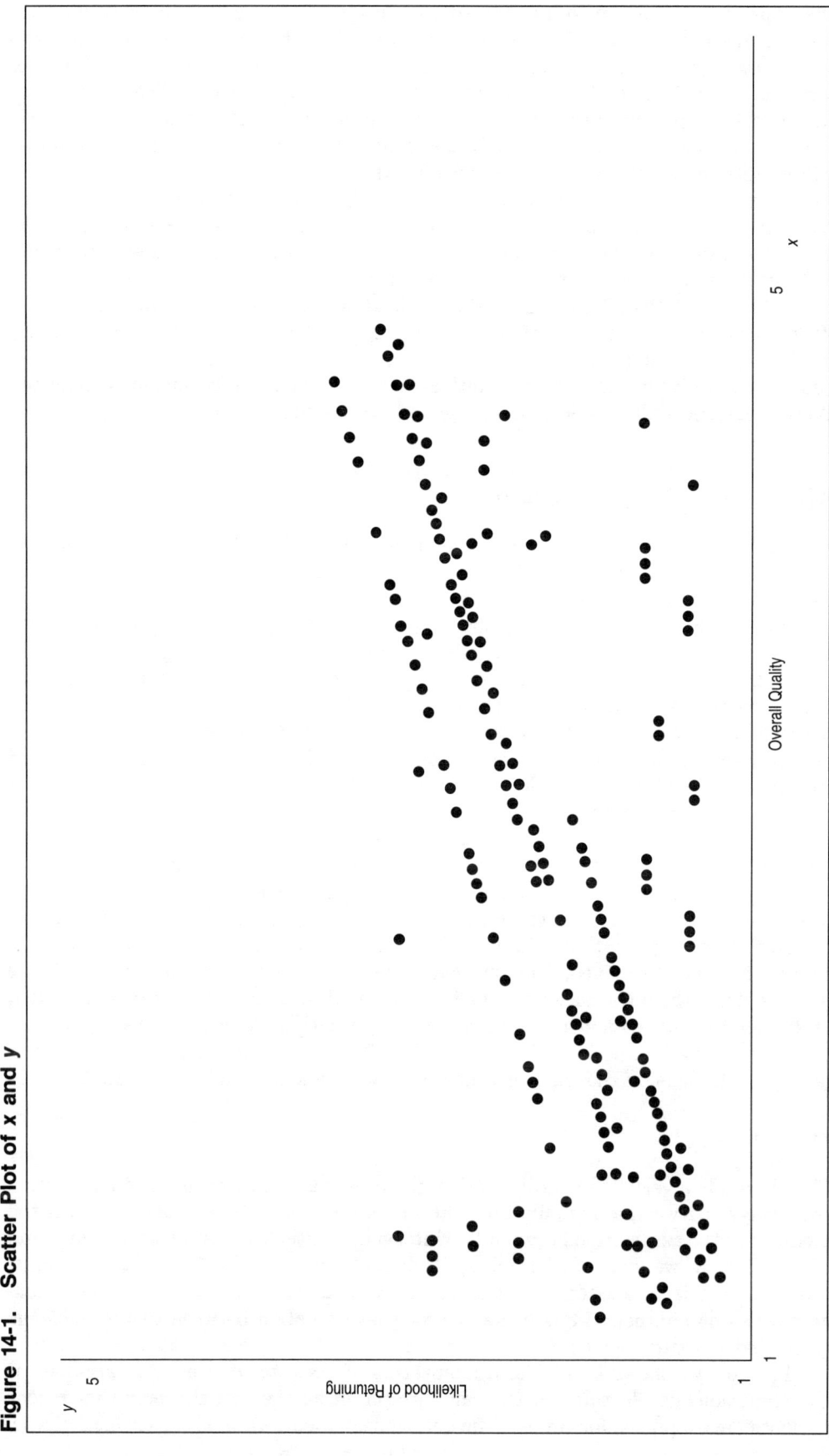

224

the overall quality of care received are plotted on the x axis and their associated scores on likelihood of returning for future needs are plotted on the y axis. Thus, the graph illustrates precisely how an individual patient rates both the quality of care and brand loyalty (likelihood of returning). Visual inspection of the scatter plot suggests a relationship between these two dimensions, one that has been tested in a number of concrete ways using the other tests already documented in this chapter. What can correlation add to this picture? The answer is, a line.

Figure 14-2 builds on the first graph by adding the line that describes the general association between quality of care and repeat likelihood. Because the line moves from the lower left of this graph to the upper right, we can say that in general, as responses to one question become more positive, so do the responses to the other question. The correlation coefficient r reaffirms this with a value of 0.58 which says that yes, the association is positive (both variables increase or decrease in concert) and modestly strong (it approaches its maximum of 1.0). Does it say that perceived quality predicts or causes loyalty? The answer to this is an unequivocal no, because correlation is simply a measure of how close the dots in this graph are to the line. It is *not* a measure of how well one variable predicts the other. For the answer to questions of predictability or causality, we must turn to a more sophisticated statistic referred to as the *regression coefficient*.

Regression

Correlation describes a general association between two variables, in a somewhat limited way. This association can be roughly described with a line. Regression provides additional, important information about the predictive nature of the relationship between the two variables. True predictive ability comes from a data set in which the variable to be predicted is measured at a point in time after the variable doing the predicting. Even without the benefit of such a time-series methodology, however, regression can tell us how knowing the performance on one variable will help us predict performance on another. It does so with the help of a simple formula.

After calculating the regression statistic, a regression model produces the following formula, which affords a predictive interpretation of the relationship between two variables, X and Y:

$$Y = a + bX,$$

where Y is the variable being predicted (the dependent variable), X is the variable doing the predicting (the independent variable), a is the intercept (the value of Y at which the line intersects the vertical axis), and b is the regression coefficient (the amount Y increases for every 1.0 increase in X).

The values for the now familiar example of overall perceived quality and likelihood of returning after outpatient care are 1.87 for a and 0.61 for b. In words, if a given outpatient rated the visit a 3.00 on overall perceived quality, we now can calculate that patient's likelihood of returning for future needs as $1.87 + 0.61(3.00)$, or 3.70. As a check for any skeptics, we have already independently confirmed that the mean satisfaction with quality rating is 4.72 and the mean likelihood of return rating is 4.75. One can be predicted from the other by inserting the appropriate numbers:

$$Y = 1.87 + 0.61(4.72).$$
$$Y = 4.75.$$

But as superior as regression is to correlation, it, too, still misses the fundamental point that correlation could not capture. Life is a bit more complicated than simply one factor leading unequivocally to another. Other factors beyond a single independent

Chapter 14

Figure 14-2. Relationship between x and y

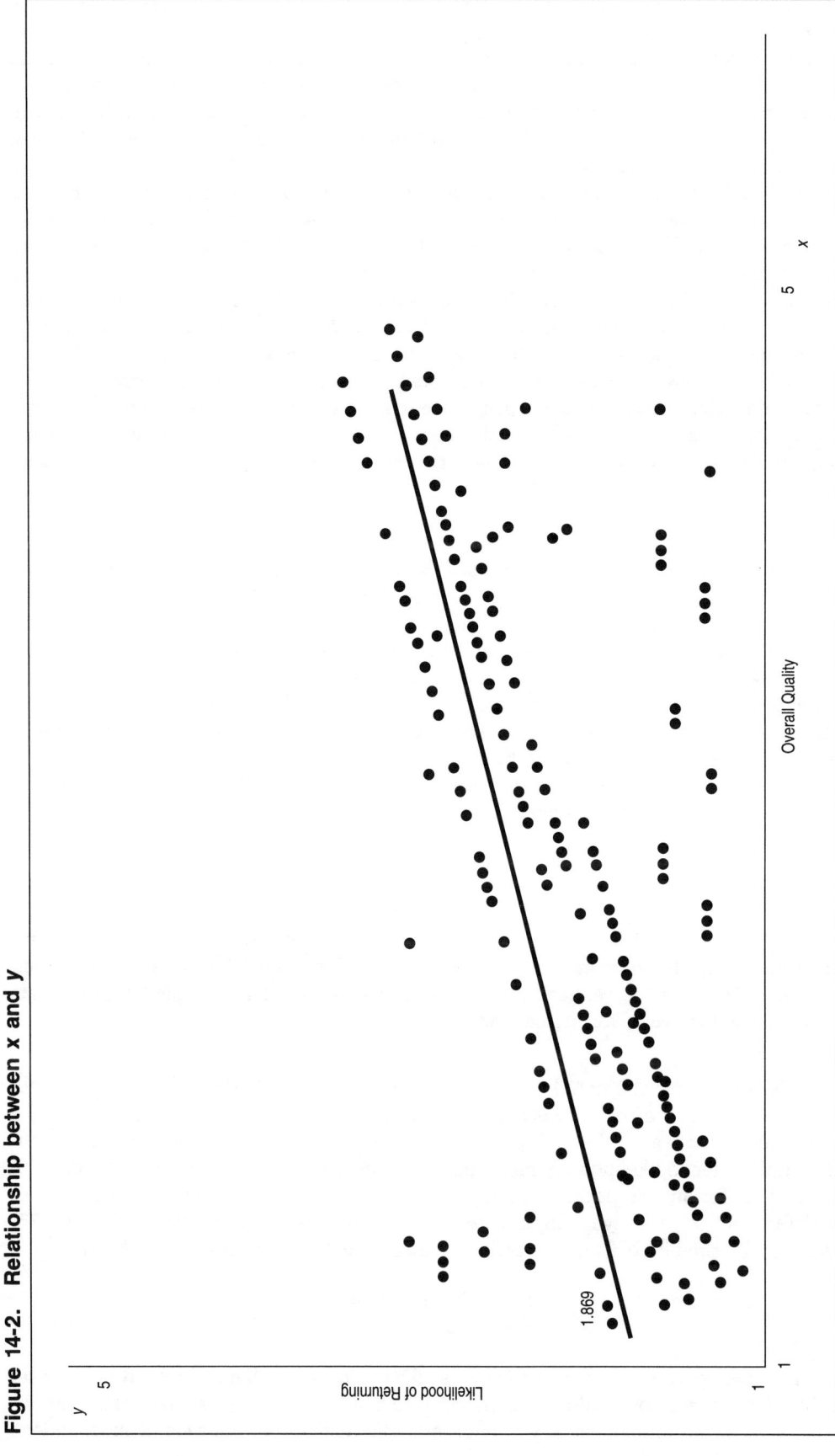

variable can be expected to have some sort of impact on the outcome, or dependent, variable. Just calculating a series of two-variable equations will not help, because reality takes into account all these factors net of one another. In other words, in a given service experience, a patient sorts through how cheery the reception person was, then discounts a long wait, then adds a plus for a great talk with the physician, then discounts even this by a large bill, and so on. What is needed to accurately capture the patient's complex service experience (and to give management sound feedback) are multivariate models, which, as the term suggests, take into account more than one or two variables.

Multivariate Models

Thus far, all the examples in this chapter have referred to the differences in one variable across categories of another or the statistical association between two variables. These *bivariate* techniques can offer insights into the relationships they describe, but they fail to take into account the fuller reality the customer experiences in any given service setting. What we are seeking is some sort of model that will capture as many different aspects of the service experience as possible, and the relationships among those aspects. Such models are generically called *multivariate* models because they explicitly take into account multiple influences on overall patient satisfaction. Although the totality of the patient experience can never be fully captured, multivariate models are superior to bivariate models due to their abilities to account for more of the variability in an outcome like overall satisfaction.

Multivariate statistical methods apply some of the same basic tools as their simpler bivariate cousins, but they do it on a grander scale. Very broadly speaking, multivariate methods seek to aggregate a variety of measures together into a model that will then have enhanced statistical precision as a result of this more broad-based approach, or they sort through the details of the experience in order to assess differentially which inputs "cause" (more strictly speaking, "are associated with") which outputs. As with the bivariate methods, there are a host of multivariate statistical techniques, but only a few of the more generalizable and useful of these techniques are presented in this chapter.

Factor Analysis

Chapter 3 pointed out how multi-item scales can be used as a broad-based method to assess patients' perspectives on service. Chapter 11 discussed in greater detail the issues of reliability and validity of question items or scales. The construction and statistical refinement of multi-item scales have the distinct advantage of producing a series of items that can be used with measurable statistical confidence or reliability. By combining a number of items with statistically determined "scalability," we reduce the amount of error variance in the data, increase the variability of the summated score, and obtain a more normal distribution of scores.

The method used in chapters 2 and 3 to create multi-item scales was *factor analysis*. *Exploratory factor analysis* offered a perspective on what should be included in an attitude scale that captured the essence of the patient experience. Factor analysis allows us to look at all of the variability contained in the original questions of a patient questionnaire and, out of that variability, determine common groupings. The common groupings are defined, in part, by a matrix of the correlation coefficients of each question with every other question in the data set. In this case, it was determined that a subset of the original questions actually explained most of the variance across all the questions. In other words, knowing how patients rated a relatively modest number of questions was able to tell us what had the most impact overall on patients' experience with a provider. *Confirmatory factor analysis* then helped to refine what exploratory analysis initially told the researcher, sometimes using an independent set of data and sometimes using the same initial set.

Factor analysis also suggested where a provider should put resources to have the greatest impact on the patient's perceptions. Factor analysis could not afford the same level of detail at the next level, however. That next level naturally asks what we should do specifically in order to see the impact on patient evaluations or opinions that can be derived by investing in the elements that define the major "factors." That is, where should we specifically invest quality improvement efforts, and what is our return on investment likely to be? It is at this point that another method might help in sorting the details that ultimately assist in giving a total quality improvement effort the direction it needs to begin to "move the needle" on customer satisfaction. But we will defer discussion of that method for a moment while we describe a close cousin of factor analysis, cluster analysis.

Cluster Analysis

In some research efforts it can be helpful to determine if there are unique groups of patients defined by their common service experiences. Instead of looking for groups of questions that logically work together, as happens during factor analysis, the researcher looks for groups of patients whose responses to questions logically link them together. For such applications, cluster analysis is the tool of preference. Patients situated within the same clusters are statistically more similar to one another and more dissimilar to patients situated in other clusters.

Cluster analysis can perform this function using the same measure of association that underlies factor analysis, a correlation matrix. Even so, the rest of the procedure is very different. Cluster analysis has been relatively limited in its application to the patient experience, but one of its more noteworthy applications historically has had profound implications for Medicare reimbursement for more than a decade—diagnosis-related groups (DRGs). DRGs initially used cluster analysis to define and refine specific kinds of medical cases; the underlying assumption was that similar procedures should consume similar amounts and kinds of resources. Once DRGs had been defined, then, it was possible to look for outliers within DRG classifications in order to target cost-cutting efforts.

Multiple Regression Analysis

Go downtown to virtually any metropolitan area in any state, and you will see one thing that they all have in common—very tall buildings. If you look more closely at the corporate names on them, you will be sure to see at least one—perhaps several—with a life insurance imprimatur emblazoned across it in large letters. The reason why life insurance companies can raise such tall buildings is because they have learned to apply multiple regression techniques (plus great marketing) to answer an age-old question: How long is an individual going to live?

The question is simple and at the same time challenging, because no one knows how long he or she personally will live. But the life insurance companies have learned some very valuable generalizations about longevity that help them calculate the rates to charge, based on their assessment of life expectancy for a large group of insured individuals. Their regression model is based on a mass of accumulated actuarial information that tells them that smoking behavior will have a predictable impact on an insured's life expectancy. Someone who smokes pays more for life insurance. An insured who drives too fast pays more, an insured with a family history of heart disease pays more, and so on.

Providers trying to sort the dimensions of health care service that affect a patient's evaluation of care face the same challenge that life insurance companies have faced. In the case of health services, knowing which facility or service dimensions contribute the most to patient satisfaction and perceived quality of care allows decision makers to manage services more effectively. The technique that helps achieve this insight (and consequent improvement opportunities) is multiple regression analysis.

The utility of the multiple regression model comes only in part from now understanding what sorts out the patient who gives high scores from the one who gives low scores in our database. Rather, the utility of the model comes from the ability to use this model's results as a predictive tool that says if we can improve our performance on nursing (because it is the largest coefficient), then we can begin to improve the overall perception of service we are providing our customers. And this will affect brand loyalty, which in turn will have revenue consequences.

So, the model that we first explored earlier, under Measures of Association, applies to multiple regression; the solution just gets more complex. We are still attempting to find how well understanding performance on X helps us to predict, or manage toward, Y. The equation now looks like this:

$$Y = a + b_1 X_1 + b_2 X_2 + b_n X_n$$

where all the variables have the same meaning as before. We simply have as many as n independent variables.

It is appropriate to introduce a few precautions about multiple regression. Some apply what is referred to as "stepwise regression," which is as good as saying the researcher does not know what to expect from the analysis. Stepwise regression is simply a way of allowing the software to think for us, and we should avoid it. A better approach is to test alternative models that we can specify based on theory or experience, and statistically evaluate one's ability to explain one reality versus the other. This statistical testing, however, is beyond the scope of this book.

A second precaution has to do with the number of variables that can be used in a regression model. The practical fact of the matter is that most software packages allow as many as one fewer variables as the researcher has respondents, but anything even approaching a fraction of this limit introduces potentially spurious results. By spurious, we mean that the actual significance of a given independent variable may be masked entirely, exaggerated beyond its real influence or even reversed. A more appropriate limiting factor would be one in which the number of respondents exceeds the number of categories in any independent variable to the nth power, where n equals the number of independent and dependent variables. If there are five responses codes in each question, and there are one dependent and five independent variables, then the number of respondents should be 5^6, or $5 \times 5 \times 5 \times 5 \times 5 \times 5 = 15,625$. Now, in the real world, we rarely have this luxury, so we often relax this requirement to a fraction of the ideal; it is feasible to apply multiple regression analysis with samples as small as 500 to 1,000, so long as the number of independent variables remains modest (5–10).

A third important precaution regarding the use of multiple regression analysis concerns the relationships among independent variables themselves. The underlying regression model requires that independent variables not be too highly related to one another, because this will interfere with the efficiency of the algorithm as it attempts to predict the dependent variable. An examination of the correlations among independent variables is part of the researcher's due diligence as data are analyzed.

The researcher should also pay attention to the distributional qualities of the variables, the nature of the error variance in the model, and whether all factors which define the customer experience have been included in the model. Such precautionary discussions are beyond the scope of this book. Also beyond the scope of this book are more recent innovations in multiple regression analysis that can accommodate dichotomous, or two response code, dependent variables. Models with more than one equation also can be helpful, when applied appropriately, as can models that specify nonlinear or interactive effects as well as latent or manifest variables.

Summary

The ultimate goal of analyzing customer satisfaction data is not to find out how statistically sophisticated the researcher is but how effectively the analysis can guide the service provider toward opportunities for improvement. The leap to actual management changes is discussed in the next chapter. The statistical techniques reviewed in this chapter allow researchers to gain insight into the customer experience and to measure movement over time. The reader wishing more detailed information about research statistics is referred to Chisnall (1986), Emory and Cooper (1991), and Blalock (1972). For specific information about cluster analytic methods, the reader should consult Cooley and Lohnes (1971). For further details on factor analysis, Bryant and Yarnold (1995) is an excellent source. Finally, Horton (1978) offers a thorough review of the essential elements of multiple regression.

CHAPTER FIFTEEN

Plotting a Course of Action

What direction can patient satisfaction data offer to management? In an era of constrained resources, where should management devote its energies to see maximum payoff? How can management "close the loop"—use patient satisfaction data to improve those dimensions of care that will in turn boost satisfaction ratings? And how can this be implemented as a systemwide, ongoing philosophy?

Patient satisfaction surveys should be used to show more than just high scores and low scores. As emphasized throughout this book, these surveys, when analyzed using more sophisticated methods, can also show which specific service attributes drive overall satisfaction, return visit intentions, and other outcomes of interest to management. This is not to say that a good statistician will be the answer to all management challenges or that multivariate methods alone will remedy service shortfalls. But such methods can provide insight into service areas where changes can be instituted, with some predictive promise of improving patients' perceptions of services. In a global sense, then, measurement not only is a necessary step in management but itself can become a key driver of management.

This chapter details the final link between measurement and management of patient satisfaction. Keeping patient satisfaction firmly at center stage, we introduce into this picture some action steps for management. The chapter begins by discussing basic ways to use patient satisfaction data in setting priorities for quality improvement efforts. The chapter then presents a number of specific methods or tools for quality improvement that can be applied to the patient experience and to patient satisfaction data. Although these tools do not exhaust all the possibilities for translating research findings into action, they illustrate important ways in which the management of patient satisfaction can build on measurement. Finally, the chapter offers a simple case study to illustrate how patient satisfaction research can be integrated into management's ongoing satisfaction-driven, quality improvement efforts.

Patient Satisfaction Goals

Recall that in case study 3-B (chapter 3), nursing was identified as the most important statistical determinant of a patient's overall evaluation of quality of care received. The average score recorded for the hospital unit in question was 4.5 on a 5-point Likert-format scale, where 5 = "very satisfied" and 1 = "very dissatisfied." Should management follow up by establishing a realistic and tangible goal toward which the nursing department's efforts can be directed?

It sounds like a great idea, but, as with many management applications, the devil is in the details. The regression model clearly orients our thinking to nursing care, among other dimensions, but how do we quantify our opportunities for quality improvement, our goals? And how do we take meaningful and measurable action? These are the core challenges to management once a useful and valid patient satisfaction measurement system is in place.

Case study 3-B offered valuable perspective on a typical inpatient satisfaction survey by showing that nursing ought to be an important focus of any subsequent management efforts. But this specific focus exists within the context of a larger service delivery environment and a commensurately larger satisfaction survey in which nursing care was but one of many elements measured. Nursing is also, therefore, only one of many service elements that potentially can bear on the inpatient experience. (Case study 3-B is an *inpatient* case study with nursing as a defining element of the service; the core elements around which quality improvement activities will be built for other delivery modalities will be different.) Case study 3-B offered two key pieces of information about nursing care: (1) It displayed how well nursing care was performing from the point of view of the patient, and (2) it offered a statistical translation of the importance of nursing as a driver of overall perceived quality.

Four Service Dimension Quadrants

Figure 15-1 offers a generalizable vehicle in which such statistically significant variables as nursing could be arrayed in a single presentation. It is a two-dimensional graph in which the performance of each factor is plotted on the horizontal axis and the importance of each factor is plotted on the vertical axis. In very general terms, there are four quadrants in which one can place all the dimensions of service for which a patient has offered feedback through the satisfaction survey. Each quadrant is associated with different management action steps. A quadrant can be high in quality rating and high in quality importance, it can be low in rating but high in importance, it can be low in rating and low in importance, or it can be high in rating and low in importance. These combinations are labeled respectively 1 through 4 on the graph. Each represents specific opportunities for management response.

1. *Market:* The upper right quadrant identifies those elements on which the provider performs very well and which are also very important to patients. This quadrant is labeled the "market" quadrant because these elements afford the provider an opportunity to take a message to the market that should be salient to consumers at large and reflect well on the institution.
2. *Manage:* The upper left quadrant identifies service dimensions important to patients but on which the provider does not perform as well. This quadrant is labeled the "manage" quadrant because the dimensions located here afford management an opportunity to make quality improvements that will be valued by patients. Improvements in this quadrant will yield the greatest return on resource investment.
3. *Monitor:* The lower left quadrant identifies elements that are both relatively unimportant to patients and low performers for the provider. Improvement may not be warranted, but the provider will wish to monitor these dimensions over the long run for any sign that they are becoming important to patients and therefore moving into the "manage" quadrant. For the present, no further action is recommended.

4. *Maintain:* The lower right quadrant identifies elements on which the provider is performing well but to which the patients assign less importance. This quadrant is referred to as the "maintain" quadrant, because although these elements are not as important to patients in relation to other dimensions, the provider will wish to maintain its high performance levels. At present, the dimensions would require no added investment of time or resources, but it is desirable that they not slip. No further actions would be recommended.

This figure, then, roughly sorts potential actions that management could implement on different dimensions according to patients' perceptions and evaluations of quality. Within this context, nursing care in general and its defining elements specifically would most likely cluster in the "manage" or "market" quadrant. But nursing is not the only driver of patient satisfaction, and nursing itself is not a unitary thing but consists of several dimensions, each potentially occupying a different area on the graph. Thus, management is likely to find a large number of service components occupying various locations across all four quadrants of figure 15-1. In that case, how does management set priorities, and how does a quality researcher measure movement over time?

Most management priorities will appear, by definition, in the manage quadrant, and those that will give the greatest return on investment will be higher on the vertical dimension of the graph. If there are five elements populating the manage quadrant, highest priority is likely to be given to that element that is highest in importance, but this decision on allocation of resources must be weighed against a consideration of the relative starting point of the element as well. Improving some of the less important variables may contribute only modestly to the desired outcome but, because they are so easy to improve, it makes sense to tackle them early in the continuous quality improvement (CQI) process. For instance, low environmental temperature may be a minor factor diminishing overall satisfaction with a provider, but it would be so easy to raise the temperature to a more comfortable level that this becomes a first order of priority. The proverbial "low-hanging fruits" may, in fact, be only modestly important to the overall picture of patient satisfaction, but with such overwhelming opportunity for change, they can become a top priority. Setting priorities, then, is not strictly a numerical exercise. It is also something of an art that one develops with experience.

Figure 15-1. Setting Satisfaction Priorities

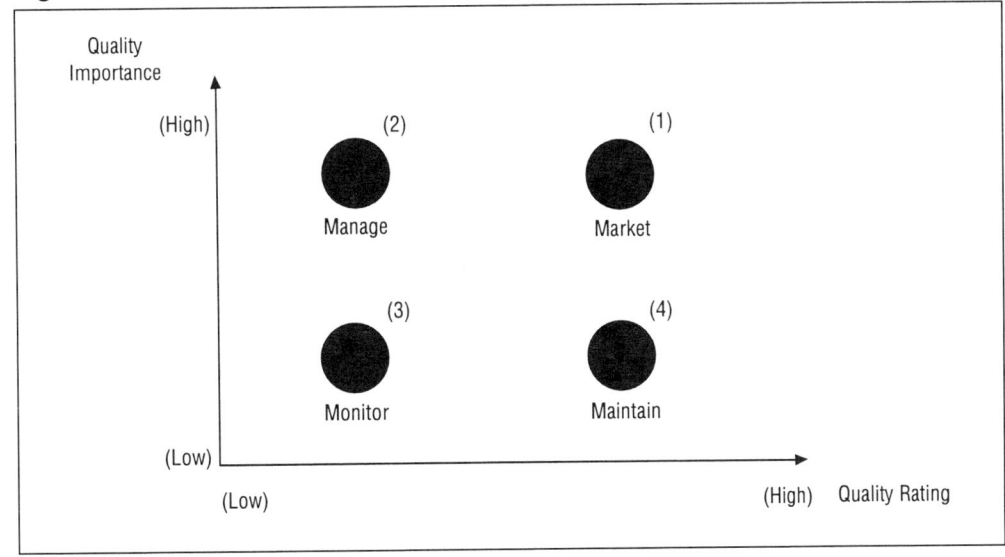

Chapter 15

Meaningful Change

"Meaningful change" can be defined quantitatively either in terms of *percentage* movement in a given response category for a question of interest or in terms of movement in the overall *mean* of responses to a question of interest. Recall from chapter 14 that one may measure the former using a difference of proportions test and the latter using a t-test. Other measures are available to the researcher as well, but they all effectively ask whether we have seen significant movement in the response to a given category or whether we have seen the overall distribution of responses shift to a more favorable score. Which method ought one employ?

On the surface, it might appear that we are asking the same fundamental question with both statistical tools, but research by Jones and Sasser (1995) suggests that one of these approaches is better suited to questions of customer loyalty than the other. In their analyses, Jones and Sasser suggest that merely looking at a statistical average or at a simple dichotomy between generally favorable versus generally unfavorable responses may cause management to miss the boat entirely. It is critically important, they contend, that one measure the percentage of customers responding within the "top score" on a scaled response and track this category's change over time for meaningful trends.

In many of the examples used throughout this book, we have applied a Likert-format response that employs a 5-point scale where 5 equals "very satisfied" or "strongly agree" and 1 equals "very dissatisfied" or "strongly disagree." In research case studies across local telephone, airline, personal computer, automobile, and hospital customers, Jones and Sasser showed that the critical datum to track is the percentage of respondents who are in the "very satisfied" or "strongly agree" categories. They report research from Xerox Corporation that demonstrated that "*totally satisfied* customers were six times more likely to repurchase Xerox products over the next 18 months than its *satisfied* customers. . . . Merely satisfying customers who have the freedom to make choices is not enough to keep them loyal. The only truly loyal customers are totally satisfied customers" (p. 91).

Although industries differ in the extent to which they offer consumers freedom of choice, we have found results very consistent with Jones and Sasser's results in a variety of health care delivery settings. Those who reportedly are "very satisfied" or its equivalent are between 50 percent and 100 percent more likely than those who are "somewhat satisfied" to also report they will return to the provider for any future needs. Jones and Sasser find such "self-reported" brand loyalty to be the best surrogate measure of actual repeat purchase in populations where the purchase cycle can be fairly protracted. We therefore have a clearer idea of *what* we will track—the percentage of responses in the top rating category. The question now is how best to track *movement* in this top category.

As we track movement in the percentage of customers who endorse the provider at the highest level for any given question item, we will need either a great deal of movement or a very large sample for this change to register at conventional levels of significance. Although the traditionally accepted level of significance is the 95 percent level, we may relax this requirement somewhat and content ourselves with the 68 percent level, which is the equivalent of saying that we will be impressed with 1 standard deviation of movement (68 percent level) over approximately 2 standard deviations of movement (95 percent level). We may also be better able to track movement over time if we have a broad-based measure of customer satisfaction rather than one that is narrowly defined. A broad-based measure can subsume several different dimensions in a single measure. A narrow measure might use only a single dimension; it is analogous to putting all of one's eggs in a single basket.

Historically, psychometric researchers have found that they have a more reliable reading on any behavioral or perceptual dimensions if they employ a statistically derived, broad-based measure. Such measures typically take the form of a summated scale or battery of interview questions. This is the equivalent to tracking stock market movement using a portfolio of measures such as the Dow-Jones Industrial Average rather than a single stock's value. If a $55 stock moves 55 cents on the Big Board, it rarely attracts much attention, but if the Dow (currently around 5500) moves 55 points, people take note. Both are increments of only 1 percent, but the broader-based measure is perceived (and rightly so) to be a better indicator of important "market movement."

Figure 15-2 shows an example of how one might create a Dow-Jones-like "index of quality," building on case study 3-B. While not going into great detail, figure 15-2 shows that we will sum the performance of all items that are statistically significant within each of the overall measures such as nursing, admitting, physician care, testing, meal service, parking, and perhaps even more. (A refinement of this same approach would involve weighting these items by their loadings from factor analysis or their

Figure 15-2. Creating an Index of Quality

Nursing Care
  _____ #
  _____ #
  _____ #

Admitting
  _____ #
  _____ #
  _____ #

Physician Care
  _____ #
  _____ #
  _____ #

Testing
  _____ #
  _____ #
  _____ #

Meal Service
  _____ #
  _____ #
  _____ #

Parking
  _____ #
  _____ #
  _____ #
            Total   ##

regression coefficients from a multiple regression model.) In our experience the scale is more sensitive than tracking a single item, for we have found that relatively more modest movement on a summated scale typically is statistically significant when the same absolute change on a single item is not.

An index has the virtue of being able to track statistically discernible change if substantial quality improvement progress has been made on only a modest number of dimensions. The index also is sensitive to the combined impact of more modest movement over a larger number of items. And, of course, the more important the dimension is to the patient's experience (on a weighted scale), the easier it is for that dimension to "move the needle." This trade-off between breadth of movement and intensity of movement is captured in figure 15-3. The actual distance of each of the lines moving up and out from the intersection of the axes is determined by one's determination of acceptable levels of measurable quality improvement as translated into levels of statistical significance.

We mentioned that one may wish to relax the rigor of a 95 percent level of confidence (2 standard deviations of movement) and accept change at a 68 percent level (1 standard deviation of movement). When one relaxes assumptions of statistical significance levels, there is a proportionately increased risk that ostensibly significant changes may, in fact, be spurious. The researcher and client may be willing to accept this risk, however, if the advantage is that employees in the organization will be able to feel the rewards of meaningful movement earlier in the quality improvement process.

One Step at a Time

How does the researcher help management set priorities and quantitative goals simultaneously? Figure 15-4 shows that the stair steps toward higher and higher performance,

Figure 15-3. How a Quality Index Moves

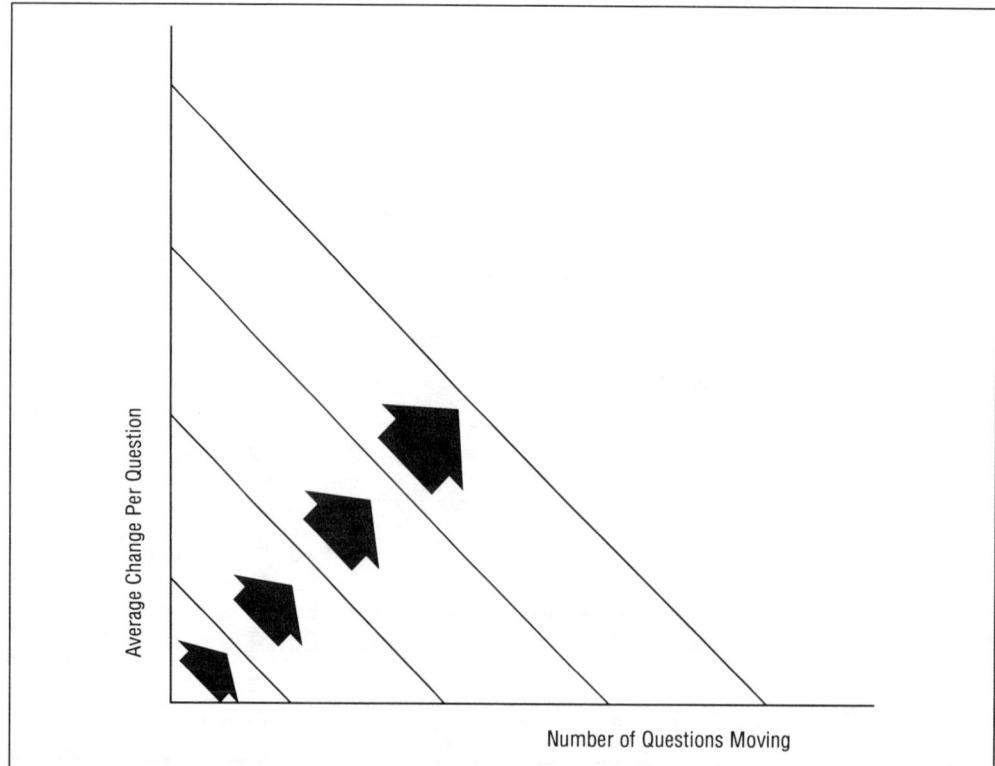

Figure 15-4. Significant Increases in Key Drivers

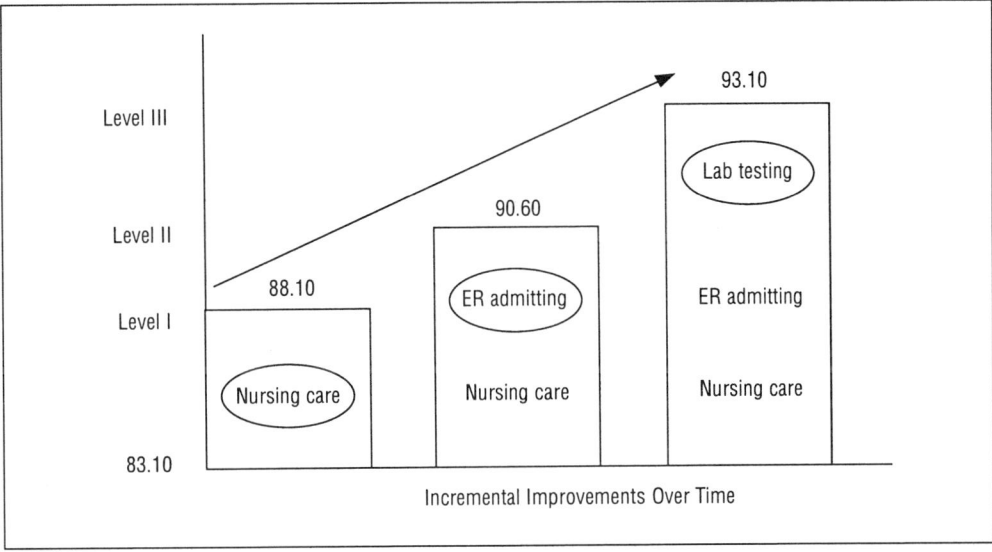

represented on the *y* axis, can come from targeting those dimensions with the greatest potential return on investment first, and others at later stages in the process. As a practical matter, however, numerous teams throughout a facility may be at work simultaneously, so the graphic presents only a hypothetical situation. If admitting were to make early strides while the laboratory department and nursing were experiencing more modest gains, then the first goals might be met at least as readily as if nursing had shouldered the exclusive responsibility for all early movement.

The discussion so far has assessed how one gains focus and sensitivity in patient satisfaction tracking. With all the metrics in place, how does one actually "make the needle move" on patient satisfaction? Without attempting to be an entire reference on CQI tactics and tools, the following sections offer some mechanisms that help close the management loop.

Research-Based Management

The late W. Edwards Deming had a reputation for beginning most of his consultative engagements with a twofold question, asking management to show their processes and their data. Most of this book has been devoted to methods for collecting meaningful customer satisfaction feedback, or data. Data collection is done within a working model of the customer experience, but we have not formally created a flowchart of health service delivery processes per se.

Figure 15-5 adapts a very basic model that flowcharts a health service process (Batalden and others, 1994). As a systems model, this flowchart begins with the *resources* on which a provider draws to render a service to a customer. As patient satisfaction researchers, however, we are not tremendously interested in the hardware or chemicals and equipment that support the clinical health care experience. We are more interested in such resources as they are ultimately brought to a focus in the service environment as *inputs,* and that is why the shaded portion of the chart begins at this point. (Had this been a pharmacoeconomic model, however, we might have traced our research design back to include resources.)

The inputs are brought to the customer in the form of *actions* whose ultimate *outputs* interface with the customer. And the outcome of this cycle in service performed is a health outcome as well as a perceptual outcome. In many ways, the flowchart is

Figure 15-5. Flowchart the Processes

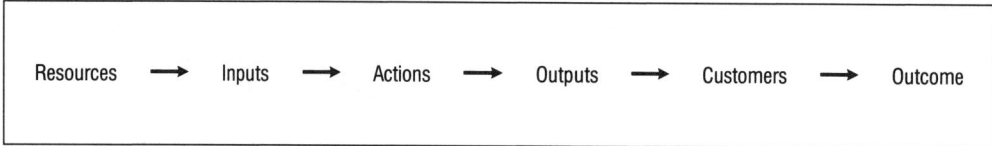

not unlike the regression model already presented, and the outcomes of this flowchart are analogous to the "overall perception of quality" or "overall satisfaction" as perceived by the patient. Just showing a provider the scores on overall satisfaction, however, does little to shed light on the processes that lead to overall satisfaction. Simply showing a professional driver the average lap time may not offer insight into ways to enhance the driver's and race car's performance and, therefore, the lap time. But breaking down the race car's performance into its component parts and the driver's detailed responses to each bend in the roadway will show opportunities to shave precious fractions of a second from the lap time. Once the process is flowcharted, it is possible to identify critical points where change in the inputs and outputs can yield change in the ultimate outcomes.

Models for Improvement

Engineering enhanced patient satisfaction into a service encounter requires a rethinking and reworking of the service processes underlying the patient experience. It is not simply a matter of showing the providers where opportunities for improvement exist and then leaving them to their own devices. Granted, talented and motivated professionals will find ways to make their own needles move, but true systemwide improvement efforts require innovation at the system level. Even talented and motivated people will occasionally fall short of the mark if they are forced to reinvent the wheel each time they render service. True quality improvement changes should be fundamental and become so systemic within a service delivery environment that they become part of the "givens" a provider brings to a customer encounter.

Figure 15-6 offers a relatively simple model that has been successfully applied within the wider context of CQI activities, and it has great utility in patient satisfaction programs. The circular design of the graphic underscores the ongoing nature of quality improvement, a chance to build on incremental success as a provider's service reaches ever higher levels of patient satisfaction. Batalden, Nelson, and Roberts (1994, p. 171) explain that this model will work optimally only when three important preconditions are met.

First, it is critical that there be a clear statement of what is to be accomplished prior to instituting any new measures: we must have a well-articulated aim for the service enhancement activity. Second—and this is tied very closely to patient satisfaction research—we must all agree on and specify what kind of change is to be expected: we must have a concrete measure of improvement. Third, we must clearly lay out a causal model that specifies how our revised actions anticipate change in some desirable direction: we must make concrete the parameters of an improvement trial before rolling it out to the entire staff.

With this foundation, patient satisfaction improvement activities begin the cycle characterized in the graphic by "Plan," "Do," "Check and Study," and "Act," or what CQI researchers have referred to as PDCA trails. The first stage, *plan*, incorporates the considerations necessary not only to be certain that any actions are in accordance with our overall goals, but that we will be able to document the extent to which changes

Figure 15-6. Model for Improvement

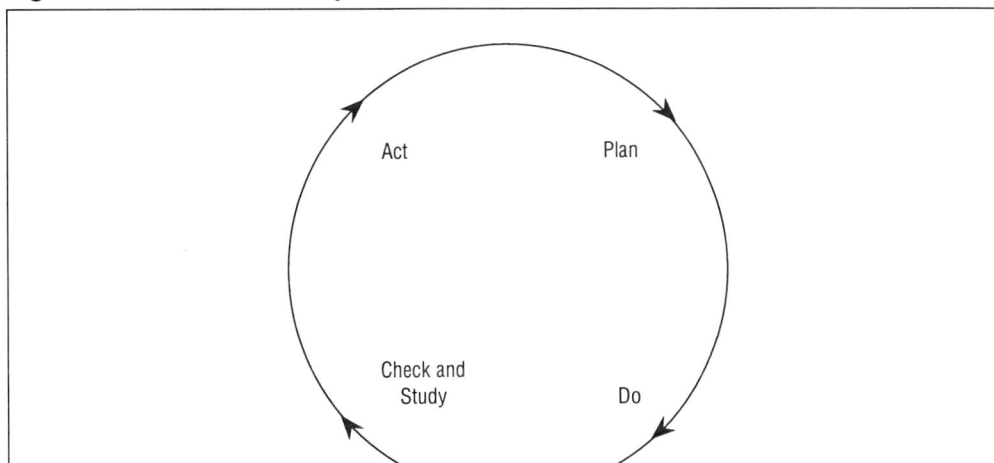

in inputs have yielded changes in outputs from the patient's point of view. The second stage, *do*, is the launch of a modestly scaled pilot project to determine the effectiveness of the proposed modifications. The third stage, *check and study*, now uses concrete before and after measurements to determine that the modifications do in fact elevate customer perceptions of quality or satisfaction. All of this is then feedback that allows the management team to implement more broad-based change (that is, to *act*) that redesigns the overall organizational processes to benefit from this learning experience.

Translated into patient satisfaction research, the initial cycle leading up to action is not intended to raise the organization's performance overall; it is a test to see if the change being considered is likely to create the opportunity for broad-based movement. Once this determination is made through a pilot test, then organizationwide change will register on the overall quality index tapping customer satisfaction more generally. At the same time as this larger implementation is being made, countless other pilot projects are in the works. Not all of these pilot projects will yield measurable and positive results, but a full CQI program organizationwide will ensure that the pipeline remains full of good ideas.

Internal Metrics

The PDCA cycle is dependent on being able to measure important elements of the patient experience and make changes in those that matter to the patient. Within this context, patient satisfaction scores are an external, or perceptual, measure of organizational effectiveness. The actual organizational changes that result in improved patient satisfaction scores may best be measured internally using metrics captured in real time. Patient satisfaction with the time spent waiting for a nurse to respond to a call button is an external, or perceptual, measure of service effectiveness, but the actual time it takes for a nurse to respond is an internal metric. Patient satisfaction with clarity of billing information is an external, or perceptual, measure of service effectiveness, but the number of telephone calls with questions about the bill is an internal metric. These internal metrics typically are very simple, and they can provide the information necessary to determine if pilot projects are delivering the impact desired long before the research team has accumulated enough patient satisfaction scores to demonstrate that impact.

Figure 15-7 shows how we can begin to make the translation to internal metrics so that we will have confidence, even before the next patient satisfaction survey report is issued, that our changes are likely to have the desired effects. We start at the top of the flowchart by recognizing that overall patient satisfaction among those receiving outpatient services is a desirable, if coarse, measure of what we wish to improve. We subsequently derive measures of importance that tell us that specific satisfaction with laboratory services is a prime contributor to overall satisfaction. Moving down to the level of laboratory service, we find that the satisfaction with time spent waiting for laboratory results is a key driver of satisfaction with the laboratory department itself. It is then a relatively small leap of faith to determine that minutes spent waiting for laboratory test results are a real-time indicator that will tell us when we are moving important processes that affect outpatient satisfaction. Although the example of excessive waiting time may have a direct, unequivocal relation to satisfaction, other variables will be less clearly related to our goal of improving services through improving satisfaction.

Improvements in elements lower down on the chart affect those higher up. Improvements in actual time spent waiting will enhance satisfaction with the time wait, which in turn will influence overall satisfaction with the laboratory experience and ultimately global satisfaction with the provider. And it will be the cumulative effect of a large number of quality improvement activities, each carving out its own focus and associated internal metrics, that will move the satisfaction needle. Once the internal metrics lend empirical support to the fact that process changes at the pilot study level are effective, they can be introduced at ever wider levels. If the pilot project has external validity, then the CQI professional will see sustained, systemwide improvements in patient satisfaction scores.

Identifying Outliers for Action

Anything that can be measured will typically produce a distribution of scores around some sort of mean or other measure of central tendency. But it is not the statistical average that tells management how loyal customers are, nor is it the mean that tells managers where to focus quality improvement activities. Instead of the middle of the

Figure 15-7. Internal Metric Translation

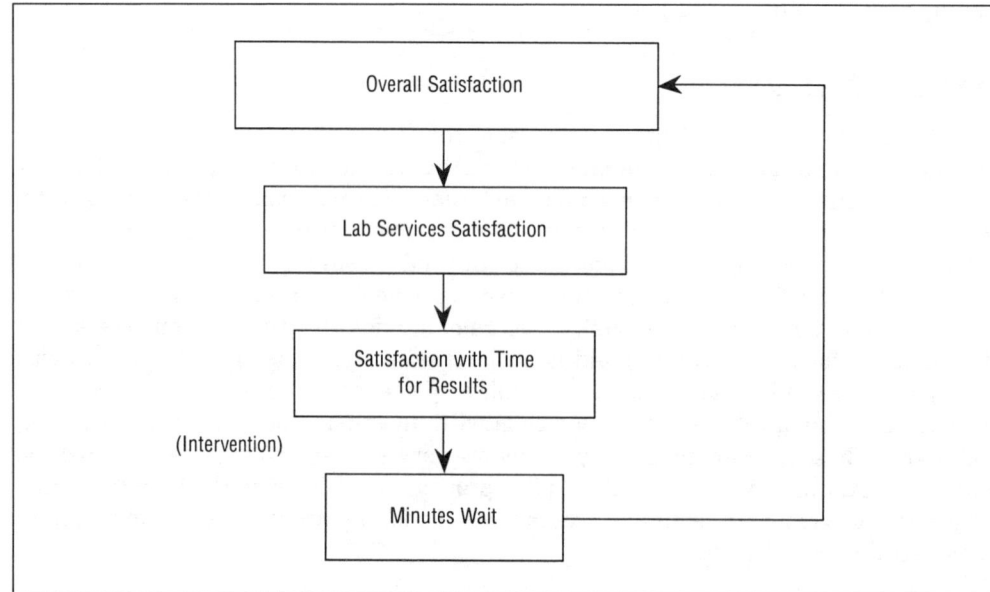

distribution, the researcher should look at the outliers, or the tails of the distribution. A normal distribution, shown in thousands of college textbooks, looks like the postcard views of Mount Fuji, with a sharp peak in the middle and the curves to the right and left of the peak falling sharply down as they move farther away from the center. The typical curve for patient satisfaction, however, is anything but normal.

Figure 15-8 shows what a distribution of patient satisfaction scores in response to a given question of services typically resembles. Note that the average score is relatively high at 4.5, and it is this high overall average that tells the story of a distribution that appears skewed (from normal) toward the high end of the scale. Although the actual middle score is only 3.0 on this 5-point scale, the average is far higher at 4.5. Categories less than a "perfect 5" on this scale are relatively less populated the farther left and away from the top score we move, and in the authors' experience, it is not uncommon to find no responses at all in the 1 and 2 categories. But, all of this notwithstanding, where does one look for quality improvement opportunities?

The classic theory underlying quality improvement suggests that one ought not look for "bad apples" (examples of poor performance) for correction as much as seek out top achievement for commendation. As one does that in this statistical context, it should be with an eye to what helps move a patient's perception into the top category from even the next category down; what distinguishes a 4 from a 5? The true outliers on the far left tail of the distribution may, in fact, be misleading, because they can be the chronic complainers. This is not to say that managers and quality researchers should discount every dissatisfied customer, but it does suggest that the problems of this population segment may not be amenable to improvement by service providers. Even jumping through hoops of fire may not move these negative outliers, if they simply represent chronic complainers.

The point of focus for improvement efforts ought to be on the top score, with an eye to elevating those only near the top (4) into the higher response category (5). What are the "moments of truth" among those rating the highest scores? What do patients report in their surveys that puts a specific department, service experience, or person up in lights? How can we institutionalize these special service encounters in order to offer far more customers a chance to edge up from 4 to 5? This is a way to use outliers

Figure 15-8. Identifying Outliers for Action

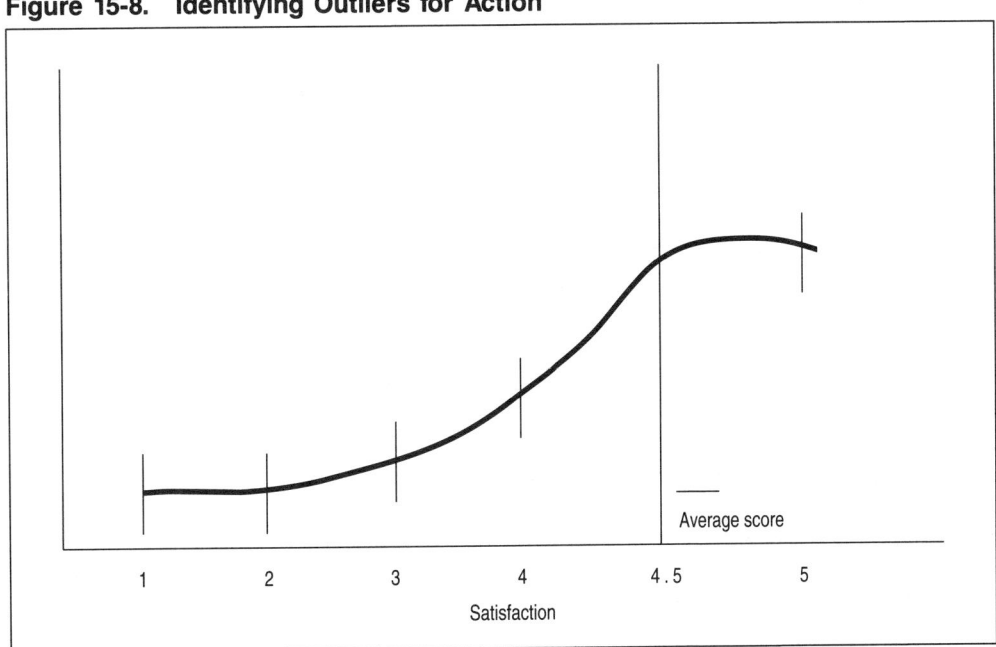

in a positive context—more carrot than stick. Once we have hoisted patients into this top category, they not only become more loyal by an appreciable magnitude, but they also become the grassroots fans of the organization, the customers Jones and Sasser (1995) call "apostles."

All of this orientation is related to the simple emphasis on catching staff members in the act of doing things right, rather than catching them in the act of doing things wrong. Many physicians' groups, both under the evolving rules of managed care and otherwise, and many other hospital-based and alternate site providers are grappling with how to move staff toward enhancing patient satisfaction. It clearly is a nice thing to do, it is better for the patient's health, and it is better for the provider's bottom line, but increasingly, management is making it good for the service provider as well. Physicians have patient satisfaction in their credentialing profiles, if not in their compensation structures. Hospital managers have quantifiable satisfaction goals with commensurate bonus rewards. All of this is done to truly close the loop from measuring patient satisfaction to now rewarding those who manage health services toward a more satisfactory patient experience.

Case Study

A hypothetical case study of modest scope that builds on research case studies presented earlier in the book affords a more encompassing look at the role of measurement and management in the CQI loop. The case also illustrates the PDCA track graphed in figure 15-6. Figure 15-9 takes a routine visit to the primary care physician's office as the starting point for a satisfaction-based CQI project. The physician's office is in a larger multi-office complex shared by nearly 20 other primary care physicians in a group practice. In step 1 of this hypothetical case study, the patient makes a routine visit to the family physician. During the examination, some standard blood work is requested. The patient's visit to the laboratory to have blood drawn and the patient's subsequent receipt of the report while still in the facility now become part of this office visit.

Step 2 occurs within two weeks after the office visit, when the patient receives either a telephone call or a letter soliciting opinions on this most recent visit to the doctor's office. Reports from the patient are not entirely glowing, given the nearly two-hour wait for blood test results, results that had been pledged by the physician to be "rapid turnaround" based on new diagnostic technology available at the laboratory. In step 3, this patient's satisfaction scores are merged with those of approximately 1,000 other patients who made office visits during the prior month. This data set becomes part of a baseline analysis to determine not merely how well physicians at the facility are performing, but also what in the overall patient experience is important to customers. Communication with the physician is determined to be the most important driver of overall patient satisfaction, but waiting time emerges as an important factor in a number of clinical sites. The wait in the reception room, the wait in the examining room, and the wait for laboratory test results all prove to have at least some bearing on how satisfied patients ultimately are with the group. Of these three, waiting time for laboratory results seems to have the greatest impact, with the average time waited for same-day blood test results reported to be approximately two hours.

In step 4, the CQI team conducts on-site observational research to gain familiarity with the laboratory service experience. Although patients initially are seen very promptly and blood samples are drawn seemingly without incident, there are selected inefficiencies later. Once patients have their blood drawn, they return to the same waiting area and join others who have yet to have their blood drawn. The latter are seen very promptly, which only adds to patients' sense that they are waiting unduly long for their results. Behind the scenes, even the rapid response tests are queued behind

Figure 15-9. Closing the Management Loop

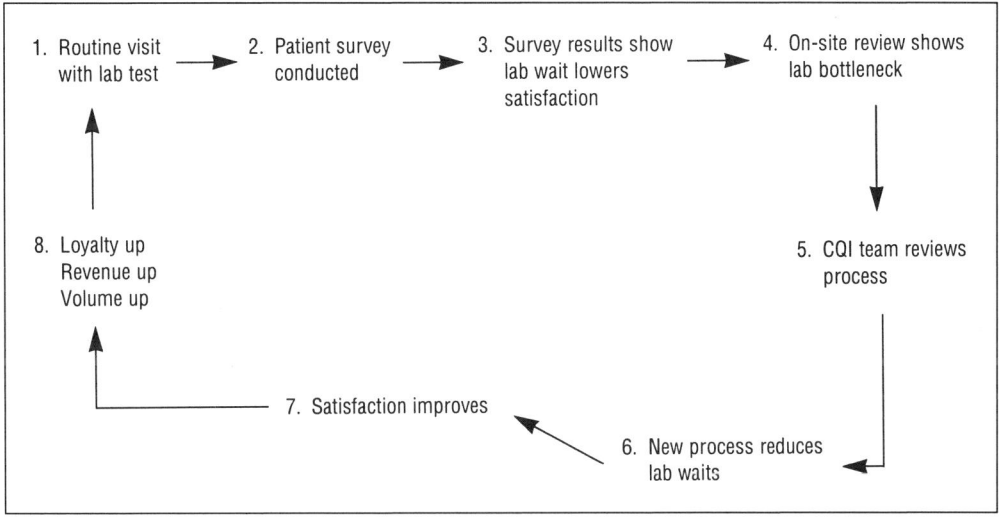

Source: Quality Expectations, Inc., Evanston, IL.

all other tests that have been ordered earlier in a first in/first out sequencing. Some tests require significant time, and this holds up all tests, including the rapid response tests.

In step 5, the CQI team convenes to discuss the satisfaction survey results as well as their own qualitative data from the on-site assessment of the laboratory. They carefully formulate a project aim for laboratory testing; they desire to reduce rapid response laboratory test turnaround time to 20 minutes or less. They will measure this not just with the patient satisfaction survey, which asks patients to state their relative satisfaction with testing as well as how long they waited to receive test results. They also will clock the turnaround time for test results with the computerized system that is part of the laboratory testing software. As part of their pilot project, the team determines that patients now will have separate waiting areas that segregate those waiting to have their blood drawn from those who are waiting for test results. At the site where patients will wait for their test results, a new clock is installed in a conspicuous site. Before having any laboratory work done, patients will be informed of the time wait they should expect, given the volume of activity at that moment as well as the complexity of the actual test or tests. All of this is slated to be implemented at only one practice site, in keeping with the limited scope of the pilot project.

The CQI team waits until this new system has been in place for one month before beginning to assess its impact on actual waiting time for rapid response testing. In step 6, the new measures are shown to reduce total time wait to 25 minutes, but the time still seems to be falling, judging from the time line over the initial month. In step 7, patient satisfaction surveys returned after the one-month period show satisfaction significantly up from the baseline. Perceived time wait is 15 minutes for the average rapid response laboratory client, a period appreciably less than the real time charted by the computer. On further investigation of this phenomenon, the CQI team determines that patients evidently do not take note of the lapse of time until they return to the waiting area for their test results. The clock, on the other hand, begins as soon as the blood samples are registered at the diagnostic site.

Because the time spent waiting for laboratory results is a key driver, the summated scale used by the CQI team to assess global satisfaction also is nominally trending up. Other positive outcomes such as patient retention and revenue are anticipated farther down the road but are not yet fully documented. The CQI team begins the cycle once again with a focus on another level of key drivers that they will strive to change positively.

And it is at the point where a measurement and management cycle begins once again that we close this book. Measuring and managing satisfaction are not one-time actions. They are milestones as we make our way through a continuous cycle of activity that has ongoing and incremental improvement as its goal.

Summary

Patient satisfaction measurement is not an end unto itself, and patient care management without the direction of patient feedback will not necessarily produce the changes management desires. The provider who can link effective measurement and effective management will deliver better service to the patient as well as outperform other facilities in the increasingly competitive health care delivery environment of the 21st century.

APPENDIX A
Table of Random Numbers

Appendix A

Row number						
00000	10097	32533	76520	13586	34673	54876
00001	37542	04805	64894	74296	24805	24037
00002	08422	68953	19645	09303	23209	02560
00003	99019	02529	09376	70715	38311	31165
00004	12807	99970	80157	36147	64032	36653
00005	66065	74717	23072	76850	36697	36170
00006	31060	10805	45571	82406	35303	42614
00007	85269	77602	02051	65692	68665	74818
00008	63573	32135	05325	47048	90553	57548
00009	73796	45753	03529	64778	35808	34282
00010	93520	17767	14905	68607	22109	40558
00011	11805	05431	39808	27732	50725	68248
00012	83452	99634	06288	98033	13746	70078
00013	88685	40200	86507	58401	36766	67951
00014	99594	67348	87517	64969	91826	08928
00015	65481	17674	17468	50950	58047	76974
00016	80124	35635	17727	08015	45318	22374
00017	74350	99817	77402	77214	43236	00210
00018	69916	26803	66252	29148	36936	87203
00019	09893	20505	14225	68514	46427	56788
00020	91499	14523	68479	27686	46162	83554
00021	80336	94598	26940	36858	70297	34135
00022	44104	81949	85157	47954	32979	26575
00023	12550	73742	11100	02040	12860	74697
00024	63606	49329	16505	34484	40219	52563
00025	61196	90446	26457	47774	51924	33729
00026	15474	45266	95270	79953	59367	83484
00027	94557	28573	67897	54387	54622	44431
00028	42481	16213	97344	08721	16868	48767
00029	23523	78317	73208	89837	68935	91416
00030	04493	52494	75246	33824	45862	51025
00031	00549	97654	64051	88159	96119	63896
00032	35963	15307	26898	09354	33351	35462
00033	59808	08391	45427	26842	83609	49700
00034	46058	85236	01390	92286	77281	44077
00035	32179	00597	87379	25241	05567	07707
00036	69234	61406	20117	45204	15956	60000
00037	19565	41430	01758	75379	40419	21585
00038	45155	14938	19476	97246	43667	94543
00039	94864	31994	36168	10851	34888	81553
00040	98086	24826	45240	28404	44999	08896
00041	33185	16232	41941	50949	89435	48581
00042	80951	00406	96382	70774	20151	23387
00043	79752	49140	71961	28296	69861	02591
00044	18633	32537	98145	06571	31010	24674
00045	74029	43902	77557	32270	97790	17119
00046	54178	45611	80993	37143	05335	12969
00047	11664	49883	52079	84827	59381	71539
00048	48324	77928	31249	64710	02295	36870
00049	69074	94138	87637	91976	35584	04401
00050	09188	20097	32825	39527	04220	86304
00051	90045	85497	51981	50654	94938	81997
00052	73189	50207	47677	26269	62290	64464
00053	75768	76490	20971	87749	90429	12272
00054	54016	44056	66281	31003	00682	27398
00055	08358	69910	78542	42785	13661	58873
00056	28306	03264	81333	10591	40510	07893
00057	53840	86233	81594	13628	51215	90290
00058	91757	53741	61613	62669	50263	90212
00059	89415	92694	00397	58391	12607	17646

Table of Random Numbers

Row number						
00060	77513	03820	86864	29901	68414	82774
00061	19502	37174	69979	20288	55210	29773
00062	21818	59313	93278	81757	05686	73156
00063	51474	66499	68107	23621	94049	91345
00064	99559	68331	62535	24170	69777	12830
00065	33713	48007	93584	72869	51926	64721
00066	85274	86893	11303	22970	28834	34137
00067	84133	89640	44035	52166	73852	70091
00068	56732	16234	17395	96131	10123	91622
00069	65138	56806	87648	85261	34313	65861
00070	38001	02176	81719	11711	71602	92937
00071	37402	96397	01304	77586	56271	10086
00072	97125	40348	87083	31417	21815	39250
00073	21826	41134	47143	34072	64638	85902
00074	73135	42742	95719	09035	85794	74296
00075	07638	77929	03061	18072	96207	44156
00076	60528	83441	07954	19814	59175	20695
00077	83596	35655	06958	92983	05128	09719
00078	10850	62746	99599	10507	13499	06319
00079	39820	98952	43622	63147	64421	80814
00080	59580	06478	75569	78800	88835	54486
00081	38508	07341	23793	48763	90822	97022
00082	30692	70668	94688	16127	56196	80091
00083	65443	95659	18238	27437	49632	24041
00084	27267	50264	13192	72294	07477	44606
00085	91307	06991	19072	24210	36699	53728
00086	68434	94688	84473	13622	62126	98408
00087	48908	15877	54745	24591	35700	04754
00088	06913	45197	42672	78601	11883	09528
00089	10455	16019	14210	33712	91342	37821
00090	12883	97343	65027	61184	04285	01392
00091	21778	30976	38807	36961	31649	42096
00092	19523	59515	65122	59659	86283	68258
00093	67245	52670	35583	16563	79246	86686
00094	60584	47377	07500	37992	45134	26529
00095	53853	41377	36066	94850	58838	73859
00096	24637	38736	74384	89342	52623	07992
00097	83080	12451	38992	22815	07759	51777
00098	16444	24334	36151	99073	27493	70939
00099	60790	18157	57178	65762	11161	78576
00100	03991	10461	93716	16894	66083	24653
00101	38555	95554	32886	59780	08355	60860
00102	17546	73704	92052	46215	55121	29281
00103	32643	52861	95819	06831	00911	98936
00104	69572	68777	39510	35905	14060	40619
00105	24122	66591	27699	06494	14845	46672
00106	61196	30231	92962	61773	41839	55382
00107	30532	21704	10274	12202	39685	23309
00108	03788	97599	75867	20717	74416	53166
00109	48228	63379	85783	47619	53152	67433
00110	60365	94653	35075	33949	42614	29297
00111	83799	42402	56623	34442	34994	41374
00112	32960	07405	36409	83232	99385	41600
00113	19322	53845	57620	52606	66497	68646
00114	11220	94747	07399	37408	43509	23929
00115	31751	57260	68980	05339	15470	48355
00116	88492	99382	14454	04504	20094	98977
00117	30934	47744	07481	83828	73788	06533
00118	22888	48893	27499	98748	60530	45128
00119	78212	16993	35902	91386	44372	15486

Appendix A

Row number						
00120	41849	84547	46850	52326	34677	58300
00121	46352	33049	69248	93460	45305	07521
00122	11087	96294	14013	31792	59747	67277
00123	52701	08337	56303	87315	16520	69676
00124	57275	36898	81304	48585	68652	27376
00125	20857	73156	70284	24326	79375	95220
00126	15633	84924	90415	93614	33521	26665
00127	92694	48297	39904	02115	59589	49067
00128	77613	19019	88152	00080	20554	91409
00129	38688	32486	45134	63545	59404	72059
00130	25163	01889	70014	15021	41290	67312
00131	65251	07629	37239	33295	05870	01119
00132	36815	43625	18637	37509	82444	99005
00133	64397	11692	05327	82162	20247	81759
00134	04515	25624	95096	67946	48460	85558
00135	83761	60873	43253	84145	60833	25983
00136	14387	06345	80854	09279	43529	06318
00137	51321	92246	80088	77074	88722	56736
00138	72472	00008	80890	18002	94813	31900
00139	05466	55306	93128	18464	74457	90561
00140	39528	72484	82474	25593	48545	35247
00141	81616	18711	53342	44276	75122	11724
00142	07586	16120	82641	22820	92904	13141
00143	90767	04235	13574	17200	69902	63742
00144	40188	28193	29593	88627	94972	11598
00145	34414	82157	86887	55087	19152	00023
00146	63439	75363	44989	16822	36024	00867
00147	67049	09070	93399	45547	94458	74284
00148	79495	04146	52162	90286	54158	34243
00149	91704	30552	04737	21031	75051	93029
00150	94015	46874	32444	48277	59820	96163
00151	74108	88222	88570	74015	25704	91035
00152	62880	87873	95160	59221	22304	90314
00153	11748	12102	80580	41867	17710	59621
00154	17944	05600	60478	03343	25852	58905
00155	66067	42792	95043	52680	46780	56487
00156	54244	91030	45547	70818	59849	96169
00157	30945	57589	31732	57260	47670	07654
00158	69170	37403	86995	90307	94304	71803
00159	08345	88975	35841	85771	08105	59987
00160	27767	43584	85301	88977	29490	69714
00161	13025	14338	54066	15243	47724	66733
00162	80217	36292	98525	24335	24432	24896
00163	10875	62004	90391	61105	57411	06368
00164	54127	57326	26629	19087	24472	88779
00165	60311	42824	37301	42678	45990	43242
00166	49739	71484	92003	98086	76668	73209
00167	78626	51594	16453	94614	39014	97066
00168	66692	13986	99837	00582	81232	44987
00169	44071	28091	07362	97703	76447	42537
00170	41468	85149	49554	17994	14924	39650
00171	94559	37559	49678	53119	70312	05682
00172	41615	70360	64114	58660	90850	64618
00173	50273	93113	41794	86861	24781	89683
00174	41396	80504	90670	08289	40902	05069
00175	25807	24260	71529	78920	72682	07385
00176	06170	97965	88302	98041	21443	41808
00177	60808	54444	74412	81105	01176	28838
00178	80940	44893	10408	36222	80582	71944
00179	19516	90120	46759	71643	13177	55292

Table of Random Numbers

Row number						
00180	49386	54480	23604	23554	21785	41101
00181	06312	88940	15995	69321	47458	64809
00182	60942	00307	11897	92674	40405	68032
00183	92329	98932	78284	46347	41209	92061
00184	77936	63574	31384	51924	85561	29671
00185	38101	77756	11657	13897	95889	57067
00186	39641	69457	91339	22502	92613	89719
00187	84054	40455	99396	63680	67667	60631
00188	47468	03577	57649	63266	24700	71594
00189	43321	31370	28977	23896	76479	68562
00190	64281	61826	18555	64937	13173	33365
00191	66847	70495	32350	02985	86716	38746
00192	72461	33230	21529	53424	92581	02262
00193	21032	91050	13058	16218	12470	56500
00194	95362	67011	06651	16136	01016	00857
00195	49712	97380	10404	55452	34030	60726
00196	58275	61764	97586	54716	50259	46345
00197	89514	11788	68224	23417	73959	76145
00198	15472	50669	48139	36732	46874	37088
00199	12120	86124	51247	44302	60883	52109

APPENDIX B
Distribution of t

	Level of significance for one-tailed test					
	.10	.05	.025	.01	.005	.0005
df	Level of significance for two-tailed test					
	.20	.10	.05	.02	.01	.001
1	3.078	6.314	12.706	31.821	63.657	636.619
2	1.886	2.920	4.303	6.965	9.925	31.598
3	1.638	2.353	3.182	4.541	5.841	12.941
4	1.533	2.132	2.776	3.747	4.604	8.610
5	1.476	2.015	2.571	3.365	4.032	6.859
6	1.440	1.943	2.447	3.143	3.707	5.959
7	1.415	1.895	2.365	2.998	3.499	5.405
8	1.397	1.860	2.306	2.896	3.355	5.041
9	1.383	1.833	2.262	2.821	3.250	4.781
10	1.372	1.812	2.228	2.764	3.169	4.587
11	1.363	1.796	2.201	2.718	3.106	4.437
12	1.356	1.782	2.179	2.681	3.055	4.318
13	1.350	1.771	2.160	2.650	3.012	4.221
14	1.345	1.761	2.145	2.624	2.977	4.140
15	1.341	1.753	2.131	2.602	2.947	4.073
16	1.337	1.746	2.120	2.583	2.921	4.015
17	1.333	1.740	2.110	2.567	2.898	3.965
18	1.330	1.734	2.101	2.552	2.878	3.922
19	1.328	1.729	2.093	2.539	2.861	3.883
20	1.325	1.725	2.086	2.528	2.845	3.850
21	1.323	1.721	2.080	2.518	2.831	3.819
22	1.321	1.717	2.074	2.508	2.819	3.792
23	1.319	1.714	2.069	2.500	2.807	3.767
24	1.318	1.711	2.064	2.492	2.797	3.745
25	1.316	1.708	2.060	2.485	2.787	3.725
26	1.315	1.706	2.056	2.479	2.779	3.707
27	1.314	1.703	2.052	2.473	2.771	3.690
28	1.313	1.701	2.048	2.467	2.763	3.674
29	1.311	1.699	2.045	2.462	2.756	3.659
30	1.310	1.697	2.042	2.457	2.750	3.646
40	1.303	1.684	2.021	2.423	2.704	3.551
60	1.296	1.671	2.000	2.390	2.660	3.460
120	1.289	1.658	1.980	2.358	2.617	3.373
∞	1.282	1.645	1.960	2.326	2.576	3.291

APPENDIX C
Chi-Square Test

Appendix C

Degrees of freedom df	P = .99	.98	.95	.90	.80	.70	.50	.30	.20	.10	.05	.02	.01
1	.000157	.000628	.00393	.0158	.0642	.148	.455	1.074	1.642	2.706	3.841	5.412	6.635
2	.0201	.0404	.103	.211	.446	.713	1.386	2.408	3.219	4.605	5.991	7.824	9.210
3	.115	.185	.352	.584	1.005	1.424	2.366	3.665	4.642	6.251	7.815	9.837	11.341
4	.297	.429	.711	1.064	1.649	2.195	3.357	4.878	5.989	7.779	9.488	11.668	13.277
5	.554	.752	1.145	1.610	2.343	3.000	4.351	6.064	7.289	9.236	11.070	13.388	15.086
6	.872	1.134	1.635	2.204	3.070	3.828	5.348	7.231	8.558	10.645	12.592	15.033	16.812
7	1.239	1.564	2.167	2.833	3.822	4.671	6.346	8.383	9.803	12.017	14.067	16.622	18.475
8	1.646	2.032	2.733	3.490	4.594	5.527	7.344	9.524	11.030	13.362	15.507	18.168	20.090
9	2.088	2.532	3.325	4.168	5.380	6.393	8.343	10.656	12.242	14.684	16.919	19.679	21.666
10	2.558	3.059	3.940	4.865	6.179	7.267	9.342	11.781	13.442	15.987	18.307	21.161	23.209
11	3.053	3.609	4.575	5.578	6.989	8.148	10.341	12.899	14.631	17.275	19.675	22.618	24.725
12	3.571	4.178	5.226	6.304	7.807	9.034	11.304	14.011	15.812	18.549	21.026	24.054	26.217
13	4.107	4.765	5.892	7.042	8.634	9.926	12.340	15.119	16.985	19.812	22.362	25.472	27.688
14	4.660	5.368	6.571	7.790	9.467	10.821	13.339	16.222	18.151	21.064	23.685	26.873	29.141
15	5.229	5.985	7.261	8.547	10.307	11.721	14.339	17.322	19.311	22.307	24.996	28.259	30.578
16	5.812	6.614	7.962	9.312	11.152	12.624	15.338	18.418	20.465	23.542	26.296	29.633	32.000
17	6.408	7.255	8.672	10.085	12.002	13.531	16.338	19.511	21.615	24.769	27.587	30.995	33.409
18	7.015	7.906	9.390	10.865	12.857	14.440	17.338	20.601	22.760	25.989	28.869	32.346	34.805
19	7.633	8.567	10.117	11.651	13.716	15.352	18.338	21.689	23.900	27.204	30.144	33.687	36.191
20	8.260	9.237	10.851	12.443	14.578	16.266	19.337	22.775	25.038	28.412	31.410	35.020	37.566
21	8.897	9.915	11.591	13.240	15.445	17.182	20.337	23.858	26.171	29.615	32.671	36.343	38.932
22	9.542	10.600	12.338	14.041	16.314	18.101	21.337	24.939	27.301	30.813	33.924	37.659	40.289
23	10.196	11.293	13.091	14.848	17.187	19.021	22.337	26.018	28.429	32.007	35.172	38.968	41.638
24	10.856	11.992	13.848	15.659	18.062	19.943	23.337	27.096	29.553	33.196	36.415	40.270	42.980
25	11.524	12.697	14.611	16.473	18.940	20.867	24.337	28.172	30.675	34.382	37.652	41.566	44.314
26	12.198	13.409	15.379	17.292	19.820	21.792	25.336	29.246	31.795	35.563	38.885	42.856	45.642
27	12.879	14.125	16.151	18.114	20.703	22.719	26.336	30.319	32.912	36.741	40.113	44.140	46.963
28	13.565	14.847	16.928	18.939	21.588	23.647	27.336	31.391	34.027	37.916	41.337	45.419	48.278
29	14.256	15.574	17.708	19.768	22.475	24.577	28.336	32.461	35.139	39.087	42.557	46.693	49.588
30	14.953	16.306	18.493	20.599	23.364	25.508	29.336	33.530	36.250	40.256	43.773	47.962	50.892

References

Akers, D., and Myers, J. *Advertising Management.* Englewood Cliffs, NJ: Prentice-Hall, 1987.

American College of Healthcare Marketing Institute. The dubious achievement award. *HealthMarketing* 10(2):7, 1990.

American Hospital Association. *1993 AHA Hospital Statistics.* Chicago: AHA, 1993.

American Medical Association. *Code of Medical Ethics.* Chicago: AMA, 1994.

Anders, G. Drug makers help manage patient care. *Wall Street Journal,* May 17, 1995, pp. B.1, B.4.

Bassili, J. N. The how and why of response latency measurement in telephone surveys. In: N. Schwarz and S. Sudman, editors. *Answering Questions: Methodology for Determining Cognitive and Communicative Processes in Survey Research.* San Francisco: Jossey-Bass, 1996.

Batalden, P. B., Nelson, E. C., and Roberts, J. S. Linking outcomes measurement to continual improvement. *Journal on Quality Improvement* 20(4):167-80, 1994.

Bellenger, D. N., Bernhardt, K. L., and Goldstucker, J. L. Qualitative research techniques: focus group interviews. In: J. B. Higginbotham and K. K. Cox, editors. *Focus Group Interviews: A Reader.* Chicago: American Marketing Association, 1979.

Bergman, R. The measuring stick. *Hospitals and Health Networks* 36:36-42, Dec. 1993.

Bickart, B., and Felcher, E. M. Expanding and enhancing the use of verbal protocols in survey research. In: N. Schwarz and S. Sudman, editors. *Answering Questions: Methodology for Determining Cognitive and Communicative Processes in Survey Research.* San Francisco: Jossey-Bass, 1996.

Billiet, J., and Loosveldt, G. Improvement of the quality of responses to factual survey questions by interviewer training. *Public Opinion Quarterly* 52(2):190-211, 1988.

Blair, E., Sudman, S., Bradburn, N. M., and Stocking, C. B. How to ask questions about drinking and sex: response effects in measuring consumer behavior. *Journal of Marketing Research* 14(3):316-21, Aug. 1972.

Blalock, H. M., Jr. *Causal Inferences in Non-Experimental Research.* Chapel Hill: University of North Carolina Press, 1964.

Blalock, H. M., Jr. *Social Statistics.* New York City: McGraw-Hill, 1972.

References

Bloch, T., and Nebenzahl, I. Respondents' bias in mail surveys. *Psychological Reports* 53(1):227-30, 1983.

Bolton, R., and Drew, J. A longitudinal analysis of the impact of service changes on customer attitudes. *Journal of Marketing* 55(1):1-9, 1991.

Bowers, M., and others. What attributes determine quality and satisfaction with health care delivery? *Health Care Management Review* 19(4):42-50, 1994.

Box, G. E. P., and Jenkins, G. M. *Time-Series Analysis: Forecasting and Control.* San Francisco: Holden-Day, 1976.

Brook, R., Brutoco, R., and Williams, K. *The Relationship between Medical Malpractice and Quality of Care.* The Rand Paper Series, Santa Monica: The Rand Corporation, 1975.

Brook, and others. Malpractice claims data as a quality improvement tool: epidemiology of error in four specialties. *Journal of the American Medical Association* 266(15):2087-92, 1991.

Brown, S., and Swartz, T. A. A gap analysis of professional service quality. *Journal of Marketing* 53(2):92-98, Apr. 1989.

Bryant, F. B., and Yarnold, P. R. Principal components analysis and exploratory and confirmatory factor analysis. In: L. G. Grimm and P. R. Yarnold, editors. *Reading and Understanding Multivariate Statistics.* Washington, DC: American Psychological Association, 1995, pp. 99-119.

Campbell, D. T., and Fiske, D. W. Convergent and discriminant validation by the multitrait/multimethod matrix. *Psychological Bulletin* 58(2)81-105, 1959.

Campbell, D. T., and Stanley, J. C. *Experimental and Quasi-Experimental Designs for Research.* Chicago: Rand McNally, 1963.

Carmines, E. G., and Zellar, R. A. *Reliability and Validity Assessment.* Beverly Hills, CA: Sage Publications, 1979.

Center for Health Policy Research. *Physician Market Place Statistics.* Chicago: American Medical Association, 1994.

Chisnall, P. M. *Marketing Research.* London: McGraw-Hill, 1986.

Clifford, D., and Cavanaugh, R. E. *The Winning Performance: How America's High-Growth, Mid-Size Companies Succeed.* Toronto: Bantam Books, 1985.

Cook, T. D., and Campbell, D. T. *Quasi-Experimentation: Design & Analysis Issues for Field Settings.* Boston: Houghton Mifflin, 1979.

Cooley, W. W., and Lohnes, P. R. *Multivariate Data Analysis.* New York City: John Wiley and Sons, 1971.

Cronbach, L. J. Coefficient alpha and the internal structure of tests. *Psychometrika* 16:297-334, 1951.

Cronin, J. J., and Taylor, S. A. SERVPERF versus SERVQUAL: reconciling performance-based and perceptions-minus-expectations measurement of service quality. *Journal of Marketing* 58(1):125-31, Jan. 1994.

Cryns, A. G., Nichols, R. C., Katz, L. A., and Calkins, E. The hierarchical structure of geriatric patient satisfaction: an older patient satisfaction scale designed for HMOs. *Medical Care* 27(8):802-16, 1989.

Data archives. Evanston, IL: Quality Expectations, Inc., 1995.

Davies, A. R., and Ware, J. Involving consumers in quality care assessment. *Health Affairs* 7(1):33-48, Spring 1988.

de Lafuente, D. Stark bill may limit satellite sites. *Modern Healthcare* 24(14):36, Apr. 4, 1994.

Dillman, D. A. *Mail and Telephone Surveys: The Total Design Method.* New York City: John Wiley and Sons, 1978.

DiMatteo, M. R., and DiNicola, D. D. *Achieving Patient Compliance: The Psychology of the Medical Practitioner's Role.* New York City: Pergamon Press, 1982.

Drucker, P. F. *Managing in a Time of Great Change.* New York City: Truman Talley Books, 1995.

Drucker, P. F. The new productivity challenge. *Harvard Business Review* 69(6):69–79, Nov.–Dec. 1991.

Edwards, A. L. The relationship between the judged desirability of a trait and the probability that the trait will be endorsed. *Journal of Applied Psychology* 37(2):90–93, 1953.

Emory, C. W., and Cooper, D. R. *Business Research Methods.* Homewood, IL: Irwin, 1991.

Ericsson, K. A., and Simon, H. A. *Protocol Analysis: Verbal Reports as Data.* Cambridge: MIT Press, 1984.

Fiebelkorn, S. L. Retail service encounter: model and measurement. In: J. A. Czepiel, M. R. Solomon, and C. F. Surprenant, editors. *The Service Encounter: Managing Employee/Customer Interaction in Service Businesses.* Lexington, MA: Lexington Books, 1985, pp. 181–94.

Filron, F. Estimating bias due to non-response in mail surveys. *Public Opinion Quarterly* 39:482–92, 1976.

Fitzpatrick, R., and Hopkins, A. Problem in the conceptual framework of patient satisfaction research: an empirical exploration. *Sociology of Health and Illness* 5(3):297–312, 1983.

Fitzpatrick, R., and others. Satisfaction with health care. In: R. Fitzpatrick, editor. *The Experience of Illness.* Tavistock, U.K.: Routledge, Chapman and Hall, 1984, pp. 154–75.

Fox, R. J., Crash, M. R., and Kim, J. Mail survey response rate. *Public Opinion Quarterly* 52(4):467–91, Winter 1988.

Franks, E. Targeting excess-of-benchmark returns. *Journal of Portfolio Management* 18(4), Summer 1992.

French, K. Methodological considerations in hospital patient opinion surveys. *International Journal of Nursing Studies* 18:7–32, 1981.

Garvin, D. A. How the Baldrige Award really works. *Harvard Business Review* 69(6):80–95, Nov.–Dec. 1991.

Gaughan, C., and Muneta, L. Let patients define quality. *Quirk's Marketing Research Review* 6(7):29, Nov. 1993.

Geigle, R., and Jones, S. B. Outcomes measurement: a report from the front. *Inquiry* 27:7–13, 1990.

Gerteis, M., Edgman-Levitan, S., Walker, J., Stokes, D., Cleary, P., and Delbanco, T. What patients really want. *Health Management Quarterly* Third Quarter, pp. 2–6, 1993.

Ghali, J. K., Cooper, R., and Ford, E. Trends in hospitalization rates for heart failure in the United States. *Archives of Internal Medicine* 150:769–73, 1990.

Goode, W. J., and Hatt, P. K. *Methods in Social Research.* New York City: McGraw-Hill, 1952, pp. 209–14.

Greater Cleveland Health Quality Choice Program. Asking the right questions in your "satisfaction" survey. *Health Care Performance Reporting* 1(1):7–8, Jan. 19, 1995.

Hall, J. A., and Dornan, M. C. Patient sociodemographic characteristics as predictors of satisfaction with medical care: a meta-analysis. *Social Science and Medicine* 30(7):811–18, 1990.

Hall, M. F. Patient satisfaction or acquiescence? Comparing mail and telephone survey results. *Journal of Health Care Marketing* 15(1):54–61, 1995.

Hansen, M. H., Hurwitz, W. N., and Madow, W. G. *Sample Survey Materials and Theory.* Vol. 1. New York City: John Wiley and Sons, 1953.

Health Care Advisory Board. *Service Quality at U.S. Hospitals.* Washington, DC: The Advisory Board Company, 1988.

Health care policy standards. Five large employers require HMOs to meet NCQA accreditation standards. *BNA's Health Care Policy* p. 2097, July 19, 1993.

References

Helmstadter, G. C. *Principles of Psychological Measurement.* New York City: Appleton-Century-Crofts, 1964.

Herberlein, T. A., and Baumgartner, R. Factors affecting response rates to mailed questionnaires: a quantitative analysis of the published literature. *American Sociological Review* 43(4):447-62, Aug. 1978.

Hill, R. C. When the going gets rough: a Baldrige Award winner on the line. *Academy of Management Executives* 7:75-79, Aug. 1993.

Horton, R. L. *The General Linear Model.* New York City: McGraw-Hill, 1978.

Hospitals. Reduce malpractice risks through better communication. *Hospitals* 20:50, Nov. 1987.

Jacobson, R., and Aaker, D. A. The strategic role of quality. *Journal of Marketing* 51:31-44, Oct. 1987.

Jobe, J. B., White, A. A., Kelley, C. L., and others. Recall strategies and memory of health-care visits. *The Milbank Quarterly* 68(2):171-89, 1990.

Joint Commission on Accreditation of Healthcare Organizations. *1995 Comprehensive Accreditation Manual for Hospitals.* Oakbrook Terrace, IL: JCAHO Department of Publications, 1994.

Jones, T. O., and Sasser, W. E., Jr. Why satisfied customers defect. *Harvard Business Review* 73(6):88-99, Nov.-Dec. 1995.

Juran, J. M., and Gryna, F. M. *Juran's Quality Control Handbook.* 4th ed. New York City: McGraw-Hill, 1988.

Katzer, J., Cook, K. A., and Crouch, W. W. *Evaluating Information: A Guide for Users of Social Science Research.* Reading, MA: Addison-Wesley, 1982.

Kerlinger, F. N. *Foundations of Behavioral Research.* New York City: Holt, Rinehart and Winston, 1973.

Koeske, G. F. Some recommendations for improving measurement validation in social work research. *Journal of Social Service Research* 18(3/4):43-71, 1994.

Kravitz, R. L., Rolph, J. E., and McGuisan, K. Malpractice claims data as a quality improvement tool: epidemiology of error in four specialties. *Journal of the American Medical Association* 266(15):2087-92, 1991.

LeVois, M., Nguyen, T. D., and Attkisson, C. C. Artifact in client satisfaction assessment. *Evaluation and Program Planning* 4(2):139-50, 1981.

Ley, P. Satisfaction, compliance and communication. *British Journal of Clinical Psychology,* pp. 241-54, 1982.

Likert, R. A technique for the measurement of attitudes. *Archives of Psychology* 140(1):1-55, 1932.

Linder-Pelz, S. Toward a theory of patient satisfaction. *Social Science and Medicine* 16(5):577-82, 1982.

Linder-Pelz, S., and Struening, E. L. The multidimensionality of patient satisfaction with a clinic visit. *Journal of Community Health* 10(1):42-54, Spring 1985.

Locander, W. B., and Burton, J. P. The effect of question form on gathering income data by telephone. *Journal of Marketing Research* 13:189-92, May 1976.

Mages, P. The Dubious Achievement Award: the punitive effect of poor customer relations. *Health Marketing* 10:2, May-June 1990.

Malcolm Baldrige National Quality Award. Health Care Pilot criteria. National Institute of Standards and Technology, 1995.

Marquis, M. S., Davies, A. R., and Ware, J. E., Jr. Patient satisfaction and change in medical care provider: a longitudinal study. *Medical Care* 21(8):821-29, Aug. 1983.

McAlexander, J., Kaldenberg, D., and Keonis, H. Service quality measurement. *Journal of Health Care Marketing* 14:34-40, Fall 1994.

McIver, J. P., and Carmines, E. G. *Unidimensional Scaling.* Beverly Hills, CA: Sage, 1981.

Med Ad News. The compliant patient is well-informed. *Med Ad News,* Mar. 1995.

Miller, P. V. Alternative question forms for attitude scale questions in telephone interviews. *Public Opinion Quarterly* 48(4):766-78, Winter 1984.

Muirhead, G. Pharmacoeconomics: a still-fuzzy buzzword. *Drug Topics* 138(9):74-75, 1994.

National Committee for Quality Assurance. NCQA announces results of public call for measures. Press release. Washington, DC: NCQA, 1996.

Nelson, E., and Larson, C. Patients' good and bad surprises: how do they relate to overall patient satisfaction? *Quality Review Bulletin* 19(3):89-94, Mar. 1993.

Nelson, E., Rust, R., Zahorik, A., Rose, R., Batalden, P., and Siemanski, B. Do patient perceptions of quality relate to hospital financial performance? *Journal of Health Care Marketing* 12(4):6-13, 1992.

Nunnally, J. C. *Psychometric Theory.* New York City: McGraw-Hill, 1978.

Nunnally, J. C., and Durham, R. L. Validity, reliability, and special problems of measurement in evaluation research. In: E. L. Struening and M. Guttentag, editors. *Handbook of Evaluation Research.* Beverly Hills, CA: Sage, 1975.

Nunnally, J. C., and Wilson, W. H. Method and theory for developing measures in evaluation research. In: E. L. Struening and M. Guttentag, editors. *Handbook of Evaluation Research.* Beverly Hills, CA: Sage, 1975.

Oksenberg, L., Coleman, L., and Cannell, C. F. Interviewers' voices and refusal rates in telephone surveys. *Public Opinion Quarterly* 50(1):97-111, Spring 1986.

Oloroso, A. Managed care will get a reality check. *Crain's Chicago Business* 17(45):1, 58, 1994.

Opinion Research Corporation. *National Healthcare Consumer Survey.* Evanston, IL: Opinion Research Corp., 1996.

Ouchi, W. G. *Theory Z: How American Business Can Meet the Japanese Challenge.* New York City: Avon Books, 1982.

Parasuraman, A., Zeithaml, V., and Berry, L. A conceptual model of service quality and its implications for future research. *Journal of Marketing* 49:41-59, Fall 1985.

Parasuraman, A., Zeithaml, V., and Berry, L. SERVQUAL: a multiple-item scale for measuring customer perceptions of service quality. *Journal of Retailing* 64(1):12-40, 1988.

Parasuraman, A., Zeithaml, V., and Berry, L. *SERVQUAL: A Multiple-Item Scale for Service Quality.* Cambridge: Marketing Science Institute, 1986.

Parmley, W. W. Pathophysiology and current therapy of congestive heart failure. *Journal of the American College of Cardiology* 13(4):771-85, 1989.

Parten, M. *Surveys, Polls and Samples: Practical Procedures.* New York City: Harper and Row, 1950, p. 106.

Pascoe, G. C. Patient satisfaction in primary health care: a literature review and analysis. *Evaluation and Program Planning* 6(3/4):185-210, 1983.

Patrick, D. L., Scrivens, E., and Charlton, J. R. H. Disability and patient satisfaction with medical care. *Medical Care* 21(11):1062-76, Nov. 1983.

Patton, M. Q. *Qualitative Evaluation Methods.* Beverly Hills, CA: Sage, 1980.

Payne, S. L. *The Art of Asking Questions.* Princeton, NJ: Princeton University Press, 1951.

Pearl, D., and Fairley, D. Testing for the potential for non-response bias in sample surveys. *Public Opinion Quarterly* 49:553-60, 1985.

Peters, T. J. *The Tom Peters Seminars: Crazy Times Call for Crazy Organizations.* New York City: Vintage Books, 1994, pp. 227-28.

References

Peters, T. J., and Waterman, R. J., Jr. *In Search of Excellence: Lessons from America's Best-Run Companies.* New York City: Harper and Row, 1982.

Peterson, K. *The Strategic Approach to Quality Service in Health Care.* Rockville, MD: Aspen, 1988.

Phillips, L. W., and others. Product quality, cost position and business performance: a test of some key hypotheses. *Journal of Marketing* 47:26-43, Spring 1983.

Priest, D. Health care organizations back national database to rate their plans. *Washington Post,* Jan. 15, 1993, p. 1.

Rolph, J. E., Kravitz, R. L., and McGuisan, K. Malpractice claims data as a quality improvement tool: is targeting effective? *Journal of the American Medical Association* 266(15):2093-96, 1991.

Rosenthal, R. *Experimenter Effects in Behavioral Research.* New York City: Appleton-Century-Crofts, 1966.

Rosenthal, R., and Jacobson, L. *Pygmalion in the Classroom.* New York City: Holt, Rinehart and Winston, 1968.

Ross, C. E., and Mirowsky, J. The worst place and the best face. *Social Forces* 62:529-36, 1983.

Rudnick, J., and Dougherty-Draper, E. The direct effect of health managers on quality control, assessment, assurance. *Health Care Strategic Management* 5:12-16, Nov. 1987.

Rummel, R. J. *Applied Factor Analysis.* Evanston, IL: Northwestern University Press, 1970.

Rust, R. T., Zahorik, A. J., and Keiningham, T. L. Return on quality (ROQ): making service quality financially accountable. *Journal of Marketing* 59:58-70, Apr. 1995.

Schlackman, N. Quality and physician compensation: performance-based incentives in managed care. *Quality Letter for Healthcare Leaders* 6(2):18-23, Mar. 1994.

Schoenfeldt, R. C., Seale, W. B., and Hale, A. W. Survey alerts hospital to needs of consumers. *Health Progress* 68(7):61-66, Sept. 1987.

Schwarz, N., and Sudman, S., editors. *Answering Questions: Methodology for Determining Cognitive and Communicative Processes in Survey Research.* San Francisco: Jossey-Bass, 1996.

Selltiz, C., Wrightsman, L. M., and Cook, S. *Research Methods in Social Relations.* New York City: Holt, Rinehart and Winston, 1976.

Simon, J. L. *Basic Research Methods in Social Science.* New York City: Random House, 1969, pp. 109-17.

Singer, E., Frankel, M. R., and Glassman, M. B. The effect of interviewer characteristics and expectations on response. *Public Opinion Quarterly* 47(1):68-83, Spring 1983.

Sommers, P., and Thompson, M. The best malpractice insurance of them all: customer satisfaction. *Health Marketing Quarterly* 1(1):83-91, 1983.

Steiber, S. R. Advertising cuts represent marketing shakeout. *Hospitals* 62(22):33-35, Nov. 20, 1988a.

Steiber, S. R. Americans accept foreign-born physicians. *Hospitals* 62(3):79, Feb. 5, 1988b.

Steiber, S. R. Conclusions probably 180 degrees off. *Journal of Health Care Marketing* 15(2):6, 1995.

Steiber, S. R. How consumers perceive health care quality. *Hospitals* 62(7):84, Apr. 5, 1988c.

Steiber, S. R. *The National Hospital Marketers' Survey.* Evanston, IL: Quality Expectations, Inc., 1989.

Steiber, S. R., and Krowinski, W. J. *Measuring and Managing Patient Satisfaction.* 1st ed. Chicago: American Hospital Publishing, 1990.

Stephan, F. F. History of the uses of modern sampling procedures. *Journal of the American Statistical Association* 43(1):12-40, 1948.

Stewart, M. A., and Wanklin, J. Direct and indirect measures of patient satisfaction with physician services. *Journal of Community Health* 3:195–204, 1978.

Sudman, S., and Bradburn, N. M. *Asking Questions: A Practical Guide to Questionnaire Design.* San Francisco: Jossey-Bass, 1982.

Sudman, S., Bradburn, N. M., and Schwarz, N. *Thinking About Answers: The Application of Cognitive Processes to Survey Methodology.* San Francisco: Jossey-Bass, 1996.

Swan, J. E., Sawyer, J. C., VanMatre, J. G., and McGee, G. W. Deepening the understanding of hospital patient satisfaction: fulfillment and equity effects. *Journal of Health Care Marketing* 5(3):7–18, 1985.

Taylor, K. S. New integrators on the block. *Hospitals and Health Networks* 68(23), Dec. 5, 1994.

Walker, A. H., and Restuccia, J. D. Obtaining information on patient satisfaction with hospital care: mail versus telephone. *Health Services Research* 19(3):291–306, Aug. 1984.

Walton, M. *The Deming Management Method.* New York City: Dodd Mead, 1986.

Ware, J. E., Jr. Effects of acquiescent response set on patient satisfaction ratings. *Medical Care* 16(4):327–36, Apr. 1978.

Ware, J. E., and Davies, A. R. Behavioral consequences of consumer dissatisfaction with medical care. *Evaluation and Program Planning* 6(4):291–97, 1983.

Ware, J. E., Jr., and Snyder, M. K. Dimensions of patient attitudes regarding doctors and medical care services. *Medical Care* 13(8):669–82, Aug. 1975.

Ware, J. E., Snyder, M. K., and Wright, W. R. Development and validation of scales to measure patient satisfaction with health care services: volume I of a final report. Part A. Review of literature, overview of methods and results regarding construction of scales. Springfield, VA: National Technical Information Services, 1976.

Ware, J. E., Snyder, M. K., Wright, W. R., and Davies, A. R. Defining and measuring patient satisfaction with medical care. *Evaluation and Program Planning* 6(3):247–63, 1983.

Weeks, M. F., Kulka, R. A., and Pierson, S. A. Optimal calling schedule for a telephone survey. *Public Opinion Quarterly* 51(4):540–49, Winter 1987.

Weiss, C. H. Interviewing in evaluation research. In: E. L. Struening and M. Guttentag, editors. *Handbook of Evaluation Research.* Beverly Hills, CA: Sage, 1975.

Wiesendanger, B. Deming's luster dims at Florida Power & Light. *Journal of Business Strategy* 14(5):60–61, Sept.–Oct. 1993.

Wiesendanger, B. The post-Deming diet: dismantling a quality bureaucracy. *Training* 28:41–43, Feb. 1991.

Woodside, A., Frey, L., and Daly, R. Linking service quality, customer satisfaction and behavioral intention. *Journal of Health Care Marketing* 9(4):5–17, 1989.

Yates, R. Game plan. *Chicago Tribune Magazine*, Feb. 16, 1992, pp. 14–16, 18–22.

Zismer, D. K., and Collins, J. J., Jr. Physician incentives in a managed care world. *Healthcare Forum Journal* 37(5):39, Sept.–Oct. 1994.

Index

Abbott Laboratories, value-added consulting services at, 4-5
Action, plotting course of, 231-44
Administration and design problems in mail-out surveys, 70
Allied Signal, 21
Ameritech, 21
Analysis of research data
　chi-square test in, 220-21
　cluster analysis in, 228
　correlation in, 223, 225
　difference of means test in, 222-23
　difference of proportions test in, 221-22
　factor analysis in, 227-28
　measurement levels in, 218-19
　measures of association in, 223-30
　multiple regression analysis in, 228-30
　multivariate models in, 227-30
　qualitative, 217-18
　quantitative, 218
　regression in, 225-27
　simple tests of differences in, 219-23
Assimilation model, 33
Attitude scaling approach, 55-56
Award winning, focus on, 5

Baldrige, Malcolm, 3-4
Baldrige, Malcolm, National Quality Award, 3-5, 5
　Health Care Pilot of, 4
Baldrige, Malcolm, National Quality Improvement Act, 3-4
Bias, selection, interaction effects of, 196-97
Biased questions, 130-31, 184

Causal inference, principles of, 191-94
Causal relationships, 82
Causality, three conditions of, 192
Chi-square test, 220-21, 254
Cleveland Health Quality Choice Program, 25
Closed-ended questions, 133-35
Cluster analysis, 228
Cluster sampling, 94-95
Coding in mail questionnaire administration, 155
Communication problems
　in in-person surveys, 68-69
　in telephone surveys, 69
Competition and patient satisfaction, 25-28
Confidence interval, 89
Constant errors, 182
Construct validity, 189-90
Content validity, 187-88
Contrast model, 33
Control group interrupted time series design, 204-5
Control group pretest posttest designs, 200-201
Correction factor in sampling, 90-91
Correlation, 223, 225
Cost-benefit analysis, 45-46
Cost-effective analysis, 45
Cost-minimization analysis, 46-47
Cost-utility analysis, 47
Criterion validity, 188-89
Customer-centered service, evolution of, 2-6
Customer satisfaction. *See* Satisfaction
Customers
　acquisition and retention of, 5-6
　patient satisfaction and provider benefits of, 6-12
　service model for, 35-36

Data analysis, 114-18
Data, qualitative, 217-18
Deming, W. Edwards, 2, 237
　and customer-centered service, 2
Descriptive research, 82
Difference of means test, 222-23
Difference of proportions test, 221-22
Discrete service encounters, 53-54
Discrete service inputs, linkage to satisfaction outcomes, 55-64
Dissatisfaction
　financial benefits of addressing, 12-16
　financial consequences, 9-12
Domain sampling model, 184-85
Drucker, Peter, 5-6

Electronic questionnaire versus written questionnaire, 155-56
Empathic interviewing, 105
Employers, stake in patient satisfaction, 20-21
Errors
　constant, 182
　random, 182
Evaluation designs
　control group interrupted time series, 204-5
　control group pretest posttest, 200-201
　one group interrupted time series, 201-4
　one group pretest posttest, 197-99

(Continued on next page)

Index

Evaluation designs (continued)
  principles of causal inference, 191-94
  randomized control group posttest only, 199-200
  randomized control group pretest posttest, 199
  threats to validity, 194-97
Evaluation plan
  analyzing data in, 211
  choosing evaluation design in, 209-10
  collecting data in, 210-11
  describing service and its problem in, 207-8
  establishing improvement objectives in, 208-9
  reporting results in, 211-12
  sample, 212-15
  specifying service modification in, 208
Evaluations, 122
Exhaustive categories in closed-ended questions, 134-35
Experimental procedures, reactive effects of, 197
External validity, threats to, 196

Face validity, 187
Factor analysis, 38-39, 56-58, 227-28
Fiebelkorn, Sandra, 35-36
Financial benefits of addressing dissatisfaction, 12-16
Financial consequences of dissatisfaction, 9-12
Financial return on quality, 16-18
Florida Power & Light, 5
Focus areas in qualitative research, 99-101
Focus groups, 107-12
  guide to, 111
  number of sessions in, 110
  observation of, 113
  opening remarks for, 111-12
  participant recruitment for, 110-11
  sample selection and assignment for, 109
  setting for, 109
  size of, 108-9
  techniques for leading discussions in, 112-13
  telephonic, 113
Follow-up methods in mail questionnaire administration, 152-55
Formal interviews, 102-7
Frequency scales, 139

Gallup, George, Sr., 87
Global questions, 128-29
Global satisfaction, 54-55
Goals
  patient satisfaction, 231-36
  and sample size in sampling, 91

Graphic scales, 139-40
Greater Cleveland Health Quality Choice Program, 22
GTE, 21

Health Care Advisory Board, 12-13
Health care, ten attributes of, 33-34
Health Plan Employer Data and Information Set (HEDIS), 23, 24-25
Historical threat, 195
Home management versus hospitalizations, 48-49
Hospital
  impact of patient dissatisfaction on, 9-11
  and patient satisfaction, 25, 27-28
Hospitalizations versus home management, 48-49

Improvement, models for, 238-39
In-depth interviews, 102-7
Informal interviews, 101-2
Information, categories of, 121-24
Informed consent, 8
Inpatient experiences, patient satisfaction in, 39-40
In-person surveys, timing and communication problems in, 68-69
In Search of Excellence (Peters and Waterman), 3
Instrumentation threat, 195
Insurer, stake of, in patient satisfaction, 20
Interaction effects of selection bias, 196-97
Internal consistency reliability, 185-86
Internal metrics, 239-40
Internal validity, threats to, 195-96
Interrater reliability, 186-87
Interval scales, 81
Interviews
  empathic, 105
  formal, 102-7
  in-depth, 102-7
  informal, 101-2

Joint Commission on Accreditation of Healthcare Organizations (JCAHO), 22-24, 37-38
Juran, Joseph, 2
  and quality management, 2

Letter of transmittal in mail questionnaire administration, 149-51
Likert-type scales, 140
Linder-Pelz, Susan, 33, 38
Literary Digest, 87-88

Mail surveys
  administration, 148-55
  administration and design problems in, 70
  prenotification of, 151-52
Malpractice suits, 8-9
Management commitment to patient satisfaction, 64-65
Maturation threat, 195
Measurement levels in analysis of research data, 218-19
Medical advice, compliance with, 7
Modeling as management tool, 63-64
Mortality threat, 196
Multiple regression, 58-63
Multiple regression analysis, 228-30
Multiple-service interference, 197
Multivariate models, 227-30
Mutually exclusive response categories in closed-ended questions, 135

National Committee for Quality Assurance (NCQA), 21, 23, 24-25
National Hospital Marketers' Survey, 25, 27
National Institute of Standards and Technology (NIST), 4
Nominal scales, 80
Nonrandom sampling, 95-96

Objectionable questions, 129-30
Objectivity, lack of, 67-68
Observations in qualitative research, 98-101
One group interrupted time series design, 201-4
One group pretest posttest design, 197-99
Open-ended questions, 132-33
Ordinal scales, 80-81
Outliers, identifying for action, 240-42
Outpatient experiences, patient satisfaction in, 40-41
Overgeneralizations, 68

Participation in qualitative research, 99
Pascoe, Gregory, 33
Patient reactivity, 68
Patient satisfaction
  categories, attributes, and processes in, 36-43
  and the competition, 25-28
  defining terms of, 29-49
  definition of, 33
  efficacy and value, 44-49
  employers' stake in, 20-21
  and the hospital, 25, 27-28

insurers' stake in, 20
management commitment to, 64-65
and physicians, 18-19
purchaser demands for, 19-21
and regulators, 22-25
Patients
benefits of customer satisfaction to, 6-12
loyalty of, to primary care physicians, 8
quality of life of, 20
PDCA cycle, 239
Pepsico, 21
Peters, Thomas J., 2, 3
Peterson, Kristine, model of service delivery, 52-53
Physicians
impact of patient dissatisfaction in office of, 11-12
patient loyalty to, 8
and patient satisfaction, 18-19, 42-43
Picker/Commonwealth Program for Patient-Centered Care, 22
Predischarge questionnaire administration, 148
Prenotification of surveys in mail questionnaire administration, 51-52
Pretesting
questionnaires, 142-43
reactive effects of, 197
Primary care physician. *See also* Physician
patient loyalty to, 8
Providers
benefits of customer satisfaction, 6-12
increased loyalty to, 7-8
Pseudonormative samples, 73
Purchaser
demands for patient satisfaction, 19-21
drive for quality measurement, 21-22

Qualitative data, 217-18
Qualitative research, 79
appropriate uses for, 79
combining quantitative research and, 82
data analysis in, 114-18
focus groups in, 107-12
formal interviews in, 102-7
informal interviews in, 101-2
interview process in, 105-7
scheduling, 104-5
timing and length in, 104
observations in, 98-101
pitfalls in, 67-68
researcher qualifications in, 118

review of existing data sources in, 97-98
telephonic focus groups in, 113
Quality
financial return on, 16-18
focus on, 5
purchasers' drive for measurement of, 21-22
statistical interrelationships of satisfaction and, 43-44
Quality management
and Juran, 2
Quality movement, 3
Quality scales, 137
Quantitative data, 218
Quantitative research
abbreviations in, 125
appropriate uses for, 82
biased questions in, 130-31
categories of information in, 121-24
combining qualitative research with, 82
descriptive and causal, 82
double-barreled questions in, 125
double negatives in, 124-25
evaluations in, 122
frequency scales in, 139
global questions in, 128-29
graphic scales in, 139-40
interval scales, 81
irrelevant questions in, 125-27
jargon in, 125
Likert-type scales in, 140
nominal scales, 80
objectionable questions in, 129-30
ordinal scales, 80-81
pitfalls in, 68-70
pretesting questionnaires in, 142-43
quality scales in, 137
question construction in, 124-32
rating scales in, 136-42
ratings in, 122
ratio scales, 81
reports of facts in, 121-22
reports of intended behavior in, 122-23
response construction in, 132-35
satisfaction scales in, 136-37
service attribute scales in, 138-39
summated scales in, 140-42
vague questions in, 129
Questionnaires
mail
administration of, 70, 148-55
prenotification of, 151-52
self-report
administration
mail, 148-55
predischarge, 148
take-home, 148
construction, 145-48
question ordering and grouping, 147-48
question-response formatting, 146-47

electronic versus written, 155-56
telephone
adapting for, 164-68
analyzing, 172-73
Question-response formatting, 146-47
Questions
biased, 130-31, 184
closed-ended, 133-35
construction in quantitative research, 124-32
double-barreled, 125
global, 128-29
irrelevant, 125-27
objectionable, 129-30
open-ended, 132-33
in survey construction, 71
vague, 129

Random errors, 182
Random numbers, table of, 246-49
Random sampling, 92, 93
Randomized control group
posttest only design, 199-200
pretest posttest design, 199
Randomness in sampling, 88
Rating scales, 136-42
Ratings, 122
Ratio scales, 81
Reactive effects
of experimental procedures, 197
of pretesting, 197
Regression in analysis of research data, 225-27
Regulators and patient satisfaction, 22-25
Reliability. *See also* Validity
assessment of, 184-87
attribute characteristics of respondent, 183
biased sampling of questions, 184
definition of, 181
internal consistency, 185-86
interrater, 186-87
lack of clarity, 184
model of domain sampling, 184-85
need for assessment, 181-82
situational factors, 183
sources of error, 182-83
test-retest, 186
transient personal factors, 183
variations in administration, 183-84
Reports
of facts, 121-22
of intended behavior, 122-23
Representativeness in sampling, 91-92
Research-based management, 237-38
Research design
case study for ambulatory surgery center, 78-79
defining patient satisfaction, 78
determining objectives, 78
identifying decision makers, 77
selecting methodology, 79-82

265

Index

Research plan, developing, 82-83
Research process, potential pitfalls in, 67-75
Response formats in surveys, 71-72
Roosevelt, Franklin D., 87-88

Sampling
  cluster, 94-95
  correction factor in, 90-91
  error in, 88-90
  goals in, 91
  history of, 87-88
  nonrandom, 95-96
  random, 88, 92, 93
  representativeness in, 91-92
  sample size in, 91
  sequential, 94
  stratified, 94
  systematic, 92-93
Satisfaction
  measurement as blunt instrument, 65
  outcomes
    linkage of, to discrete service inputs, 55-64
    and service encounters, 51-65
  and quality statistical interrelationships, 43-44
  scales, 136-37
Scales
  frequency, 139
  graphic, 139-40
  Likert-type, 140
  as management tool, 63-64
  quality, 137
  rating, 136-42
  satisfaction, 136-37
  service attribute, 138-39
  summated, 140-42
Selection bias, interaction effects of, 196-97
Selection threat, 196
Self-report questionnaires
  administration
    mail, 148-55
    predischarge, 148
    take-home, 148
  construction, 145-48
  electronic versus written, 155-56
  question ordering and grouping, 147-48
  question-response formatting, 146-47

Sequence of experiences in qualitative research, 100-101
Sequential sampling, 94
Service attribute scales, 138-39
Service delivery system, 52-55
Service dimension quadrants, 232-33
Service encounters and satisfaction outcomes, 51-65
SERVQUAL, 34-35
Setting in qualitative research, 99-100
Situational factors, 183
Specific outcomes, 54-55
Spiral of progress in quality model, 2
Stakeholders, 4
Standard deviation, 89
Statistical regression threat, 196
Stratified sampling, 94
Summated scales, 55, 140-42
  construction and statistical refinement of, 56
Survey construction, pitfalls in, 70-72
Survey response and processing, pitfalls in, 73-75
Survey sampling, pitfalls in, 72-73
Systematic sampling, 92-93

t distribution, 252
TakeCare, 19
Take-home questionnaire administration, 148
Telephone interviews
  adapting questionnaires for, 164-68
  adapting ranking questions in, 166
  adapting response scaling in, 165-66
  asking income questions in, 168
  conducting in, 162-63
  editing completed questionnaires in, 163
  facilities and supervision in, 164
  formatting in, 168-70
  incorporating responses mentioned within questions in, 168
  ordering and grouping questions in, 166-67
  pretesting in, 170-72
  recording responses in, 163
  scheduling in, 163-64
  selecting interviewers in, 159-61
  timing in, 164
  training interviewers in, 161-63
  using transitional statements in, 167-68
Telephone satisfaction questionnaire, inpatient, 174-79
Telephone surveys, timing and communication problems in, 69
Telephonic focus groups, 113
Testing threat, 195
Test-retest reliability, 186
Third variables, 192-94
Timing problems
  in in-person surveys, 68-69
  in telephone surveys, 69
Transient personal factors, 183
Transitional statements in telephone interviews, 167-68
Treatment regimens, improved compliance with, 7
Turnaround time and reenrollment, 47-48

Vague questions, 129
Validity. *See also* Reliability
  assessment of, 187-90
  attribute characteristics of respondent, 183
  biased sampling of questions, 184
  construct, 189-90
  content, 187-88
  criterion, 188-89
  definition of, 181
  external, 196
  face, 187
  internal, 195-96
  lack of clarity, 184
  model of domain sampling, 184-85
  need for assessment, 181-82
  situational factors, 183
  sources of error, 182-83
  threats to, 194-97
  transient personal factors, 183
  variations in administration, 183-84

Waterman, Robert J., Jr., 2, 3
Written questionnaire versus electronic questionnaire, 155-56

Xerox Corporation, 21

Leadership Resources for a Changing Health Care Environment

Mary K. Kohles, RN, MSW, William G. Baker, Jr., MD, and Barbara A. Donaho, RN, MA
Transformational Leadership
Renewing Fundamental Values and Achieving New Relationships in Health Care

> "Transformational leadership speaks to creating a new organization that results in the alignment of personal, organizational, and community goals. When accomplished, everyone has achieved recognition as a valued individual, everyone has learned the skills of challenging and questioning the present reality, and everyone has the opportunity to take their place as leaders in order to build a stronger, more humanistic health care delivery system,...thus transforming the systems of health care for the benefit of the people served."
> —from the Preface

Examine the pivotal role of leadership in transforming your organization.
Drawing on the first-hand experience of health care leaders who have faced the challenges and reaped the rewards of transformative change, *Transformational Leadership* moves beyond the conceptual ideas of cultural change to detail the specific processes required for action. For hospital executives, trustees, physicians, and other professionals in the field, the authors offer a proven framework to show how any organization confronting the demands of today's changing health care environment can create a vision of the future and realize the opportunities for improved health care delivery.

Catalog no. 001116 • October 1995 • 304 pages, 14 figures, 1 table, 3 appendixes • $40.00 (AHA members, $32.00)

Winnie Schmeling, PhD, RN, FAAN
Facing Change in Health Care
Learning Faster in Tough Times

> "With the rate of change accelerating as it is, a key leadership skill for the 1990s is leading during times of change. This book is a must read for any health care executive or manager who is facing the challenge of great change in their organization, and who isn't?"
> —Jo Manion, Manion & Associates

Much has been written about learning organizations as a model for organizational change—changing how we think and what we do. But how do you go about *building* such an organization and *creating* such change? Author Winnie Schmeling, project director for the Program to Improve Patient Care at Tallahassee Memorial Regional Medical Center, outlines the experiences of more than 60 health care facilities to present scores of practical ideas and tools to *create* a learning organization. Presenting several proven learning models, this book offers advice and guidance on how to customize these models to meet the particular needs of your institution and to create the kind of change that leads to improved effectiveness, efficiency, and customer satisfaction.

Catalog no. 174400 • January 1996 • 298 pages, 55 figures, 6 tables, 3 appendixes • $69.00 (AHA members, $55.00)

Call 1-800-AHA-2626 to place your order.
Prices and availability subject to change.

American Hospital Publishing, Inc.
Dedicated to realizing the vision of improving health through information.

In partnership with our authors, we strive to provide the latest insights and innovations to help our readers participate fully in the changing health care environment and to meet the new requirements of a world in which leadership is demanded of us all. Our books present the essential tools and resources that executives, managers, educators, administrators, consultants, and other health care professionals need to manage change responsibly—for the health of individuals and their organizations, our communities, and our nation.